10th IADIS International Conference on Information Systems 2017

Budapest, Hungary
10 – 12 April 2017

Editors:

Miguel Baptista Nunes
Pedro Isaias
Philip Powell
Luis Rodrigues

ISBN: 978-1-5108-4821-4

Printed from e-media with permission by:

Curran Associates, Inc.
57 Morehouse Lane
Red Hook, NY 12571

Some format issues inherent in the e-media version may also appear in this print version.

Printed by Curran Associates, Inc. (2017)

For permission requests, please contact International Association for Development of the Information Society (IADIS) at the address below.

International Association for Development of the Information Society (IADIS)
Rua Sao Sebastiao Da Pedreira
No. 100, 30, 1050-209
Lisbon, Portugal

Phone: 351 21 3151373
Fax: 351 21 3151244

secretariat@iadis.org

Additional copies of this publication are available from:

Curran Associates, Inc.
57 Morehouse Lane
Red Hook, NY 12571 USA
Phone: 845-758-0400
Fax: 845-758-2633
Email: curran@proceedings.com
Web: www.proceedings.com

PROCEEDINGS OF THE 10th IADIS INTERNATIONAL CONFERENCE

INFORMATION SYSTEMS 2017

BUDAPEST, HUNGARY

10 - 12 APRIL, 2017

Organised by

iadis

international association for development of the information society

Edited by Miguel Baptista Nunes, Pedro Isaías and Philip Powell

Associate Editor: Luís Rodrigues

TABLE OF CONTENTS

FULL PAPERS

SHORT PAPERS

REFLECTION PAPER

FOREWORD

These proceedings contain the papers of the 10th IADIS International Conference Information Systems 2017, which was organised by the International Association for Development of the Information Society in Budapest, Hungary, 10 - 12 April 2017.

The IADIS Information Systems Conference 2017 aims to provide a forum for the discussion of IS taking a socio-technological perspective. It aims to address the issues related to design, development and use of IS in organisations from a socio-technological perspective, as well as to discuss IS professional practice, research and teaching. A set of key areas has been identified. However, these do not aim at being prescriptive, or set in stone, and any innovative contributions that do not fit into these areas have also been considered.

The following main tracks have been object of paper submissions:

- IS in Practice, Technology Infrastructures and Organisational Processes
- IS Design, Development and Management Issues and Methodologies
- IS Professional Issues
- IS Research
- IS Learning and Teaching

The IADIS Information Systems Conference 2017 had 132 submissions from more than 28 countries. Each submission has been anonymously reviewed by an average of 4 independent reviewers, to ensure the final high standard of the accepted submissions. Out of the papers submitted, 20 got blind referee ratings that published them as full papers, which means that the acceptance rate was 15%. Some other submissions were published as short papers and reflection paper. Extended versions of the best papers will be selected to be published in a special issue of the Journal of Electronic Commerce in Organizations (JECO) journal (ISSN: 1539-2937) and also in the IADIS Journal on Computer Science and Information Systems (ISSN: 1646-3692) indexed by Emerging Sources Citation Index by Thomson Reuters.

The conference, besides the presentation of full, short and reflection papers, also includes a keynote presentation from an internationally distinguished researcher. We wish to thank Professor Albert Boonstra, Vice Dean of the Faculty of Economics and Business and Professor of Information Management, University of Groningen, The Netherlands, for accepting our invitation as keynote speaker.

As we all know, a conference requires the effort of many individuals. We would like to thank all members of the Program Committee for their hard work in reviewing and selecting the papers that appear in the book of the proceedings. We would also like to thank all the authors who have submitted their papers to this conference. We wish to thank all members of our organizing committee.

Last but not the least, we hope that everybody will have a good time in Budapest, and we invite all participants for the next year edition of the IADIS International Conference of Information Systems 2018.

Professor Philip Powell, Executive Dean, University of London, UK
Conference Chair

Miguel Baptista Nunes, School of Information Management, Sun Yat-sen University, Guangzhou, China
Pedro Isaías, The University of Queensland, Australia
Program Co-Chairs

Budapest, Hungary
April 2017

PROGRAM COMMITTEE

CONFERENCE CHAIR

Professor Philip Powell, Executive Dean, University of London, UK

PROGRAM CO-CHAIRS

Miguel Baptista Nunes, School of Information Management, Sun Yat-sen University, Guangzhou, China
Pedro Isaías, The University of Queensland, Australia

COMMITTEE MEMBERS

Adam Wojtowicz, Poznan University of Economics and Business, Poland
Amelia Badica, University of Craiova, Romania
Anastas Mishev, University of Ss Cyril and Methodius, Macedonia
Anastasia Constantelou, University of the Aegean, Greece
Andrea Kienle, University of Applied Sciences Dortmund, Germany
Betim Cico, South East European University, Macedonia
Bulend Terzioglu, Australian Catholic University, Australia
Christos Kalloniatis, University of the Aegean, Greece
Demetrios Sarantis, National Technical University of Athens, Greece
Dimitar Trajanov, Ss Cyril and Methodius University, Macedonia
Dimitris Karagiannis, University of Vienna, Austria
Dimitris Kardaras, Athens University of Economics and Business, Greece
Eddie Soulier, Université de Technologie de Troyes, France
Edward Bernroider, Vienna University of Economics and Business, Austria
Efthimios Tambouris, University of Macedonia, Greece
Eija Koskivaara, University of Turku, Finland
Eleutherios Papathanassiou, IST College, Greece
Elli Georgiadou, Middlesex University, United Kingdom
Euripides Loukis, University of the Aegean, Greece
Faiez Gargouri, Institut Superieur d'Informatique et de Multimedia, Tunisia
Fang Zhao, Edith Cowan University, Australia
Francisco Jose Silva Mata, Cenatav, Cuba
François Bergeron, TELUQ, Canada
Frank Bannister, Trinity College, Ireland
George Dafoulas, Middlesex University, United Kingdom
Goran Velinov, University Ss. Cyril and Methodius Skopje, Macedonia

KEYNOTE LECTURE

UNDERSTANDING AND MANAGING INFORMATION SYSTEM CONFLICTS

By Professor Albert Boonstra,
Vice Dean of the Faculty of Economics and Business and
Professor of Information Management, University of Groningen,
The Netherlands

Abstract

Dilemmas, tensions and conflicts are an inherent part of organizational life and managers deal with this on an almost daily basis. Information system implementations are a type of change that often leads to open or hidden tensions and conflicts. Managers and others involved can only deal with such conflicts effectively if they understand the nature and causes of information system conflicts (IS conflicts). Despite this, in many situations, IS project managers demonstrate a low degree of 'conflict sensitivity'. IS project proposals are frequently presented from an implicit unitarist view of organizations. Within this view, organizations are perceived to be essentially harmonious, with conflicts both unlikely and undesirable. As such, new information systems are often heralded as innovative and beneficial for the organization, and therefore as progress for all involved. For this reason, design and implementation plans often follow approaches that reflect a lack of awareness of conflicting characteristics of the IS. This keynote addresses the causes, the analysis and the management of IS conflicts. In so doing we both seek to advance theoretical understanding and practical insights that aim to help implementers to become more competent IS conflict managers.

Full Papers

THE TEACHING-LEARNING OF A SECOND LANGUAGE, USING AUGMENTED REALITY AS A TECHNOLOGICAL TOOL

Maily A. Quintero E
Universidad Distrital Francisco Jose de Caldas, Bogotá, Colombia

ABSTRACT

It is well known that in our country learning English is truncated, among other reasons for the lack of appropriate teaching materials to the educational demands of the time, and the use of traditional methodologies. Given this situation, the Augmented Reality becomes a fundamental element in teaching learning English at school, because it has the ability to optimize the process of teaching and learning, adding virtual elements to the real environment, providing information of interest to the user, taking advantage of the ICT infrastructure (Information and Communication Technologies), with highly positive results. This article proposes the development of the implementation of a board game that allows the teaching of English in a playful way using ICT, allowing the student to interact in real time with the virtual contents.

KEYWORDS

Augmented Reality, Education, English, Technology, Teaching, Learning

1. INTRODUCTION

The General Education Act (Act 115 of 1994) provides learning a second language as an added value in the formation of the student and whose impact is reflected in the direct access to sources of knowledge, as well as being an element It allows global interaction with peers from other latitudes [1].

It is well known that learning a second language, English in this case, from an early age, power linguistic intelligence, and develop communication skills that lead the child to develop a complex thought more structured than a monolingual child. According to Lora, "learning new languages can change brain structure" [2], thesis is supported by Grandinetti stating that "people who have knowledge of at least one foreign language, is more likely to advance their career" [3].

The start learning English should be given at the same time the child begins to relate the concepts of mathematical worlds, scientific, linguistic and even playful, as it is essential to enable interconnections to the knowledge that incorporates their cognitive apparatus. Studies by educators and psychologists have determined that children are subjects that easily learn due to those deep capabilities of imitation and abstraction.

In this context, Augmented Reality, acting as a virtual technological tool, has been gaining space and acceptance in different fields, allowing interaction between the virtual and real worlds, using computers and smartphones (mobile devices). The latter are those that offer greater range of application usage as they are powerful, portable and versatile devices for services offered and sensors that allow.

Thanks to these technological conditions, the use of smartphones has spread in society as fundamentally as education, which allows the creation of meaningful learning environments into truly fields [4].

Similarly, one can think that school as an initial area of knowledge, although it does not depend on these new tools, if required, as the learning dynamics have been changing substantially, in these times a process of teaching and learning is inconceivable without the presence of a technological device, as they have been becoming a sensitizer element that arouses interest for knowledge in students, in areas that have traditionally been classified as difficult learning.

By combining real and virtual events, is creating an alternative space that allows interaction, questioning and feedback real-time issues that would otherwise be left out [5].

2. PROBLEM STATEMENT

In the process of teaching-learning a second language, English, in Colombian public schools, it has shown a number of shortcomings that prevent their impact to be highly positive at the end of the school year because the methodologies used are not in line with the changes that have been taking place in the behavior of new generations of individuals; besides not take into account possible changes in the operational structure of the brain. In addition to this, not taking advantage of computing resources and technology available in the market to facilitate the teaching-learning process.

The latter has led us to raise the question of how to develop cognitive abilities significantly to students in Preschool degree in Colombian public schools from the use of ICT in the process of learning a second language, English.

However, some scholars of pedagogy have been given the task of investigating about the learning process, and in turn propose strategies to its improvement, is the case of American pedagogue Edgar Dale, who has made significant contributions in analysis visual and auditory, focused on deciphering the phases of a learning process. After a long period of observation Edgar Dale, it has concluded that there are several percentage learning studies which may be intervened and improved by Augmented Reality. In the cone of learning Dale, shows ways of teaching a particular discipline in relation to the amount of acquired knowledge, which allows us to conclude that requires an alternative methodology to modify these percentages in ascending order, and Augmented Reality now becomes relevant tool for this situation because it allows a significant and real interaction [6].

The proposal is to design and provide a board game for mobile devices that contribute to learning a second language, English, in children of preschool level, from the formulation previously developed with Augmented Reality questions, so that create an experimental universe where students interact. Studies by psychologists and pedagogues confirm that, hear and see provides a comprehensive and cognitive development of the child. Thus the use of the proposal as didactic and pedagogical ICT tool ensures a really significant learning a second language due to this experience is integrated by a greater number of senses simultaneously, hence the success of teaching using Augmented Reality.

3. AUGMENTED REALITY

There is a commonly accurate definition of Augmented Reality today. One of them was given by Ronald Azuma in 1997 the definition of Azuma says Augmented Reality: It combines real and virtual elements, is interactive in real time and is recorded in 3D [7].

Augmented Reality is understood as incorporating digital information data of a real environment, through pattern recognition which is done through software; in other words, it is an interactive tool that is gradually implemented in video games, mass media, architecture, education and even in medicine, etc.

It uses Augmented Reality in order to confront the events of virtual procedures with objective reality, allowing effective development of projects in each discipline where it is implemented. In a primary conception, it can be understood as Augmented Reality technology that according to Azuma "includes elements of virtual reality with real world elements coexist in the same space" [8].

Trying to establish a liaison relationship between these two concepts is not an easy task since, it is not simply to incorporate images or virtual to our real world information, so it becomes necessary to propose different methods to achieve that objective.

It is very important to differentiate Augmented Reality from virtual reality, although they are concepts that are closely linked, there is a thin line that marks the boundary between technology and the other; this difference starts when the user is completely immersed in a world by making it impossible for computer interact with real elements generated, which causes the system to use more resources to generate precisely this virtual world, while Augmented Reality builds on real world and this integrates the virtual information, which makes the user can interact with real and virtual element, while reducing the use of resources, but increasing the complexity [9] [10] [11] [12] [13] [14] [15].

4. AUGMENTED REALITY IN LEARNING

Augmented Reality has become an effective technology platform as it determines a very particular way of perceiving physical reality by students, allowing them to break it down into its various dimensions, and thus facilitate the capture of certain particular situations, sometimes undetectable using traditional teaching methods. From the implementation of Augmented Reality in school, it is feasible to generate models that simplify the multidimensional complexity of the surrounding world, which, from an academic perspective, allows a holistic view of any learning experience [16].

The application of Augmented Reality in the design and development of training materials and learning activities are, however, many heterogeneous in the preschool level because as is well known, the first relationship of children with the world of knowledge is given from the playful interaction; for that reason learning a second language is given as a significant event, as the paradigms of spatiotemporal traditional classroom break, knowledge is contextualized and a transverse relationship between reality and the learning situation is established, in addition to any space physical can become a stimulating learning environment.

In some of the works consulted [17] [18] [19] concludes that Augmented Reality provides valuable tools that can enable reinforce learning and increase student motivation. These tools use 3D applications to enrich the explanatory methodology collaborating with the understanding of the concepts and achieving a better field for practice and experimentation.

Through the use of interface metaphors, they can be used to manipulate physical objects virtual information in an intuitive way and allows the transition between the real world and the virtual naturally. These interfaces allow promote and enhance collaborative work [20].

While the use of Augmented Reality has been gaining space in the process teaching and learning many of its possible applications are in arrears to be developed, and the tangible results being conditioned more to pedagogical applications than technological skills.

5. IMPLEMENTATION AND ANALYSIS OF AUGMENTED REALITY

The proposed tool is a game; by a plane containing boxes is deployed on a physical board, preconfigured content, selected and stored Augmented Reality. The process is that each participating student can touch the virtual dice to record his advance through the boxes of the physical board. In each box corresponding to the topic (English) will appear a question which can be presented through a video or text where the answer comes through animated options which the player will choose by tapping on the screen that appears in the device, so it can move forward. If the answer is incorrectly, the player will lose the turn and the game will continue with another student. If hit, the student still playing. When the student reaches the goal, he not only achieves the target to complete the course of the game, but also gets a score of the game with details of his obtained successes and mistakes, which are saved as the contents that the student could not overcome.

5.1 Process Creation of Augmented Reality Game

The implementation of Augmented Reality is done with the programming language C Sharp (C #) [21]. By UNITY 3D software, this platform is a flexible, powerful development to create 3D and 2D games and cross-platform [22] interactive experiences. Along with the SDK (software development kit [23]) of Vuforia (image recognition engine).

Board's processing creation was performed as a marker that recognizes the application, these can be done from any software able to create or edit images; once created the image, it has to be transformed into a markup format to be recognized by UNITY 3D, this is done on the official website of Vuforia, after creating the marker is unloaded and loaded into the project.

It starts with the creation of 3D animation software made in the blender (3D modeling program) [24], which is exported and loaded into Unity 3D, to combine with the marker.

Once all prototypes loaded 3D Unity, their respective configurations and adjustments in the position, size, quality, and informational texts that each marker or 3D model are made when you have finished the project and then is passed to compile the application.

5.2 Mode of Use of the Application

The users must have a Smartphone with Android operating system and the application filed previously installed. To play users should focus Board; see Figure 1, with your device so that the virtual elements can be visualized through the display of the device. At the beginning of the shift, the student who participates plays the given virtual, see Figure 2, to determine how many boxes advance. Then, the tab, see Figure 3, associated with the student turn player will move to the position which was determined by the random number returned to roll the die. Then shows, a video or a text to perform a question associated with markers with different topics, such as: animal, see Figure 4, colors, see Figure 5, family, see Figure 6, fruit, see Figure 7, and numbers, see Figure 8. At the end of the video playback or reading the text, animated options in which you must choose one response will be displayed. As a result we can expect the player to continue with their turn, if answered correctly. Otherwise, misses the turn to lend it to other participating student. The game ends when a participant reaches the goal.

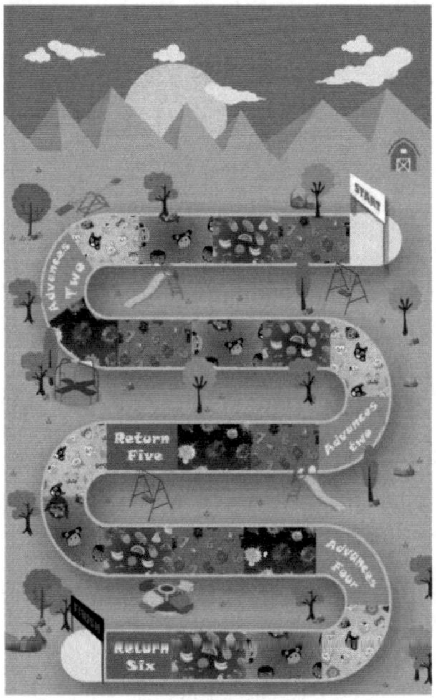

Figure 1. Game Board

Figure 2. Given Virtual

Figure 3. Tab of the Players

Figure 4. Bookmark Animals

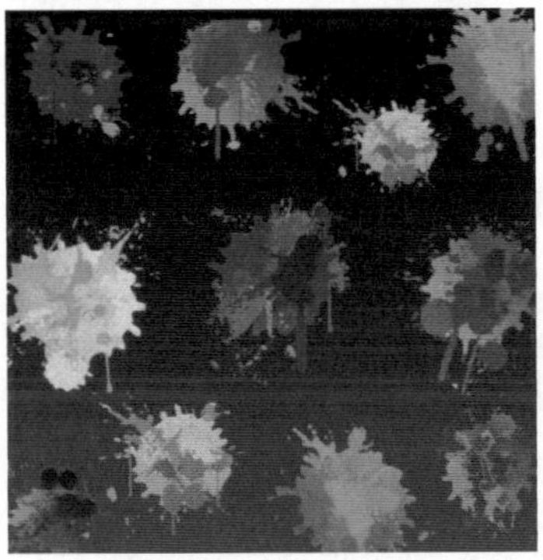

Figure 5. Bookmark Color

Figure 6. Bookmark Family

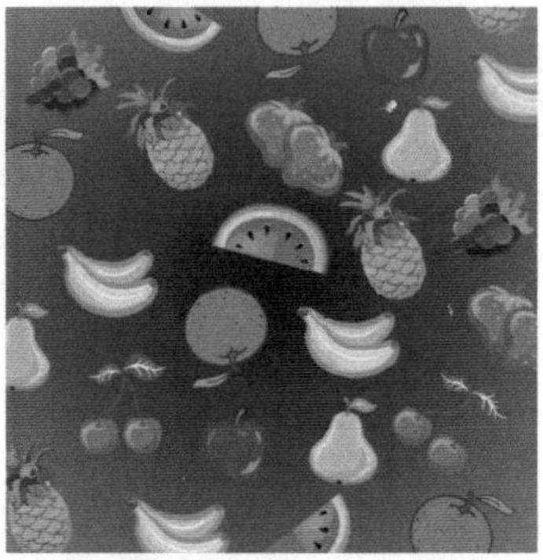

Figure 7. Bookmark Fruits

Figure 8. Bookmark Numbers

5.3 Analysis of Test and Result

Tests were conducted in Almenar School, located in the town of Kennedy, Bogota, Colombia, where 20 students were selected in preschool level, two groups, each one of 10 students, which were asked 20 questions of English equal for both groups covering topics like animals, colors, family, fruits and vocals.

The first group was asked the questions in the form of written test and the second group was asked with questions in an Augmented Reality game.

As you can see the figure 9 shows the result of incorrect and correct answers of the two groups, the highest number of correct answers took place in the group that tried the game due to it can be observed they had satisfactory results where students showed great interest in the mechanics of the game because it rewards knowledge and learning in a high level of incorporation of the exposed contents.

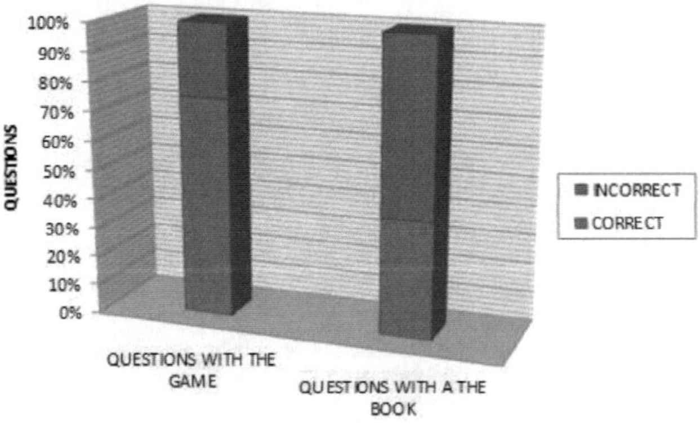

Figure 9. Graphic of Results of Surveys

In addition, students who answered questions with the game made comments such as: "What I like the game was able to turn the elements to see the images in 3D," Use of mobile is an attractive resource for most participating children. "I learned to pronounce many words in English that did not know", this can be because many textbooks do not allow sound reproduction. "The difference of study English book and with this game is that the game amuses children playing and easing", also stressed that the information has more details and looks more real than a 2D image as offering in any book text.

6. CONCLUSION

It is pertinent, learning a second language starting from the pre-school level, since children develop communication skills from the imitation of certain paradigms of teaching that allows them to incorporate into their cognitive universe different knowledge and ways of relating to the world. In this vein it can be concluded that: the application of the augmented reality system helps structuring the cognitive ability of the child, in such a way that, given a different development of complex thought, compared with those who do not have access to the application.

The use of cellular technology is the most widely accepted among children, because it allows a playful handling of different systems, including augmented reality that allows them to the learning of a second language, from the permanent manipulation of the mobile.

From the results obtained, after testing the application proposed in this article, with children from the preschool level of the college Almenar, in relation to the learning of a second language, it was observed that those involved with the new didactic element reached a high percentage of correct answers against those who made it through a traditional text book; qualitative aspects that make up the game could also be analyzed in order to correct it and set it.

Implementation in the school of ICT in these times is almost as mandatory, because thanks to them can be developed, in real time and space, a second language teaching and learning methodologies, consistent with the real educational needs.

For a better understanding of everything related with augmented reality, defined the basic principles that constitute it and the ways how you can access and manipulate the application, in order to have a basic knowledge and from it, discover all its didactic possibilities.

The possibilities that it brings augmented reality, are evident and practices, however the difficulty, is the creation of interactive content, because it is a task that is as wasteful as the elaboration of a text book.

REFERENCES

1. Congreso de Colombia, *ley 115 de 1994*. Retrieved from: http://www.alcaldiabogota.gov.co/sisjur/normas/Norma1.jsp?i=292.0
2. Raquel M.T. 2004. *Estrategias Instruccionales Constructivistas en la Formación de Docentes de Inglés*. Retrieved from: http://dspace.casagrande.edu.ec:8080/bitstream/ucasagrande/418/1/Tesis709MAQe.pdf.
3. Lora, Anderson A. 2011. *La importancia de aprender una segunda lengua*. Retrieved from: https://www.gvsu.edu/cms3/assets/F8585381-E4E9-6F8EF7EE2083CCE4F9AC/2011/nuestros_ensayos_la_importancia_de_aprender_una_segunda_lengua.pdf, pp. 2.
4. Carmen C. V., Margarita R. R., Ana S. P., 2012 *Tendencias actuales en el uso de dispositivos móviles en educación* Retrieved from: http://educoas.org/portal/la_educacion_digital/147/pdf/ART_UNNED_EN.pdf, pp. 8-9.
5. Florez, C.J., Dominguez, J.C., Rodriguez, V.J.: *La realidad Aumentada como herramienta para mejorar los procesos educativos en la USMP*. Retrieved from: http://www.anobium.es/docs/gc_fichas/doc/6CFJNSalrt.pdf.
6. Dale, E, 1966. *Métodos de enseñanza audiovisual*, Mexico.
7. Realidad aumentada. Retrieved from: http://wwwavancesdelcelular. weebly.com/definicion.html
8. Azuma, 2001: R.T. Azuma "*Augmented Reality: Approaches and Technical Challenges*", Fundamentals of Wearable Computers and Augmented Reality, W. Barfield, Th. Caudell (eds.), Mahwah, New Jersey, 2001, pp 27-63.
9. A. A. Toro. Modelo de Contexto para Realidad Aumentada.
10. A. Ruiz, C. Urdiales, J. A. Fernández-Ruiz, and F. Sandoval, 2004. *Ideación Arquitectónica Asistida mediante Realidad Aumentada*. Innovación en Telecomunicaciones.

11. T. Maldonado, 2004. *Mundo virtual y mundo real*. Debats, pp. 20 – 27.

12. D. Levis, 1997. *¿Qué es la realidad virtual*.

13. C. Boj and D. Díaz, 2007. *La hibridación a escena: Realidad aumentada y teatro*. UNAM. MX. Revista Digital Universitaria,Vol 8, pp 6.

14. M. I., i Melchor Herrero, and G. A. García. 2006. *Realidad Aumentada: ARToolKit para animación de personajes*.

15. J. M. Andujar, A. Mejias, and M. A. Marquez, 2011. *Augmented Reality for the Improvement of Remote Laboratories: An Augmented Remote Laboratory*. Education, IEEE Transactions on, 54(3) pp 492 – 500.

16. Jacqueline C. M., Alejandro H. G., Angélica T. T., Sidley V. R., 2015, *Implementación de realidad aumentada como herramienta para el aprendizaje en los estudiantes de ii ciclo de la carrera técnica profesional de computación e informática del instituto superior bitec de la ciudad de Chimbote*. Retrieved from: http://www.docfoc.com/ pp. 14

17 Fombona C. J., Goulão, M.., Tamargo G., 2014. Melhorar a atratividade da informação através do uso da realidade aumentada. Perspectivas em Ciência da Informação. Retrieved from: http://www.scielo.br/pdf/pci/v19n1/04.pdf. Vol.19, n.1, pp. 37-50.

18 D. Ruiz Torres, 2011. Revista Icono14, Realidad Aumentada, educación y museos, Volumen 2. pp. 212-226. Retrieved from: http://www.icono14.net.

19 Su Cai, Xu Wang, Feng-Kuang C., 2014. A case study of Augmented Reality simulation system application in a chemistry course, Computers in Human Behavior, Volume 37, pp. 31-40. Retrieved from: http://dx.doi.org/10.1016/j.chb.2014.04.018.

20 Haller M., Billinghurst, M., Thomas, 2007. Emerging Technologies of Augmented Reality – Interfaces and Design. Idea Group Publishing. ISBN 1-59904-067-0.

21. Microsoft, (s.f.). Visual C#. Retrieved from: https://msdn. microsoft.com/es-es/library/kx37x362.aspx.

22. Unity3D, (s.f.). La mejor plataforma de desarrollo para crear juegos. Retrieved from: https://unity3d.com/es/unity.

23. programaciondesarrollo. 2011. ¿Qué es sdk?. Retrieved from: http://programacion desarrollo.es/¿que-es-sdk.

24. renderati, (s.f.). ¿Qué es Blender?. Retrieved from: http://www.renderati.com/render/%C2%BFque-es-blender/.

RULE-BASED EXPERT SYSTEM TO LEAD FRESHMEN STUDENTS IN CHOOSING A SUITABLE COLLEGE MAJOR IN PALESTINE POLYTECHNIC UNIVERSITY

Bashar Albakri, Samaher Abuhamdeiyeh and Musa Alrefaya
Palestine Polytechnic University, College of Information Technology and Computer Engineering
Wadi Alhareya, Hebron, Palestine

ABSTRACT

Choosing a suitable college major is a challenging process for freshman students. This research focuses on switching the process of selecting a college major form the traditional method into a systematic and computerized method by deploying artificial intelligence and an expert system. In order to lead freshman students to a suitable college major, the research proposes to use rule-based expert system with multi-criteria analysis such as student general ability, personality character and market analysis for future careers. Results revealed that the proposed system has provided accurate outcomes based on the knowledge extracted from the domain experts. The outcomes of the proposed system suggested a minimum number of major alternatives, these alternatives were sorted based on the importance of each assessed criteria. Keeping into consideration that the proposed system was found to lead and help freshman students in choosing a suitable college major, but not to replace human experts within the same domain.

KEYWORDS

Expert System, Decision Support System, College Major, College Major Selection

1. INTRODUCTION

In recent years, statistics have revealed relative increase in the total number of high school graduates who are planning to be enrolled in universities, with a total number of 77772 in 2016 according to (Palestinian Ministry of Education and Higher Education, 2016).

It should not be a surprise that the majority of those freshman students didn't receive any advice related to the college major selection process, the fact is, they count on their own judgment and evaluation to choose a suitable college major. However, (Arcidiacono Peter, 2012) stated that choosing an appropriate college major is absolutely necessary and important for determining the student's future attainment. Studies such as (Douglas, 2016) highlighted the importance of the selected college major on financial values, and other studies indicate that the academic major plays a significant role in work value and individual differences (Balsamo Michela, 2013).

Colleges and universities offer hundreds of choices, and it is a challenge for students to decide what major they are going to be enrolled in. However, most colleges and universities depend on admission and enrollment criteria, which primarily depend on the student's academic records as an indicator of general academic abilities. Nevertheless, studies such as (Bartolj Tjaša, 2012) suggest that it's not good enough, and other researches discussed the importance of using artificial intelligence theories in education (Gardner, 1995) and personality matching to college majors and career fields (Barak Azy, 1982), since the students' personality impacts the students' satisfaction, thus affecting the students' performance (Pawlowska, 2014).

Nowadays, Decision Support System DSS and Expert System ES have been widely used, and researchers from many disciplines studied and implement DSS and ES for almost 40 years (Burstein Frada, 2008) in Medical Issues (Patra, 2010), Business management and process (Arias-Aranda, 2010) (Hettiarachchi, 2016), Environmental (Pincinato, 2009), Architecture and Engineering (Ibáñez, 2016) and Education (Engin, 2014) (Kamarthi, 1992).

Considerable things can be done with DSS and ES to lead freshman students in their college major selection process. The presented work describes developing, implementing and testing the decision support system (expert system) to advice freshman students the most suitable college major. Thus, the overall objective of this research is to reduce number of students who drop-out due to bad choice by using artificial intelligence and expert system.

2. SYSTEM SPECIFICATION

The domain of this research can be summarized from the previous discussion as a system that aims to switching the college major selection process from the traditional method into a knowledge based expert system. Thus, the proposed system assesses the most important criteria that any student takes into consideration when choosing a college major, these include:

2.1 Admission and Enrollment Criteria

Being enrolled in a specific major primarily depends on set of predefined requirements in a particular college or university which any student has to satisfy, these predefined requirements including: general examination score and the field of study (Art, Science, Economy, Occupational and Technology) which differ from one university to another. As a case study, Palestine Polytechnic University has been selected to develop and implement this system; the university offers two, four and five years programs that include more than 50 majors, divided into 6 faculties (Palestine Polytechnic University, 2016).

2.2 Personality Match

Many empirical researches found relations between a students' personality theme and suited college major, they stated that the college major and personality match led to locating student's future occupation and more work satisfaction (Prediger, 1992). However, in this research Holland's hexagon theory will be proposed as personality indicator and will be assessed as one of the selecting college major criteria.

Holland has defined six personality themes including: realistic, investigative, artistic, social, enterprising, and conventional, commonly identified by only the first letter I, A, S, E, and C. He suggested that people usually have more than one theme characteristic, usually two or more, and few people said that a person has a unique personality theme (Holland, Making vocational choices; a theory of careers, 1973,1985). However, a personality theme can be declared by two dominant themes such as RI, SE, EC or other, with strongest theme donated by primary and second strongest theme donated by secondary theme. Thus, an individual can be identified as some researchers suggest to use strongest three letters (Holland, Some speculation about the investigation of person-environment transactions, 1987).

2.3 Market Analysis and Future Career

Choosing a suitable college major can lead to a better job opportunity, job satisfaction and guaranteed financial security. Since most students will be classified as a job seeker after completing one particular program in college or university, therefore it is increasingly important to think carefully about where their studies will lead them. The proposed system continuously assesses future careers as important criteria that must be taken into consideration when choosing a college major.

3. PROPOSD METHODOLOGY

The proposed methodology of this research is to develop an effective method to lead freshman student to choose the most suitable college majors using an expert system. This can be done by identification, conceptualization and formalization of all the proposed college major criteria. An expert system relies on two basic components as illustrated in figure 1,

1- Knowledge base, which is a set of organized facts about the system's domain.
2- Inference engine interprets and evaluates the facts in the knowledge base.

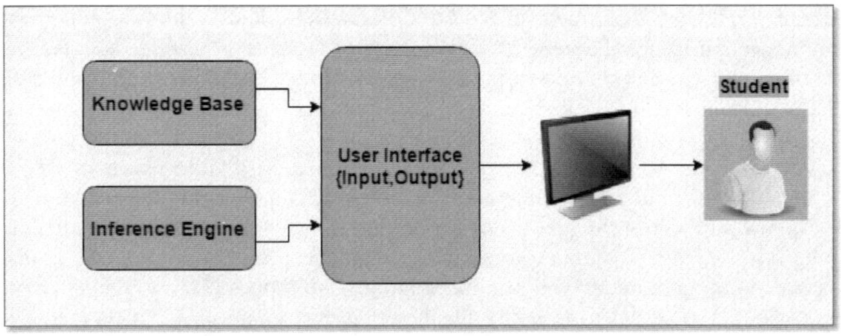

Figure 1. Basic Components of Expert System

However, the proposed system will pass through the following methodology illustrated in figure 2 which attempts to represent all major selection criteria. The methodology includes: Knowledge elicitation, knowledge representation and models design, Implementation and Testing and accuracy assessment.

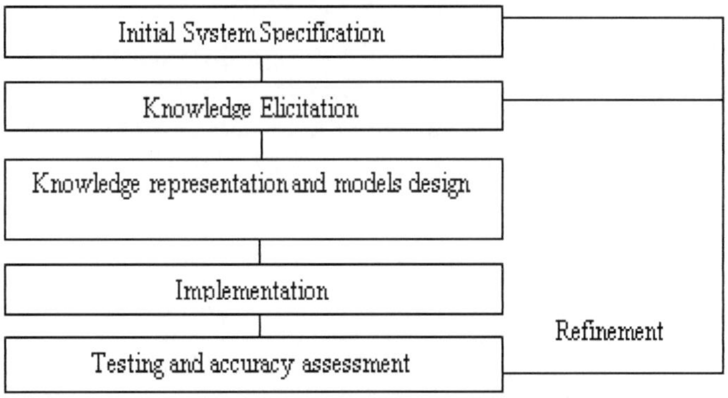

Figure 2. Proposed Methodology

3.1 Knowledge Elicitation

Knowledge elicitation, known as the process in which all the information and facts that are related to one specific domain are extracted from closely related experts, the sources of the knowledge in this research is extracted from the admission and enrollment department in Palestine Polytechnic University, interviews and literature review.

Official admission and enrollment criteria has been acquired, since it's basic information that must be taken into consideration, the interviews were primarily based on human experts, advisors and specialists to provide greater understanding of the reasoning behind the selection process. In addition to admission/enrollment criteria and interviews with experts, previous research and empirical studies have been reviewed as part of literature review to provide greater understanding of the system domain.

3.2 knowledge Representation and Models Design

What comes after knowledge elicitation is a set of logical models and decision tables to represent the acquired knowledge in a way that all selection criteria are connected to each other. In this research, the system has been divided into sub-models in which each model represents one criterion.

3.2.1 Admission and Enrollment

A deep analysis has been done for admission and acceptance criteria based on the information obtained from the admission and enrollment department in Palestine Polytechnic University, students must belong to the predefined requirements in which the university asks students to satisfy, these include: General Examination score and field of study (Art, Science, Economy, Occupational and Technology). Table (1) clarifies colleges and majors that a student is allowed to be enrolled in, based on General Examination score and Filed of Study.

A build-in coding model has been developed for the purpose of dividing students into a set of groups based on their suitability; the build-in coding model assesses the degree in which General Examination score, Field of study and α contribute to the process of classifying students to university faculties. However, α was derived from the fact that some majors require high mathematical skills, critical thinking and logical skills. Such as engineering programs and applied science programs, we proposed that if the value of α is more than 80 % then the student is more suited to apply for the college of engineering. If the value of α is between 70 – 80 % then the student is suited to apply for the college of applied science or the college of information technology and computer science, and if the value of α is less than 70 % then the student is more suited to apply for other colleges.

α can be calculated by the average scores of Mathematics, Physics and English:

$$\alpha = \frac{\text{Mathmatics \%} + \text{Physics \%} + \text{English \%}}{3}$$

The result of the build-in coding model is a set of total points divided into intervals in which each interval represents one faculty that the student is allowed to be enrolled in.

Table 1. Admission and Enrollment Criteria in Palestine Polytechnic University

Field of study / College	Science	Art	Economy	Occupational
College of Engineering	Accepted with an average score above 80%	Not Accepted	Not Accepted	Accepted with an average score above 80%
College of Administrative Sciences and Informatics	Accepted with an average score above 70%	Accepted with an average score above 70%	Accepted with an average score above 70%	Accepted in Information system with an average score above 70%
College of Information Technology and Computer Engineering	Accepted with an average score above 70%, except computer engineering with an average score above 80%	Not Accepted	Not Accepted	Accepted with an average score above 70%, except computer engineering with an average score above 80%
College of Applied Sciences	Accepted with an average score above 65%	Not Accepted	Not Accepted	Accepted in applied electronics with an average score above 65%
College of Applied Professions (Two years program)	Accepted with an average score above 50%	Computer information technology program, Administrative Science Program and Banking and Finance program	Computer information technology program, Administrative Science Program and Banking and Finance program	Computer information technology program and Engineering professions programs

Table 2 illustrates how the build-in coding model is working and how the total points is calculated, while Table 3 clarifies how the total points could be associated with the appropriate faculty.

Table 2. Build-In Coding Model Decision Table

Build-In coding model		
Field of Study	Science	300 Points
	Art	150
	Economy	150
	Occupational	250
General Examination score	80 – 100 %	300
	70 – 79.9 %	250
	65 – 69.9 %	100
	50 – 64.9 %	0
α	80 ↑	150
	70 – 80	99
	70 ↓	0

Table 3. The Appropriate Faculty Based on Build-In Coding Model

Total Points	faculty
0.0-399	College of Applied Professions (Two years program)
400-499	College of Administrative Sciences an Informatics
500-699	College of Applied Sciences and College of Information Technology an Computer Engineering
700 or more	College of Engineering

Now the whole process of selecting a major based on admission and enrollment criteria is moving on this track. First of all, the student must provide information about the program type that he/she may wish to belong to, and then provide an academic record and the general examination score. The system will assess this information and then lead the student to the accepted majors with reference to admission and enrollment criteria as illustrated in table 4.

3.2.2 Personality Match

As discussed before, the students' general ability is an important factor to choose a college major but counting only on it is not good enough. Thus, in this research we link the students' general ability with his/her personality theme. Holland Personality Theme HPT which is based on HPTs theory stated that the personality is basically divided into six categories including: realistic, investigative, artistic, social, enterprising, and conventional. These donated by the first strongest letter and second strongest letter. This research proposed to use the two strongest personality theme to identify the students' general character as shown in table 5, and then define the college majors associated with each personality theme. All the majors offered by Palestine Polytechnic University were examined and represented with the help of human experts within the same domain.

3.2.3 Market Analysis and Future Career

As discussed before, choosing suitable college major will lead to career success and more job satisfaction. The final stage of the analysis is assessing the degree in which has an increasing demand for current and future careers contribute in major selection process. The proposed system was based on local, regional and global indicators, this will help students to take into consideration the alternative majors they seek to apply for.

Table 4. Admission and Enrollment Criteria Decision Table

Conditions	Program Type	4 Years Program	N	N	N	N	Y	Y	Y	Y
		2 Years Program	Y	Y	Y	Y	N	N	N	N
	Total Points	0 – 399	N	N	N	Y	N	N	N	Y
		400 - 499	N	N	Y	N	N	N	Y	N
		500 - 699	N	Y	N	N	N	Y	N	N
		700 or more	Y	N	N	N	Y	N	N	N
Alternatives		College of Engineering					√			
		College of Applied Sciences					√	√		
		College of Information Technology and Computer Engineering					√	√		
		College of Administrative Sciences and Informatics					√	√	√	
		College of Applied Professions	√	√	√	√				√

Table 5. Holland Personality Theme HPT Matrix

		Secondary					
		R	I	A	S	E	C
Primary	R	RR	RI	RA	RS	RE	RC
	I	IR	II	IA	IS	IE	IC
	A	AR	AI	AA	AS	AE	AC
	S	SR	SI	SA	SS	SE	SC
	E	ER	EI	EA	ES	EE	EC
	C	CR	CI	CA	CS	CE	CC

The system assessed the expanding industries and sector, careers availability in the future, wages and salaries and the employment growth, even in regional, if available, or global base, and then linked this information majors that Palestine Polytechnic University offers. In case of information unavailability about a specific major, then we proposed to use the most related information based on human experts and consolers.

3.3 Implementation

After data and domain knowledge has represented in set of models and decision tables to retrieve required knowledge, the next stage was implementing the system in a way which achieves its primary objective. This has been done through the use of basic architecture of expert system presented in figure 1.

A Rule- based method was used to implement all the decisions tables within the system. Since all criteria of the major selection is a symbolic criterion, it can be logically transformed to IF-THEN format. The proposed expert system was developed with an Object-Oriented Database which can symbolize all data and domain knowledge.

The system was developed as Web-Based expert system. PHP with MySQL environment was used to build up and structure the logical process flowchart. Figure 3 illustrates logical schema of proposed system.

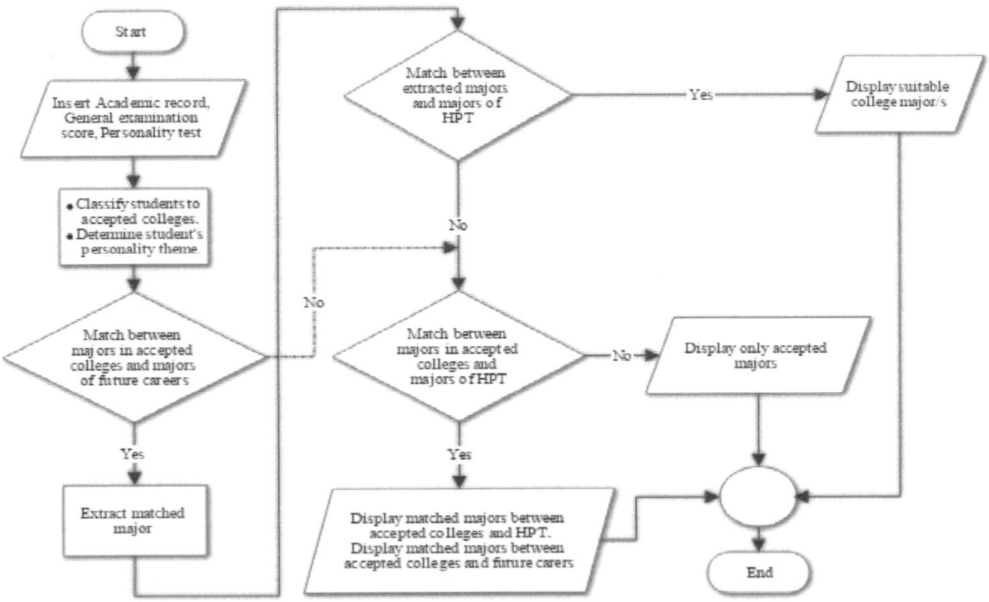

Figure 3. Logical Schema of Proposed System

3.4 Testing and Accuracy Assessment

A sample data were collected from students (n= 887, 443 Female and 443 Male) at Palestine Polytechnic University and analyzed for the purpose of applying testing process. The testing process which includes verification and accuracy assurance was applied to ensure that the proposed system meets its primary objective and provides accurate results based on the predefined criteria. However, functional testing and random data testing were applied as a part of the testing process. In functional testing, sub-functions inside the proposed system such as testing accepted colleges based on admission and enrollment criteria and majors of HPT were separately tested and examined to ensure that each sub system functions as planned. Random data testing process examines system results if random data was provided by a student.

Accuracy assurance testing process which assesses the degree to which the proposed system provides an accurate result, this is basically done through presenting results to human experts and counselors.

4. RESULTS AND DISCUSSION

The proposed system was successfully implemented in a way which meets its predefined primary objectives. the system provides either one of two alternatives that include: 1) most suitable college major/s that would be student's academic record, personality general character and career availability, 2) majors that would be eligible for personality general character or career availability.

The results offered by the system was fully accurate based on information provided by the student and knowledge-based acquired by the domain experts. The results were previewed by academic advisors and the discussion of these results stated that it can be reliable based on the fact that all analyzed criteria were significant for the process of choosing the college major.

Discussion of the results revealed that 11% of the students touched by their gender aspect when choosing their major. Females tend to choose a college major which will usually lead them to desk jobs, while males more likely tend to choose majors which will lead them to on field and vocational jobs. Further, 7 % of the students choose a major based on family suggestion and their parent's jobs, while 21 % said that funding issues and financial aspect affect their decisions

The knowledge that related to the market analysis and future career must be continuously updated, in this research the knowledge was derived from global statistics, but local and regional market trends must be assessed and taken into consideration to provide more accurate results.

5. CONCLUSION

In this research, a rule-based expert system for leading freshmen students to select the most appropriate college major has been proposed, designed, implemented and tested. The proposed system considered criteria such as student general ability, personality character and market analysis for future careers. Each used criteria has been analysed and discussed. The system provides reliable and accurate results based on information provided by students and knowledge extracted from experts and specialists. Extra environmental and cultural factors can be easily merged in the proposed system.

REFERENCES

Arcidiacono P. et al, 2012. *Modeling college major choices using elicited measures of expectations and counterfactuals. National Bureau of Economic Research*, Cambridge, UK.

Arias-Aranda, D. et al, 2010, December. A fuzzy expert system for business management. *Expert Systems with Applications*, 37(12), 7570-7580. doi:10.1016/j.eswa.2010.04.086.

Pawlowska, D. K. et al, 2014, December. Student personality, classroom environment, and student outcomes: A person–environment fit analysis. *Learning and Individual Differences*, 36, 180-193. doi:10.1016/j.lindif.2014.10.005.

Balsamo M. et al, 2013. Work values and college major choice. *Learning and Individual Differences*, 24, 110-116. doi:10.1016/j.lindif.2012.12.022

Barak A. et al, 1982, April. Predicting persistence, stability, and achievement in college by major choice consistency: A test of Holland's consistency hypothesis. *Journal of Vocational Behavior*, 20(2), 235-243. doi:10.1016/0001-8791(82)90011-2.

Logaj, T., & Polanec, S, 2012, July. College major choice and ability: Why is general ability not enough? *Economics of Education Review, 31(6), 996-1016. doi:10.1016/j.econedurev.2012.07.010.*

Burstein, F., & Holsapple, C. W, 2008. *Handbook on decision support systems.* Springer, Berlin.

Douglas, W, 2016, Augest. Are college costs worth it? How ability, major, and debt affect the returns to schooling. *Economics of Education Review*, 53, 296-310. doi:10.1016/j.econedurev.2016.04.007.

Engin, G. et al, 2014. Rule-based Expert Systems for Supporting University Students. *Procedia Computer Science*, 31, 22-31. doi:10.1016/j.procs.2014.05.241.

Gardner, H., 1995. December. Multiple Intelligences" as a Catalyst. *The English Journal, 84(8), 16. doi:10.2307/821182.*

Hettiarachchi, C.et al, 2016, January. Risk-based test case prioritization using a fuzzy expert system. *Information and Software Technology*, 69, 1-15. doi:10.1016/j.infsof.2015.08.008.

Holland, J. L, 1973,1985. *Making vocational choices; a theory of careers.* Prentice-Hall, Englewood Cliffs, NJ.

Holland, J. L, 1987. Some speculation about the investigation of person-environment transactions. *Journal of Vocational Behavior*, 31(3), 337-340. doi:10.1016/0001-8791(87)90048-0.

Ibáñez, A. J. et al, 2016, April. Expert system for predicting buildings service life under ISO 31000 standard. Application in architectural heritage. *Journal of Cultural Heritage*, 18, 209-218. doi:10.1016/j.culher.2015.10.006.

Kamarthi, S. et al, 1992. ADVISOR—An expert system for the selection of courses☆. *expert Systems with Applications*, 5(1-2), 153-165. doi:10.1016/0957-4174(92)90104-z.

Palestinian Ministry of Education and Higher Education, 2016. *Publications and Studies*. Retrieved from moehe.gov: http://www.moehe.gov.ps

Pawlowska, D. et al, 2014. December. Student personality, classroom environment, and student outcomes: A person–environment fit analysis. *Learning and Individual Differences*, 36, 180-193. doi:10.1016/j.lindif.2014.10.005.

Pincinato, F. et al, 2009. September. Modelling an expert GIS system based on knowledge to evaluate oil spill environmental sensitivity. *Ocean & Coastal Management*, 52(9), 479-486. doi:10.1016/j.ocecoaman.2009.08.003.

Prediger, D. J., & Vansickle, T. R, 1992, April. Locating occupations on Holland's hexagon: Beyond RIASEC. *Journal of Vocational Behavior*, 40(2), 111-128. doi:10.1016/0001-8791(92)90060-d.

VIRTUAL REALITY: A TECHNOLOGICAL TOOL FOR TEACHING THE LOGIC OF PROGRAMMING WITH THE HELP OF A SERIOUS GAME

Michael Valencia R.
Universidad Distrital Francisco Jose de Caldas, Bogotá, Colombia

ABSTRACT

Currently it is essential that the student develops his logic and even more a good logic of programming. In this perspective, it is intended to turn programming logic into a teaching-learning tool, developing different kind of competences in the student, which will help him achieve positive results during the school and work stages, as well as provide tools that allow him to solve problems or situations of daily life using algorithmic formats. The teacher's activity must be rethought when faced with a wave of changes between which information technology compels the search for new forms and learning environments, knowing the way students learn, allowing the teacher to establish strategies and resources that favor the educational process; therefore, the development of pedagogical tools that integrate the use of Virtual Reality, can achieve an effective multisensory communication in the classrooms, taking into account that students have different learning abilities. This work proposes the development of a serious game through the application of Virtual Reality, which improves the abilities with respect to the concepts of sequencing, defined iteration, nesting, modularization and structuring, concepts that are part of the programming logic without to emphasize some particular language, since everything is directed to the design of algorithms.

KEYWORDS

Virtual Reality, Serious Games, Programming Logic, Teaching, Learning

1. INTRODUCTION

Virtual Reality is a technology that has been taken a major boom in all fields of the current productive society, as it is part of the recent technological revolution of ICT [1], the consequences can be displayed on the decline materials costs to produce hardware and software. Similarly, it has enhanced the acquisition, processing and reproduction of information, making this technology into a tool that is applicable in processes such as teaching and learning, as they have allowed transform traditional teaching methods of teaching in school, facilitating access to information in real time and space, making it possible to obtain highly positive results, in the case of the teaching of logic programming [2] [3].

It is noteworthy that in Colombia the teaching of logic programming in primary and secondary school is not part of the curriculum, since this subject mistakenly only pertaining to undergraduate programs in engineering and technical programs in the computer area, a situation that deserves to be reviewed by the Ministry of Education.

The programming logic is designed to solve different types of problems, to achieve this, it is necessary to consider three fundamental aspects: analyze and understand the meaning of the problem to be solved; also specify the requirements that warrant the problem, for example, inputs, outputs and processes and finally propose an appropriate solution.

The game as a mechanism for learning and improving skills is characteristic of living beings. In the academic context, the game can be considered an auxiliary tool in the construction of systematized knowledge. There are many studies indicating the importance of play in the teaching-learning because it allows the development of communication skills as well as the structuring of mathematical logical thinking, and sensorimotor revitalization. Seen transversely above, is the basis that allows troubleshooting with algorithmic [4] principles.

The game is a must in all teaching-learning process as it generates motivation, increases self-esteem, in addition to promoting habits and commitments on the student.

2. PROBLEM STATEMENT

Non-teaching logic programming in primary and secondary schools has contributed to learning levels do not prove satisfactory when being measured, basically admission tests to higher education and national or international, SABER and PISA.

To overcome this obstacle has implemented a series of strategies at the level of the curriculum, as well as the restructuring of textbooks and adjustment in teaching methodologies, however this has not been enough for them is necessary to implement ICT, as are endless studies supporting its effectiveness in teaching and learning processes [5].

Is very likely to develop programming logic for people, they are able to understand a problem, for instance, abstracting, model and analyze its content, ask a relevant and effective solution [6], however, this means a whole methodological cognitive process that ultimately leads to the design of an algorithmic solution, understood as the set of ordered sequences [7].

With the aim of solving many of the problems of teaching and learning in primary and secondary school I created a serious game, in which people are able to develop their logic programming and thus strengthen and improve their skills regarding sequencing concepts defined iteration, nesting, modularization and structuring [8] [9] [10]. The serious game consists of an intuitive and attractive interface, from the Virtual Reality, so that allows access to an experience of personal interaction, as different levels of difficulty lead a search for possible effective solutions.

3. VIRTUAL REALITY

The concept of Virtual Reality is defined by, its breakdown, thus: reality means anything that is perceived as real, i.e truthfully that exists and that is not part of fantasy or imagination; and virtual is related to everything that has the virtue to exist, so apparently, although it is not real [11].

In recent times have been generating definitions that differ according to the concept we have, is the case of Manetta C. and R. Blade in 1995, who proposed that the "Virtual Reality: a computer system used to create a artificial world in which the user has the impression of being and the ability to navigate and manipulate objects in it "; Hodder and Stoughton and propose that "Virtual Reality allows you to explore a world generated by computer through your presence in it."

Based on the above it can be concluded that the Virtual Reality is a computer system that generates real-time representations of scenes, objects and situations real appearance; pretending simulate sensory reactions, so enabling it to perceive the virtual world, which is not an illusion, because it is a perceptual reality no physical support and which only occurs within computers [11].

For an event of Virtual Reality This should take into account the following principles: immersion, interaction and imagination, so that a space where the user does not have the ability to differentiate the real from the unreal is generated, see Figure 1 [12]".

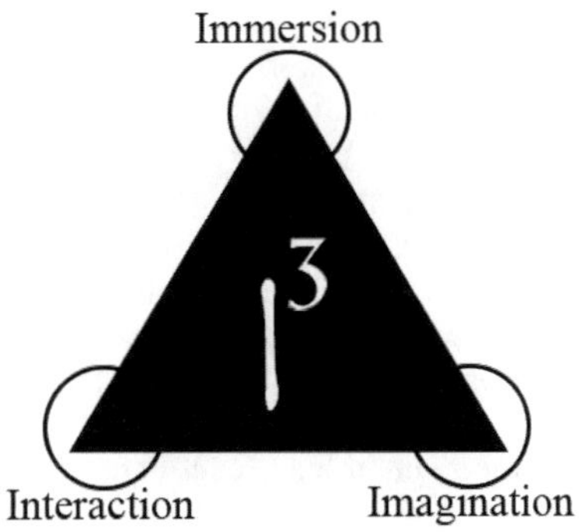

Figure 1. Triangle of Virtual Reality

Immersion is a moment in which the user loses touch with reality to perceive only the stimuli of the virtual world, then a phenomenon of interaction with the elements of the virtual world is presented through input devices, so that modifies sensory behaviors, upon receiving the response through the senses, then emptying into the world of imagination realities that do not exist in a tangible way, as in art spaces [13] are perceived.

4. SERIOUS GAMES FOCUSED ON EDUCATION

Game is an innate human condition, just observe how fleeting relationships of friendship between children, young people or adults, even without knowing it, and the effect that this generates in the cognitive, physical, social and emotional development are established. It is commonly played for fun and socialisation; According to Crawford, it is primarily played to learn, even though it is an unconscious intention. Huizinga, Gros, Gee considered the game as a voluntary, primarily social, activity where it is in relation to others and learned patterns of behavior, values and culture [14]. On the other hand wheat points out that the game is a determining factor for the structuring of language and thought, acts systematically on the psychosomatic balance; allows learning of strong significance; It reduces the sensation of gravity against mistakes and failures; It invites active participation by the player; It develops creativity, intellectual competence, emotional strength and personal stability. Finally, it can be said that play is an essential strategy to stimulate the comprehensive development of people in general [15].

The term "serious game", seems to be contradictory, since the word "game" is synonymous with fun, joy and fantasy, are conceived as an action that "serious" things of life. The term 'serious' refers to liability, common sense, reality and actions with consequences to consider.

The serious games according to Michael and Chen, are basically used to educate, train and inform. The term has been used since the 60's by Clark Abt, referring to games that simulated events of World War I, in which the strategies of war in the classroom are recreated. However, at present, is assigned this name to a group of video games and simulators whose aim is the formation before the entertainment [16].

5. LEARNING LOGIC PROGRAMMING USING VIRTUAL REALITY

In recent years, Virtual reality, has been becoming an alternative to traditional learning experiences [17] approach, on the basis of the ability that has this technology to provide a highly interactive visual environment, approximate to the one offered by the real world, moreover, allowing people to experience the feeling of being present in the environment with the possibility as well as interact with objects within it. Current research has shown that the use of Virtual reality, is highly significant in the process of teaching - learning.

Now, to better understand the concepts related to the teaching of programming logic, is necessary to adapt in a practical way of virtual environments, since this is its raison d ' être, and so has dip, as a fundamental tool, since the process is always developed within the virtual context with a result interactive, complemented by the representation of the concept. For Gordin et al. (Cited by Fallman, Backman & Holmlund 1999), different academic disciplines such as physics, chemistry, algebra and even Linguistics, success for a student depends largely on its ability to anticipate and handle abstract information, so that the handling of Virtual reality, is a determining factor, which helps people to recognize the different conceptual patterns to qualitatively understand the physical processes, to move between the different frames of reference and to more easily understand the dynamic models that can contain intangible information. It should be noted that, to the initiates the process of solving a problem, no matter if it is ordinary or not, always we are faced with the difficulty of having to precisely find a solution, leaving the structural way that that implies, because prima power media on the analytical side. It is in this range of thinking, where the knowledge of programming logic meets a very important role, because through algorithmic elements has to build the relevant to the problem solution.

However, so algorithmic response is relevant, it is necessary to have clarity of what we want to solve, and so design the algorithm, understood as one sequence ordinate of moments that allow a target [18]. An example of how it operates an algorithmic solution, find it in the following situation: the acquisition of a book in the library.

Algorithm 1 Purchase_of_a_Book

Beginning
Know what is the book that you want to purchase.

Scroll down to the library.

Ask if you have the book you need.

If they do not boy it and stop there (in the algorithm). If not, GO to step 2 (to another library).

End

The RV is a tool very useful for programming logic learning significantly, by its multimedia features and the possibility to involve people in a synthetic environment similar to a large extent to the reality, making them feel really within the virtual stage, facilitating learning. The features have and the ability to allow people to visualize complex or abstract concepts. RV offers many advantages in learning, including the delivery of information through multiple channels, addressing different learning styles and learning based on experience [19].

6. IMPLEMENTATION OF VIRTUAL REALITY

The proposal is the creation of a serious game, which serves for the learning of concepts from logic of programming from the solution of any problem, creating structural paths to reach a solution, called algorithm, the game is given in such a way that for each level that the user go beyond, increase the difficulty, in order to identify strengths and weaknesses.

Programming logic, should be used to solve the levels of the game, each level challenges, these are given in the form of a question, in the form of text and animations; each level is divided into two challenges: the first challenge is an introduction, the steps of the algorithm which are randomly and are located on the right side of the interface should be organized to resolve it the user has to go by selecting them in where they are going to be adding to a list that is located in the lower part of the interface, the selected steps must comply with the correct order of the established algorithm and thus meet the challenge, see Figure 2, otherwise indicate to the user that the selected steps do not comply with a logical order and you have to start the challenge see Figure 3, where it meets with the logical order should advance to the second part of the challenge, where the user has to help the protagonist to solve a problem of everyday life, to overcome the challenge, the user must first select the input data, selected once is to create logical due process with the help of a few words actions and a few diagrams with their respective representation in order to resolve the problem, see Figure 4, and as the last part you click on the button run resulting in the right or wrong solution to the problem, if you hit the user, progresses to the next level, where there is a level of greater complexity.

Figure 2. Graphical Interface Challenge One, Solved Correctly

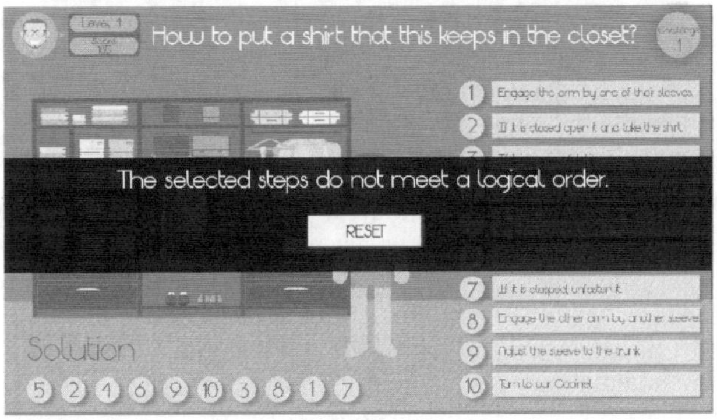

Figure 3. Graphical Interface Challenge One, Solved Incorrectly

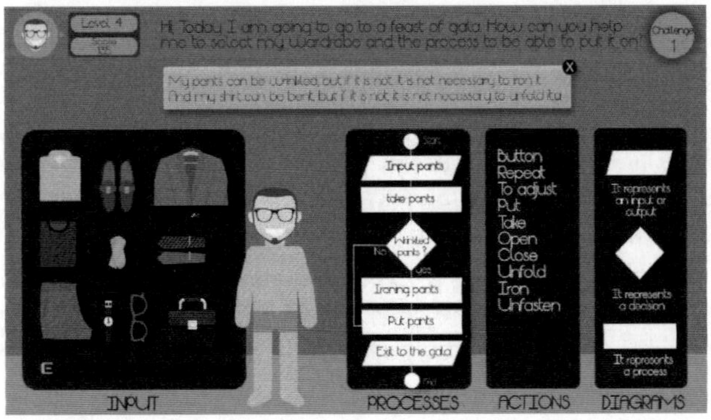

Figure 4. Graphical Interface Challenge Two, Solved Correctly

6.1 Serious Game with Virtual Reality Creation Process

It creates a virtual world, and to access, the student must use an optical device designed, in such a way that it allows interaction and thanks to the movement of the head begins relationship with the game in its different manifestations. The game was developed completely with the C Sharp programming language (C#) [20]. Using the UNITY 3D v4.6 graphics engine, this is a flexible and powerful development platform for creating

games and interactive experiences in 3D and 2D [21]; In addition it requires development kit Google Cardboard, which allows work with a stereo camera and thus trace the orientation of the user's head and Photoshop software is used for editing the elements involved in the game.
The interface of the game is completely visual, is divided into 6 parts, as shown in Figure 5. The first is located at the top left, level that is being played is displayed and the current score of the player, the second is located at the top right displays options for executing the algorithm, enable / disable the sounds of the game and background music, the third is located in the top center shows the problem to solve , the fourth is on the left side shows the space where the student can select the input data to define the algorithm in a sequential manner, the fifth is located in the central part shows the main character of the game showing what the problem to solve in a lively manner, and the sixth is located on the right side shows three blocks : the first is the block process, where the user makes use of the program logic to create the algorithm, the second block is the one containing the actions that you can use to solve the problem and in the third block types of diagrams that you can use to perform the algorithm.

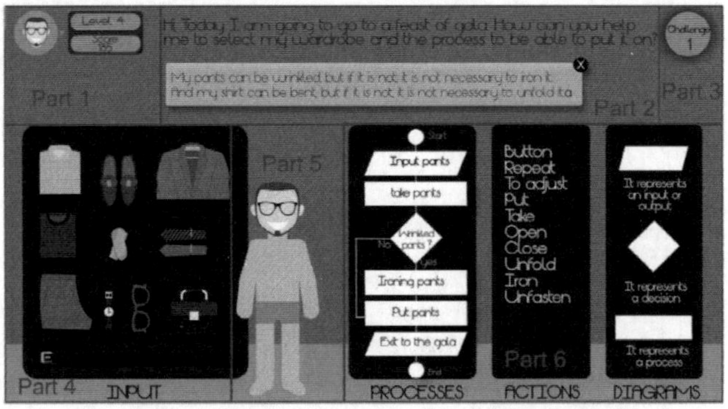

Figure 5. Graphical Interface Split Into Parts

The game has eight levels, where each of them will be gradually increasing difficulty, mechanics that is used in various games to keep the interest of the players, also has a pedagogical purpose in the sense that it presents a natural order to address concepts seeking to teach in this game in particular. I.e., the first few levels have to do with the concept of sequencing; the following added the concept of defined iteration and the last of nesting of instructions.

7. ANALYSIS AND TESTING

Ernesto Guhl - Bogota, Colombia school students performed a test with the Beta version of the game. In total there were 25 students from sixth grade to eleventh, see table 1 who tested the game and requested who after interacting with it complete the survey.

Table 1. List of Students who used the Name Level Punctuation

Name	Level	Punctuation
Daniel Correa Botero	8	870
Willington Vega	7	635
Juan Camilo Osorio	7	575
Andrés Felipe González	7	575
Miguel Andrés Gómez	7	475
Mayra Pazú	6	435
Cristian Sandoval	6	435
Marina Basabe	5	335
Valery Valencia	6	305
Sebastián Aristizabal	5	305
Leidy Fonseca	3	215
Juan Rodríguez	4	185
Sebastián Ramírez	4	120

Tatiana Ríos	4	120
Clara Valencia	4	105
Carlos Castro	4	100
Claudia Patricia Gutiérrez	3	90
Diana María Pérez	3	70
Daniel Buitrago	3	60
Oscar Martinez	3	45
Viviana Taque	3	45
Ximena Galindo	2	35
Efrén Beltrán	1	35
Omar Barriga	2	30
Mabel Aguilera	2	25

Table 2. Questions to the Participants of the Game

Name	Punctuation
1. In a general way, How would you rate the game	1-10
2. From the academic point of view, what rating would give you the game as a tool to strengthen skills before entering the University?	1-10
3. From the point of view graphics, animation, sounds, effects, how would you rate the game?	1-10
4. On the interface of the game, what rating would give you regarding ease of use, clarity, etc.?	1-10
5. The degree of difficulty of the levels found it appropriate?	Yes/No
6. If you have any comments on how to play, interface, levels, characters, design, or any other aspect of the game, please enter i below.	Free

Table 3. Responses of the first Four Questions that were Made

Question	Average
1	9.12
2	8.56
3	9.67
4	9.57

As it can be seen in Tables 2 and 3, the survey responses are satisfactory and the students showed great interest in the mechanics of the game that rewards knowledge and learning. In addition to Question 5, all students responded affirmatively and the vast majority of students were able to play intuitively without explanation of the game, and the most common comment referred to the lack of instructions in the game.

8. CONCLUSION

Virtual reality is an applicable technology in the teaching-learning process, basically because it displays the processes in study or development, in such a way that the person is immersed in artificial scenarios, allowing you to experience and interact with an environment, becoming an active subject of the process. This is the enormous potential of Virtual reality, stimulate the pedagogical practices. In addition, interest and motivation aroused by the virtual reality, the user, is very significant, because, somehow, subverts the traditional pedagogical practices and is positioned as an alternative dynamic that facilitates any learning. The use of serious games, has been taking force in recent decades and there are numerous studies that validate its use in classrooms. In this context, the work presented in this article is an important contribution in that, it points to a domain specific knowledge, in this case, the logic of programming, in which there are many developments and even less with the educational and emotional strengths which includes the game seriously, because this, explores the concepts of sequencing defined iteration and nesting, making it a fun and challenging way.

During the application of the test and subsequent to it, students College Ernesto Guhl, showed interest in the game, not only because of its visual and auditory attraction but also by the way as it was intended, since the segmentation in levels with increasing difficulty, forced them to associate and enabling their knowledge. Its usefulness was also validated to secure the domain of knowledge for which it was created, as well as encourage analysis of the efficiency of the proposed solutions. The applied test results, corroborated the importance of play as a pedagogical tool, since it encourages the development of other cognitive abilities, such as memory, apart from logic and abstract reasoning.

As a continuation of this work it is proposed to apply the game, with students of engineering undergraduate programs and technical programmers in the area of information technology, in order to validate a precisely, the impact that would have on the learning process. Would be of interest analysis, the serious game, can help students with academic performance bass, to consolidate the concepts explored.

REFERENCES

[1] Servicios TIC:. (2006*)*. Definición de TIC. Retrieved 30 November 2016, from: http://www.serviciostic.com/las-tic/definicion-de-tic.html.

[2] García, R.M, Waterman:. (2002). La tecnología de realidad virtual aplicada a la educación: el futuro ya está aquí. Retrieved 20 November 2016, from: http://www.hrl.uoit.ca/~miguelga/Realidad_ virtual_educacion_Iridia.pdf.

[3] Vera, O.G., Ortega, C.J.A, González, A.B:. (2004). La realidad virtual y sus posibilidades didácticas. Retrieved 3 November 2016 from: http://www.ugr.es/~sevimeco/revistaeticanet/Numero2/Articulos /Realidadvirtual.pdf

[4] Klopfer, E., & Yoon, S:. (2005). Developing Games and Simulations for Today and Tomorrow's Tech Savvy Youth TechTrends. Linking Research & Practice to Improve Learning, 49(3), pp. 33-41.

[5] James, J., Beaton, B., Csete, J., Vogel, D:. (2003). Mobile educational games. In: Lassner, D., McNaught, C. (eds.) Proceedings of ED-MEDIA 2003, pp. 801– 802.

[6] Bonwell C, Eison J:. (1991). Active Learning: Creating Excitement in the Classroom . Jossey-Bass publishers.

[7] Cassola, E. Elaboración de material educativo para la formación de profesionales en desarrollo de software. Congreso Iberoamericano de Educación Superior en Computación (CIESC), Conferencia Latinoamericana de Informática (CLEI). Perú, 2004.

[8] Herrera, J., Giraldo, O*:. (2008).* Apropiación de Conocimiento en Instituciones de Educación Superior Privadas: Factores Inhibidores y Potencializadores, Paradigma: Revista Electrónica en Construcción de Software, B ogotá – Colombia.

[9] Humphrey, W.S:. (1997). Introduction to the Personal Software Process. SEI Series In Software Engineering. Addison-Wesley. Cupi2 – Una Solución al Problema de Aprender/Enseñar a Programar. 36.

[10] Jenkins T:. (2001). The motivation of students of programming. Proceedings of the 6th annual conference on Innovation and technology in computer science education, Canterbury, United Kingdom.

[11] Levis, D:. (1997/2006). *¿Qué es la realidad virtual?* Retrieved 18 December 2016 from: http://www.diegolevis.com.ar/secciones/Articulos/Que_es_RV.pdf.

[12] Zapatero, G:. (2005). La realidad virtual como recurso y herramienta útil para la docencia y la investigación. Retrieved 15 November 2016 from: http://teyet-revista.info.unlp.edu.ar/nuevo/files/No6 /TEYET6-art02.pdf

[13] Vasquez, S.B:. (2010). Inteligencia Artificial. Retrieved 27 November 2016, from: https://solvasquez. wordpress.com /2010/08/15/inteligencia-artificial.

[14] Huizinga, J:. (1996). Homo Ludens. Madrid, España: Alianza Editorial.

[15] Abt, C. (1987) Serious Game. Lanham. University Press of América.

[16] Crawford, C (1982) The art of game desing.. Retrieved 18 November 2016 from: http://www.vancouver.wsu.edu/fac/peabody/game-book/Coverpage.html.

[17] AI-LIM, Elinda; WAI, Kok, & FUNG, Chun:. (2010). "Learning with virtual reality: its effects on students with different learning styles". In Transactions on edutainment IV, Zhigeng Pan, et al. (Eds.). Lecture Notes In Computer Science, 2010, Vol. 6250. Springer-Verlag, Berlin, Heidelberg 79-90.

[18] Trejos, B., Omar, I:. (1999). La Esencia de la Lógica de Programación. Retrieved 23 November 2016, from: http://blog.utp.edu.co/programacionmecatronica/files/2012/07/EsenciaLogica.pdf, Pereira, Colombia.

[19] Bell, John. T. & FOGLER, Scott:. (1995*)*. "The Investigation and Application of Virtual Reality as an Educational Tool". En actas de American Society for Engineering Education, Annual Conference, Anaheim, CA.

[20] Microsoft:. (2011). Visual C#*,* Retrieved 3 December 2016, from: https://msdn. microsoft.com/es-es/library/kx37x362.aspx.

[21] Unity3D:. (2015). *The best development platform for creating games.* Retrieved from: https://unity3d.com/unity.

STUDENT DEVELOPMENT AND SOFT SKILLS: IT-STUDENTS AT A UNIVERSITY IN SOUTH AFRICA

Estelle Taylor
North-West University, Potchefstroom Campus, South Africa

ABSTRACT

The aim of this paper is to determine whether IT-students are aware of soft skills and the importance thereof, and to research the students' perceptions on the importance and development of their own soft skills. More and more corporations recognize the importance of soft skills, but employers complain about a lack in soft skills among graduates from tertiary education institutions. This has significance for educational programs such as Computer Science (CS) and Information Systems (IS). A questionnaire was distributed electronically to the students doing IT-subjects at a university in South Africa. Quantitative research and qualitative research was done, as the researchers wanted to measure certain variables as well as understand the students' own perceptions on the development of soft skills. Results of this study show that students feel most confident about their willingness to learn, their work ethic and their skill for self-management. They feel least confident about their skill for cross-cultural relationships, leadership, multi-disciplinary thinking, time-management and teamwork. Decision making was rated as the most important skill, followed by work ethic, positive attitude, communication skills and time-management. According to the respondents, cross-cultural relationships and interpersonal relations are least important. Comparisons show that the male students perceive their emotional intelligence as higher than the female students perceive their emotional intelligence, while first year and second year students perceive their conflict management and cross-cultural relationship skills as higher than the third and fourth year students perceive theirs.

KEYWORDS

Soft Skills, Teaching, IT, Curricula, Tertiary Education

1. INTRODUCTION

The aim of this paper is to determine whether IT-students are aware of soft skills and the importance thereof, and to research the students' perceptions on the importance and development of their own soft skills. The paper starts with background and problem statement. The next section is the literature review, followed by the methodology used in this research. Finally the results and the conclusion are discussed.

2. BACKGROUND AND PROBLEM STATEMENT

More and more corporations recognize that, in order to gain competitive advantage, they need to make sure employees know how to handle themselves at work and how to communicate with their customers and colleagues. Industry recruiters emphasize the importance of soft skills (Russell et al., 2005). Joseph et al. (2010) refer to a growing awareness that technical skills alone are insufficient for success in IT. A broader set of skills are required, and these are labelled soft skills. The realization of importance of soft skills is on the increase (Azim et al., 2010). Though there are many differences between hard skills and soft skills, they complement each other, and in recent year recognition for the relationship between soft skills of employees and the overall success of the organization has grown (Dixon et al., 2010). The results of a study by Lee et al. (1995) showed that respondents considered technical specialties knowledge to be the least important, and business functional knowledge and interpersonal/ management skills most important for the future.

The nature of IT professionals' jobs are changing, including changes in job roles, required skills, and personal attributes required for successful IT employees (Gallivan et al., 2004). Employers complain about a lack in soft skills among graduates from tertiary education institutions (Schulz, 2008). No agreement exists about what these skills actually are, which are of importance and how they acquiring them should be approached in higher education (Adomssent et al., 2007). There is no single best approach for teaching soft skills, as the most appropriate one depends on the context under which the teaching is taking place, the specific goals of the programme and the discipline (Kechagias, 2011). Soft skills require a different strategy for both teaching and evaluating (Wilhelm et al., 2002). This has significance for educational programs such as Computer Science (CS) and Information Systems (IS) and suggest that students can benefit from formal training / education in soft skills (Wynekoop and Walz, 2000). Technical skills are a part of most educational curricula, but soft skills need further emphasis in the university curricula (Robles, 2012). The challenge for educators and educational institutions is to change the curriculum to accommodate teaching and learning for a diversity of career paths (Lee et al., 1995).

When soft skills topics are introduced into a technical training program, it is very important to start by getting the students to realize the importance of learning soft skills. Bancino and Zevalkink (2007) wrote: "*The more linear-thinking, task-oriented personalities will roll their eyes and disengage when they perceive the topic has shifted to subjects they consider fluff.*" (Schulz, 2008) suggested that the first step in improving soft skills is to raise the students' awareness about the importance of soft skills and the consequences of shortcomings in this regard. This brings us to the research question of this paper. Are IT-students aware of soft skills and the importance thereof? What are their perceptions on the development of their own soft skills?

3. LITERATURE REVIEW ON SOFT SKILLS

Terminology being used include soft skills, applied skills and 21st-century skills (Gewertz, 2007); practical intelligence (Joseph et al., 2010); nontechnical skills, general skills, generic skills, essential skills and employability skills (Johnston and McGregor, 2004); behavioural skills (Wilhelm et al., 2002); enabling skills, generic skills, core skills, key competencies, essential skills and necessary skills Kechagias (2011). There is no globally accepted definition of soft skills. Each discipline, educational sector and country defines soft skills according to their own needs (Kechagias, 2011, Chamorro-Premuzic et al., 2010). For the purpose of this study, the term soft skills is used and it is defined as intra- and inter-personal skills, essential for personal development, social participation and required to function in a specific employment environment.

Lists of soft skills varies widely from one study to another and included a wide range of attributes (Chamorro-Premuzic et al., 2010). In a previous study (Taylor, 2016) a list was compiled of the most important soft skills after research of relevant literature and feedback from stakeholders (lecturers, industry and students). This list can be seen in table 1. The soft skills listed in table 1 are used as starting point in this research.

Table 1. List of Important Soft Skills (Taylor, 2016)

Client management
Communication (verbal and written)
Conflict management
Critical thinking
Cross-cultural relationships
Decision-making
Emotional intelligence
Flexibility / ability to cope with uncertainty
Interpersonal relations
Leadership
Multi-disciplinary thinking
Negotiation
Positive attitude
Professionalism

Table 1. List of Important Soft Skills (Taylor, 2016)

Self-confidence
Self-management
Teamwork
Time-management / punctuality
Willingness to learn
Work ethic / Integrity

4. METHODOLOGY

The questionnaire was distributed electronically to all students doing IT-subjects at a university in South Africa. The questionnaire was completed by 142 first year, second year, third year and fourth year students. Quantitative research was done as the researchers wanted to measure certain variables. To do this statistical analysis was done on 40 questions. The aim of these questions was to measure the students' perceptions on the level of development of specific skills and the importance of these skills. Qualitative research was also done, as the researchers wanted to understand the students' own perceptions on the development of soft skills. The answers to 2 open questions were analyzed interpretively.

5. RESULTS

5.1 Statistical Analysis of Data

Most of the respondents (74.65%) were male. This is representative of the group studied, and corresponds to international trends for IT-studies. There were more female respondents in the first year group (32%) than in the fourth year group (20%).

40.85% were first year students, 26.76% second year students, 23.94 % third year students and 8.45 % fourth year students. This is a representation of the actual number of students in each year group, as the institution has, for instance, approximately 250 first year students in the IT-modules, +- 80 third year students and +- 30 fourth year (post graduate) students.

Students were asked to evaluate themselves on the 20 different skills mentioned in table 1. To guide the students, each skill was described in a brief sentence. The results can be seen in table 2.

Table 2. Evaluation of Level

Description of soft skill	Not at all like me (1)	Very little like me (2)	Somewhat like me (3)	To a great extent like me (4)	Mean
1.1 I have strong writing and speaking skills (communication).	0.0	9.22	46.10	44.68	3.35
1.2 I can handle and resolve conflict (conflict management).	1.42	4.96	53.90	39.72	3.32
1.3 I use knowledge and skills to guide my behaviour (critical thinking).	0.0	2.82	40.14	57.04	3.54
1.4 I find it easy to interact with people from other cultures (cross-cultural relationships).	1.41	21.13	37.32	40.14	3.16
1.5 I can choose between possible solutions through a reasoned process (decision-making).	0.0	6.38	52.84	41.13	3.35
1.6 I can control my emotions, or at least my reactions to them (emotional intelligence).	0.71	9.22	34.75	55.32	3.45
1.7 I am flexible and adapt to circumstances when necessary (flexibility).	0.0	7.75	33.80	58.45	3.50

1.8 I get along well with others (interpersonal relations).	0.0	9.86	37.32	52.82	3.43
1.9 I can lead and motivate people (leadership).	2.11	15.49	44.37	38.03	3.18
1.10 I can use knowledge of different disciplines to reach solutions based in complex situations (multi-disciplinary thinking).	0.0	10.56	57.04	32.39	3.22
1.11 In a work environment I will be able to maximize client satisfaction (client management).	0.0	7.09	47.52	45.39	3.38
1.12 I can negotiate with others to find a solution that will benefit all parties (negotiation).	0.0	7.75	47.18	45.07	3.37
1.13 I have a positive attitude even in difficult circumstances (positive attitude).	1.41	10.56	42.25	45.77	3.32
1.14 I behave professionally at all times (professionalism).	0.70	11.27	48.59	39.44	3.27
1.15 I have confidence in my own abilities (self confidence).	1.41	9.86	45.07	43.66	3.31
1.16 I manage myself and take responsibility for my own behaviour (self-management).	0.0	4.93	33.80	61.27	3.56
1.17 I am an effective team player and work well in a group (teamwork).	2.13	14.89	41.84	41.13	3.22
1.18 I am always on time and keep to the set schedule (time-management).	2.82	16.20	37.32	43.66	3.22
1.19 I am willing and eager to learn new things (willingness to learn).	0.0	2.11	22.45	75.35	3.73
1.20 I value integrity above all else (work ethic).	0.0	4.23	30.99	64.79	3.61

According to the results in table 2 students feel most confident about their willingness to learn (mean of 3.73), their work ethic (mean of 3.61) and their skill for self-management (mean of 3.56). They feel least confident about their skill for cross-cultural relationships (3.16), leadership (3.18), multi-disciplinary thinking (3.22), time-management (3.22) and teamwork (3.22).

Because this was an availability sample Cohen's effect size d was calculated to determine the practical impact of differences between male students and female students. Included in the report are p–values, for completeness sake. The perceptions of male students and female students on the development of their own soft skills do not differ significantly, except for emotional intelligence. These results can be seen in table 3.

Table 3. *t*-Test Done Using Effectiveness Factor on Gender: Emotional Intelligence

Factor	*Group*	N	*Mean*	*Standard deviation*	**p-value** (when random sampling is assumed)	**d-value**
Effectiveness	1	105	3.55	0.64	< 0.05*	0.54
	2	36	3.14	0.76		

Note: Group 1 – Male
Group 2 – Female
* Statistically significant at 0.05 level according to t-test results for independent groups
** Statistically significant at 0.01 level according to t-test results for independent groups

The male students perceive their emotional intelligence as higher than the female students perceive their emotional intelligence, with a medium practical effect, thus noticeable with the 'naked eye' (Cohen, 1988).

Cohen's effect size d was also calculated to determine the practical impact of differences between first year and second year students in one group, and third and fourth year students in another group. The perceptions of first year and second year students and those of third and fourth year students on the development of their own soft skills do not differ significantly, except for conflict management and cross-cultural relationships. These results are presented in table 4 and table 5.

Table 4. *t*-Tests Done Using Effectiveness Factor on Year Groups: Conflict Management

Factor	*Group*	N	*Mean*	*Standard deviation*	**p-value** (when random sampling is assumed)	**d-value**
Effectiveness	1	95	3.41	0.63	0.01**	0.5
	2	46	3.13	0.62		

Note: Group 1 – First and second year students
Group 2 – Third and fourth year students
* Statistically significant at 0.05 level according to t-test results for independent groups
** Statistically significant at 0.01 level according to t-test results for independent groups

Table 5. *t*-Tests Done Using Effectiveness Factor On Year Groups: Cross-Cultural Relationships

Factor	*Group*	N	*Mean*	*Standard deviation*	p-value (when random sampling is assumed)	d-value
Effectiveness	1	96	3.28	0.79	0.01**	0.5
	2	46	2.91	0.78		

Note: Group 1 – First and second year students
Group 2 – Third and fourth year students
* Statistically significant at 0.05 level according to t-test results for independent groups
** Statistically significant at 0.01 level according to t-test results for independent groups

The first year and second year students perceive their conflict management and cross-cultural relationship skills as higher than the third and fourth year students perceive theirs.

Next, the students were asked their opinion on the importance of each one of the soft skills for a successful career. The results can be seen in table 6, in order of importance.

Table 6. Importance of Soft Skill

	Soft skill	Not important at all	Somewhat important	Important	Very Important	Mean
1	Decision-making	0.0	0.0	16.20	83.80	3.83
2	Work ethic / Integrity	0.0	0.0	18.31	81.69	3.81
2	Positive attitude	0.0	0.70	18.31	80.99	3.80
4	Communication (verbal and written)	0.0	0.7	18.31	80.99	3.80
5	Time-management / punctuality	0.0	0.70	22.54	76.76	3.76
7	Professionalism	0.0	1.43	23.57	75	3.74
6	Critical thinking	0.0	1.41	23.94	74.65	3.73
8	Willingness to learn	0.0	1.42	26.95	71.63	3.70
9	Self-management	0.0	2.11	27.46	70.42	3.68
10	Leadership	0.0	4.26	26.95	68.79	3.65
11	Conflict management	0.0	2.11	33.8	64.08	3.62
12	Self-confidence	0.0	0.0	35.92	64.08	3.64
13	Teamwork	0.0	4.93	35.21	59.86	3.55
14	Flexibility / ability to cope with uncertainty	0.0	2.82	40.14	57.04	3.54
15	Emotional intelligence	0.0	7.04	36.62	56.34	3.49
16	Negotiation	0.0	5.63	39.44	54.93	3.68
17	Client management	0.0	2.11	45.07	52.82	3.50
18	Multi-disciplinary thinking	0.0	3.52	49.30	47.18	3.44
19	Cross-cultural relationships	0.0	9.15	47.18	43.66	3.35
20	Interpersonal relations	0.0	6.34	50.7	42.96	3.37

All of the skills were seen as important on some level (mean between 3.37 and 3.83). According to the results in table 3, decision making is rated as the most important skill, followed by work ethic, positive attitude, communication skills and time-management. According to the respondents, cross-cultural relationships and interpersonal relations are least important.

5.2 Interpretive Analysis of Open Questions

The first question was: Do you think enough is done at university to develop these soft skills (listed in table 1)? Motivate or explain your answer.

Of the 142 respondents who answered the questionnaire, 138 answered this open question. Of these 90 felt that enough is done at university to develop these skills, and 48 felt that enough is not done to develop these skills.

Of the 90 students that felt that enough is done to develop soft skills, 24 mentioned team work as important in the development of soft skills. Examples of answers were:

Yes. Like there are several modules that do group work. Sometimes I think we have too much group work and it becomes irritating (and I tend to lose my temper because sometimes your group members contribute so little).

Yes. Multiculturalism is encouraged and students are made to work together in random groups. Public speaking is practiced as well as leadership skills.

Yes, there are designated subjects as well as a strong emphasis on group projects (even though the entire group project does more harm than good in my opinion).

Some students mentioned that, according to them, soft skills are mainly developed during non-academic activities at university. Examples of answers:

I do, however, think that it is developed mostly at the university within the student structures and on and off campus housing, where one has to use your people skills to create relationships and build new relationships for the future.

Yes, there are enough committees and structures in place to engage in activities that allows you to develop these skills.

Other students felt that it may not be the responsibility of the university to develop these skills:

Your skills will only develop if you get exposed to a work environment.

When you are in university you should already have mastered all or most of these skills.

I am not sure that a university will be able to change the soft skills of a person. It should come from within each student.

Of the 48 students who felt that not enough is done at university to develop soft skills, some mentioned specific skills as not being developed: team work (3), problem-solving skills (2), interpersonal skills, professionalism and work ethics. An example is:

Some of the skills yes, but not all. Skills like teamwork, communication, and time management are learned. Work ethics for example is not learned.

There were some negative comments about team work. Two of these are:

In many cases where we are put into teams and told to work together there are always those who do not do their part. And as the leader of such a team you do not have any real influence so people can ignore you.

No, very little is done to improve these skills aside from being forced to work in groups which is more a 'sink-or-swim' approach and does not fairly evaluate all members.

Recommendations made were for additional free courses for the development of soft skills, or a module specifically for the development of soft skills.

The second question was: How do you think these soft skills can be developed? What can your lecturer do to help develop these soft skills?

Of the 142 respondents who answered the questionnaire, 90 answered this open question. Of these, most mentioned teamwork (38), some including recommendations on how teamwork can be improved:

It's not a good idea to force people to work together, encouragement is key, the problem with this on university is the fact that not all people in a group do their part as needed as the leader has to pick up an extra workload or two, this puts too much strain on the group which usually end with internal fighting and the leader or other group members have no way to punish the people that slack off but still get the full participation and marks.

They can't force a student to develop these skills, the best way is to motivate the students, because in some groups there will be always someone that will not bring their part. I have been the leader of several groups so far and always struggle to get the group to come together and do their part, and every time there is a student that does nothing or brings everything a day before the deadline that gives me as the leader too much work and I have no way of reporting or exclude the student, as my own marks will suffer.

You can have more projects. With the same teams but with each project a new leader is chosen so each person can be criticized on these skills as well as that you will be expected to dress formally and act professionally at all times or marks will be deducted.

Stop forcing group projects down our throats! No one is willing to work with a group and most of the time people just copy previous years work!

Some of the students (16) mentioned more practical assignments specifically focusing on development of soft skills, including interdisciplinary assignments:

Give students certain tasks in which you need to have a 'Big-Picture' thinking mindset to solve problems, and approach problems from different angles.

Other students (11) felt that capable lecturers should be able to lead by example in showing these skills.

Students (8) also recommended that the development of soft skills should be a constant concern in every lecture and should receive more focus.

Other recommendations (8) were that outside professionals could be used to lecture and that students should be more exposed to the real world.

Some students (6) felt that the development of these skills is the students' own responsibility:

There is not much that the lecturer can do in my opinion. The student themselves should take initiative to learn things on their own.

It is something someone must be able to improve and build on their own. We are at university not high school or college. Students should be professional and capable of self management.

Soft skills are developed over time and can't really be taught! By forcing students to work together in groups where only 2 persons out of a 5 person group actually work won't help soft skills development in a person and would actually discourage students from developing soft skills!

6. CONCLUSION

Students feel most confident about their willingness to learn, their work ethic and their skill for self-management. They feel least confident about their skill for cross-cultural relationships, leadership, multi-disciplinary thinking, time-management and teamwork.

All of the skills were seen as important. Decision making was rated as the most important skill, followed by work ethic, positive attitude, communication skills and time-management. According to the respondents, cross-cultural relationships and interpersonal relations are least important. Research can be done on why these skills are seen as less important and how to raise awareness of their importance.

Comparisons show that the male students perceive their emotional intelligence as higher than the female students perceive their emotional intelligence, while first year and second year students perceive their conflict management and cross-cultural relationship skills as higher than the third and fourth year students perceive theirs. No other significant differences could be found between male students and female students, and first year and second year students compared to third and fourth year students. This is only the students' own perceptions and not a test of the actual level of development of soft skills. More research must be done on how to test these skills, because it would be very interesting to know if the development of skills is actually as the students perceive them to be. According to these results there is no improvement in the skills from first and second year level to third and fourth year level. The actual meaning of these results can only be speculated on, and it may be that the third and fourth year students have a better and truer perception of the development of their skills than the first and second year students?

Although most students feel that enough is done to develop soft skills, there are also many students who do not agree with this. Some students feel that soft skills are mainly developed during non-academic activities at university, while others felt that it is not the responsibility of the university to develop these skills, as soft skills will only develop when you get exposed to a work environment. There were also the perception that the development of soft skills is a personal thing, depending on the individual and his or her decisions. This perception is the same as found in other studies, for instance Chamorro-Premuzic et al. (2010) wrote that how well students may benefit from opportunities to develop their soft skills may partly depend on their actual competencies; while Hazzan and Har-Shai (2013) wrote that soft skills cannot be studied and taught formally and, rather, should be learned and over a period of time, based on students' engagement, active learning, and reflection.

Team work was mentioned frequently as contributing to the development of soft skills. Some students have a negative perception of team work, mentioning factors such as team members not contributing, members being forced to work together, and evaluation of team work not being done in a fair manner. Research can be done on how to improve the practical implementation of teamwork in teaching and learning.

Reasons mentioned for indicating that enough is not done at university to develop soft skills were lecturers not interacting enough with students and subjects not being challenging enough.

From the results of this research some recommendations can be made for the development of soft skills. These are:

- Making available additional (free) courses for the development of soft skills.
- Adding a module specifically for the development of soft skills to the programme. Schulz (2008) had the same suggestion for lecturers on enhancing their students' soft skills, namely incorporating soft skills subjects into a programme's curriculum. However, very often the curricula are already overloaded with hard skills courses, making it almost impossible to add or substitute courses.
- More focus on practical work / assignments and less on theory.
- Including interdisciplinary assignments in the programme.
- The development of soft skills being a constant concern in every lecture. This corresponds to what Schulz (2008) wrote, that another way of offering soft skills training to students is to embed it into the teaching of hard skills. This way, no changes to a programme's curriculum are necessary; instead the change will be reflected in the lecturers' teaching methodology. For instance, an increase in group discussions and letting students do presentations can be applied throughout the program (Schulz, 2008).
- Using outside professionals to lecture; and exposure to the real world. Research by Joseph et al. (1999) showed that there is a difference between the soft skills of experienced I/S professionals and inexperienced undergraduates, suggesting that exposure to work situations is extremely important in developing soft skills. Real-world examples can help students relate to the importance of soft skills, with emphasis on the end result (Bancino and Zevalkink, 2007).

Further study should be done to compare these results with those of other studies, and to research what can be done to change perceptions where necessary.

REFERENCES

ADOMSSENT, M., GODEMANN, J., MICHELSEN, G., BARTH, M., GODEMANN, J., RIECKMANN, M. & STOLTENBERG, U. 2007. Developing key competencies for sustainable development in higher education. *International Journal of Sustainability in Higher Education,* 8, 416-430.

ANDREWS, J. & HIGSON, H. 2008. Graduate employability,'soft skills' versus 'hard'business knowledge: A European study. *Higher education in Europe,* 33, 411-422.

AZIM, S., GALE, A., LAWLOR-WRIGHT, T., KIRKHAM, R., KHAN, A. & ALAM, M. 2010. The importance of soft skills in complex projects. *International Journal of Managing Projects in Business,* 3, 387-401.

BANCINO, R. & ZEVALKINK, C. 2007. Soft Skills: The New Curriculum for Hard-Core Technical Professionals. *Techniques: Connecting Education and Careers (J1),* 82, 20-22.

CASNER-LOTTO, J. & BARRINGTON, L. 2006. *Are They Really Ready to Work? Employers' Perspectives on the Basic Knowledge and Applied Skills of New Entrants to the 21st Century US Workforce*, ERIC.

CHAMORRO-PREMUZIC, T., ARTECHE, A., BREMNER, A. J., GREVEN, C. & FURNHAM, A. 2010. Soft skills in higher education: Importance and improvement ratings as a function of individual differences and academic performance. *Educational Psychology,* 30, 221-241.

COHEN, J. Statistical power analysis for the behavioral sciences. Second Edition (1988) Hillsdale, NJ: Erlbaum. 567 p.

DIXON, J., BELNAP, C., ALBRECHT, C. & LEE, K. 2010. The importance of soft skills. *Corporate finance review,* 14, 35.

GALLIVAN, M. J., TRUEX III, D. P. & KVASNY, L. 2004. Changing patterns in IT skill sets 1988-2003: a content analysis of classified advertising. *ACM SIGMIS Database,* 35, 64-87.

GEWERTZ, C. 2007. Soft skills in big demand. *Education Week,* 26, 25-27.

GONZÁLEZ-MORALES, D., DE ANTONIO, L. M. M. & GARCÍA, J. L. R. Teaching “Soft” skills in software engineering. Global Engineering Education Conference (EDUCON), 2011 IEEE, 2011. IEEE, 630-637.

HAZZAN, O. & HAR-SHAI, G. Teaching computer science soft skills as soft concepts. Proceeding of the 44th ACM technical symposium on Computer science education, 2013. ACM, 59-64.

JOHNSTON, S. & MCGREGOR, H. 2004. Recognising and Supporting a Scholarship of Practice: Soft Skills Are Hard!

JOSEPH, D., ANG, S., CHANG, R. H. & SLAUGHTER, S. A. 2010. Practical intelligence in IT: assessing soft skills of IT professionals. *Communications of the ACM,* 53, 149-154.

JOSEPH, D., ANG, S. & SLAUGHTER, S. Soft skills and creativity in IS professionals. Systems Sciences, 1999. HICSS-32. Proceedings of the 32nd Annual Hawaii International Conference on, 1999. IEEE, 5 pp.

KECHAGIAS, K. 2011. Teaching and assessing soft skills. *MASS Project, September.*

LEE, D. M., TRAUTH, E. M. & FARWELL, D. 1995. Critical skills and knowledge requirements of IS professionals: a joint academic/industry investigation. *MIS quarterly*, 313-340.

ROBLES, M. M. 2012. Executive perceptions of the top 10 soft skills needed in today's workplace. *Business Communication Quarterly,* 75, 453-465.

RUSSELL, J., RUSSELL, B. & TASTLE, W. J. 2005. Teaching soft skills in a systems development capstone class. *Information Systems Education Journal,* 3, 3-19.

SCHULZ, B. 2008. The importance of soft skills: Education beyond academic knowledge.

TAYLOR, E. 2016. Investigating the Perception of Stakeholders on Soft Skills Development of Students: Evidence from South Africa. *Interdisciplinary Journal of e-Skills and Lifelong Learning,* 12, 1-18.

WILHELM, W. J., LOGAN, J., SMITH, S. M. & SZUL, L. F. 2002. Meeting the Demand: Teaching" Soft" Skills.

WYNEKOOP, J. L. & WALZ, D. B. 2000. Investigating traits of top performing software developers. *Information Technology & People,* 13, 186-195.

FINDING ICT NON-ACCEPTANCE FACTORS BY GROUNDED THEORY: A CASE OF ONLINE PAYMENT SYSTEM 'KAKOPAY'

Woong-Kyu Lee
Department of Business Administration, Daegu University
201, Daegudae-ro, Gyeongsan-si, Gyeongsangbuk-do, 38453, Republic of Korea

ABSTRACT

The tremendous previous studies attempted to explain information and communication (ICT) acceptance using a range of theoretical models, which have the important implications for understanding the users' behavior in the earlier stage of the ICT usage life cycle. However, few studies have attempted to explain the other side, non-acceptance, the phenomenon that people do not accept a given ICT. The principal aims of this study is to identify inductively the factors influencing ICT non-acceptance using grounded theory that is a methodology for the discovery of theory from qualitative data, which are obtained and analyzed systematically using a code paradigm to ensure conceptual development and density. The target technology is Kakaopay, which is one of online payment systems in Korea, provided by Kakaotalk, one of world famous social network service providers. Data was collected from a total of 72 Korea university students (Male: 52, Female: 20) and, the codes were extracted and classified using two coding methods: open coding and axis coding. From open coding, the following four codes were extracted from the data: newness aversion, visibility, relative advantage, and risk concern. Via axis coding, a process to find classifications of codes extracted from open coding, these codes are classified into two main groups, status quo maintenance and expected value: the former includes newness aversion and visibility and the latter relative advantage and rick concern. In a view of dual-processing theory, status quo maintenance is included in system 1 thinking and expected value in system 2 thinking.

KEYWORDS

ICT Non-Acceptance, Status Quo Maintenance, Expected Value, System 1 Thinking, System 2 Thinking

1. INTRODUCTION

Various attempts have been made to explain information and communication (ICT) acceptance using a range of theoretical models, such as the technology acceptance model (TAM) (Davis, 1989; Davis et al., 1989), the theory of reasoned action (TRA), and the theory of planned behavior (TPA) (Taylor and Todd, 1995). Despite the important implications for understanding the users' behavior in the earlier stage of the ICT usage life cycle, most of these trials focused on the behavior of people who were willing to accept a given ICT, which is only one side of the earlier stage. Few studies have attempted to explain the other side, non-acceptance, the phenomenon that people do not accept a given ICT.

Despite the tremendous studies in ICT acceptance, the reasons for the scarcity in ICT non-acceptance studies are as follows. First, many ICT acceptance studies have the implicit or explicit assumption that the factors for ICT acceptance can also explain non-acceptance. For example, perceived usefulness, which is one of the most influential variables for ICT acceptance studies (Davis, 1989; Davis et al., 1989), can be assumed to explain non-acceptance only if it has a lower or negative value. This means that ICT acceptance studies may imply non-acceptance studies. On the other hand, ICT non-acceptance behavior may be independent of acceptance; there may be the variables that explain the non-acceptance variables but not the acceptance variables (Cenfetelli, 2004). For example, while the tedium of installing an ICT may influence non-acceptance, acceptance would not be influenced by resolution of such tediousness.

Second, the methodology adopted in most ICT acceptance studies may have some limitations for non-acceptance. Most studies adopted quantitative and statistical approaches, such as a structural equation model for their research methodology. These approaches assume that the ICT acceptance is a frequentative action, which is non-continuous and can be perceived consciously and measured quantitatively. For example, the dependent variable of TAM, which is one of the most theoretical models for ICT acceptance, is the extent of using or the using intention of a given ICT, which can be measured quantitatively. Non-acceptance, however, is a state of being that has no extent and cannot be measured in quantitative form. This suggests that quantitative or statistical approaches are not appropriate in non-acceptance studies. Based on the above discussions, this study addresses the following research questions.

Which codes are hidden in the phenomenon that people do not accept a new given ICT, i.e., ICT non-acceptance?

To answer these research questions, this study, with reviewing the contributions and limitations of previous studies, identifies inductively the factors influencing ICT non-acceptance using grounded theory, a qualitative methodology. Based on these factors, a research model for ICT non-acceptance is suggested.

2. CRITICAL REVIEW ON PREVIOUS STUDIES

As mentioned in the introduction, there are few studies of ICT non-acceptance. On the other hand, resistance is the most similar subject constantly studied for a long time. Resistance is the opposition of users to change involved in a new information system (IS) implementation. Most studies focused on threats or loss of power due to IS implementation in organizations (e.g. Bhattacherjee and Hikmet, 2007; Joshi, 1991; Markus, 1983; Kim and Kankanhalli, 2009; Lapoint and Rivard, 2005; Maraks and Hornik, 1996 Martinko et al., 1996). Resistance, which is one of classical topics in IS communities, is still one of the important research issues in recent organizations, particularly under smart environments (Park and Chae, 2014).

Nevertheless, there are some conceptual differences between resistance and ICT non-acceptance. First, while resistance has been witnessed in organizations where the use of ICTS is mandatory, ICT non-acceptance is involved in behavior or decisions as to whether a given ICT is to be used or not. Second, there is difference in the analysis target. While resistance is used to analyze employees in organizations in view of change management, ICT non-acceptance would be applied to general users in addition to organization members.

The studies for investigating the negative impacts for ICT acceptance are also similar to ICT non-acceptance (e.g. Bhattacherjee and Park, 2014; Cenfetelli and Schwarz, 2011; Polite and Karahanna, 2012; Venkatesh and Brown, 2001). Most of these studies tried to explain the behaviors under traditional ICT acceptance theories, such as TAM and TPB, which assume the deliberation of ICT acceptance decision based on reasoning. This suggests that ICT acceptance is a very new and important job (Fishbein and Ajzen, 2011). Currently, however, ICT is no longer used for new and important jobs but rather it is one of the tools for daily lives. Moreover, non-acceptance is decision making for doing nothing rather than doing something, which may be not dependent on rational judgments. Therefore, studies based on traditional ICT acceptance theories, such as TAM, TRA, and TPB, which may have contributed to elaboration of ICT acceptance, have limitations in understanding the behaviors in non-acceptance.

3. METHODOLOGY

Grounded theory was adopted as a main research methodology. Grounded theory is a methodology for the discovery of theory from qualitative data, which are obtained and analyzed systematically using a code paradigm to ensure conceptual development and density (Glaser and Strauss, 1967; Strauss, 1987). According to Urquhart et al. (2010), grounded theory has the following four distinct characteristics. First, the main purpose is theory building. Second, researchers should not depend on prior knowledge of the field. Third, analysis and conceptualization are enriched by data collection and constant comparison, where every slice of data is compared with all existing concepts and constructs. Fourth, the slices of data of all kinds are selected by theoretical sampling, where the researcher decides on analytic grounds where to sample from the next. Therefore, grounded theory is appropriate for explaining the phenomenon of ICT non-acceptance, which has poor theoretical backgrounds and is difficult to apply using quantitative or statistical approaches.

One of core concepts in grounded theory is a coding paradigm. This study adopted two types of coding, open coding and axis coding. Open coding aims to find some codes by describing the concepts in data that may define a significant occurrence, or incident, about the phenomenon. Axis coding requires a comparison of the codes to classify them under common themes, thus entailing the production of hierarchical classifications (Abraham et al, 2013). Open coding and axis coding are repeated until no more theories are developed. In this study, the factors for explaining ICT non-acceptance are found by open coding, whereas the relationships among factors are identified by axis coding.

The target technology is Kakaopay, which is one of online payment systems in Korea, provided by Kakaotalk, one of world famous social network service providers. Data was collected from May 1st to July 31st, 2015 from a total of 72 Korea university students (Male: 52, Female: 20) according to the following three phases:In the first phase, the interviews were conducted on ten university students. Among them, while five students are users, the other five students do not use Kakaotalk. The result of the first phase provided overall directions for both the second and third data collections. In the second phase, through a survey by questionnaires, sixty two non-accepters who did not have any intention of using Kakaopay were selected and asked the open ended question, "Why do you not intend to use Kakaopay?". In the third phase, in-depth interviews were conducted with ten people selected from non-accepters in the second phase. These interviews were repeated until no new concepts were found, i.e., theoretical saturation was met. The questions during the interviews were started from a very comprehensive one, "Why do you not intend to use Kakaopay", to detailed ones. After the data collected from all phases were recorded and documented, the codes were extracted and classified using two coding methods: open coding and axis coding.

4. ANALYSIS OF CODING

4.1 Open Coding

The following four codes were extracted from the data: newness aversion, visibility, relative advantage, and risk concern. The first one is newness aversion. Many non-accepters averted tedium and tiresomeness in adoption of new system such as installation and registration. They have inclinations toward inertia in maintaining their incumbent systems. They raised questions about the reasons for changing the current system to a new system, as seen in the following illustrative interview.

"I hate a new way. Yes, it is somewhat inconvenient, but I am used to my system. I do not have any reason to change my system." (Interviewee No. 6)
"I am using a similar online payment system."(Interviewee No.16)
"I am sure I can have an easy life without Kakaopay."(Interviewee No. 5))

In particular, a few people thought changing to a new system is a very tiresome job.

"The change due to a new payment way is not comfortable and is a hassle." (Interviewee No. 16).
"System installation and credit card registration appear to be so cumbersome."(Interviewee No. 5)

Interestingly, these judgments may be dependent on the subjective biases or heuristics rather than rational judgments, such as usefulness and risks, as shown in the following.

"I am willing to change my payment system but information re-input is a hassle."(Interviewee No. 19)
"I know installation is not a difficult job but I do not really want it. I do not want a new one."(Interviewee, No 17)

These inclinations appear to be similar to switching costs, which are incurred in many cases of using ICT (e.g.: Polites and Karhanna, 2013; Ray et al., 2012). On the other hand, while the switching costs were calculated based on rational judgments, this is not dependent reasoning regarding the use of a system but rather no-reasoning. That is, rational judgments do not maintain the status quo in using an incumbent system, but the status quo governs the attitude and intention towards using a system.

The second one is visibility. Many people, who hesitate to accept a new system, try to see how many people around them use the system before making rational judgments. If the users of the new system are seen to be few, their decision will be non-acceptance.

"I have not seen people using Kakaopay near me. It seems that very few people use it, but I do not know why I use it. (Interviewee No. 8)
"Maybe I will use it when I see my friends use it. I have not seen that so I will not use it." (Interviewee No. 10)

However, although they would see only a few people use the system, their decision may not be inclined to accept a new system. They would try to find reasons for non-acceptance rather than reasons for why they should accept new system based on the number of users. Therefore, visibility, in addition to a code for non-acceptance, can be considered a mechanism for justifying the maintenance of the status quo. Naturally, visibility is also dependent on a heuristic without cognitive efforts.

The third code is relative advantage of a new system. A low perceived advantage against other alternatives would lead to non-acceptance. This code involves traditional ICT acceptance variables, such as usefulness and easy to use also works in the case of non-acceptance: the negative perceptions of these variables would influence non-acceptance. Many non-accepters doubted new system's usefulness and versatility.

"Payments by Kakaopay have limitations in buying diverse contents."(Interviewee No. 16)
"Because few stores accept Kakaopay, I will not use it." (Interviewee No. 29)

This code follows the traditional ICT acceptance theories' view of non-acceptance, in which non-acceptance can be explained by the acceptance factors; the factors with opposite values will influence non-acceptance. Unlike the above codes, this code is based on conscious reasoning.

Finally, risk concern is included. This code means the unexpected negative results from using a new system. For a long time, the use of ICT involved psychological and financial losses due to disclosure of sensitive private information. These concerns still exist.

"Hearing that lost cellphones would be sold overseas, I would be more anxious and more nervous if I lost a Kakaopay installed cellphone. Moreover, Kakopay-involving crimes, such as voice phishing, will emerge."(Interviewee No. 5)

4.2 Axis Coding

Axis coding is a process to find classifications of codes extracted from open coding. The four codes from open coding were classified into two categories: status quo maintenance and expected value. One of the most common and distinctive characteristics in non-accepters is status quo maintenance, which implies the adherence to current status or situation without considering new alternatives. Both codes, newness aversion and visibility, are included in this category. Averting a new system and searching for the new system's users is to find out the justification for using a current system, that is, status quo maintenance.

The second one is expected value. This category follows traditional ICT acceptance theories view. Non-acceptance is determined based on low expected value for a given system considering pros and cons. Relative advantage and risk concern are included in this category. Contrary to status quo maintenance, expected value is based on rational judgment.

In addition to the characteristics of each code, this study also focused on the interviewees' cognitive efforts for understanding a given ICT (Kakaopay). Most interviewees' answers for questions involved 'maintenance of the status quo' and 'visibility' are relatively simple without much deliberation and inferences, as seen in the following example.

"Kakaopay installation is a hassle to me." (Interviewee No. 19)

On the other hand, in the cases of 'expected values' or 'risk concern', the answers were observed to involve detailed explanations with more cognitive efforts, even giving concrete illustrations.

"I have an experience of charging due to a credit card registered in a hacked account independent of my willingness. Fortunately I could cancel it because I can see it through messages from my cellphone. Afterwards, I have presented a petition to a police station, but the response from Korea National Police Agency Cyber Bureau was 'It is not easy to trace the hackers because they appear to be a bypass hacking from China.'. This experience makes me hesitate to use a payment system, in which sensitive information is saved online." (Interviewee No. 18)

From these discussions, this study classified the codes into two groups. While 'newness aversion' and 'visibility' are developed from intuition with little cognition, the other two codes, 'relative advantage' and 'risk concern' are formed from conscious reasoning with cognitive efforts. According to dual process theory (Stantovich and West, 2000) in behavioral economics, human beings process information using two different systems, so called system 1 thinking and system 2 thinking. System 1 thinking is fast and a responsive automatic association system based on intuition without cognitive efforts. System 2 thinking is a slow and controlled inference system controlled by logical reasoning based on cognitive efforts. Dual-processing theory can be applied to the categories classified in this study: status quo maintenance is included in system 1 thinking and expected value in system 2 thinking. Therefore, ICT non-acceptance can be explained by Figure 1.

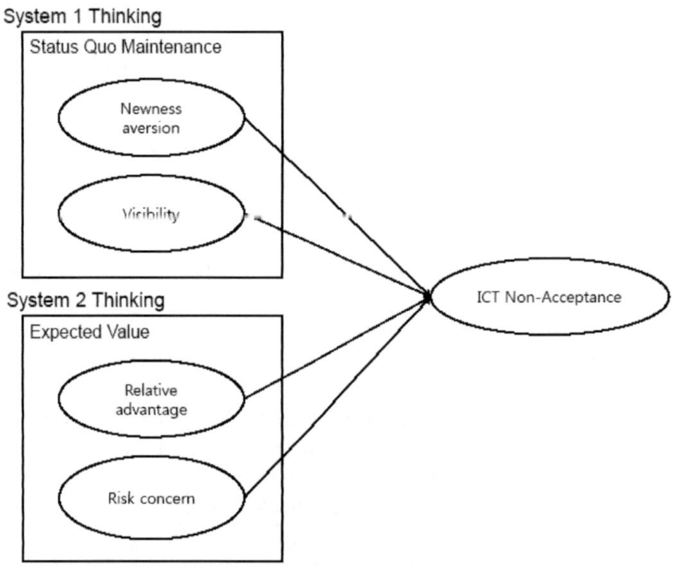

Figure 1. Research Model for ICT Non-Acceptance

5. CONCLUSION

The aim of this study was to identify the factors influencing ICT non-acceptance and suggest a theoretical model for explaining ICT non-acceptance. For this purpose, the limitations of previous studies are discussed. Following ground theory, by open coding based on the data from three phased collection, interviews and open ended questions survey, four codes, 'maintenance of the status quo', 'visibility', 'relative advantage, and 'risk concern' were extracted. Through axis coding, these four codes were classified into two categories: status quo maintenance and expected value. Our classification is supported theoretically by dual process theory.

Despite the tremendous amount of ICT users' behavioral studies, particularly ICT acceptance, non-acceptance is still an under researched area. This study examined ICT non-acceptance independently of the previous ICT acceptance theories. The contributions and implications are summarized as follows: First, this study found the codes in determination of ICT non-acceptance. As expected, some codes are independent of ICT acceptance variables. For example, newness aversion is independent of ICT-acceptance. Moreover, the categories found in this study was theoretically supported by system 1 thinking and system 2 thinking. This is unlike the case of ICT acceptance, which is controlled by system 2 thinking. This suggests that theories derived from TRA, such as TAM and TPB, have some limitations for explaining ICT non-acceptance.

Second, grounded theory, which is one of qualitative approaches, was shown to be a very effective research methodology for ICT non-acceptance. Because there have been few studies, the theoretical model suggested in this study was not developed deductively from existing theories but inductively from interviews and open-ended questionnaires. The data were analyzed independently of statistical tools without researchers' involvement but based on open coding and axis coding with researchers' qualitative interpretations and insights. This approach, which developed the theory, was clearly differentiated from most previous ICT acceptance approaches, which proved the suggested hypotheses.

Despite the contributions, this study has the following limitations. First, the data were collected from only university students. A limited sampling strategy can cause biased analyses and interpretations, even though university students may be one of the major samples for ICT non-acceptance. Therefore, the model suggested in this study should be formalized cautiously. For example, a different theory may be drawn if older people aged over seventy were sampled.

Second, the dynamics of non-acceptance were not identified. Non-acceptance is a state of being that may change over time. For example, a given technology, at a first glance, is not accepted because it is evaluated by system 1 thinking, but over time it may evaluated based on system 2 thinking, which may lead to acceptance. Therefore, a more intensive study with more careful sampling will be needed to understanding these dynamics.

ACKNOWLEDGEMENT

This research was supported by the Daegu University Research Grant 2012-0033.

REFERENCES

Abraham, C., Boudreau, M. C., Junglas, I., and Watson, R., 2013, Enriching our theoretical repertoire: the role of evolutionary psychology in technology acceptance, *European Journal of Information Systems,* Vol. 22, pp. 56-75.

Bhattacherjee, A., and Hikmet, N., 2007, Physicians' resistance toward healthcare information technology: a theoretical model and empirical test, *European Journal of Information Systems*, Vol. 16, NO. 4, pp. 725-737.

Bhattacherjee, A., and Park, S. C., 2014, Why end-users move to the cloud: a migration-theoretic analysis, *European Journal of Information Systems*, Vol. 23, No. 3, pp. 357-372.

Benbasat, I., and Barki, H., 2007, Quo Vadis TAM? *Journal of the Association for Information Systems, Vol. 8, No. 4,* pp. 211-218.

Cenfetelli, R. T., and Schwarz, A., 2011, Identifying and testing the inhibitors of technology usage intentions, *Information Systems Research,* Vol. 22, No. 4, pp. 808-823.

Davis, F. D., 1989, Perceived usefulness, perceived ease of use, and user acceptance of information technology, *MIS Quarterly, Vol.* 13, No. 3, pp. 319-340.

Davis, F. D., Bagozzi, R. P., and Warshaw, P. R., 1989, User acceptance of computer technology: a comparison of two theoretical models, *Management Science, Vol.* 35, No. 8, pp. 982-1003.

Fishbein, M., and Ajzen, I., 2011, *Predicting and Changing Behavior: The Reasoned Action Approach,* Taylor & Francis,.

Glaser, B. G. and Strauss, A. L., 1967, *The Discovery of Grounded Theory: Strategies for Qualitative Research*, Aldine Publishing Company, Chicago, USA.

Joshi, K., 1991, A model of users' perspective on change: the case of information systems technology implementation, *MIS Quarterly,*Vol. 15, No. 2, pp. 229-242.

Kim, H. W., and Kankanhali, A., 2009, Investigating user resistance to information systems implementation: A status quo bias perspective, *MIS Quarterly,* Vol. 33, No. 3, pp. 567-582.

Lapointe, L., & Rivard, S., 2005, A multilevel model of resistance to information technology implementation, *MIS Quarterly,* Vol. 29, No. 3, 461-491.

Marakas, G. M., & Hornik, S., 1996, Passive resistance misuse: overt support and covert recalcitrance in IS implementation, *European Journal of Information Systems,* Vol. 5, No. 3, pp. 208-219.

Martinko, M. K., Zmud, R. W., & Henry, J. W., 1996, An attributional explanation of individual resistance to the introduction of information technologies in the workplace, *Behavior & Information Technology,* Vol. 15 No. 5, pp. 313-330.

Markus, M. L., 1983, Power, politics, and MIS implementation, *Communication of the ACM,* Vol. 26, No. 6, pp. 430-444.

Park, C.P. and Chae, S. W., 2015, A study of user's resist and productivity using smart device in the smartwork context", *The Journal of Information Systems*, Vol. 23, No. 3, pp. 189-208.

Polites, G. L., and Karahanna, E., 2012, Shackled to the status quo: the inhibiting effects of incumbent system habit, switching costs, and inertia on new system acceptance, *MIS Quarterly,* Vol. 36, No. 1, pp. 21-42.

Strauss, A. L., *Qualitative Analysis for Social Scientists*, Cambridge University Press, Cambridge, UK., 1987.

Ray, S., Kim, S.S., and Morris, G., 2012, Users' Switching Costs: Their Nature and Formation, *Information Systems Research*, Vol. 23, No. 1, pp. 197-213.

Stanovich, K. E., and West, R. F., 2000, Individual differences in reasoning: implications for the rationality debate, *Behavioral and Brain Sciences,* Vol. 23, pp. 645-665.

Taylor, S., and Todd, P. A., 1995, Understanding information technology usage: a test of competing models," *Information Systems Research*, Vol. 6, No. 2, pp. 144-176.

Urquhart, C., Lehmann, H., and Myers, M, D., 2010, Putting the 'theory' back into grounded theory: guidelines for grounded theory studies in information systems, *Information Systems Journal,* Vol. 20, No. 4, pp. 357-381.

Venkatesh, V., and Brown, S., 2001, A longitudinal investigation of personal computers in homes: adoption determinants and emerging challenges, *MIS Quarterly*, Vol. 25, No. 1, pp. 71-102.

CONTEXT AWARENESS AS A PREREQUISITE FOR DECISION SUPPORT SYSTEMS: A SPATIAL EXAMPLE

Hardy Pundt
Harz University of Applied Sciences, Friedrichstr. 57-59, 38855 Wernigerode, Germany

ABSTRACT

A typical characteristic of spatial problem-solving is the multi-disciplinarity, i.e. different actors from various sectors have to be involved in decision making processes. To satisfy as many actors as possible it is necessary, to consider all relevant fields, and contexts. This can be a problem due to the complexity of a project, especially if the goal of a project is ill defined or broadly scoped. The actors, however, have different goals, perceptions and ideas of how a place, a landscape, a village or city should develop in the future. They see problems necessarily within their specific context. The idea of a holistic approach to decision making is to consider possibly all relevant contexts, in which a spatial problem is embedded. Ignoring specific contextual information can lead to bad and unsustainable decisions. This problem is not new, but this paper does not argue from a perspective of human communication. It raises the question, whether *applications* can *support a holistic approach* in spatial decision making through improved context integration.

KEYWORDS

Spatial Decision Support Systems, GIS, Mobile GIS, Context, Holistic Approach

1. INTRODUCTION

Most spatial applications are embedded in multi-contextual frameworks. Spatial decision making requires often data that are related to different sectors, e. g. urban planning, agriculture, forestry, road and traffic infrastructure, water management, soil protection, etc. Geographical Information Systems (GIS) are tools that own the ability to integrate information from different sectors in a suitable way. This combined with the fact that the great appeal of GIS stems from their ability to integrate great quantities of information about the environment and to provide a powerful repertoire of analytical tools to explore this data, makes GIS very useful tools for decision making concerning the natural and man-made environment (Foote and Lynch 2015). Mount described the role of context adequately when writing: "Context is an important aspect of any decision-making process. The constraints and opportunities surrounding decisions play causal roles in determining the outcomes of activities. In other words, context causes things to happen" (Mount 2013, p 1). The analysis of such data leads to new insights into spatial patterns. The question, which data layers are relevant within the framework of a complex spatial problem setting, relies still on human assessment. The identification of relevant sectors and related data can be a challenging task. This is especially true if the problem is very complex, only semi-structured, ill-defined or broadly scoped (Mount 2013, Densham and Goodchild 1994). There is always a risk that relationships between sectors are not, or insufficiently, considered and that specific information is ignored, under- or overrepresented, or not adequately evaluated.

This paper focuses on the question, if applications can assist users in identifying relevant contexts based on a problem-setting, aiming at integrating relevant context-information from different sectors. This would require a formalization of both, the problem setting, and the sector-specific context information. Following, a brief review of context-aware research and developments will throw light onto existing approaches to deal with context information. Thereafter, a use case is presented, aimed at two goals:

- Presenting *multi-contextual decision making* as a prerequisite for a holistic approach to adequate problem solutions, respected by all relevant actors that are included in the decision-making process
- Presenting a very first assumption of how a technological approach could support the enablement of spatial applications to identify relevant context information automatically.

After a brief discussion of what holistic decision making means, an overview of research on context-sensitive systems is presented. The following section deals with an exemplary use-case. Furthermore, a suggestion is made how to formalize context information, aiming at making it available for applications.

2. APPROACHING SPATIAL DECISION MAKING HOLISTICALLY

Spatial decision support systems (SDSS) are seen close to a definition of Densham et al. (1996) who stated that SDSS have been developed to address ill-structured problems with spatial query, modeling, analysis, and display capabilities. The authors identified a mismatch between the widespread single-user model of GIS and SDSS use and the group-based approach to decision-making that is often adopted when ill-structured problem-settings are addressed. The group-based approach relates to the need of considering different contexts for spatial decision making. Densham et al. came to the conclusion that SDSS-based spatial analysis and display methods must be expanded to encompass group decision-making processes, and new tools must be developed that will enable group members to generate, evaluate, and illustrate the strong and weak points of alternative scenarios and come to a consensus about how to proceed toward a decision. In such a sense, an SDSS can occur in various forms, aiming at helping decision makers in developing improved decisions (Gupta 2015). The authors found even more reasons for the necessity of such "group-based" approaches toward SDSS, e. g. the fact that complex spatial problems often have multiple, conflicting objectives for their solutions and that a solution, to be acceptable by all actors, must reconcile these conflicting goals. Many problems occurring in practice are still solved in a one-dimensional ("single-user") manner and they tend to solve them in a piecemeal way, instead of using an integrated approach.

There are various attempts aimed at improving SDSS. Many of them are still single-user focused, not taking into account multiple sectors adequately. In this paper, the idea of collaborative decision making supported by SDSS is coupled with the term of *holistic decision making*. 'Holistic' means to take into account most of the sectors that occur within the framework of a problem, instead of tackling them in a piecemeal way. Holistic problem-solving is hence the result of transdisciplinary cooperation of relevant actors (Odum and Barrett 2004; Velasquez-Manoff 2009). From a GIS perspective, holistic means that as many *relevant* datasets, and considerations of *different actors*, as possible are taken into account.

In computer science various approaches exist to integrate context information (see tables 2 and 3). Concerning *spatial* applications, context integration hasn't been dealt with comprehensively up to now. Whereas context-awareness has been identified as a property of mobile geo-applications, only few ideas have been published about how to achieve context integration in spatial decision making in general.

3. RELATED WORK

Dey and Abowd asked many years ago: "How do we as application developers provide the context to the computers, or make those applications aware and responsive to the full context of human-computer interaction?" (Dey & Abowd 2000, p. 2). To approach an answer with a *focus on geo-applications*, the following issues should be analysed:

- Which context types and which context representations are existing?
- Which approaches for context information integration and –processing are available?
- Are there opportunities to use such existing approaches in spatial applications?

3.1 Context Types

Meanwhile, it has been understood in computer science that developing context-aware applications should be supported by adequate context information modeling and reasoning techniques. The aims of such techniques are to reduce the complexity of context-aware applications and improve their maintainability and evolvability (Bettini et al. 2010). In table 1 basic context types are specified, taking into account results from (Sagl et al. 2015, Topcu 2010, Bettini et al. 2010, Hong et al. 2009). Whereas these authors, and others, discuss context aware systems in general, this paper focuses on the need of *context integration in spatial applications*.

Therefore, table 1 includes an example related to a mobile geo-application that is used for data collection purposes, namely an app aimed at acquiring road specific information.

Table 1. Basic Context Types

Context type	Brief description	Example: Data collection app for road information
Computer-specific context	The device including its properties, as well as the data network	Employee has a smartphone incl. GPS-receiver and digital maps; sporadic Internet connection
User-context	Personal data, preferences, individual goals	Employee is well trained in mobile apps; goal is to collect road specific information
Physical context	Location, temperature and further weather conditions, other facts and circumstances close to the current location	Start- and goal point and the track on which data will be collected are fixed; weather conditions and possibly specific conditions and needs to be considered
Temporal context	Current date and time, planning period	Start time and duration of data collection; physical properties of the employee and weather conditions
Social context	Near Groups or individuals	Other data collectors spatially close? Have citizens delivered road information which can be integrated?

3.2 Surveys on Context-Aware Systems

There have been different reviews of context-aware systems during the foregoing years (e. g. Hase and Vaidya 2013, Truong and Dustdar 2009, Hong et al. 2009). Publications in the field of pervasive and ubiquitous computing are prone to consider context information (e. g. Ou et al. 2006). Carvalho and da Silva (2012) pointed out that „The purpose of software is to help people to perform their activities and fulfill their objectives. In this regard, the human-software relationship could be enhanced if software could adapt to changes automatically during its utilization". Chen and Kotz (2005) surveyed the literature related to mobile systems. The following overview (table 2) provides information gathered from various papers.

Table 2. Methodologies and Technologies to Integrate Context Information into Computer Applications

Method	Brief description	Authors / Source
Proximate selection approach	The focus is on the user interface: Objects are related with other objects which are spatially „close" to them	Schilit et al. 1994
Automatic contextual reconfiguration approach	New components replace existing, if the context changes (then a reconfiguration of the system is carried out).	Kwon (2006)
Context-triggered actions	If the user gets into a new situation or if new data play a role, the system adapts using if-then-rules.	Chen & Kotz (2005)
Extending standard context models	An extension for a standard context model	Wieland et al. (2011); Sagl et al. (2015)
Ontological context-integration	The adaptation of a system to different users through context-related ontologies.	Gruber (1995); Wang et al. 2004); Welty (2010); Topcu (2011); Pundt (2012)

Another survey is from Baldauf et al (2007). Here, different approaches which are aimed at the integration of context information are mentioned (Baldauf et al, 2007; see also Kokinov et al., 2007). Later, Hong et al. (2009) presented a detailed literature review of context-aware systems (table 3).

Aiming at answering the question, whether context-awareness is only a matter of mobile geo-applications or if it is relevant for SDSS in general, section 4 introduces a conceptual approach.

Table 3. Layers of Context and Related Approaches (Hong et al (2009); Baldauf et al., (2007); and others)

Layer (classification framework)	Approaches	Goal
User-Infra-structure (incl. direct sensor access)	Mobility is at its core the essence of context-awareness. The dynamic environment sets special requirements for usability and acceptance of context-aware systems. Clients gather context information directly from sensors.	Optimizing usability of context-aware systems, focusing on the GUI.

Application	• Computing device to operate independently of human control (customizable by user context and preference) • Systems that not only handle a current task, situation and action but also anticipate future behavior • Systems that recognize each other at a certain distance because proximal devices are important factors to offer appropriate services to users • Applications that provide a rich set of capabilities and services to the nomad moving from place to place in a transparent form	Supporting users in many different situations and smart environments such as home, hospital, museums, shops, etc. These applications include, among others, decision support systems, and web services.
Middle-ware Infrastructure (incl. networked services)	• Mobile agents (emerge as technology suitable to develop context-aware systems) • Reflective middleware (possesses the unique ability to model itself through self-representation) • Methods of encapsulation used to separate e.g. business logic and graphical user interfaces • Metadata based middleware (facilities perform binding management actions based on metadata and context and locations visibility)	Allowing agents to acquire contextual information easily, reason about it using different logics and then adapt themselves to changing contexts.
Network Infra-structure	Internet protocol, handoff management, sensing, network requirements, network implementation	Dynamic adaptation to changes in contexts.
Context server	Introducing an access managing remote component and thus permitting multiple clients access to remote data sources.	Usage of a context server to relieve clients of resource intensive operations.
Concept & Research	• Designing and modeling algorithm, message bus encoded by XML, role and communication methods of agents • Increasing accuracy and efficiency of algorithm for extracting context • Development of algorithms to recommend appropriate service considering the user context	Develop theories and foundations to construct context-aware systems

4. INTEGRATION OF CONTEXT INFORMATION: A CONCEPTUAL APPROACH

Context information is related to a specific sector, such as water management, forestry, agriculture, urban planning, traffic infrastructure, or tourism. An application that considers different, relevant contexts needs access to descriptions of potentially *relevant* context models. A formalized description of the data acquired and stored by single sectors would lead to a sector-specific meta model. Such a meta model could be implemented using, for instance, textual tags in XML. If different sectors provide meta models, these can be compared automatically. The comparison can lead to the identification of equal or similar tags in the XML descriptions. If such identities, or similarities, are detected this hints on potential relationships between different contexts, or sectors. A problem-setting, however, could also be formalized in a tag-based manner and analysed together with the meta models. Equalities between the problem-setting and sector-specific meta models would either represent relationships between the problem, and possibly concerned sectors. The component that compares the XML models should work on a syntactical, and a semantic basis. If syntactically equal terms are identified, this is a hint on a contextual relationship between sectors, and/or between the problem-setting and sectors. The claim is that all sectors that show any such relationships should be considered when decisions within the framework of the spatial problem are made. Semantic similarities can be detected grounded on appropriate published algorithms (e. g. UMBCSim 2016, Rus et al. 2013).

4.1 An Examplary Use Case: Identifying Contextual Relationships between Two Sectors: "Road Infrastructure" and "Environment"

To avoid criticism about decisions, often uttered after the decisions have been implemented (e. g. criticisms on ‚incompleteness' of problem solutions, ‚overemphasis' of specific aspects, 'ignorance' of certain actors or lacking ‚sustainability'), the identification of potentially relevant contexts within a spatial problem-setting could help to make more comprehensive, and therefore better decisions.

The exemplary scenario is as follows: in urban planning, road infrastructure and green areas (lawns, parks, green corridors along roads, etc.) play an important role. Particular urban management purposes may require the collection of data about road conditions, as well as information about the vitality of trees along the roads. Data collection is mostly done using GPS-supported, mobile geo-applications. The data is stored using GIS. Of course, such data are collected primarily for usage within a single sector. But once digitized, such data could be relevant for different other applications as well.

Two mobile apps are supposed, an app to collect road data, and another app to acquire information about urban vegetation. Such tasks are often carried out by different administrational units.

However, the data, collected using the mobile GI apps, is potentially interesting in many different contexts. To make this more explicit, the following table considers a road infrastructure (or traffic-) department and an environmental department. The table shows sector-specific issues and, additionally, it hints on contexts in which other sectors the data could play a role as well. The use-case serves only as a theoretical framework, and table 4 raises some issues to demonstrate the goal of making the "SDSS" context-aware. To achieve this, it needs to be expanded by a functionality that, in a first step, tries to identify all relevant contexts within the framework of the underlying problem-setting. This is envisaged using the formalized meta models.

The challenge is to consider multi-contextuality *not only on the human level* but on the *level of geo-software* that supports communication and data sharing needs.

Table 4. Contexts that are potentially relevant a) for mobile mapping apps and b) for urban planning purposes in general

Specific contexts, potentially relevant for the mobile apps	
Sector: Road infrastructure; *Using: "Road Infrastructure Mapping App"*	*Sector: Environment;* *Using: "Urban Vegetation Mapping App"*
• requirements of passengers • requirements of cyclists • harmonization of pavement of roads with noise minimization demands • integration of road improvement and historical, as well as aesthetical aspects	• Influences of pavement and road infrastructure elements on the vitality of road trees • Influences of road improvement on water provision for road vegetation • Limiting effects of road trees on traffic (e. g. visibility of traffic signs) • Selection of suitable species for road vegetation in case of tree replacement • Consideration of legal aspects concerning cutting and replacing of road trees • Consideration of urban-aesthetical aspects
Other contexts, potentially identified by the SDSS (which must be expanded by formal descriptions aiming at accessing sector specific meta models and identifying dependencies between the problem, and relevant sectors)	
• *Traffic security context* (e. g. road trees may affect traffic security aspects) • *Environmental context (e. g.* role of road trees for urban microclimate) • *Urban aesthetics context (*e. g. coincidence of the improved road, and road vegetation, concerning the aesthetical urban picture that is envisaged) • *Urban development context* (e. g., consideration of underground engineering; telecommunication measures (hauling of pipes, wires, etc.) during the renewal of roads and the planting of new trees) • *Political context* (e. g. integrated urban development plan) • *Economic context* (e. g. improvement of overall urban traffic infrastructure) • *Climate Change adaptation context* (e.g. consideration of climate protection (CO_2-reduction) and climate adaptation (generation of shadow through trees)) • *Citizens participation context (1)* (e. g. requirements of elderly people, children, handicapped people) • *Citizens participation context (2)* (e. g. resistance against planned road- and vegetation modifications)	

4.2 A First Step toward Formalization of Meta Models

Neither table 3, nor figure 4 substantiate a claim that they are complete. They indicate exemplarily that multi-contextuality is a crucial prerequisite for proper and comprehensive spatial decision-making. „The association between Web-Services [or geo-applications] and context is not easy to achieve because the adequate mechanisms are not offered to developers in order to support the description and representation of context-related information and its later utilization (…).” (Carvalho & da Silva 2012, p 63). The claim is that technology can contribute to improve spatial decision-making quality through the application of techniques to integrate context information, thus supporting a holistic approach.

A prerequisite for the suggested approach is the description of context-specific meta models. There are XML derivates which own the capabilities for formalizing textual descriptions, e. g. RDF and/or OWL. RDF gains popularity for its ability to manage semi-structured data without a predefined database schema and therefore suitable for meta-model descriptions (Brodt et el. 2011). The difference between such a meta-model, and an ontology, for which formalization in RDF/OWL is possible, can be scrutinized. Ontology-based spatial models, however, have been considered as useful in many publications (e. g. Gruber 1995, Bolchini et al. 2006, Klien et al. 2006, Ou et al., 2006, Kuhn et al. 2007, Obrst et al. 2010, Pundt 2012).

The following figure presents the proposed interplay of the formal models under the assumption that the SDSS was expanded with a formal description of the problem setting, e. g. within the framework of an “urban road improvement project”. Based on the underlying models, two specific contexts are identified as being *relevant*. Whereas information on the age of trees can be found in one sector-specific model (Sector: “Road Infrastructure”), the question could come up, how the vitality of old trees looks like. This information is available in another context-model (Sector: “Environment”). In such a way, both pieces of information can be provided to the decision makers through the context integration procedure. The information can afterwards be taken into account in the decision making process, thus avoiding wrong decisions, e. g. cutting of road trees only due to their age, even if they are still quite healthy.

Concerning the formal representation, in a first step not XML (or RDF/OWL) has been used, but N-triples. This is a line-based, plain text format, capable of storing and transmitting data. It relies on the components subject, predicate, object and in such a way it provides a means to represent spatial features. A basic format of an n-triple is as follows (W3C 2014):

```
<http://one.example/subject1> <http://one.example/predicate1>
<http://one.example/object1> .
_:subject1 <http://an.example/predicate1> "object1" .
_:subject2 <http://an.example/predicate2> "object2" .
```

According to this basic structure, the following figure represents an example in that two meta-models represent the context-specific description using n-triples. The triples are applied to find corresponding contexts, hinting on their relevance within the framework of the decision making process.

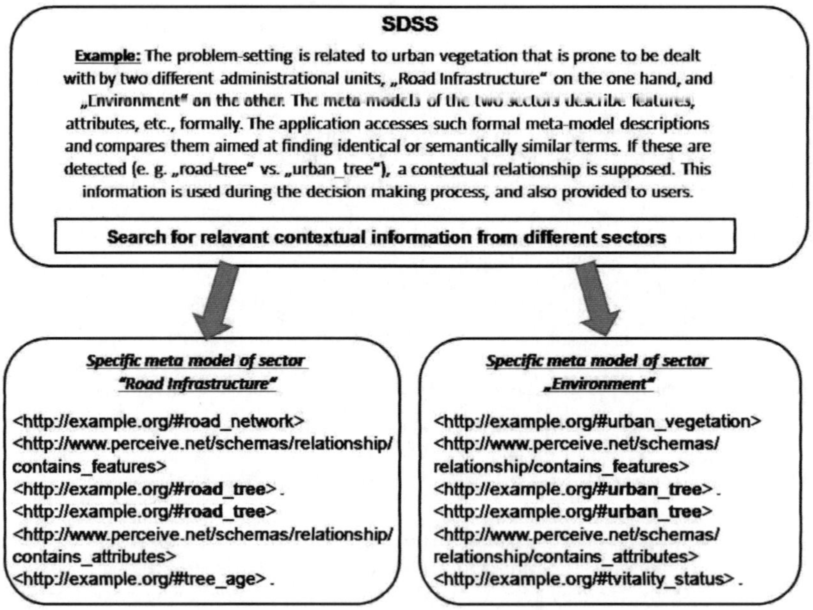

Figure 4. An n-triple-based example of how a spatial application (SDSS) can deal with specific, formal meta-models to identifying contextual relationships between different sectors (and using this information as decision support)

The figure shows only a very first idea of how to approach context integration in SDSS. Further studies should be carried out to investigate if such an approach is vital, and could be combined with solutions that have been mentioned in tables 2 and 3.

5. CONCLUSIONS

Spatial decision support systems (SDSS) should be completed by components that enable the system to identify and possibly integrate relevant contextual information from different sectors. This capability would support a holistic approach in decision making, thus aiming at considering as many relevant contexts as possible. The *application-steered identification* of relevant context information, and *its provision* would support decision making especially in complex, multi-dimensional problem settings.

Extracting information from different representations, e. g. meta models as mentioned before, is a tough task to do. However, the growing need for more transdisciplinarity and cross-sector thinking in spatial decision making, require action for more substantial, sector-wise formal context representations. If they exist, applications would be enabled to identify relationships and dependencies between different contexts which would contribute to more sustainable decisions.

In this paper, related work has been investigated critically; a use case has been defined to make the problem more transparent, and an idea to formalize context information is presented. A next step should be to implement the exemplary use case and to test if the approach supports the goals defined previously.

However, the overall aim of making SDSS context-aware is to minimize the danger of producing deficient, ignorant or wrong decisions. Such support would also avoid workflows that are carried out uniquely, sector-specific ("piecemeal"), instead of integrative.

REFERENCES

Baldauf, M.; Dustdar, S.; Rosenberg, F., 2007. A survey on context-aware systems. *Int. Journal Ad Hoc and Ubiquitous Computing*, Vol. 2, No. 4, pp 263 - 277.

Beigl, M.; Christiansen, H.; Roth-Berghofer, T.; Kofod-Petersen, A.; Coventry, K.R.; Schmidtke, H.R. (Eds.), 2011. *Modeling and Using Context - 7th International and Interdisciplinary Conference CONTEXT 2011*, Karlsruhe. Lecture Notes in Computer Science, Springer.

Bettini, C., Brdiczka, O., Henricksen, K., Indulska, J., Nicklas, D., Ranganathan, A. , Riboni, D., 2010. A survey of context modelling and reasoning techniques. *Pervasive and Mobile Computing*, Vol. 6, Issue 2, Pages 161–180.

Bolchini, C., Curino, C., Schreiber, F.A., Tanca, L., 2006. Context integration for mobile data tailoring. 7th Conference on Mobile Data Management, Nara, Japan, *Proceedings*.

Brodt, A., Schiller, O., Mitschang, B., 2011. Efficient resource attribute retrieval in RDF triple stores. *Proceedings of the 20th ACM conference on information and knowledge management* (CIKM).

Carvalho, L.P.; da Silva, P.C., 2012. CCMF, Computational Context Modeling Framework - An Ontological Approach to Develop Context-Aware Web Applications. In: *Afzal, M.T. (ed.) Computer and Information Science, "Computer Science and Engineering, Semantics in Action - Applications and Scenarios".*

Chen, G.; Kotz, D., 2005. A Survey of Context-Aware Mobile Context Research. https://mmlab.snu.ac.kr/courses/2005_advanced_internet/handout/ppt/36%20-%20context_aware.pdf (accessed 19.02.2016)

Densham, P.J., M.P. Armstrong and K.K. Kemp, 1996. Collaborative Spatial Decision-Making: Scientific Report for the Specialist Meeting. Techn. Rep. 95-14, Nat. Center for Geogr. Information and Analysis, Sta Barbara, CA., 184 pp.

Densham, P.J., Goodchild, M.F., 1994. Spatial Decision Support Systems Closing Report. University of New York at Buffalo, University of California, Santa Barbara. http://www.geog.ucsb.edu/~good/papers/218.pdf (accessed 04.01.2017)

Dey, A.K.; Abowd, G.D, 2000. Towards a better understanding of context and context-awareness. In: *Proceedings of the Workshop on the What, Who, Where, When and How of Context Awareness,* affiliated with the CHI 2000 Conference on Human Factors in Computer Systems, New York, NY: ACM Press.

Foote, K., Lynch, M., 2015. Geographic Information Systems as an Integrating Technology: Context, Concepts, and Definitions. Univ. Colorado: http://www.colorado.edu/geography/gcraft/notes/intro/intro_f.html (accessed 10.01.17).

Gruber, T., 1995. Toward principles or the design of ontologies used for knowledge sharing. *International Journal of Human-Computer Studies*, Vol. 43, Issue 5-6, pp 907-928.

Gupta, S., 2015. Using Real-Time Data: How Geospatial Connect Provides Better GIS Decision Support. http://blog.hexagongeospatial.com/using-real-time-data-gsif-provides-better-gis-decision-support/(accessed 11.01.17)

Hase, S.K., Vaidya, M.B., 2013. A survey on context aware system & intelligent Middleware's. *Journal of Computer Engineering*, Vol. 15, Issue 3, pp 26 – 29.

Hong, J., Suh, E., Kim, S.J., 2009. Context-aware systems: A literature review and classification. *Expert Systems with Applications 36*, pp 8509–8522.

Kokinov, B.N.; Richardson, D.C.; Roth-Berghofer; Vieu, T.L. (Eds.), 2007. Modeling and Using Context, 6th International and Interdisciplinary Conference CONTEXT 2007, Roskilde, Denmark, August 20-24, 2007, *Lecture Notes in Computer Science 4635*, Springer.

Klien, E., Lutz, M., Kuhn, W., 2006. Ontology-based discovery of geographic information services - An application in disaster management. *Computers, Environment and Urban Systems. 30(1),* pp 102 - 123.

Kuhn, W., Raubal, M., Gärdenfors, P., 2007. Cognitive Semantics and Spatio-Temporal Ontologies. *Introduction to a Special Issue of Spatial Cognition and Computation 7(1),* pp 3-11.

Kwon, O., 2006. The potential roles of context-aware computing technology in optimization-based intelligent decision-making. In: *Expert Systems with Applications.* Volume 31, Issue 3, October 2006, Pages 629 – 642.

Mäs, S.; Henzen, C.; Müller, M.; Bernard, L., 2014. Glues GDI - Eine Geodateninfrastruktur für wissenschaftliche Umweltdaten. In: *gis.science 4/2014*, S. 129 - 137.

Mount, J. 2013. The role of context in spatial decision-making in GIScience. PhD (Doctor of Philosophy) thesis, University of Iowa, 2013. http://ir.uiowa.edu/etd/5027. (accessed 08.01.2017).

Obrst, L., Janssen, T., Ceusters, W. (eds.), 2010. *Ontologies and Semantic Technologies for Intelligence.* IOS Press Amsterdam, Berlin, Tokyo, Washington DC.

Odum, E., Barrett, G.W., 2004. *Fundamentals of Ecology*. Thomson Brooks Cole, Australia, Canada.

Ou, S., Georgalas, N., Azmoodeh, M., Yang, K., Xiantang, S., 2006. A Model Driven Integration Architecture for Ontology-Based Context Modelling and Context-Aware Application Development. *Lecture Notes in Computer Science 4066*, Springer, pp. 188 – 197.

Pundt, H., 2012. Semantically Enriched POI as Ontological Foundation for Web-Based and Mobile Spatial Applications. In: Podobnikar, T., Ceh, M. (eds.): *Universal Ontology of Geographic Space*. IGI Global, USA, pp. 186 - 206.

Rus, V., Lintean, M., Banjade, R., Niraula, N., and Stefanescu, D., 2013. SEMILAR: The Semantic Similarity Toolkit. *Proceedings of the 51st Annual Meeting of the Assoc. for Computational Linguistics,* Sofia, Bulgaria.

Sagl, G., Resch, B., Blaschke, T., 2015. Contextual Sensing: Integrating Contextual Information with Human and Technical Geo-Sensor Information for Smart Cities. *Sensors* 2015, *15*(7).

Schilit, B., Adams, N., Want, R., 1994. Context-Aware Computer Applications. http://graphics.cs.columbia.edu/courses/mobwear/resources/schilit-mcsa94.pdf, Zugriff 01/15.

Topcu, F., 2011. Context Modeling and Reasoning Techniques. SNET Seminar 2011 TU Berlin. http://www.snet.tu-berlin.de/fileadmin/fg220/courses/SS11/snet-project/context-modeling-and-reasoning_topcu.pdf (accessed 01.02.2016)

Truong, H.L., Dustdar, S, 2009. A survey on context-aware web service systems. *Int. Journal of Web Information Systems* 5(1), pp. 5-31.

UMBCSim, 2016. UMBS Semantic Similarity Service. http://swoogle.umbc.edu/SimService/ (accessed 13.02.2017)

Velasquez-Manoff, M., 2009. http://www.csmonitor.com/Environment/Bright-Green/2009/1016/ environmental-problems-need-a-holistic-approach (accessed 30.05.2016)

Wang, X.H., Zhang, D.Q., Gu, T., Pung, H.K., 2004. Ontology based context modeling and reasoning using OWL. *IEEE Annual Conference on Pervasive Computing and Communications Workshops, Proceedings*, pp 18-22.

Welty, C., 2010. Context Slices: Representing Contexts in OWL. In: Blomqvist, E., Chaudri, V., Corcho, O., Presutti, V., Sandkuhl, K. (eds.), Workshop on Ontology Patterns. *Proceedings of the 2nd International Workshop on Ontology Patterns - WOP2010*; http://ceur-ws.org/Vol-671/.

Wieland, M., Nicklas, D., Leymann, F., 2011. Context Model for Representation of Business Process Management Artifacts. In: Lin, Chun Hua (Hrsg); Zhang, Ming (Hrsg): *International Proceedings of Economics Development and Research: IPEDR*. Economics and Business Information 9, pp. 46-51.

W3C, 2014. RDF 1.1 N-Triples. https://www.w3.org/TR/n-triples/ (accessed 05.06.2016)

TOWARD DEVELOPING THE MODEL OF EMERGING TECHNOLOGY ADOPTION (META)

Mohanad Halaweh
Al Falah University, Dubai, United Arab Emirates

ABSTRACT

This paper aims to conceptually develop a model of emerging technologies adoption (META). Although technology acceptance and adoption have been intensively investigated using well-established theories called the Technology Acceptance Model (TAM) and Innovation Diffusion Theory (IDT), this paper claims that emerging technology (ET) has particular characteristics that differentiate it from the adoption of traditional technology that has been used for a long time. Therefore, it argues that TAM and IDT are not sufficient to investigate the adoption of ET. Investigating the adoption of ET requires additional, unique, non-traditional factors (constructs). To achieve the objective of this paper, first, TAM and IDT will be reviewed. Then, this paper will use the characteristics of ET as the basis for developing the factors that influence the adoption of ET. A discussion of META applications and implications for future research are also provided.

KEYWORDS

META, Emerging Technologies, TAM, IDT, Adoption Factors, Technology Acceptance

1. INTRODUCTION

The literature review encompasses extensive research that has investigated users' and organisations' intention to adopt and use new technology in different contexts (e.g. e/m-commerce, e/m-banking, m/e-learning, and enterprise systems (EPR), just to name a few (Chen, Tsai, & Tseng, 2016; Asunka, 2016; Abdelghaffar & Moustafa, 2013; Pham et al., 2011; Lin, 2011; Lee, 2011; Sundarraj and Manochehri, 2011; Sadi and Noordin, 2011). Although technology acceptance and adoption have been intensively investigated using well-established theories called the Technology Acceptance Model (TAM) and Innovation Diffusion Theory (IDT), this paper claims that ET has particular characteristics that differentiate it from the adoption of traditional technology that has been used for a long time. For example, e-commerce has become traditional technology (i.e. it is not labelled as an emerging technology). On the other hand, Big Data, Internet of Things (IOT), Virtual Reality, and Near Field Communication (NFC), for example, are labelled as emerging technologies (ETs). Therefore, this poses a question: Are the factors that influence the adoption of traditional technology identical to or different from those that influence the adoption of ET? This paper argues that TAM and IDT are not sufficient to investigate the adoption of ET. Investigating the adoption of ET requires additional, unique, non-traditional factors (constructs). Therefore, this paper proposes a model of emerging technologies adoption (META).

The remainder of this paper is organised as follows: Section 2 presents a review of TAM and IDT. Section 3 presents the characteristics of ET which are used as a foundation to develop META. Section 4 discusses the questions and implications that might rise from developing and applying META. Finally, the research conclusion is provided by highlighting the main research contribution.

2. ADOPTION THEORIES (TAM AND IDT)

This Most technology adoption research is based on two predominant theories: TAM (Davis, 1989) and IDT (Rogers, 1995, 2003). They are used to explain, predict and test the factors that influence the acceptance and adoption of technology. These two theories were selected, as they are well-established and considered the basis for most adoption and acceptance of technology research (Monchak and Kim, 2011; Williams et al., 2009). However, other models were extended based on them (Williams et al., 2009), for example,

Venkatesh, Morris, Davis & Davis (2003) developed Unified Theory of Acceptance and Use of Technology (UTAUT) which in fact was developed on the basis of TAM. The TAM model includes two main factors: perceived usefulness, and perceived ease of use (Davis, 1989). Williams et al. (2009) systematically reviewed the literature on IT adoption, acceptance and diffusion by examining 345 papers published in 19 peer-reviewed journals between 1985 and 2007. Their findings suggest that the survey method and TAM theory (and its associated constructs) are primarily used in the examined papers. Monchak and Kim (2011) also analysed recent IDT research published in the top eight IS journals and the International Conference on Information Systems (ICIS) from the period of 2003 to 2011, as it is widely used in IS research, in order to determine the trends and directions for future adoption research. Rogers (1995) refers to five factors that are the attributes of innovation and could explain new technology adoption: relative advantage, complexity, compatibility, trialability, and observability. Table 1 provides a description of these factors. However, Davis' factors (i.e. ease of use and usefulness) are equivalent to Rogers' perceived complexity and perceived relative advantage factors (Moore and Benbasat, 1991). Therefore, the comparison and discussion in the current paper will focus on IDT, as it is broader than TAM, and TAM's basic constructs (i.e. perceived usefulness and perceived ease of use) are already covered by IDT. However, more discussions about TAM criticisms can be found in Bagozzi (2007) and Benbasat and Barki, (2007).

Table 1. Constructs of TAM and IDT

Construct/Factor	Description	Reference
Perceived usefulness	Degree to which a person believes that using a particular system would enhance his or her job performance	Davis (1989)
Perceived ease of use	Degree to which a person believes that using a particular system would be free from effort	Davis (1989)
Relative advantage	Degree to which an innovation is perceived as better than the idea it supersedes	Rogers (1995)
Compatibility	Degree to which an innovation is perceived as consistent with the existing social values and beliefs, past experiences, and needs of potential adopters	Rogers (1995)
Complexity	Degree to which an innovation is perceived as difficult to understand and use	Rogers (1995)
Trialability	Degree to which an innovation may be experimented or tested before deciding to adopt it or not	Rogers (1995)
Observability	Degree to which the results of an innovation are observable/visible to others	Rogers (1995)

Rogers (1995) developed variables that affect the adoption rate of any innovation. These include 1) perceived attributes of innovations (described in Table 1), 2) type of innovation decision, 3) communication channels, 4) nature of the social system, and; 5) extent of change of the agents' promotion efforts. However, the model of the attributes/characteristics of the innovation relationship with the rate of adoption of innovations (ROAI) is described as the basic IDT research model because characteristics of the innovations (described in Table 1) are theorised to explain much of the variance in the ROAI (Monchak and Kim, 2011).

Monchak and Kim (2011) highlighted two meanings of technology adoption: 1) adoption is the decision to use an innovation, 2) adoption by putting the innovation into use. In this research, adoption refers to the decision to use new ET, not the actual use of the technology per se.

Rogers (1995) defined the diffusion of innovation as "the process by which an innovation is communicated through certain channels over time among the members of a social system" (p. 5). He stated that diffusion is a special type of communication concerned with the spread of messages that are perceived as new ideas. Although IDT has been widely used in IS research, it has faced many criticisms. Firstly, Maloney (2010) noted that Rogers' definition focuses on 'communication' rather than the 'adoption' of new innovations, and this is perhaps due to the fact that Rogers was a communications academic. He continued, stating that, by definition, 'members of a social system' may restrict the theory to one home market. He further argued that the rise of the global economy has meant that new innovations are no longer merely launched and diffused in one market in isolation, but in many countries across the world at the same time. Therefore, Rogers' theory was developed with only one market in mind (Maloney, 2010). Secondly, Rogers's theory does not take into account the particularities of complex information technologies (Lyytinen and Damsgaard, 2001). Rogers states that innovation can be a new idea or object. However, not all innovations are homogeneous. Technology is not like medical products or marketing ideas. Innovated ideas or objects are treated similarly by Rogers. In this regard, Lyytinen and Damsgaard (2001) pointed out that not all technological innovations should be characterised with the same set of attributes. Thirdly, some argue from the interpretive and critical thought schools (Lyytinen and Damsgaard, 2001; Beynon-Davis and Williams, 2003; Light and Papazafeiropoulou, 2004; Stahl et al., 2010; Stahl, 2011) that technologies are socially constructed and subject to multiple interpretations according to the contexts and user perceptions, which Rogers' theory does not take into account.

These criticisms are taken into consideration when developing META, as subsequent sections will discuss.

3. META

In this section we first present definition of ET and its characteristics and then use them as foundation for developing META. There is no widely agreed-upon definition of ET. However, Halaweh (2013) provided a very good comprehensive definition for ET which was developed based on reviewing several definitions (Stahl 2011, Day & Schoemaker, 2000; Srinivasan, 2008; Doering & Veletsianos; 2007; Miller et al., 2005; Daniel et al., 1998). Halaweh (p.110) pointed out:

"ETs are not necessarily new and are not limited to a fixed period of time. Technology is labeled as emerging in a particular context (domain or place). Technology is also considered emerging when it is not widespread in that particular context. Technology is defined as emerging when it causes a radical change to business, industry and society."

He stated that some might consider ET as new technology, which is not entirely accurate. This is one of the main misconceptions about ET. Technology can still be considered emerging in one context even though it has been considered established in another. The context here is related to place, domain, or application. For example, Radio Frequency Identification (RFID) is not considered emerging in developed countries, whereas it is described as an ET in other poor and developing countries in the world where the Internet and communication technology infrastructures are still poor. Social Media are considered established tools in the Media industries, but they are still considered to be emerging in the education sector. A technology is still emerging if it is not yet a "must-have", meaning that it is not widespread in that particular context. For example, a few years ago email or smartphone were an optional technology. Today, it is a must-have, must-use technology for most people in all organizations. Another misconception about ET is to set specific range of time in a technology's lifecycle (5- 10 years) to determine if it is emerging. For example, virtual worlds were described as an ET in the mid-1990s (Dede, 1996). However, virtual worlds are still now described as an ET. For example, Second Life (a 3D virtual world) is labeled as an ET. This means that the life of a technology can exceed 10 years and the technology can still be considered emerging, as is Second Life, which is still in its early revolution and is being discovered by many business models. Finally, ET causes radical change on business and society. It creates a new industry or transforms an existing one. For example, record label companies and the DVD market were destroyed because of the emerging Apple store and the iPod.

Halaweh (2013) referred to six characteristics that describe the ET which are presented in Table 2. In his paper entitled "Emerging Technology: What is it?" he provided several examples of ETs to prove the concepts related to these characteristics.

Table 2. ET Characteristics (Halaweh, 2013)

Characteristics	Characteristics Description
ET uncertainty	The uncertainty associated with ET takes several forms with unknown and unpredictable values and outcomes, such as standards and specifications (maturity), business models, price, and adoption rate uncertainties.
ET network effect	The value of an ET increases by increasing the number of ET users.
ET costs	The cost of owning the ET is high, and the cost of substituting traditional technology with the ET is high.
Unobvious ET impact	The social and ethical impacts associated with the use of ET are unseen, unknown, or unexpected before its adoption/use or at an early stage of the ET life cycle.
ET is limited to creator or inventor country	ET is usually available first for use in a particular context or in the country that creates or invents it.
ETs are not fully investigated and researched	Most of the materials on ET are white papers and technical reports produced by the manufacturers of the ET with little scientific/academic research

This paper proposes using these characteristics as foundation to study the factors that influence the adoption of ET. As indicated before that ET is not equal to T (traditional technology or established technology) so the influencing factors should not be same, which existing adoption theories (IDT and TAM) did not take into consideration. Thus, this paper suggests developing META. Table 3 shows the main elements of META by considering the definition and characteristics of ET as the basis for defining the factors that influence on adoption.

Table 3. META Elements Based on the Aforementioned Characteristics

META Description	META is a theory that posits that ETs have special characteristics that differentiate them from traditional technologies. This implies that unique and non-traditional factors influence their adoption and correspond to the nature of *emerging*. This pertains to a future that is uncertain and unknown. The core characteristic of META is uncertainty, which is a vacuum for any unique emerging contextual factors that influence the adoption of a particular ET.	
META Goal	Predict the influencing factors on the decision to adopt ET rather than using the ET itself. TAM and IDT predict factors that mainly influence *using* a technology/innovation such as ease of use, complexity and triability, which concern the actual use of the technology per se.	
Unit of Analysis	Investigate the adoption at different levels: user, organisation, and country. Country as a whole is taken as one unit, as the adoption of an ET sometimes requires governmental support and industry collaboration, or both users and organizations together.	
Factors	**Description**	**Influence on Adoption**
Uncertainty	Degree to which the outcomes and implications of the adoption of the ET are unknown and unpredictable	Decrease adoption
ET Network Effect	Degree to which the value of an ET increases by increasing the number of network users (users of ET)	Increase adoption
ET Maturity	Degree to which ET standards and specifications are well established	Increase adoption
ET Cost	Degree to which the cost of owning the ET is high and the cost of substituting traditional technology for the ET is high	Decrease adoption
Clarity of ET Impact	Degree to which the social and ethical impact of the technology is observable before its adoption or at an early stage of the ET life cycle	Increase adoption
Availability of ET	Degree to which ET is available for use in a particular context (e.g. community or country)	Increase adoption
Timing	Degree of elapsed time in which ET needs to become widespread. As time passes, the ET becomes more diffused and the number of adopters also increases	Increase adoption

Uncertainty is a core factor in META, which means that adoption is determined by many uncertain variables. This is due to the nature of ET, whose future is unknown or unpredictable. Under this factor, any contextual factors that underline the particularity of a certain context or certain ET features are included. Uncertainty here is like a vacuum that has capacity to any emerging thing related to a particular context. Thus, uncertainty here is related to two categories. The first one is uncertainty about different variables whose values or descriptions are unknown, unpredictable or unstable such as cost, penetration rate, standards and specifications. The second category is related to those variables that are unknown and related to a particular context and ET (contextual factors). These variables (rather than those mentioned in the first category) change across applications, contexts and users. For example, revolutions occurred in the Arab world (Called Arab Spring) was one of the main factors that influence on many people's decision to adopt Facebook. This contextual factor was not mentioned in the adoption theories (IDT or TAM) nor investigated by researchers until 2011 when Arab Spring occurred.

Figure 1 shows the correlation between time and ET adoption rate and how other factors are correlated with these two constructs. The ET adoption rate increases over the time; it starts with low availability (in market, society, and country) and a low network effect. However, availability increases over time as the number of ET manufactures and providers increase, spread across borders and developed industrial countries (for example, smartphones are produced by many manufacturers in Europe and Asia, resulting in increased market availability). However, ETs can be available but not adoptable or neither available nor adoptable because of economic conditions or exclusive restrictions of an ET to the manufacturer's country or inventors in a particular country. Figure 1 also shows that the ET network effect increases over time. For example, the network effect of Web 2.0 applications (e.g. Facebook, Twitter, and YouTube) increases over time as a result of increasing the number of network users. The initial value of Facebook was very low, but its value gradually increases as the number of users who join the Facebook network increase.

ET also starts with low technology maturity with incomplete specifications and non-uniform standards. For example, some near field communication (NFC) specifications were defined in 2011 and some are underway (NFC Forum, 2011), although its first trials application started earlier in 2006.

ET also begins with few or unobservable ethical and social problems. However, as time passes, the number of ethical and social concerns gradually increases. The reason is that when ET is used in different applications, new unexpected concerns arise. For example, RFID technology is used in many applications. When it was used for managing and tracking goods in supply chain and inventories, the ethical concerns were very minor. However, when it was later used for human tracking by implanting an RFID under the skin, it raised new concerns (i.e. privacy). When a new application is identified, new social and ethical concerns are expected to emerge. However, this will increase to a certain point where no more applications are expected to appear and where similar concerns such as privacy are repeated across different applications.

In contrast, as time passes the cost of ET gradually drops and the level of uncertainty decreases. If many manufacturers offer it, its price decreases due to strong competition. However, before ET is produced by many manufacturers, its standards and specifications need to mature. Once they become matured and unfirmed across different manufacturers, the cost and uncertainty decrease.

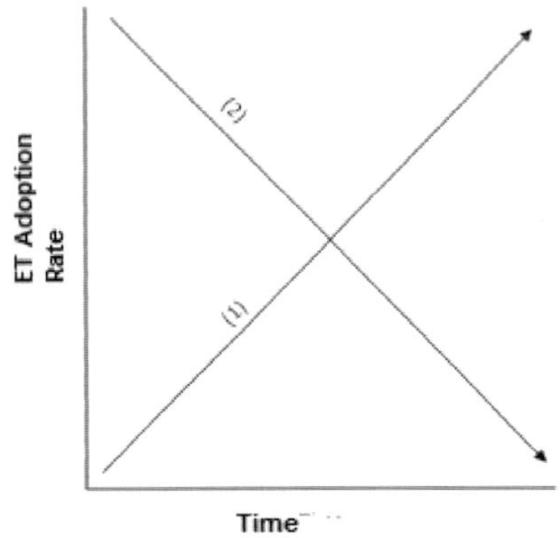

Figure 1. Correlation between Timing and ET Adoption Rate and How Other Factors are Correlated with These Two Constructs

(1) Availability, Network Effect, ET Maturity, ET Impact

(2) Uncertainty and Cost

4. DISCUSSION AND IMPLICATIONS FOR FUTURE RESEARCH

As mentioned previously, Davis' constructs of TAM were covered by IDT (Moore and Benbasat, 1991), which enables a direct comparison of META with IDT theory. First, Rogers' theory (1995) focuses on user perceptions of using the innovation itself. The META factors in this paper do not focus on the use of the technology (how easy or complex), but rather about the decision to adopt new ET. It is important to mention that the main intrinsic of META is that ET has certain characteristics that require emerging, unique and non-traditional factors to understand their adoption. This is the most important feature that IDT failed to consider. Nonetheless, other IDT criticisms discussed before are also addressed, for example, responding to the criticism that not all technological innovations should be characterised with the same set of attributes. The *uncertainty* of technology is considered here as factor that reflect that meaning. Uncertainty is a core factor considered to address any emerging factors relevant to a particular context, users or technology features on one hand. On another hand, they conform to the nature of emergency, as ETs involve unpredictable related variables and concerns. In this regard, one of the implications for future research that aims to apply META, researchers need to establish the issues surrounding uncertainty and measure that construct. Uncertainty is changing across contexts and different ETs. If the value of uncertainty is low, this predicts high adoption. Conversely, if the uncertainty value is high, the adoption rate will be low.

The IDT criticism relates to the fact that new innovations are no longer merely being launched and diffused in one market in isolation, but simultaneously in many countries across the world, is also addressed in META. The "availability" factor is developed based on the characteristic that ET is limited to developed countries. This means that consumers might be ready to adopt the new technology, but they are unable to adopt it because it is not available to them for several reasons, mainly the economic conditions. In addition, ET maturity is relevant in this context, as globally standardising the technology and interoperability between different product manufacturers increases production and lowers the price, thus increasing the adoption. Finally, regarding the criticism related to the notion that technologies are socially constructed and subject to multiple interpretations according to the context and user perception, the factors of *uncertainty* and *ET impact* are developed, as they respond to this perfectly and leave space for contextual factors.

For other META constructs, cost is a major factor that influences the adoption rate. Previous Adoption theories have not mentioned the cost factor. However, some technology adoption studies have mentioned it (Dahlberg et al., 2008). Nevertheless, here it is linked with ET, as we provide a general conceptual basis that is applicable to many emerging technologies. The reason is that ETs are science-based and usually involve research and development costs. Also, ET creates substitution costs as sometimes leads to replacing the traditional/established technology (for example, users might have to replace smartphone with another one NFC-enabled which is costly). It is also important to mention that if a particular technology is not new but labeled as an ET in a particular context, cost is still an issue. The cost is not for the technology per se rather for organisational change and substitution, as ETs usually transforms business and industry radically. Finally, Timing also is a new factor that TAM and IDT do not mention. It has been shown how other factors are correlated with time.

As META is a new model, IS/IT researchers might pose several questions about its application and use. Firstly, is a new theory for adoption necessary? The answer to this question is yes. META is used to predict the adoption of ET not use of the technology per se. Moreover, traditional technology acceptance and adoption theories do not consider the special characteristics of ET such as uncertainty, ET maturity, network effect, cost and other factors. META is independent from other adoption theories. In another words, it is not an extension of TAM and/or IDT.

Secondly, can META be used to predict the adoption of traditional technology? The answer is Yes and No. Yes, if some ET characteristics also describe the traditional technology like cost, but this is not always the case. No, as other factors such as ET maturity may not applicable in the case of traditional technology that has been well established and defined in particular context.

Thirdly, can META be used to investigate the adoption from the perspective of users or organisations? The unit of analysis can be organisations and users. There are no restrictions for that, as the factors are flexible and fit both.

Fourthly, can META be used under qualitative or quantitative research methods? In fact, it can be used with both methods. The core characteristic of META is uncertainty, which is a vacuum for any unique emerging contextual factors. These factors are constructed based on that particular context and user perceptions, as well as the unique features of each ET. Therefore, although other factors such as timing and cost appear to be constant and predefined constructs for the adoption of ET, there is space for other factors to emerge under "uncertainty". This conforms to qualitative/impetrative research, and responds to the problem of labeling all innovations/technologies as homogeneous with similar characteristics (Lyytinen and Damsgaard, 2001).

Finally, what are the limitations of META? Can it be used with TAM or IDT? META is only used to predict the adoption rate, but it cannot predict or measure the actual use and interaction (such as ease of use/complexity) with the adopted ET. Therefore, one interesting approach is to predict the adoption and use of an ET by integrating META with IDT or TAM, where META is a prerequisite or antecedent to IDT/TAM. Another limitation is when a technology is labeled as emerging in one context but considered traditional in another context. Can one still use META? Yes, but attention must be paid, as the ET in this case is mature and stable. Hence, *ET maturity*, for example, is not a relevant factor in this case. Therefore, one can state that META is fully applicable when the technology is emerging and completely new.

Future research needs to develop a survey instrument to measure the factors with specific observable indicators. Future empirical research is required to validate the model with three different cases: 1) adoption of ET that is completely new 2) technology that is emerging in a particular context 3) adoption of the same ET by two different units of analysis (organisation and users). In addition, empirical research might be conducted to investigate both the adoption and actual use of ET by integrating META and IDT.

5. CONCLUSION

This paper has made a contribution by extending the theoretical knowledge about technology adoption research by developing a new theory called META, which predicts the factors that influence the adoption of ET. The justification for developing META was also discussed by highlighting the criticisms and deficiencies of traditional adoption theories such as TAM and IDT, which are not well equipped with the special characteristics of ET.

REFERENCES

Abdelghaffar, H., and Moustafa. H., 2013. Exploring the Factors Affecting the Intention to Use C2C Auction Websites in Egypt. *International Journal of E-Adoption*, Vol. 5, No. 2, pp 1-13.

Asunka, S., 2016. Are We There Yet?: An Exploratory Predictive Study of Instructor Acceptance of an Educational Tablet Computer. *International Journal of E-Adoption*, Vol. 8, No. 1.

Bagozzi, R.P., 2007. The legacy of the technology acceptance model and a proposal for a paradigm shift, *Journal of the Association for Information Systems*, Vol. 8, No. 4, 244-254.

Benbasat, I., Barki, H., 2007. Quo vadis, TAM?. *Journal of the Association of Information Systems,* Vol. 8, No. 4, pp 211–218.

Beynon-Davis, P. and Williams, M. D, 2003. The diffusion of information systems development Methods, *Journal of Strategic Information Systems,* Vol. 12, No. 1, pp 29-46

Chen, Y. Tsai, C. & Tseng, Y., 2016. Factors Influencing Consumer Adoption for Network Fellowship Auction in Taiwan. *International Journal of E-Adoption*, Vol. 8, No. 1.

Dahlberg, T., N. Mallat, J. Ondrus, and Zmijewska, A. 2008. Past, Present and Future of Mobile Payments Research. *Electronic Commerce Research and Applications,* Vol. 7, No. 2, pp.165-181.

Daniel, Man, Johns and Mendenhall. 1998. Technical Assessment of Residential and Small Commercial Emerging Technologies. San Francisco, CA: Pacific Gas & Electric Company.

Davis, F.D., 1989. Perceived usefulness, perceived ease of use, and user acceptance of information technology. *MIS Quarterly*, Vol. 13, No. 3, pp 319-349.

Day, G. and Schoemaker, P., 2000. *Wharton on managing emerging technologies*. New York, NY: John Wiley and Sons, Inc.

Dede, C., 1996. Emerging technologies and distributed learning. *American Journal of Distance Education,* Vol. 10, No. 2, pp 4–36.

Doering, A. and Veletsianos, G., 2007. An investigation of the use of real-time, authentic geospatial data in the K–12 classroom. *Journal of Geography*, Vol. 106, No. 6, pp 217–225.

Halaweh, M. 2013. Emerging technology: What is it? *Journal of Technology Management & Innovation*, Vol. 3, No. 8, pp 108-115.

Lee, Y.-H., Hsieh, Y.-C., and Hsu, C.-N. 2011. Adding Innovation Diffusion Theory to the Technology Acceptance Model: Supporting Employees' Intentions to use E-Learning Systems. *Educational Technology & Society*, Vol. 14 No. 4, pp 124–137.

Light, B. and Papazafeiropoulou, A., 2004. Reasons behind ERP package adoption: A diffusion of innovations perspective. *Proceedings of the 13th European Conference on Information Systems,* 2004, Turku, Finland, June 14-16, 2004.

Lin, H., 2011. An empirical investigation of mobile banking adoption: The effect of innovation attributes and knowledge-based trust. *International Journal of Information Management*, Vol. 31, pp 252–260

Lyytinen, K. J. and Damsgaard, J., 2001. 'What's wrong with the Diffusion of Innovation Theory'. *Proceedings of Diffusing software product and process innovations*, Banff, Canada, 7-10 April 2001.

Maloney, C., 2010. The Newton Ball Multi-National Diffusion Acceleration Effect: An Apple iPhone Case Study, eBook, Smashwords. http://www.smashwords.com/books/view/31424

Miller, J., Green, I., & Putland, G., 2005. *Emerging Technologies: A Framework for Thinking*. Australian Capital Territory Department of Education and Training. Viewed 21 January 2012, http://www.det.act.gov.au/__data/assets/pdf_file/0010/74485/ACT_EmTech_Report_v1_2.pdf

Moore, G.and Benbasat, I., 1991. Development of an Instrument to Measure the Perceptions of Adopting an Information Technology Innovation. *Information Systems Research,* Vol. 2, No. 3, pp. 192–222.

Monchak A., and Kim, D., 2011. Examining Trends of Technology Diffusion Theories in Information Systems. *Proceedings Thirty Second International Conference on Information Systems (ICIS 2011), Shanghai 2011* China.

NFC research Forum http://www.nfc-research.at/, Accessed 10th November 2016

Pham, L. and Teich, J., 2011. A Success Model for Enterprise Resource Planning Adoption to Improve Financial Performance in Vietnam's Equitized State Owned Enterprises. *International Journal of Enterprise Information Systems*, Vol. 7, No.1, pp 41-55.

Rogers, E.M., 2003. *Diffusion of Innovations*, (Fifth ed.). New York, NY: The Free Press, A Division of Simon & Schuster.

Sadi, A.H.M. and Noordin, M., 2011. Factors influencing the adoption of M-commerce: An exploratory Analysis. *Proceedings of the 2011 International Conference on Industrial Engineering and Operations Management,* Kuala Lumpur, Malaysia, January 22 – 24, 2011

Srinivasan, R., 2008. Sources, characteristics and effects of emerging technologies: Research opportunities in innovation. *Industrial Marketing Management*, Vol. 37, pp 633–640

Stahl, B. C., 2011. What does the Future Hold? A Critical View of Emerging Information and Communication Technologies and their Social Consequences In: Chiasson, Mike, Henfridsson, Ola, Karsten, Helena, & DeGross, Janice I. (eds.), 2011. *Researching the Future in Information Systems:* IFIP WG 8.2 Working Conference, Future IS 2011, Turku, Finland, June 6-8, 2011, Proceedings, Springer , Heidelberg, 59-76

Sundarraj, R. P. and Manochehri, N., 2011. Application of an Extended TAM Model for Online Banking Adoption: A Study at a Gulf-region University, *Information Resources Management* Journal, Vol. 24, No. 1, pp 1-13.

Veletsianos, G., 2010. *Emerging Technologies in Distance Education*. Athabasca University Press. Edmonton : AU Press.

Venkatesh, V., Morris, M.G., Davis G.B., & Davis, F.D., 2003. User acceptance of information technology: Toward a unified view. *MIS Quarterly*, pp. 425-478.

Williams, D. M., Dwivedi, Y., Lal, B. and Schwarz, A., 2009. Contemporary trends and issues in IT adoption and diffusion research. *Journal of Information Technology,* Vol. 24, pp 1-10.

BIG DATA VISUALIZATION TOOL: A BEST-PRACTICE SELECTION MODEL

Ayaallah Marawan Hassan[1] and Ahmed Elragal[1, 2]
[1]*German University in Cairo, Cairo, Egypt*
[2]*Luleå University of Technology, Luleå, Sweden*

ABSTRACT

Big data visualization tools are analytical tools used by organizations for the purpose of discovering knowledge. With the support of interactive visual interfaces, methods and techniques for analyzing big data are applied to facilitate the knowledge discovery process and provide domain relevant insights. Many studies, both academic and industrial, have been conducted in order to investigate visualization tools. However, little research has been conducted in order to study how big data visualization tools could be selected. Consequently, this research is setout to fill-in this gap. Accordingly, a three phases (literature review, Delphi method, and exploratory case study) research process is conducted to propose a big data visualization tool best-practice selection model. The use of this model would help organizations in selecting and obtaining the appropriate visualization tool. The results of this research revealed a number of criteria elements, which formulate the best-practice model for big data visualization tool selection. A total number of 36 criteria have been agreed upon by a number of 14 big data experts. Such criteria belong to six main types: technical, visualization, collaboration & mobility, operational, data governance and managerial requirements. An exploratory case study was conducted on a multi-national telecommunication company in order to test the usability of the model, which attained positive feedback results.

KEY WORDS:

Big Data Analytics, Big Data Visualization Tools, Selection Procedure, Delphi Method

1. INTRODUCTION

Big data is characterized by being large in size, variety, and volume. This is also known as 3 V's of big data (Russom, 2011). It combines data that is collected from within the organization, as well as from the outside e.g., social media, IoT sensors, etc. As a result, such sheer amounts of data calls for analysis in order to uncover hidden value (Olshannikova et al, 2015; Zaslavsky et al, 2013). Studying big data entails three main areas: big data storage, data preprocessing, and analytics (Elgendy and Elragal, 2014). One of the big data analytics options adopted extensively and have been considered to have the strongest potential for growth, for discovering knowledge and insights from large datasets is advanced data visualization (ADV) tools (Elgendy and Elragal, 2014; Zhang et al, 2012). Such tools are also referred to as big data visualization tools (BDVT), which are tools that apply methods and techniques for analyzing big data, supported by the interactive visual interface to facilitate the process of data analysis. It has been recognized that as the generation and production of big data increases, the demand for BDVT increases (Olshannikova et al, 2015).

However, little research was conducted in order to provide comprehensive criteria for BDVT selection. Moreover, there is no formal method that would guide the selection of a visualization tool taking into consideration big data requirements, which indicated the pressing need for further research to fill this gap. In an attempt to cover this gap, this research proposes a BDVT: best-practice selection model. The use of this model would help organizations in selecting, and obtaining the appropriate visualization tools, which are capable of handling, and analyzing big data. This research is composed of five sections. The first section is an introduction to the research. Section two and three cover the literature review, investigating big data, and BDVT respectively. Consequently, a research gap is defined, and accordingly section four explains the study and its research methodology. Lastly, section five presents the conclusion indicating contribution, and limitations.

2. BIG DATA ANALYTICS

Availability of sheer data amounts at enormously unprecedented rates has raised interest in big data (Bughin et al, 2010). Earlier on, such technology was restricted to the use of big internet companies e.g., Google, Microsoft, and Yahoo. However, recently many organizations have become capable of generating and storing big data due to the development of technologies with advanced processing and storage functionalities (Zaslavsky et al, 2013). Big data has been defined – quite often – through the three Vs volume, variety, and velocity (Zaslavsky et al, 2013; Russom, 2011). Additionally, Demchenko et al (2013) have added value and veracity to the already known three V's, making them five. Consistently, Ward and Barker (2013) have stated that although there is a wide range of varying definitions, any one-presented definition will emphasize on at least one of the following aspects: size, complexity and technologies.

Some reported benefits of big data include: enhancing the data-driven decision making process (Joshi, 2015), future outcomes prediction (Zaslavsky et al, 2013), market prediction, social groups activity predictions (Demchenko et al, 2013), and making real-time personalization possible (Brown et al, 2011).

There are various database platforms, developed for handling big data storage. Among the most advanced and highly usable technologies, are the in-memory databases (Stimmel, 2014), such as: SAP HANA (Ivan, 2014), platforms that are based on distributed file systems and MapReduce (Russom, 2011), Hadoop (Zikopoulos et al, 2015; White, 2012), non-relational databases, including Not Only SQL (NoSQL) (Moniruzzaman and Hossain, 2013; Han et al, 2011; Elgendy and Elragal, 2014).

Once big data is gathered and stored, it must go through various transformations, and processing, before data analysis and visualization (Demchenko et al, 2013). There are three typical preprocessing techniques performed: integration, cleansing and redundancy elimination (Hu et al, 2014). On the other hand, there are four essential requirements for big data processing: fast data loading, fast query processing, the highly efficient utilization of storage space, and finally, the strong adaptability to highly dynamic workload patterns (Elgendy and Elragal, 2014). Some of the technologies used for big data processing are: MapReduce (White, 2012; Stimmel, 2014), YARN - Yet Another Resource Negotiator, Apache spark (Zikopoulos et al, 2015). Other frameworks developed specifically for big data stream processing, include: Storm, S4, SQLstream, Splunk, Apache Kafka, SAP Hana (Chen and Zhang, 2014), Esper, Spark Streaming (Ranjan, 2014), and Complex Event Processing (Russom, 2011; Stimmel, 2014).

After preprocessing, data should be ready for analysis through various types of techniques e.g., data mining, machine learning, as well as statistical analysis (Stimmel, 2014; Chen et al, 2012). ADV tools produce visualized results and reports, which represent tremendous data points that belong to various data types (Russom, 2011).

3. BIG DATA VISUALIZATION TOOLS

Although, data visualization is not a new concept, recently it has drawn the attention of many practitioners in several fields, due to the growth of new powerful technological capabilities, and the great accessibility to the huge amounts of data available today. As a result, these factors have led to the continuous study, development, and usage of visualization tools (Kirk, 2012; Friendly, 2008). The main goal of visualization tools is to provide relevant information, and insights of data, visually in the least duration of time possible (Saraiya et al, 2004).

Moreover, the emergence of big data, with the eagerness to make sense out of it, has brought some challenges to traditional visualization tools such as data volume and speed of change.

3.1 Big Data Visualization Tools Main Features

BDVT, like other types of big data analytics tools, should acquire a number of features and functionalities that are essential for performing efficient analysis and visualizations (Chen and Zhang, 2014; Olshannikova et al, 2015). Some of these features are: the ability to collaborate between multi-users, the ability to export reports, the ability to explore real-time data stream, rapid processing time, mobile intelligence and touch optimization, and the ease of access from mobile devices. Also, there should be governance and data lineage features for protected visualized reports (Stimmel, 2014). Additionally, a BGVT main feature is the ability to operate either standalone or easily integrate with existing information infrastructure (Zhang et al, 2012). Moreover, BDVT should be able to apply dynamic projection, interactive filtering, scaling images, interactive distortion, interactive combination, and advanced visualization techniques in order to provide rapid multi-dimensional volumetric visualizations for big data analysis that include: tag cloud, dendrogram, motion charts, and dashboards (Olshannikova et al, 2015; Chen and Zhang, 2014).

Nonetheless, some of the major big data visualization challenges are perceptual scalability, interactive scalability, and interactive exploration in real-time. Several techniques and methods were developed to address perceptual scalability through data reduction methods, including filtering capabilities, sampling, binned aggregation, model-based abstraction, and hybrid reduction methods. In terms of visualization, such methods could be applied visually through [multi] dimensional binned plots, scatter plots representing regression models, and multi-scale histograms of network statistics to visually summarize large networks. Also, to support interactive scalability, there are two techniques suggested for real-time visual querying. Firstly, the pre-compute of multivariate data tiles to develop pre-computed image tiles that enable scalable panning and zooming, instead of having image tiles intended for direct display, for efficient pre-processing and dynamic loading of data, to enable scalable interaction. Secondly, parallelize data processing and rendering; that is achieved through the use of a dense indexing scheme that simplifies parallel query processing (Liu et al, 2013).

A number of academic studies have been conducted, to investigate well-established commercial BDVT such as: Tableau (Chen and Zhang, 2014), Spotfire (Xavier, 2013), QlikView (Zhang et al, 2012), and Cytoscape (Praneenararat et al, 2012; Olshannikova et al, 2015).

3.2 Big Data Visualization Tools: Deriving a Best-Practice Selection Model

Despite their high-adoption rates nowadays, little research was conducted to provide a comprehensive selection model. Zhang et al (2012) have compared a number of selected BDVT, as well as other big data analytics, documenting their functionalities, determining which ones are better for what applications, and identifying future recommendations. On the other hand, some industrial studies have been conducted to serve the same purpose. In accordance to Machlis (2015), in the "Computerworld IT" publication website; digital magazine, a chart of open data visualization tools compare between a number of selected BDVT and arrange them in an ascending order, based on ease of use. Furthermore, as published in the Forrester report (2015) "Agile Business Intelligence Platforms, Q3 2015", a number of BDVT are evaluated in terms of strengths and weaknesses of functionalities.

Although, the formerly mentioned studies have researched BDVT, there seems to be a lack of a best-practice model that is comprehensive upon which criteria, BDVT could be properly selected (Harger and Crossno, 2012; Zhang et al, 2012).

Accordingly, we are setout to fill-in this research gap. Therefore, the research question this paper seeks to answer is: "*how could big data visualization tools be selected by organizations?*". That also include answering the related research question: *"what are the criteria to use in such selection process?"*

Thus, in an attempt to fulfill this gap, and answer the research question, the following section represents the methodological approach conducted, to investigate the best practice, for selecting BDVT.

4. THE STUDY

A model, by definition, is an abstraction for reality (Dunn, 2007). This model aims to present BDVT best practice selection criteria elements, in order to help organizations in selecting the appropriate visualization tool, which is capable of handling and analyzing big data. The research methodology is conducted throughout three phases, as follows: the literature review phase, the Delphi method phase and the exploratory case study phase. An illustration of the research model is represented in figure (1), as follows.

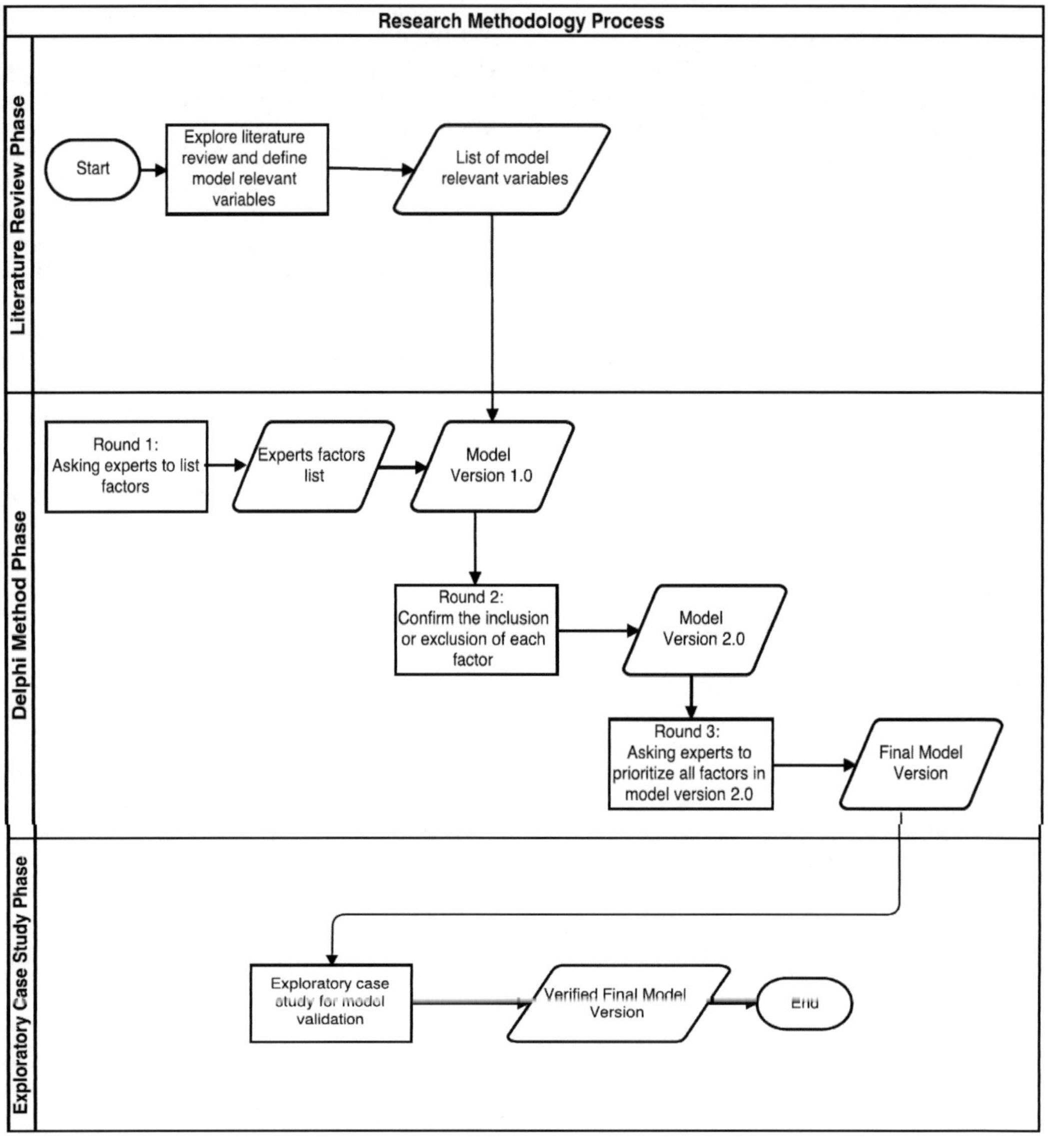

Figure 1. Research Process

4.1 The Literature Review Phase

In this phase, a research was conducted to explore previous academic and industrial studies, in order to identify criteria for the BDVT best practice model. Such outcome of this phase is being fed into the first round of the Delphi method. The outcome of this phase is a set of model relevant variables that represent an aggregated list. The list - of 39 criteria - is divided into two main sections: big data requirements and general requirements.

4.2 The Delphi Method Phase

Experts in the field of big data were invited to participate in a study, utilizing a Delphi technique for building a best practice model throughout three rounds. In this section, the reason behind the selection of the Delphi method was stated, and then experts were asked to select variables.

4.2.1 The Selection of the Delphi Method

The Delphi method is used to answer the main research question as it is a broadly known and accepted method for exploratory studies, and it is accomplished by gathering information from respondents within their domain of expertise. It is used for consensus building, through the use of a series of questionnaires in more than one round; where it attempts to address the question of "What could/should be", since one of its objectives is to "To seek out information which may generate a consensus on the part of the respondent group" (Hsu and Sandford, 2007). Additionally, the Delphi method has been confirmed to be a popular method in information systems research, and it is well suited for exploratory studies (Okoli and Pawlowski, 2004). Similarly, Habibi et al, (2014) explained that the Delphi method is well suited for exploratory research, as it can be used as a qualitative method that aims to identify the nature and fundamental elements in a certain phenomenon. Adding to that, one of its main applications is identifying the items and criteria in operations' research problems, and of multi-criteria decision- analysis techniques (MCDA).

4.2.2 Expert Selection Procedure

According to Hsu and Sandford (2007), ten to fifteen experts could be sufficient for a Delphi method, if they have related homogeneous backgrounds and experiences in the field of the target issue. This study included 14 international big data experts, from various countries and backgrounds including both practitioners and academics. The experts included: Big Data [Analytics] Professors; Senior BI Developers, CIO, IT Managers and IS Consultants with an average of 10 years of experience.

4.2.3 Data Collection and Analysis Method

The Delphi process could continue, until consensus is built. However, many studies have conducted the Delphi process in two or three rounds to achieve study objectives (Habibi et al, 2004). Regarding data analysis, the criteria used for developing the consensus of experts is subject to interpretation. Data analysis involves both qualitative and quantitative data. Qualitative data is gathered and analyzed in the initial iteration through the open-ended questions, in order to gather opinions from experts. On the other hand, quantitative data is gathered and analyzed in the subsequent iterations, to detect and reach the preferred and prescribed level of consensus, as well as any changes of judgments among panelists. Basically, the consensus is developed when a certain percentage of votes fall within a prescribed range. One of the criteria used in the literature prescribes that the consensus is developed, when having the same agreement that presents at least 70% of experts (Hsu and Sandford, 2007). The Delphi questionnaires were administrated, during 5 months duration, using e-mail and online survey development cloud-based software. The identities were kept anonymous.

4.2.4 Round 1: Devising a Beta Model

Experts were sent an open-ended questionnaire, asked to list the criteria elements that should be taken into account in building a BDVT best-practice selection model, as well as classifying each of the criteria into main areas e.g., technical, managerial, etc. All 14 experts engaged, and filled in the first round questionnaire.

After collecting and analyzing all the respondents input into round 1, and consolidating alike responses, "BDVTs: Best-practice selection model - version 1.0" was built, by aggregating all respondents' input to round 1 with relevant variables, identified in the literature review phase. The model consisted of 107 criteria that were divided into six main sections: technical, visualization, collaboration & mobility, operational, data governance, and managerial requirements.

4.2.5 Round 2: Updated Model

The purpose of this round was for each expert to assess, and verify other experts input, as well as their initial input, if needed, and reach a consensus on BDVT criteria elements. Accordingly, a structured closed questionnaire was developed, consisted of all the 107 criteria, each represented in a question with three answer options: 1) Include, 2) Exclude, 3) Other, for providing any modifications. 13 experts engaged, and filled in round 2 questionnaires.

After collecting and analyzing all respondents input into round 2, BDVT: best-practice selection model - version 1.0 was updated by narrowing down the 107 criteria, to include elements yielding 80%, or more, of what the respondents have voted to include. This was for building a model, with criteria that represented the consensus, and agreement of big data experts.

The updated model BDVT: best-practice selection model - version 2.0 consists of 48 criteria that are divided into six main sections: technical, visualization, collaboration & mobility, operational, data governance, and managerial requirements.

4.2.6 Round 3: Final Prioritized Model

The purpose of this round was for each expert to rate the importance level of each criterion, included in BDVT: best-practice selection model - version 2.0, to build a prioritized final model to present end users with how important each criterion is.

Accordingly, a structured closed questionnaire, covering all the 48 criteria was developed, where each respondent would classify each criterion, as one of the following three levels: extremely important, moderately important, and slightly important. 12 experts engaged, and filled in round 3 questionnaires.

After collecting, and analyzing all the respondents input into round 3, it was found that out of the 48 criteria, 36 criteria classified, reached a consensus of 70% or more of the respondents. Moreover, the consensus on the 36 reached, were of the same level, and that is "Extremely important" i.e. 36 criteria were classified to be "Extremely important" by 70% or more respondents. On the other hand, the other 12 criteria did not reach consensus by respondents to be classified, as any of the three levels. Hence, BDVT: best-practice selection model - version 2.0" was updated to include only the criteria elements that reached a consensus of 70% or more of the respondents.

The final version of the BDVT: best-practice selection model is represented in table (1), in the following page.

4.3 The Exploratory Case Study Phase

This phase was conducted to test the usability of the developed model. This is an exploratory case study combined with a structured interview. The case study was conducted on a multi-national telecommunication company that adopts and uses a number of big data visualization tools, whereas big data analytics projects and activities are essential in their daily operations.

The target respondent of the research included employees, who are involved in the selection process of big data analytics tools, particularly visualization. In this research, a number of 4 employees were chosen, from two departments: IT department, and the big data department. From the IT department, the IT manager and a technical expert from the big data analytics team participated, also from the big data department, the big data manager, and big data and channels development manager participated.

The interview included open-ended evaluation questions to assess the usability of the model. Interviews were conducted with participants at the company. They were face-to-face, individual interviews, to be able to record both verbal and nonverbal behavior, to gain as much details as possible, and to avoid any biased opinions, and responses. Each of the four interviews lasted from one to two hours. At first, the participant was provided with the model, and was given all the time needed to review. Afterwards, all the interview questions were asked to the participants and they were recorded. Participants were encouraged to state any difficulties or struggles faced while using the model, and suggest recommendations for better usability.

All participants have confirmed the usability of the developed model, asserting that they did not find any difficulties or struggles, while usage, and suggested no modifications for better usability. Moreover, declaring that they would be using the model in the future, for evaluating proposals of BDVT to select from. Therefore no modifications have been made.

Table 1. BDVT: Best-Practice Selection Model

BDVTs Criteria Elements	
Technical	1) Flexible and easy access to various data sources
	2) Ability to access big data environment (e.g. Hadoop cluster)
	3) Ability to access traditional databases
	4) Support various data types
	5) Drill-down and drill-up capability
	6) Support real-time data analysis
	7) Support real-time processing
	8) Simplicity in integrating various analyses
	9) Scalability
	10) Ability to handle high volume of data
	11) Variety of equations and algorithms that give varieties of outputs for analysis
	12) Ability to visualize and explore data in-database as well as in-memory
	13) Ability to perform and utilize in-memory data compression techniques to enable handling of large datasets without driving up hardware costs
	14) Ability to export the data to different formats (e.g. CSV, excel, PDF)
	15) Dashboard integration capability
	16) Filtering capabilities
Visualization	17) Availability of various types of graphics that can interact with complex data
	18) Map and Heat Map visualization capabilities
	19) Efficient grouping techniques(e.g. maps, tag clouds, charts and graphs)
	20) Binning to visualize big data volume
Collaboration & mobility	21) Ability to provide web-based reports
	22) Ability to share reports by various means (e.g. email, links, web)
Operational	23) Drag and drop components
	24) Ease-of-use
	25) Robust and user-friendly presentation layer
	26) Proper manuals and documentation for tool
	27) Availability of training and support for tool
	28) Good customer service and response to inquiries for help with tool
	29) Easy to upgrade
Data Governance	30) Allow users to share and collaborate results securely
	31) Drilldown capabilities with ability to link to the user's security profile
	32) Comprehensive security for all internal and external user groups
Managerial	33) High quality of visuals to be put in presentations and other communication means
	34) Reasonable licenses cost
	35) Interactive reports and charts
	36) Enabled what-if scenarios and scenario analysis

4.4 Practitioner Guide: How to Use the Model

This section provides a practitioner guideline on how to use the BDVT best-practice selection model. The steps involved in the process of BDVT selection are illustrated below:

- Step 1: Computing weights to determine the relative importance of each criterion

There are many approaches to calculate the weights of given criteria to give decision makers a reference about the relative importance of each criterion, some of which are: weighted ranking, analytic hierarchy process, trade-off method, paired comparison, and reference comparison. The choice of method relies on many concerns, including: the level of detail needed for the weights, available computing resources, and decision makers' preferences (Brown, 2007).The weights are determined by using a fixed range for determining the importance level of each criterion, afterwards all range values are normalized, by dividing each range value by the sum of weights, so that they sum up to one (Brown, 2007). For example, a scale from 1 to 3 could be used to keep it simple; with 1 being the least important, and 3 the most important. Accordingly, normalized values from 1 to 3 would be obtained.

- Step 2: Determining scores for each criterion of each tool

The scores of the relative performance of each tool on each criterion are subjective, and can be converted to diverse scales. For example, a scale from 0 to 1 could be used to determine the scores, where 0 represents the worst acceptable performance level, and 1 the best performance level. A detailed list is available and could be obtained from the authors.

- Step 3: Computing the value score for each tool

Value scores are computed for each proposal by: adding all criteria weighted scores (WS) by proposal, where each criterion weighted score (WS) is calculated by: multiplying scores times weight. It could be assumed – for simplicity – that a single rater is filling in the model. However, it is also possible to have more than one in the selection process where average score is obtained.

5. CONCLUSION

There are a number of papers that investigated visualization tools development, due to the emergence of big data, by either: stating a number of BDVT main characteristics, describing selected well-established BDVT, suggesting advanced visualization techniques, or comparing a number of selected BDVT to determine which ones are better for what applications. On the other hand, there seems to be a lack of a best-practice model that is comprehensive upon which criteria, BDVT could be properly selected (Harger and Crossno, 2012; Zhang et al, 2012).

Thus, in an attempt to fulfill this gap, and answer the research question: *"How could big data visualization tools be selected by organizations?"* That also includes answering the related research question: *"What are the criteria to use in such selection process?"* This research proposes a BDVT: best-practice selection model, represented in table (1). This model includes a comprehensive list of 36 criteria, which were obtained via Delphi method from 14 big data experts that could help organizations in selecting, and obtaining the appropriate visualization tools, which are capable of handling, and analyzing big data. These criteria covered different categories that were divided into six main sections: technical, visualization, collaboration & mobility, operational, data governance, and managerial requirements.

The research methodology, section (4), gives detail to the exploratory study conducted, throughout qualitative methods that consisted of three phases as follows: the literature review phase, the Delphi method phase and the exploratory case study phase.

The contribution of this research is two folds: First is industrial where this research proposes a best-practice selection model that could help organizations in selecting and obtaining BDVT. Second, is academic as this research identified a number of selection-relevant criteria elements that are comprehensive.

This study has some limitations. As per the requirements of the Delphi research method, it was recommended to conduct a fourth round, but due to time constraint as well as prolonged time for experts to respond, we conduced only three rounds. Added to that, we have only conducted single case study to test usability of the model, where multiple case studies e.g., confirmatory could have provided testing mechanism to our model.

REFERENCES

Brown, B. et al, 2011. Are you ready for the era of 'big data'. *McKinsey Quarterly*, Vol. 4, No.1, pp.24-35.

Brown, S., 2007. Standardized Technology Evaluation Process (STEP) User's Guide and Methodology for Evaluation Teams. *Mitre Corporation*. pp. 1-51.

Bughin, J. et al, 2010. Clouds, big data, and smart assets: Ten tech-enabled business trends to watch. *McKinsey Quarterly*, Vol. 56, No.1, pp.75-86.

Chen, C. and Zhang, C., 2014. Data-intensive applications, challenges, techniques and technologies: A survey on Big Data. *Information Sciences,* Vol. 275, pp.314-347.

Chen, H. et al, 2012. Business Intelligence and Analytics: From Big Data to Big Impact. *MIS quarterly,* Vol. 36, No. 4, pp.1165-1188.

Cooper, D. and Schindler, P., 2014. *Business research methods, 12th edition*. McGraw-Hill Education, NewYork, USA.

Demchenko, Y. et al, 2013. Architecture framework and components for the big data ecosystem. *Journal of System and Network Engineering,* Vol. 4, No. 2, pp.1-31.

Dunn, N., 2007. *The ecology of the architectural model.* Peter Lang, Pieterlen and Bern, Switzerland.

Elgendy, N. and Elragal, A., 2014, July. Big data analytics: a literature review paper. *The 14th Industrial Conference on Data Mining (ICDM), Springer International Publishing.* Petersburg, pp. 214-227.

Evelson, B., 2015. The Forrester Wave™: Agile Business Intelligence Platforms, Q3 2015. *Forrester Research Incorporated.* Link: http://go.sap.com/docs/download/2015/09/541ccd61-437c-0010-82c7-eda71af511fa.pdf

Friendly, M., 2008. *A brief history of data visualization. In Handbook of data visualization*. Springer Berlin Heidelberg, pp. 15-56.

Habibi, A. et al, 2014. Delphi technique theoretical framework in qualitative research. *The International Journal of Engineering and Science,* Vol. 3, No. 4, pp.8-13.

Han, J. et al, 2011. Survey on NoSQL database. *In Pervasive computing and applications (ICPCA), 2011 6th international conference on IEEE*, pp. 363-366.

Harger, J. and Crossno, P., 2012. Comparison of open-source visual analytics toolkits. *In IS&T/SPIE Electronic Imaging, International Society for Optics and Photonics (82940E-82940E). International Society for Optics and Photonics*. pp. 389-399

Hsu, C. and Sandford, B., 2007. The Delphi technique: making sense of consensus. *Practical assessment, research & evaluation*, Vol. 12, No. 10, pp.1-8.

Hu, H. et al, 2014. Toward scalable systems for big data analytics: A technology tutorial. *IEEE Access*, Vol. 2, pp. 652-687.

Ivan, M., 2014. Characteristics of In-Memory Business Intelligence. *Informatica Economica*, Vol. 18, No. 3, p.17-25.

Joshi, P., 2015. Analyzing Big Data Tools and Deployment Platforms. *Int J Multi Approach Studies,* Vol. 2, No. 2, pp. 45-56.

Kirk, A., 2012. *Data Visualization: a successful design process.* Packt Publishing Ltd, Birmingham, UK.

Liu, Z. et al, 2013. imMens: Real time Visual Querying of Big Data. *In Computer Graphics Forum*, Vol. 32, No. 3, pp. 421-430.

Machlis, S. (2015). Chart and image gallery: 30+ free tools for data visualization and analysis. 2015. *Computerworld.* Retrieved from http://www.computerworld.com/

Moniruzzaman, A. and Hossain, S., 2013. NoSql database: New era of databases for big data analytics-classification, characteristics and comparison. *International Journal of Database Theory and Application,* Vol. 6, No. 4, pp. 1-14.

Okoli, C. and Pawlowski, S., 2004. The Delphi method as a research tool: an example, design considerations and applications. *Information & management,* Vol. 42, No. 1, pp.15-29.

Olshannikova, E. et al, 2015. Visualizing Big Data with augmented and virtual reality: challenges and research agenda. *Journal of Big Data,* Vol. 2, No. 1, pp.1-27.

Praneenararat, T. et al, 2012. Integration of interactive, multi-scale network navigation approach with Cytoscape for functional genomics in the big data era. *BMC genomics,* Vol. 13, No. 7, pp.1-10.

Ranjan, R., 2014. Streaming big data processing in datacenter clouds. *IEEE Cloud Computing,* Vol. 1, No. 1, pp.78-83.

Russom, P., 2011. Big Data Analytics. *TDWI Best Practices Report, Fourth Quarter*, pp. 1-35.

Saraiya, P. et al, 2004. An evaluation of microarray visualization tools for biological insight. *In Information Visualization, 2004. INFOVIS 2004, IEEE Symposium On, IEEE.* pp. 1-8.

Stimmel, C., 2014. *Big data analytics strategies for the smart grid.* CRC Press, Boca Raton, Florida, USA.

Ward, J. and Barker, A., 2013. Undefined by data: a survey of big data definitions. *arXiv preprint arXiv:1309.5821.* pp. 1-2.

Ware, C., 2012. *Information visualization: perception for design (3rd edition).* Elsevier: Morgan Kaufman, San Francisco, USA. Link: https://books.google.com.eg/books?hl=en&lr=&id=UpYCSS6snnAC&oi=fnd&pg=PP1&ots=32Bz3kXMke&sig=F8LSsk5VwBPJ7vl10k7gCovtzQQ&redir_esc=y#v=onepage&q&f=false

White, C., 2012. MapReduce and the Data Scientist. *BI Research.* pp. 1-20.

Xavier, M., 2013. *TIBCO Spotfire for Developers.* Packt Publishing Ltd, Olton, Birmingham, GBR.

Zaslavsky, A. et al, 2013. Sensing as a service and big data. International Conference on Advances in Cloud Computing (ACC). Bangalore, India, *arXiv preprint arXiv:1301.0159*. pp. 21–29.

Zhang, L. et al, 2012. Visual analytics for the big data era - A comparative review of state-of-the-art commercial systems. *In Visual Analytics Science and Technology (VAST), 2012 IEEE Conference*. pp. 173-182.

Zikopoulos, P. et al, 2015. *Big Data Beyond the Hype: A Guide to Conversations for Today's Data Center*. Mc Graw Hill Education, NewYork, USA.

SCENARIO CREATION METHOD TO ELICIT REQUIREMENTS BY STAKEHOLDERS

Junko Shirogane
Tokyo Woman's Christian University, Japan

ABSTRACT

Typically software developers create use case diagrams and scenarios after stakeholders identify their requirements. However, stakeholders often have difficulty identifying their actual requirements. Consequently, the generated diagrams and scenarios may not reflect stakeholders' requirements. The previous paper proposed a support method to create use case diagrams from the operation histories of applications. When developing a new application, similar applications often exist. Thus, our method records the operation histories when stakeholders try to use similar applications. Then the use case diagrams are generated from the recorded operation histories and customized. Because stakeholders only operate similar applications, use case diagrams that appropriately reflect stakeholders' requirements can be easily obtained. Herein our method is expanded to create scenarios in a use case. When generating use case diagrams, the operation histories are divided into use cases. Because operation histories record the input and selection of widgets in windows, the input and selection sequences are constructed as event sequences in scenarios. Event sentences are often represented in a natural language. Thus, each event is represented in a natural language sentence using label names of widgets. The sequences of event sentences are generated as scenarios. Although there are several types of scenarios such as main scenario, alternative scenario, and exception scenario, all are generated as individual scenarios.

KEYWORDS

Operation History, Scenario, Requirements

1. INTRODUCTION

To elicit requirements, software developers analyze stakeholders' requirements by interviewing stakeholders and implementing questionnaires. However, stakeholders often misunderstand or do not fully recognize their requirements (Alexander & Beus-Dukic, 2009), which may lead to unsatisfied stakeholder requirements, software modifications, and project failure (The Standish Group, 1995). To resolve these problems, it is necessary for stakeholders to clearly convey their requirements to software developers.

Use case diagrams are described in a simple manner, while scenarios are often described with a natural language. Because stakeholders can easily understand use cases, they are used to communicate between stakeholders and software developers. Normally, software developers elicit stakeholders' requirements and create use case diagrams and scenarios. However, if stakeholders cannot appropriately convey their requirements, the use case diagrams and scenarios do not reflect the actual requirements.

Meanwhile, when stakeholders require a new application, similar applications may already exist. Thus, surveying existing applications is a common requirements elicitation technique (Alexander & Beus-Dukic, 2009). Stakeholders check functions, interaction sequences, and input/output items of the existing applications to complement their requirements. Applications realize use cases and scenarios, and when they are operated, use cases and scenarios are executed.

To create appropriate use case diagrams and scenarios as stakeholders' requirements, it is effective for the stakeholders to describe them. However, stakeholders often encounter difficultly describing the use case diagrams and scenarios because even if they are familiar with the concepts, they are not always familiar with software development. Meanwhile, stakeholders can operate applications.

Therefore, use case diagrams and scenarios can be generated from the operation histories when stakeholders operate existing applications. Then stakeholders select the appropriate use cases and scenarios from the generated ones. Finally, stakeholders customize the use cases and scenarios with software developers to reflect the stakeholders' requirements.

The previous paper proposed a method to generate use case diagrams from the operation histories (Shirogane, 2017). Operation histories are divided into windows of graphical user interfaces (GUIs). Then the same windows are merged, the main window of the application is identified, and use cases are extracted. After the extraction, connections between an actor (application user) and use cases are represented. Finally, use case diagrams are generated.

This paper proposes a method to generate scenarios in a use case, which is an extension of the previous paper. To generate scenarios, the operation histories in a use case are divided into event sequences. An "event" is an action that a user or the target application undertakes. Next, each widget operation is represented in a natural language sentence (event sentence). An event sequence is the sequence of widget operations (e.g., input and selection) in a use case. Then the same event sentences in a window are merged, and the event sequences are generated as scenarios. Finally, the generated scenarios are customized and completed. For the customization, stakeholders can adopt only the necessary use cases and scenarios from the generated use case diagrams and scenarios in several applications because often multiple applications are similar to the requirements. Thus, stakeholders can compare the generated scenarios for several applications and select the use cases, scenarios, and events that meet their requirements. Thus, the scenarios are cut from the generated artifacts and pasted to the stakeholders' artifacts in the customization. Although the base of the scenario generation method was proposed previously (Shirogane, 2014), the method was not based on the generated use cases. This paper describes details of scenario generation corresponding to the generated use cases.

Due to this research, stakeholders and software developers can obtain scenarios that reflect stakeholders' requirements appropriately. By operating similar applications, stakeholders' activities can be elucidated without software development knowledge, allowing use case diagrams and scenarios to be easily generated. Thus, the proposed method removes the heavy burden of understanding stakeholders' requirements appropriately. In addition, the similar applications are selected by stakeholders and developers, and the generated use case diagrams and they can be selected and customized by stakeholders and developers. Thus, stakeholders can try to use various types of applications, generate and customize use case diagrams and scenarios, and can obtain appropriate use case diagrams and scenarios for their requirements.

The rest of this paper is organized as follows. Section 2 describes related works. Section 3 summarizes our previous research, while Section 4 describes the detailed scenario generation. Section 5 shows the simulation of the scenario generation. Section 6 concludes this paper.

2. RELATED WORKS

Several works to support creating scenarios, such as generation of interaction sequences and description notations, were proposed.

For generation of interaction sequences, Haendler et al. proposed a method to generate interaction models, that is, sequence diagrams by tracing test scenario executions (Haendler, et al., 2015). They developed a meta model to trace test execution and map it to UML meta model. When stakeholders selected viewpoints, test scenarios corresponding to the viewpoints were selected, and sequence diagrams were generated. Due to this method, model-size explosion (Sharp & Rountev, 2005) could be avoided, and appropriate sequence diagrams could be obtained. Sharma et al. proposed a method to generate activity diagrams and sequence diagrams (Sharma, et al., 2014). Their method analyzed requirement statements, which represented interactions, and extracted patterns of the statements by grammatical knowledge patterns (GKP) (Hunston & Francis, 2000). Frames, which represent the structures of the statements, were created based on the patterns. Then activity diagrams were generated by arranging the actions based on the frames. Finally, sequence diagrams were generated by extracting actions and objects. Braun et al. also proposed a method to Use Case Maps (UCMs) (Buhr, 1998) that represented method execution flows (Braun, et al., 2015). First, lines of code, depth of nest, and complexity of a method were obtained as static data metrics. Numbers and times of calling/called methods, etc. were obtained from execution traces. Next, methods that had small lines of code and complexity were filtered. Then, whether each method was utility or not was analyzed by algorithms proposed in this method. If a method was specified as a utility, the method was also filtered. Finally, UCMs were generated. Although interaction sequences can be generated using these methods, stakeholders' requirements are not always reflected to the generated models appropriately.

For description notations, Aspect-oriented user requirements notation (AoURN) was a requirements engineering language combining goal-oriented, scenario based, and aspect-oriented notations (Mussbacher, et al., 2013). User requirements notation (URN) (Telecommuniocaton Standardization Sector of ITU, 2012), which was a requirements engineering language that consisted of goal-oriented requirements language (GRN) (GRN) for goal modeling and UCMs (Buhr, 1998) for scenario modeling, was extended. High-level workflows of concerns, the whole system, and impacts to stakeholders' goals were described using the AoURN. Souza et al. also proposed VL4UCD (visual language for use case description) as an extension of state chart to described interactions of use cases (Souza & Cavalcanti, 2015). VL4UCD could represent software concerns of both engineers and human computer interaction professionals and support communications between them. In the VL4UCD, states represented windows (scenes) including interaction items of users. An element representing a system process was prepared, and transitions represented switching between scenes and between scenes and system processes. Models by VL4UCD were created roughly at first and described in detail gradually. Correspondences to class and sequence diagrams were supported. In addition, Kantorowitz mentioned differences between verbal and formal to describe appropriate requirements as use case specifications (Kantorowitz, 2014). Although verbal include ambiguities, CSCW (computer supported collaborative work) team members (including stakeholders) are not always familiar with formal. This paper suggested that if a CSCW team included members that do not familiar with formal, use case specifications should be described by verbal. If a CSCW team did not include, use case specifications should be described by formal and translated into verbal. However, how to describe models easily by stakeholders is beyond scope of these researches.

3. USE CASE DIAGRAM GENERATION

The previous paper proposed a method to generate use case diagrams from the operation histories, which record the execution of scenarios (Shirogane, 2017). The main concept is that a use case has several scenarios, where each scenario represents an interaction between the application and a user. When a scenario is realized in an application, the event sequence is represented as a window switching sequence, while the event of an interaction to the user is represented an operation to a widget on a window of the GUI. Common scenario windows in the application are merged, and then the final GUIs are constructed. Based on the relationships between use cases/scenarios and GUIs, use case diagrams are generated from the operation histories in the previous research.

Operation histories record window appearances and, operations to widgets, and widget coordinates. In this paper, "window" indicates a window of a desktop application or a page of a web application. The basic concept in the previous research is that the main window is the starting point to use functions of the target application. In many cases, users initiate a function from the main window by selecting a menu item or clicking a button or a link, the function is executed, and some windows are switched. When the function is finished, the display returns to the main window.

Thus, operation histories are divided into windows. Next the same windows are merged based on the window titles. In this way, a directed graph called a "WSG" (window switching graph) is constructed. Nodes represent windows and edges represent window switchings. The number of window switchings from a certain window to another certain window is also represented on the edges. Then the window with the highest number of window switchings on the output edges is identified as the main window.

Figure 1 shows an example of a WSG. "M" and "W1"–"W10" are windows, edges represent window switchings, and the numbers attached to edges represent the number of window switchings. According to this WSG, window "M", which has a total number of window switchings of 8, is identified as the main window.

After the main window is identified, use cases are extracted based on three patterns: the basic pattern, the pre-condition pattern, and the inclusion pattern. The basic pattern is the base of the other patterns to extract use cases. Each branch of a window switching sequence from the main window is extracted as a use case. In Figure 1, two use cases are extracted using basic patterns: "U-2" ("M" → "W3" → ("W5" →) "W4" → ("W8" → "W9" →) "W6) and "U-3" ("M" → "W7" → "W8" → "W9" → "W10").

The window switching sequences before displaying the main window are extracted as use cases by the pre-condition pattern. The extracted use cases are identified as the pre-conditions of use cases after displaying the main window. For example, if a login process is executed before displaying the main window, the window switching sequences of the login process are extracted as a use case by the pre-condition pattern. In Fig. 1, one use case is extracted using the pre-condition pattern, "U-1" ("W1 → "W2"), and the execution of the use case "U-1" is identified as the pre-condition of the use cases "U-2" and "U-3".

Different use cases can have common window switching sequences. These window switching sequences are extracted as the inclusion pattern use case. For example, if a login process is executed during the execution of some use cases, the window switching sequences of the login process are extracted as a use case by the inclusion pattern. The extracted use cases are represented as an included use case for different use cases. In Fig. 1, window switching sequence "W8" → "W9" is used in the two different use cases "U-2" and "U-3". Hence, this window switching sequence is extracted as a use case ("U-4"). Use case "U-4" is identified as an included use case of use cases "U-2" and "U-3".

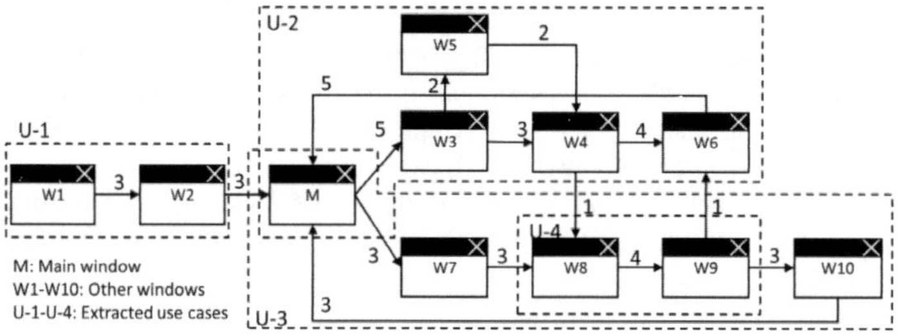

Figure 1. Example of a WSG

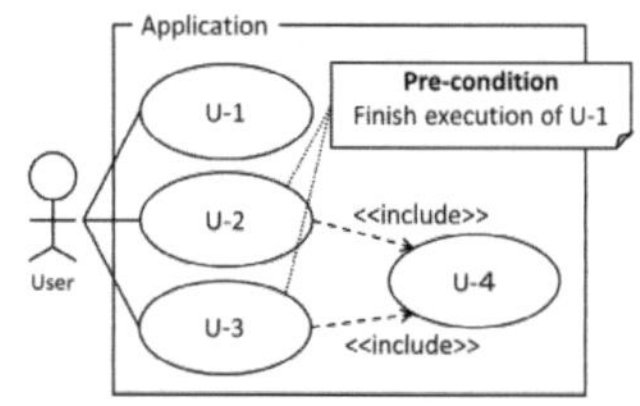

Figure 2. Example of a Generated Use Case Diagram

After extracting the use cases, use case diagrams are generated. Users of the target application are identified by the actor name "User", and the actor is connected to the extracted use cases. Figure 2 shows an example of the generated use case diagram from the WSG in Fig. 1.

4. SCENARIO GENERATION

After generating the use cases in the previous research (Shirogane, 2017), scenarios are generated based on the users' operations in the operation histories. According to Cockburn, a scenario consists of the pre-conditions, purposes, main event sequence, alternative event sequences, post-conditions, and remarks (Cockburn, 2000). Extractions of the use case names and pre-conditions are described elsewhere (Shirogane, 2017). The generation targets of this method are event sequences. Although only different event sequences from the main event sequence are described as part of the scenario where the main event sequence is described, according to the Cockburn's scenario template, the main and alternative event sequences are generated individually in this method. The generation strategy is based on that described in the literature (Shirogane, 2014). In this paper, the strategy using all the operation histories is described.

4.1 Division of the WSG

As described in Section 3, use cases are extracted by dividing the WSG. Because use cases can have several scenarios, a divided WSG in Section 3 represents every window sequence of all scenarios in a use case. The window sequence of a scenario is the window-switching path. Thus, the window sequences in a scenario are extracted by tracing all paths of the divided WSG. It should be noted that the event sequences in the operation histories are kept when windows are merged in Section 3. Even if a path can be traced on a WSG, the path is not adopted as a scenario if the event sequence of the path does not exist in the operation histories.

Figure 3 shows an example of the divided WSG of a use case. Each broken arrow represents a window sequence path. That is, the following paths for the window sequences in the scenarios are extracted:

- P1: M → W1 → W2 → W5
- P2: M → W1 → W2 → W6 → W7
- P3: M → W1 → W3 → W4→ W2 → W5

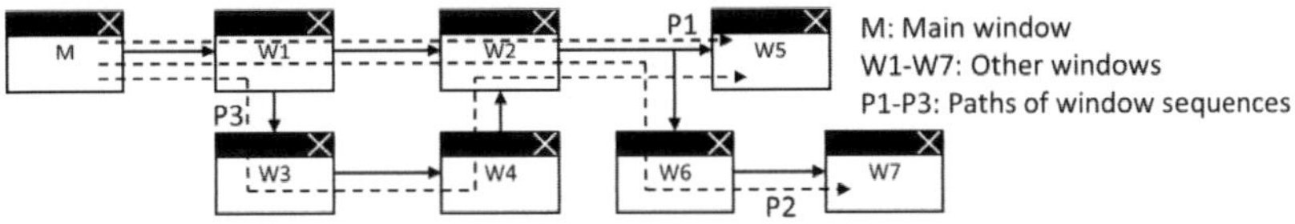

Figure 3. Example of the Paths of the Window Sequences

4.2 Construction of Event Sentences

After extracting the paths of the window sequences for scenarios, event sentences in the scenarios are constructed. Because events in the scenarios are generated as sentences of natural languages, an event is constructed by a subject, a predicate, and an object. The operation histories record the interactions between the stakeholders and applications, where stakeholders are the operators of the application and are represented as actors in the use case diagrams. The actors in the generated use case diagrams are defined as "Users" in Section 3. Thus, the subjects in a scenario event are defined as "Users". Users employ two types of widget operations: input and selection. For widgets where users input character strings with keyboards (e.g., text field and text area widgets), "input" is used as the predicate. In contrast, for widgets where users select from the selection items (e.g., radio button, check box, and combo box widgets), "select" is used as the predicate.

Widget label names are used as the objects. Some types of widgets have label names as their attributes (e.g., button widgets), while others do not (e.g., text field and combo box widgets). Widget label names without label name attributes (called "target widgets") are specified by label widgets (called "instruction labels"), which are arranged nearby. Although radio button and check box widgets have label names as their attributes, they are individual selection items and cannot be used as the object of an event sentence. However, label names of the unit for the selection items can be used as an object of an event sentence. For example, selecting from "Plan A" and "Plan B" to deposit money in a bank application, "Plan A" and "Plan B" are represented by three radio buttons. However, these plan names are unsuitable for the objects of the event sentences. When the label name of the selection is "Plan type", then "Plan type" should be used as the object.

Instruction labels are often arranged to the left or above their target widgets (Microsoft). The locations of instruction labels have been surveyed in actual applications by widget type (Shirogane & Yoshiaki, 2008). Because (Shirogane & Yoshiaki, 2008) only surveyed a few widget types, an additional survey was conducted for various applications, such as Internet Explorer, Mozilla Firefox, iTunes, Mozilla Thunderbird, Adobe Acrobat, etc. (Table 1).

Table 1. Survey Results of the Instruction Label Locations

	Left	Above	Right	Below		Left	Above	Right	Below
Check box	6	25	0	0	Radio button	13	63	0	0
Combo box	384	35	2	3	Text area	35	26	0	0
List	4	72	0	0	Text field	487	101	0	1

According to Table 1, the following locations are identified as the instruction labels of the target widgets:

- Check box widgets: Above
- Combo box widgets: Left
- List box widgets: Above
- Radio button widgets: Above
- Text area widgets: Left
- Text field widgets: Left

Based on these locations, the correspondences between label widgets and target widgets are analyzed to identify the instruction labels for target widgets by the strategy of the reference (Shirogane & Yoshiaki, 2008). The label names of the instruction labels are used as the label names of the target widgets; that is, they are the objects in event sentences. Then event sentences are constructed by arranging subjects, predicates, and objects. For example, in an event where a stakeholder selects the radio button widget and the "Plan type" item is recorded in the operation histories, the event sentence is constructed as "User selects 'Plan type'".

4.3 Generation of Sequences of Event Sentences

Based on the event sequences in the extracted paths of the window sequences in Section 4.1, the sequences of event sentences (ev-sequences) are constructed. Because the window sequence paths represent the window sequences of scenarios, the ev-sequences become the base for scenarios. Because stakeholders can try to use a function several times, the window sequence path may include several event sequences. Moreover, it should be noted that although users can quit a function in the middle, a scenario represents finishing a function, which may be successful or unsuccessful. Thus, a scenario does not represent terminating the use of a function. To quit to a function, each window usually contains a "Cancel" button (Microsof) (Apple Inc., 2016). About 85% of windows in various applications have a "Cancel" button (Shirogane, et al., 2014). Consequently, when an ev-sequence is finished by pushing the "Cancel" button, it is deleted.

Then the remaining ev-sequences in a window sequence path are integrated. Because stakeholders are not required to operate all widgets, plural ev-sequences in a window sequence path often differ. Thus, these plural ev-sequences are integrated. Concretely, the ev-sequence with the most event sentences (base sequence) is identified in plural ev-sequences as the window sequence path. If other ev-sequences have event sentences not included in the base sequence, then the event sentences complement the base sequence. Integrated ev-sequences are generated as a scenario.

Figure 4 shows an example of ev-sequences and an integrated ev-sequence. Because ev-sequence 1 has four event sentences, but ev-sequence 2 has five event sentences, ev-sequence 2 is identified as the base sequence. Comparing the two, ev-sequence 2 does not have event sentence "E1" found in ev-sequence 1. Thus, event sentence "E1" is a complement to ev-sequence 2. Ev-sequence 2 is generated as a scenario.

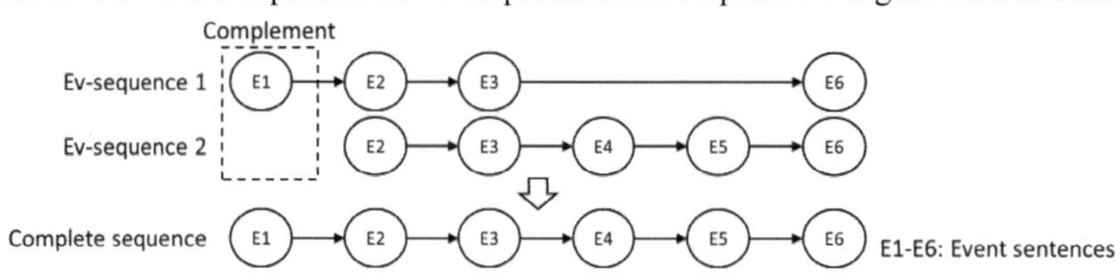

Figure 4. Example of ev-sequences

5. SIMULATION

The appropriateness of the use case diagrams and scenario generation was simulated using five applications:

- **App A**: Web banking system
- **App B**: Food delivery order system
- **App C**: Airplane ticket reservation system
- **App D**: Hotel reservation system
- **App E**: e-Learning system of a university

The purpose of this simulation was to confirm whether the strategy of scenario generation was appropriate before implementing the generation system, recording operation histories and generating scenarios were executed manually.

Table 2 shows the scenario generation results, where "Actual" indicates the number of scenarios manually (human-thinking) determined. "Generation" indicates the number of scenarios generated by this method. According to previous research (Shirogane, 2017), use case generation had some problems that might be reflected in scenario generation. If scenarios were generated based on the generated use cases, the differences between scenario numbers created by human-thinking and this method became large. Thus, the operation histories were divided into use cases by human-thinking, and scenarios were generated based on the use cases in order not to reflect the problems of use case generation.

Table 2. Results of Scenario Generation

	Actual	Generation		Actual	Generation
App A	6	6	App D	4	6
App B	3	4	App E	6	4
App C	4	4			

The scenario numbers differed between "App B" and "App D". The label names of some buttons or links were concrete names of foods in "App B" and the area in "App D". These concrete names were used for window titles as mentioned in Section 3, but the window sequence paths differed by window titles. Consequently, there were more generated scenarios. In addition, the concrete names of foods and areas were used as the objects of event sentences. As scenarios, these event sentences should represent that users select foods or areas, not concrete names (proper nouns), from some selections. To resolve these problems, proper nouns should be identified.

In addition, some other problems were found. For "App A", concrete selection items were realized as label widgets, which stakeholders could not operate, and when stakeholders clicked the corresponding buttons, the selections were performed, and windows were switched. Figure 5 (left) shows an example of this selection. In this case, although the generated event sentence was "User selects 'Select'", "User selects 'Plan selection'" was appropriate. To resolve this problem, it is necessary to extend widget-applying instruction labels and to improve strategies to identify instruction labels.

Another problem was that an input item in a scenario was divided into some text fields. Figure 5 (right) shows that examples include telephone numbers and expiration dates of credit cards.

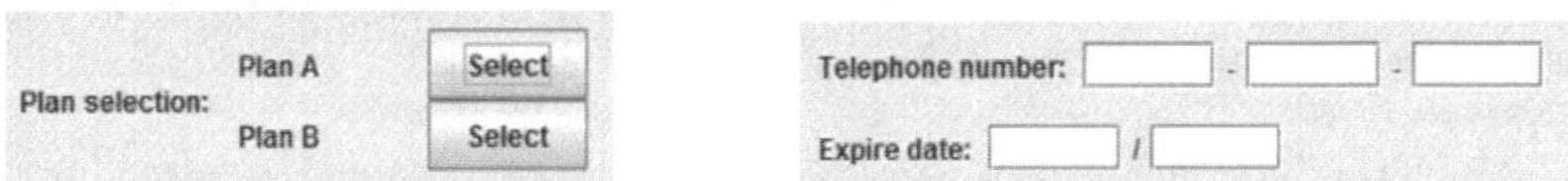

Figure 5 Examples of selection and input items

As described in Section 4.2, the instruction labels of the text field widgets are the label widgets in the left. That is, the instruction labels of the first text field widgets in Fig. 6 are "Telephone number:" and "Expiration date:". The instruction labels of the second and third text field widgets are "-" and "/". However, these two or three text field widgets should be represented as an input item in a scenario. To resolve this problem, it is necessary to survey the patterns in order to divide input items and the delimiters and improve this method so that a set of widgets and delimiters can be identified as input items, and the set of widgets can correspond to the instruction label of the first widget.

Although some problems with label names and input items were found, scenarios could be generated almost appropriately. According to the results, this method was confirmed to almost appropriately generate use case diagrams and scenarios.

6. CONCLUSION

To create use case diagrams and scenarios easily, a method to generate them from the operation histories was proposed. This paper focused on scenario generation, and the detailed generation strategies were described. Similar to the previous research, the operation histories were divided into use cases. Herein event sequences corresponding to individual scenarios were extracted from the operation histories in a use case. Next each event was represented as a natural language sentence using label names of widgets in GUIs. Then sequences of event sentences were generated as scenarios. The generated use case diagrams and scenarios were customized and completed. Using this method, use case diagrams and scenarios that appropriately reflected stakeholders' requirements could be easily obtained. Because there were no gaps between the use case diagrams/scenarios and stakeholders' requirements, misunderstandings of stakeholders' requirements by software developers were reduced. Consequently, unnecessary iterations of software development and development of applications that did not reflect stakeholders' requirements could also be reduced.

To confirm the appropriateness of the generation, five existing applications with different domains were operated. Then scenarios were generated from the operation histories. Although some problems were revealed, the scenarios were almost appropriately extracted and generated.

For future works, generation of event sentences must be improved according to Section 5. In the case where concrete selection names are used, it is necessary to identify the proper nouns in the label names. When input and selection items do not correspond to appropriate instruction labels in this method, strategies to identify the relationships between widgets and instruction labels must be improved.

REFERENCES

Alexander, I. F. & Beus-Dukic, L., 2009. *Discovering Requirements: How to Specify Products and Services.*John Wiley & Sons Ltd..

Apple Inc., 2016. *macOS Human Interface Guidelines.* [Online] Available at: https://developer.apple.com/library/content/documentation/UserExperience/Conceptual/OSXHIGuidelines/ [Accessed 5 2 2017].

Braun, E., Amyot, D. & Lethbridge, T. C., 2015. *Generating Software Documentation in Use Case Maps from Filtered Execution Traces,* Berlin, Germany: Procs of the 17th International SDL Forum on SDL 2015: Model-Driven Engineering for Smart Cities.

Buhr, R. J. A., 1998. *Use Case Maps as Architectural Entities for Complex Systems,* IEEE Transactions on Software Engineering, Volume 24, Issue 12.

Cockburn, A., 2000. *Writing Effective Use Cases.*Addison-Wesley.

GRL. [Online] Available at: http://www.cs.toronto.edu/km/GRL/ [Accessed 5 2 2017]

Haendler, T., Sobernig, S. & Strembeck, M., 2015. *An Approach for the Semi-automated Derivation of UML Interaction Models from Scenario-based Runtime Tests,* Colmar, Alsace, France: 10th International Joint Conference on Software Technologies (ICSOFT 2015).

Hunston, S. & Francis, G., 2000. *Pattern Grammar: A Corpus-Driven Approach to the Lexical Grammar of English.* John Benjamins Pub Co..

Kantorowitz, E., 2014. Verbal Use Case Specifications for Informal Requirements Elicitation. In: *Building Bridges: HCI, Visualization, and Non-formal Modeling Volume 8345 of the series Lecture Notes in Computer Science.* s.l.:Springer.

Microsoft. *Guidelines.* [Online] Available at: https://msdn.microsoft.com/ja-jp/library/windows/desktop/dn688964(v=vs.85).aspx [Accessed 5 2 2017].

Mussbacher, G., Amyot, D. & Whittle, J., 2013. Composing Goal and Scenario Models with the Aspect-Oriented User Requirements Notation Based on Syntax and Semantics. In: *Aspect-Oriented Requirements Engineering Part II.* Springer.

Sharma, R., Gulia, S. & Biswas, K. K., 2014. *Automated Generation of Activity and Sequence Diagrams from Natural Language Requirements,* Lisbon, Bortugal: Procs. of International Conference on Evaluation of Novel Approaches to Software Engineering (ENASE).

Sharp, R. & Rountev, A., 2005. *Interactive exploration of UML sequence diagrams,* Budpest, Hungary: Procs of the 3rd IEEE International Workshop on Visualizing Software for Understanding and Analysis (VISSOFT'05).

Shirogane, J., 2014. *Scenario Description Method based on Existing Software Operation History,* Vienna, Austria: Procs. of 9th International Conference on Software Technologies (ICSOFT2014).

Shirogane, J., 2017. *Generation of Use Cases for Requirements Elicitation by Stakeholders,* Macau, China: Procs. of 8th iCaste Conference on Information Science and Applications (ICISA2017).

Shirogane, J., Seitaro, S., Hajime, I. & Yoshiaki, F., 2014. *Method for Consistent GUI Arrangements by Analyzing Existing Windows and Its Evaluation,* s.l.: IEICE Transactions on Information and Systems Vol. E97-D No. 5.

Shirogane, J. & Yoshiaki, F., 2008. *Correspondence Validation Method for GUI Operations and Scenarios by Operation History Analysis,* Canary Islands, Spain: Proceedings of 2008 International Conference on Intelligent User Interfaces (IUI2008).

Souza, A. J. & Cavalcanti, A. L. O., 2015. *Visual Language for Use Case Description,* s.l.: Journal of Software: Practice and Experience, Volume 46, Issue 9.

Telecommuniocaton Standardization Sector of ITU, 2012. *Z.151: User Requirements Notation (URN) - Language definition,* s.l.: International Telecommunication Union.

The Standish Group, 1995. *The Standish Group Report CHAOS.*.

UNDERSTANDING USER LEARNING IN ITS DEVELOPMENT: APPLICATION OF ILLERIS'S LEARNING MODEL

Jan Aidemark and Linda Askenäs
Linnaeus University
Universitetsplatsen 1, 351 95, Växjö, Sweden

ABSTRACT

This paper investigates a learning model for its capabilities to improve the understanding of user learning during information systems design (ISD). We wish to explore the role of the ISD process as a learning process. Today, organizational design and development increasingly circulate around notions like "organizational learning" and "organizational knowledge creation" or is, in the general direction of organization, in a constant process of change. An information system could be the driver for new organizational routines or new produces, or the necessary component for realizing a new business strategy. The possible role of the information system might then be as a force for change or an obstacle, by the way it is used during its life time. Here we look at the development of the systems and how this process must reflect a high level of adaptation, learning and change in the user community. To add to the knowledge of ISD as a learning system we read a co-design-driven ISD case through the theory lens of Illeris (2007). We discuss the possibilities of designing an ISD process based on this learning theory and of creating users as well as an information system.

KEYWORDS

Information system Development Theory, Learning Organization, Learning Theory, Illeris.

1. INTRODUCTION

Learning could to some extent be seen as tacitly implied in all ISD; in other words, a system developer learns while doing information requirement analyses about the needs of users and the situation of usage. In this sense, all changes in the minds and actions of people imply learning. However, an explicit study of the learning dimensions should include the active use of some learning theory or models in order to narrow down the number of relevant papers and themes.

Information systems constitute a socio-technical phenomenon where technology, user and organization make up the main parts. Markus and Robey (1988) describe the development of information systems as an 'emergent process'. ISD is a dynamic multi-dimensional process, by which a system emerges from complex and reciprocal connections between people and technology within an organizational context.

Further, Newman and Robey (1992) describe ISD as a social process, which is informed by past experience and will during the process create new interaction patterns between user and developer. ISD can be seen as a sequence of events, termed by Newman and Robey (1992) either encounters or episodes, with encounters marking the beginnings and ends of episodes. Encounters, described by Newman and Robey (1992) as being of a social nature, are needed as challenges to the status quo of the users concerned and offer a possibility for changes in behavior.

The purpose of this paper is to closer investigate the nature of these learning processes going on during ISD processes. We want to propose a framework for performing this type of analysis, give a sample of what such an analysis could look like, and discuss the promises or problems of this framework. The framework of choice is a pedagogical one, which integrates both individual and contextual (group, organization, societal) levels. We apply it on a case of co-design with a somewhat different learning situation. The situation could be summarized as organizational strategy defining the needs of IS on a general level and applying a co-design process for creating a package of solutions. However, the major effort of the process was to enable the users to understand and accept the future situation of its use. They were educated in how to be technology users, and the technologies were chosen among existing solutions together with the users to fit their understanding and abilities. This is a case of user-development, that is to say, a creation of users and a technology adoption of that set of users. The learning process involved connecting organizational needs and the user situation with existing technological advances.

2. ISD AND LEARNING

Salaway (1987) presents a student-based study of the differences between learning models and their impact on the effectiveness of the ISD process. The study compares two principles of learning based on Agyris and Schön's (1996) work on organizational learning. Choosing one learning model before another could have an effect on the error levels that the system analyst/user interaction might incur. The experiment with students points towards a model where current assumptions are challenged and leads to the discovery of errors and to fewer problems in the ISD process. This study emphasizes the importance of choosing a learning model that is used actively in the ISD process in order to facilitate developer/user interactions.

End-user training as part of the implementation is a standard measure to ensure that a new system is properly used. This is one of the later steps in the ISD process, which is not aimed at changing or really affecting the design of the system. In this stage, the user is expected to adapt to the functions of the system and learn to use it as it is. In a recent study (Kaplan-Mor et al. 2011), different learning modes are compared as to their effectiveness. Here, training could be defined as "a controlled change of behavior". Three approaches were compared: traditional class instruction, a demonstration-imitation method, and behavioural learning and mentoring. These were compared with regard to the outcomes in a number of calls to a support desk about the use of the information systems. The outcome of this test in a real-time situation showed that a combination of approaches gave the best results. However, there has been no real in-depth attempt at understanding the nature of the learning efforts and the way these are connected to the outcomes.

There have been previous attempts to connect organizational learning and information systems development. Orlikowski and Robey (1991) connect information technology to the values, norms and meanings of the organization. The values and meaning of users and developers are reflected in the design of the IT artifacts, and the use of these artifacts will contribute to the development and change of the organization and its properties. In this sense, the information systems development process will be one of potential organizational learning. Stein and Vandenbosch (1996) argue that ISD creates an opportunity for higher order organizational learning. ISD methodologies are not, however, explicitly designed for learning but contain a greater or lesser possibility for this to take place. Stein and Vandenbosch (1996) examined three cases in order to find factors in an ISD process that support higher order organizational learning (Argyris and Schön, 1995). Higher order learning implies business development that involves changes in organizational principles and basic assumptions. Five success factors for achieving higher order learning are identified in this research. Stein and Vandenbosch (1996) propose that ISD should be designed in accordance with the following principles: a socio-technical perspective on the situation, process orientation, including organizational learning theories in the method, adopting a contextual view of expertise, and basing user-developer interaction on Model 2 learning (Agyris and Schön 1996). Soft systems methodology (SSM) (Checkland, 1981) has been proposed as an approach for information systems development (Hirschheim et al. 1997). SSM suggests a learning cycle of an experiential form where the experience of the implementation of a system is fed back into a new round of analysis and implementation until satisfactory results are achieved. SSM is also an approach for wicked problems with contradictory goal sets based on opposing world views. SSM was developed as a practical way of creating practical solutions in an industrial setting and has been applied in various forms of information systems development.

3. LEARNING THEORY

Learning theory has a long history and is intimately connected with the development of philosophy in general. Traditionally, two broad directions of the study of knowledge and learning are often cited: empirical/inductive and logical/deductive. These refer to the general understanding of what knowledge is and of the processes it is created of. In a more modern perspective, a psychological school was developed, sprung from the context of modern education and schooling.

Illeris (2007) provides a comprehensive human learning theory which compounds and integrates a number of existing directions in the field of learning. Learning is any process that in living organisms leads to permanent capacity change and which is not solely due to biological maturation or ageing (Illeris 2007, p. 3). An integrative learning theory needs to include the psychological, biological and social conditions for learning. The integration provides the opportunity to analyze the interconnection of its different aspects. The two central analysis dimensions include an individual and a social dimension. These two dimensions are connected in the sense that the individual is in constant interaction with the broader context and with society as a dimension or condition of learning. The individual dimension consists of a contentual and a motivational aspect. These are the "what" and the "why" aspects of learning. The individual dimension is connected to physiological and cognitive theories of learning. The individual learning process is shaped in a context that interacts with the social context in which it is embedded as well as with the broader social-cultural context.

3.1 Four Learning Types

Cumulative learning is a mechanical process of gathering experiences without any relation to previous knowledge (mental schema). This is typical at the early stages of life, or when completely new or random events are encountered. The individual has no frame of reference to process the new experience by but has to take the input at face value, for instance when learning a random set of numbers (a telephone number) by heart or memorizing a text without understanding its content. The last example could be the experience that users of a new information system encounter when being forced to use it, just by memorizing a sequence of functions to perform without any real understanding of what they do or of the real consequences. It is like receiving an instruction like "press this button, when this occurs" without any further explanation. At the same time, cumulative learning is a necessary part of the styles that a person needs, for example when learning to ride a bike. Thinking about the process of riding does not help, since the ability of riding a bike needs to be automatized into a set of reflexes like motions of the body. The outcome of cumulative learning tends to be highly localized to the situation where the memorizing takes place, and the use of this knowledge will function as in a stimulus-response manner. However, this knowledge could be a core that might evolve into more elaborate knowledge.

Assimilative learning is a process of adding cognitive and sensory information to an existing mental schema, i.e., integrating new knowledge into what is already structured and organized. The new information is understood from the point of view of what is current knowledge and fitted into that structure. This is an analytic approach to learning, involving breaking down a situation into detailed parts and refining them into a more complex schema. The refining of mental schemata turns people into experts with detailed and elaborate knowledge but creates problems when new and different situations and phenomena occur. Illeris does not present a concept for the first initiating process of creating more general mental schemata that enable more abstract thinking but only notes that this is a "built in" feature of the human mind, distinguishing humans from animals.

Accommodative learning refers to the ability to change, in part or in total, an existing mental schema. In the face of new situations, when current mental schemata do not make sense, a breakup of these is necessary. Illeris calls this a process of transcendental learning, when someone goes beyond current understanding and knowledge. In this sense, the individual accommodates towards the situation, i.e. adapts to the context in order to be able to function in it. The accommodative process might be a sudden break with old truths, or a long and cumbersome process of breaking down arguments into pieces and restructuring them. The accommodative learning process refers to decisive changes in a person's world understanding. Although the general difference between assimilation and accommodation is pretty clear, a process of gradual assimilation could in practice become the start of a process involving a more fundamental change turning into an accommodative process. In the case of the software user, when encountering a new class of system, old experiences will be used in the attempt to adapt the new situation into an old schema. For example, applying a word processing experience to a spread-sheet software will at some point require a radical change and a new schema for the use of spread sheets must be developed. The accommodating process could be associated with skills like critical thinking or reflection and with the ability to distance oneself from a paradigm, comparing different world views without bias or prejudice.

Transformative learning deals with changes that are more far-reaching then what is covered by accommodation. Transformative learning refers to a change of a large part of the total number of an individual's mental schemata. It reaches down to the basic nucleus of knowledge acquired at the cumulative process of accepting the world as it is by recording it mechanically. The change involves the whole person, skills, knowledge, emotions and self-understanding, in other words, the transformation includes everything. Illeris refers to Rogers (1969), who uses the terms "significant learning" or "pervasive learning" and attributes transformation to the level of personality change. This could apply to a software user who, when realizing how a software product is constructed, starts on a path towards becoming a programmer. Terms like the "reorganizing of everything" and the "transformation of self" are clearly distinct from accommodation. This process may be a turbulent experience including a certain amount of pain. Illeris's use of the word "transformative" relates to the work of Mezirow (2000), who defines it as "the process by which we transform our taken for granted frames of reference (meaning perspectives, habits of mind, mind-sets) to make them more inclusive, discriminatory, open, emotionally ready for change and reflective ...". Transformative change might be accompanied by a sudden realization of an identity change, followed by a new way of perceiving the world as a whole by starting to understand everyday objects in a new way. Still, the movement from accommodation to transformation is fluid, marked mostly by the importance and magnitude of change.

3.2 Learning Dimension: Content

The content of the learning process includes a great deal of what constitutes a person in terms of knowing and feeling, with learning involving the changes that lead to new ways of acting. More conservatively, knowledge and skills are seen as content, while Illeris (p. 51) sees a broader picture, consisting of aspects like opinions, insight, meaning, attitudes and qualifications. In this process of change, transforming sensorial experiences into new knowledge is seen as an internal, mental and personal process. One typical description of this process is given by Kolb, (1984), according to whom new information is acquired and diverging aspects of the cognitive information are reflected upon and assimilated with current knowledge. In the outcome, new ways of acting are devised as a ground for new actions. This picture could look somewhat different depending on the nature of new knowledge and to what extent it fits with the current knowledge triggering accommodating or transformational learning (depending on the nature and scoop of change). Still, in the end, a new content in terms of skills and knowledge is the result. A broad understanding of the content of learning is open to what could be included as important in the learning process but makes it even more important to define what should be regarded as content. Content comprises some problematic aspects with regard to conflicts of interest and novelty. Most learning theory works on the assumption of consensus, whereas a learning process that takes place under the condition of competing truths or "right ways of action" needs to be considered. Here we find ourselves in the territory of accommodating or even transformative learning, where fundamental changes might affect the outcome, if a competing set of truths ends up as the accepted new knowledge. The problem of an innovative process of learning, when a clearly prepared answer is neither available nor wanted and the process becomes a journey into an unknown future. The transformative process needs to work with the dissonances in the cognitive knowledge content and use this for innovation, while accepting that this is a painful and testing process. During a project, changes in what is understood as the content of the learning are necessary through critical reflection. It suffices to say that the design process requires an awareness of what latitude of the unknown it will have to accommodate to. Moving into a design process without a clear understanding of what the outcome will be would be anemic to most project leaders and their paymasters, as it opens the field to massive spending without any outcome whatsoever. As far as we can see, these are problems of system design that give project managers and leadership hard times, while all we can do here is to point to the potential of using learning concepts to better understand the challenges. For example, a project that takes pride in goals of innovative design could make good use of studying transformative learning and what it means to work without defining the content of a future system. In general terms, the way to the future system can be described as a learning process for the developers, and their journey of creating new knowledge (i.e. the new system) could be managed to some extent by using learning concepts. In the extreme transformative learning process, the self becomes the learning content, i.e. it is the personality and social role of the participant of the design process that comes into question and is exposed to change.

3.3 Learning Dimension: Motivation

Motivation for learning deals with the incentives that drive a learning process. While the content side of learning is often practical and logical, the forces that drive the learning are more emotional and harder to define and understand. Motivation can be found on many levels, biological, psychological and more social levels. Motivation in this part focuses on the individual, with the social dimension analyzed as individual interacting with the context, as will be further developed later. On the basic levels, we find drivers like the release of fear or pleasure hormones creating feelings and emotions that, in turn, create the need or avoidance of learning. Illeris points to the basic drivers described by Freud, including self-realization (ego), survival (avoiding death) and reproduction (sex) forces. Freud likened the brain to an engine that runs on different levels of energy, with the basic drivers producing the mental energy that drives action in general as well as learning processes. These drivers come embedded in the biological body and form part of the human condition. The mind operates on what is in focus by paying attention to a certain part of the incoming cognitive material. Attention and relevance make up a selection mechanism which decides what information is allowed to be transferred from short-term to long-term memory. This could be translated into a general statement about the inability of people to learn about matters that do not interest them. The concept of emotions is often used to sum up the set of psychological motivational forces driving learning. Strong changes in incentive patterns accompany major changes in a person, as in such cases of transformative learning experiences that could be regarded as obsessive behaviour. To learn new skills fast demands high intensity training and a total focus on the new subject or skill set. The opposite is also true, in that new information systems might trigger fear and stress responses, leading to obsessive refusal to use them if such responses are spread to many people and thus effectively sabotage the development process.

3.4 Learning Dimension: Social and Societal Interactions

The motivational and contentual dimensions of learning are seen from the individual point of view, although a great many of the concepts are connected with an individual's broader situation. Illeris sees interaction with the context as a third dimension of learning, both in a more practical, closer social context and on broader societal levels. As learning is situated, the individual exists in a context and the learning process is performed in interactions with this context. The social dimension is the immediate situation, like a class room, a work place, or a project team. The societal dimension comprises the cultures, structures and norms of the society where the social context resides. Illeris (p. 100) lists the nature of the interaction, as to the learner's level of involvement, from being passively influenced by the environment to being an active co-creator (perception, transmission, experience, imitation, participation). All learning is socially embedded to the point that it is possible to talk about social learning as a special form of learning (Banduras, 1977).

4. CASE

The project started with a number of meetings with different participant constellations. There was one group consisting of 8-10 patients and family members (the patient user group). The other group, which was made up of health-care professionals, included about 10 people with different work roles (the professional group). The patient user group and the professional group were separated for the first three rounds of meetings. To start with, health-care professionals, patients and family members were given a lecture on heart failure and self-care for this condition. The next two meetings were structured around two themes, the care process and a four-stage patient experience model of "pre/symptom, diagnosis, normalization and relapse stages". From each of these meetings researchers gathered suggestions for when and how self-care actions could improve the patient situation.

The fourth meeting was an integration meeting where health-care professionals, patients and family members discussed the situations identified and looked at possible types of support technology. An individual voting session produced a priority list of situations which needed further attention and which could form the basis for developing IT solutions. In the fifth round, all patients, family members and health-care professionals got together to present the situations ranked as the most important in the form of scenarios before an audience of IT technology experts.

In the second phase, a selection process was performed. Based on interests indicated by patients, family members and health-care professionals, a package of solutions was designed. The package was presented in user group meetings in a focus group style. Practical sessions enabled the group to make evaluations of the usefulness and of their interest in actual use. User interviews on an individual basis were performed to provide an opportunity to gather more in-depth opinions. The package consisted of technical systems, people-based activities and organizational developments.

In the third phase, a test implementation of a package of solutions was performed. New patients were invited to test the different solutions for one month each, to compare them, and share their experiences. The implementation took place in the cardiology ward of the local hospital. The process was managed in cooperation between the hospital's development department and the staff on the ward. This part of the project is not considered in the presentation, as it involves more of a testing phase than the design and development of solutions. The designed package of solutions consisted of support systems and organized activities for the patients, intended as support for better self-care. These were added to the current support given by the ward to all heart failure patients. The understanding of this co-design of support in self-care was that they were not primarily in need of a support system for self-care but of a system that focused on how to learn to become great at performing self-care.

5. CASE ANALYSIS: PATIENT LEARNING DURING DESIGN PHASE

To illustrate and give a flavour of how to apply the comprehensive and integrated learning model for better understanding of an ISD process we can only offer a minor post-mortem analysis of a known case, as described in Section 4. During the design process, the different dimensions of learning were activated, and the theory can explain how the project was driven forward through a process of user learning. The basic rationale of the analysis is that the actions of the design process had an impact on the different dimensions (content, motivation, social and societal) and that over time these form a pattern of learning that pushed the project forward. The co-design did include some elements of learning as a way of preparing the users for the process, empowering them to be active and influencing the final outcome. Here we try to understand this process better through the lens of the integrated learning model, and by this effort show how the model can be used to improve the planning of ISD processes. The basic idea of learning in the project was that users with a better knowledge about heart failure and self-care for heart failure would contribute to the design process. In this sense the content could be defined.

The project started with a clear teaching effort with content, facts about heart failure and information on how to live and act as a heart failure patient. Lectures were given by heart failure nursing professors. However, the intended users of the planned self-care support systems (patients and their next of kin) proved to possess very varying pre-knowledge and motivation for taking part. To some extent, the lectures were given first as a way of levelling out any differences and getting everyone with a stable understanding of heart failure on board the design process. However, the motivation differed greatly, with some expressing a very general interest when asked, while others believed that they would get better treatment, and others again came to complain. An IT design was very far off their agendas, if they did have any tangential understanding whatsoever of what it meant. It should be underlined that careful information about the nature and purpose of the project was given, an ethics application was granted, a pre-meeting was held where more information was given and the patients could sign up for the project. The analysis of this action could point to the problems of motivation.

The next step was a narrative session, where the patients, together with their next of kin, described their experiences, from the process of falling ill, via the first hospital contact and the recovery period, and their return to a new somewhat stable normal life. The ostensive purpose was for the design people to improve their understanding of the life world of a heart failure patient. This learning experience for the designers was very important for giving them an insight into new life worlds, almost on an accommodative level. At the same time, for the patients, listening to each other's stories gave perspectives and strengthened the understanding of the personal situation by comparing and reflecting. This process also created a social setting for the project in that patients, most of whom were new to each other, started to form a group, which became an important reference point for the continuation of the project. On the basis of their stories, the project designers devised a list of problem-oriented solutions.

The third step consisted of a solution presentation workshop, with a voting session where the users were able to rank their preferred solutions. However, there were only presentations on a general level, which were problem-oriented and contained no hands-on elements. The outcome of this was that the users on average wanted all the solutions, in "the more the better", or "this could be good too" style. From a learning perspective, this session did not push the users forward but rather served to get some kind of confirmation of the designers' understanding. It was realized that users needed a broad variety of solutions, which led to developing a toolbox of solutions. The knowledge content here was part of the problem, in that descriptions of problems and general solutions were poorly communicated and that a cumulative learning style could be observed, due to a lack of preconceptions among the users. The workshop was also attended by the group of professionals who followed the process, both as experts and co-users, and this group displayed a different pattern. These people had a clearer knowledge which they used to relate to the solution. A process of assimilative learning took place when they tried to fit the solution into the structures and norms of their care organizations. Their everyday immediate practice situation played a strong role (for example competences and work schedules). The outcome of this process was a small number of successful assimilations, while several needed accommodations of the solutions to their existing environments were rejected. These alternative views were used to influence the priorities of the future design process.

The subsequent workshop gave presentations and hands-on demonstrations of the solutions. A full day of presentations and hands-on use gave the users new perspectives. For some, these were novelties, while others had some previous experience. Most of the users in the group tried in an assimilative mode to incorporate this into their everyday reality, picturing themselves as users. Low levels of attempts at rethinking and accommodating new ways of acting could be recorded. This workshop outcome was used to create the practical solutions by tweaking and redesigning to the largest possible extent. The level of motivation for applying new ways of perceiving self-care and everyday action seemed to be low. The solutions as such did not create much driving force to extend the understanding of actual self-care or the motivation for actually performing it. In some instances of more technical solutions, there was a clear case of cumulative learning, as the technical solutions present were new to some of the users.

A roll-out workshop was held to spread the solutions to all users for the purpose of starting a real life testing period. A practical testing of the solutions was performed and instructions were given. During this day each one of the users was put into direct contact with a heart failure nurse who was to supervise the testing period. This was conducted by means of a detailed questionnaire, where the current situation of the user was explored and documented. Detailed plans for the coming months were made together with the nurse. This connection and incorporation into a practical and important social context seemed to motivate the users. The meeting did connect the solution to the user's everyday life and with the social context of the nurse, both being important motivators to engage for understanding the solutions and their connection with everyday self-care. A more intense process involving the assimilation of known actions and the adoptive learning of what was not so familiar took place. The users were sent home with a clear agenda of testing solutions, and of performing real self-care actions in practice.

After months of testing, the users were invited back for a feedback session. Now the connection to real life and practical success made a difference. Since a feedback of working solutions which affect everyday life makes people more motivated, each person came back with a clear understanding of what was good or bad. However, on an average, the "no solutions" option seemed clearly to perform better than others. The idea of allowing personal individuals to compile their own tool box of self-care support became more appealing.

6. DISCUSSION

The purpose of this paper was to explore an integrated theory of learning and how it would apply to an information systems development effort. We argued that the application of an explicit learning theory in the ISD area would contribute to the performance of an ISD project. The conclusion is that the Illeris model captures more and more elaborate aspects of the learning that actually goes on during the process and that using it will give a number of benefits as part of designing an ISD project. The use of the Illeris model creates an opportunity to understand the systems development process as the complex change and learning process that is necessary for promoting changes in behaviours and informing the design of technology to support the new ones. These new behaviours, offered by the new technology, imply learning. In our case, the system development process did work with the learning process as a key part of the technology development; in other words, users were created in a learning and change process, and a technology fitted for these new behaviours was already in place. We can study this user development process using the integrated learning model, which could be applied in a design model for planning a systems development process.

Unless working in a stable environment with users that are knowledgeable of their own situation and sufficiently able to understand technology in advance, we need to look at the greater picture of change and learning. Setting up the design process should include a good understanding of the nature of the content, ensuring that motivational forces are in place for users and other involved people, and that the social and structural environments provide a good connection for functioning interactions between people and their environment. This study points to the necessity of using an integrated learning model in order to capture the interrelated learning process that makes up the changes in the minds of all who are involved and affected by the ISD process. Connecting back to the meta-level of the systems development process, we can see different patterns giving rise to different learning situations. A process that is heavy on the organizational modelling side does stress the institutional levels (the societal dimension) but gives less room for the integration of the individual expected to adopt the new technology. This level of big picture logics could be seen as an example of being in extreme control of what is possible to do during the ISD process, and should be further investigated as to the limitations and possibilities contained.

In comparison with the SSM approach, which combines systematic, experiential organizational learning processes with the merging of opposing world views, the Illeris model offers a more complex understanding of the learning process throughout the development. The weltanschauung questions are connected with the issue of how to facilitate transformative learning and, as such, SSM does belong to a rare breed of system thinking approaches. However, the larger cycle of learning is assumed to be less complicated, as learning from the failures or successes of application is seen as an automatic process. SSM is not founded in any explicit learning model, although it is connected with a tradition of experiential learning (Kolb, 1984). In this manner, SSM or other ISD approaches could be further analyzed and possibly enhanced, on the basis of an integrated learning model.

REFERENCES

Argyris, C, Schön, DA 1996, *Organizational Learning II: Theory, Method and Practice,* Reading, Mass.: Addison-Wesley.

Bandura, A 1977, *Social Learning Theory*, n.p.: Englewood Cliffs, N.J. : Prentice Hall.

Checkland, P 1981, *Systems Thinking, Systems Practice*, John Wiley & Sons, Chichester.

Hirschheim, R, Iivari, J, & Klein, H 1997, 'A comparison of five alternative approaches to information systems development', *Australian Journal of Information Systems*, 5, 1, pp. 3-29.

Illeris, K 2007, *How We Learn : Learning and Non-Learning in School and Beyond*, n.p.: London : Routledge, 2007

Kaplan-Mor, N, Glezer, C & Zviran, M 2011, 'A comparative analysis of end-user training methods', *Journal of Systems and Information Technology*, 13, 1, pp. 25-42.

Kolb, D A 1984, *Experiential Learning: Experience as the Source of Learning and Development*, New Jersey: Prentice-Hall.

Markus, M, & Robey, D 1988, 'Information technology and organizational change: Causal structure in theory and research', *Management Science*, 5, p. 583.

Mezirow, J 2000, *Learning as Transformation : Critical Perspectives on a Theory in Progress*, n.p.: San Francisco, Calif. : Jossey-Bass.

Newman, M, & Robey, D 1992, 'A social process model of user-analyst relationships', *MIS Quarterly*, 16, 2, pp. 249-266.

Orlikowski, W, & Robey, D 1991, 'Information technology and the structuring of organizations', *Information Systems Research*, 2, p. 143.

Rogers, C R 1969 *Freedom to Learn*, Merrill, 1969.

Salaway, G 1987, 'An organizational learning approach to information systems development', *MIS Quarterly*, 11, 2, pp. 245-264.

Stein, E, & Vandenbosch, B 1996, 'Organizational learning during advanced system development: Opportunities and obstacle", *Journal of Management Information Systems*, 13, 2, pp. 115-136

AN EVALUATION STUDY OF E-COMMERCE WEBSITES THAT USE COD PAYMENT METHOD IN THE MIDDLE EAST REGION

Mohanad Halaweh
Al Falah University, Dubai, United Arab Emirates

ABSTRACT

The cash on delivery (COD) payment method has been increasingly used in the last few years as a method of payment for e-commerce transactions in the Middle East region. This mode of payment is provided as an alternative option to the existing traditional e-payment methods such as credit card, debit card, prepaid card and PayPal, for customers who are concerned about their information security (including private and monetary information) and the credibility of the website. The aim of this research paper was to evaluate e-commerce websites that accept the COD payment method. Twelve most popular e-commerce websites in the Middle East region were selected for this study and evaluated based on several criteria including acceptance of this payment option, visibility of this payment option on the website, and clarity of related terms and condition including charges, international delivery and others. The research findings revealed interesting results. The interpretation of the research findings and implications for e-commerce theory and practice, and future research are discussed.

KEYWORDS

E-commerce, Online Payment Methods, Cash on Delivery (COD), Middle East

1. INTRODUCTION

Cash on delivery (COD) is a payment method that enables customers to make a payment in cash at the time a product is delivered to their location. So, if a consumer does not like the product, he or she does not have to accept it or pay for it. It is also called a "post payment" system (Rouibah, 2015). This method of payment has been increasingly used in the last few years as an alternative option to the electronic e-payment methods which are basically initiated, processed and received electronically over the Internet. For example, in India, COD accounts for 50–80% of online transaction payments (Ernst & Young, 2013), while in the United Arab Emirates, this number is about 60% (Hamid, 2014). In Vietnam, COD is accepted by 24 out of the 33 (73%) surveyed companies (International Finance Corporation, 2014). According to much previous research, perceived security, privacy and trust were the key critical factors or reasons that make customers hesitant to adopt existing e-commerce and e-payment methods (Barkhordari et al., 2017; Bolt, Humphrey, & Uittenbogaard, 2005; Daştan & Gürler, 2016; Hamid & Cheng, 2013; Kim, Tao, Shin, & Kim, 2010; Lee, Yu, & Ku, 2001; Lim, Lee, & Kurnia, 2007; Özkan, Bindusara, & Hackney, 2010). These reasons might explain why COD has been used as an alternative or additional option to the traditional online payment methods such as credit cards, prepaid cards, and e-wallets and others. The COD method provides customers with a more convenient way not only to ensure the security of their payment, as they do not have to release their personal information online, but also to inspect the quality of the product itself at the time of delivery so they can confirm they have received the same product that they ordered. Thus, customers' perception of security and trust increase, a situation those existing e-payment methods failed to offer.

However, although the acceptance of COD payment for e-commerce transaction is increasing, there is no scientific research that has addressed this method of payment in general, and from the e-commerce companies' side, in particular. Thus, this paper was intended to shed light on this method of payment by first identifying the level of acceptance by the most popular e-commerce websites in the Middle East region, and secondly evaluating those that accept this payment method with regards the visibility of the of this option on the website, and clarity of related terms and conditions. It is worth mentioning that no previous empirical/evaluation research study exists, which makes it impossible to compare the current research results with previous research or present related literature on this method of payment as most of related research focused on other e-payment methods. Thus, this study has exploratory nature as it explores an area of research that was not clearly addressed before.

The remainder of the paper is organized as follows: Section two present a research approach methodology. Section three presents the research findings. Section four provides a discussion of the research findings, and implications for e-commerce practice and theory. Finally, the paper's conclusion is provided in the last section.

2. RESEARCH FRAMEWORK AND METHODOLOGY

This study employed content analysis where the contents (with regard COD payment method) of the websites were collected and analysed based on particular criteria: 1) whether the website accepts COD or not, 2) the visibility of this information on the homepage (visitor's ability to know that COD choice is available), 3) whether the website has used particular image/icon/logo for this payment method, and 4) clarity of terms and conditions related to this payment method including the charges, return policy and international/foreign delivery for COD e-commerce purchases. The reviewed websites' contents included any texts, image/symbols/icons, or videos related to COD payment method. Initially, we searched for most popular websites in the Middle East region. The result of search showed many sources for that (Garry, 2016; Fmeextensions, 2016; Go-Gulf, 2015; Kelkar, 2014). Some referred to the top 4 websites and another referred to top 18 websites while a third source reported the top 100 popular websites in the Middle East. Then, after reviewing all the sources, we filtered the websites and selected the most common websites that exist in all sources. In other words, we selected websites that there was agreement on them that these are very popular in the Middle East region as they appear in multiple sources. So, a total of 13 web sites were considered for the evaluation in this study. These websites were selected based on: 1) their popularity in the Middle East region in terms of traffic on the website or sales or simply people preferences to use as announced in some of the above sources, 2) most of these websites are online stores which sell various products including clothes, accessories electronics, grocery items, home appliances, and many others so the they are not very specific websites that focus on one or few products (e.g. website that sells flowers) so they have not limited number of visitors. We examined each website by browsing the homepage, terms and conditions, payment and delivery policy pages, and selecting items for purchase to see if the COD option is available at checkout point.

3. RESEARCH FINDINGS

This section provides summary of the findings which are shown in Table 1. These are described in a greater detail with practice and research implications in the following section. As shown in the table, each website is evaluated in terms of the acceptance of COD payment, the visibility of COD on the website, the use of particular sign or log for COD payment, and related terms and conditions. Snapshot screen of the logs/images that refers to COD was also included in the table.

Table 1. An Evaluation of Most Popular Websites in the Middle East Region That Accept the COD Payment

1-E-commerce website	**www.souq.com**
Acceptance of COD	Yes
Visibility on the website	Yes. It is shown on the top of the homepage
Used logo/statement	 Yes. Phrase “Cash on Delivery” was clearly shown on the top which show popup window when is clicked
Clarity of related terms and condition	No certain rules regarding COD were mentioned. It only referred to multiple payment methods that are accepted (including COD).
2-E-commerce website	**www.mumzworld.com/**
Acceptance of COD	Yes
Visibility on the website	Not directly but implicitly. On the bottom of the page there is reference to “flexibility payment options” which implicitly refers to COD that only appears when a visitor clicks on this link. However, the small icons shown on the bottom does not include this option
Used logo/statement	
Clarity of related terms and condition	Cash On delivery payment must be made in full upon receipt of goods. An additional AED 55 charge applies to COD orders outside the UAE. COD is only available in the UAE & KSA, and may not be available for certain oversized items.
3-E-commerce website	**www.letstango.com**
Acceptance of COD	Yes.
Visibility on the website	It is shown on the bottom of homepage. However, the bar below includes logos for various payment methods except the COD 
Clarity of related terms and condition	There are three main options for payment: Cash on Delivery, Credit Card Swipe on Delivery and Credit Card Online. Customers are free to use any payment method to place an order. However, there are no rules stated regarded COD if, for example, there are charges for that or if this service accepted for overseas delivery or not
4-E-commerce website	**www.jadopado.com/en-ae/**
Acceptance of COD	Yes
Visibility on the website	It is not shown on the homepage. It appears only when item is selected for purchase so customers might not know that this option is available

	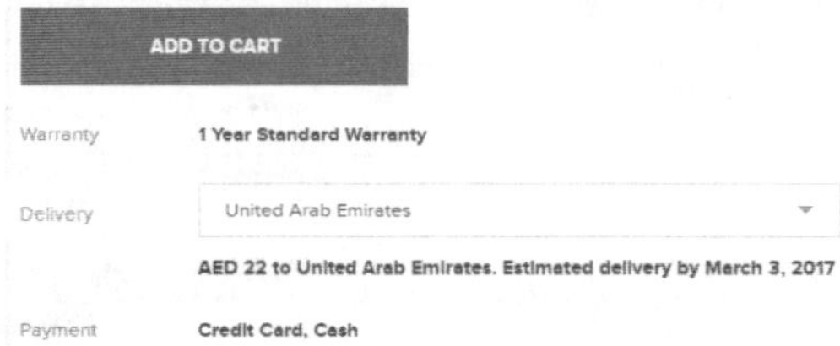
Used logo/statement	No logo or image used
Clarity of related terms and condition	There is policy which charges the customer for the following situation: For Any Orders Paid for by Cash on Delivery If your order is confiscated by customs authorities at origin or destination and cannot be delivered to the buyer, you will not receive payment for the order. You will be liable for the value of the order, the cost of shipping, customs duties, taxes, storage, demurrage, documentation fees and any other additional charges imposed by the carrier or by JadoPado for your order.
5-E-commerce website	**www.axiomtelecom.com/**
Acceptance of COD	Yes
Visibility on the website	It is not shown on the homepage. It appears only when item is selected for purchase so customers might not know that this option is available 
Used logo/statement	No logo or image used
Clarity of related terms and condition	There is clear return policy with regard using COD. It stated Cash on Delivery - If you have made a cash payment and the order has been cancelled due to the above reasons, we will offer a online voucher with the same value which can be redeemed online. No cash Refund will be provided if COD is used.
6-E-commerce website	**www.basharacare.com/**
Acceptance of COD	Yes
Visibility on the website	Yes. It is shown on the bottom of the homepage
Used logo/statement	 Yes. The phrase "Cash on Delivery" is shown on a button
Clarity of related terms and condition	It only refers to extra charges to GCC countries when COD is used.
7-E-commerce website	**www.alshop.com**
Acceptance of COD	Yes
Visibility on the website	Yes. It is shown on the bottom of the homepage
Used logo/statement	 Yes. The phrase "Cash on Delivery" beside icon for cash exchange is shown
Clarity of related terms and condition	No certain rules regarding COD were mentioned
8-E-commerce website	**www.Awok.com**
Acceptance of COD	Yes
Visibility on the website	Yes. It is shown on the bottom of the homepage
Used logo/statement	Yes. The phrase "Cash on Delivery" is shown on a button 
Clarity of related terms and condition	It has stated the COD is accepted only inside UAE. "Awok.com currently offers COD ("Cash on Delivery")..However, Cash On Delivery option is only applicable within United Arab Emirates."

9-E-commerce website	**www.markavip.com**
Acceptance of COD	Yes
Visibility on the website	Yes. It is shown on the bottom of the homepage
Used logo/statement	 Dollar $ sign is used to refer to COD
Clarity of related terms and condition	No certain rules regarding COD were mentioned. It only stated that: Shipping and taxes will be calculated based on the country and method of delivery and indicated at the time of checkout
10-E-commerce website	**www.en-ae.namshi.com/**
Acceptance of COD	Yes
Visibility on the website	Yes. It is shown on the top of the homepage
Used logo/statement	Yes. The phrase "Cash on Delivery" was clearly shown on the top and at bottom of the page besides other modes of payment. When a visitor clicks on it, a popup window appears which refer to COD and related terms and conditions 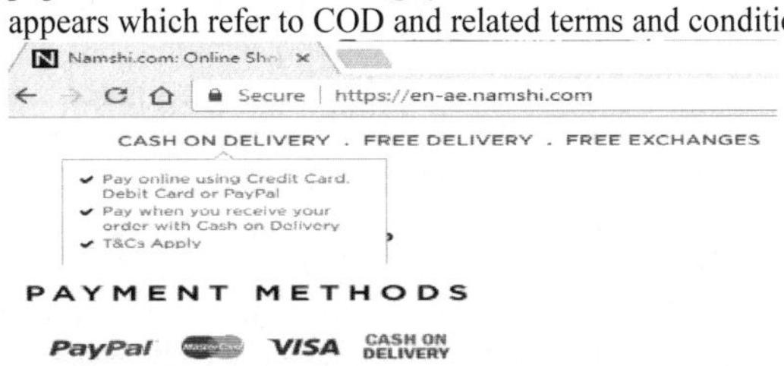
Clarity of related terms and condition	It clearly stated a policy regarding COD charge and delivery outside the country: Cash on Delivery: For customers without access to a credit card, we accept Cash on Delivery (COD) as an alternative payment method for orders less than USD 500 in GCC, 2000 in KSA and unlimited for UAE. Please note that since the COD service is costly for us to provide, cash payment orders will be charged additionally for per order no matter the number of items your order contains. The charges for cod are as follows: UAE - AED 15 KSA - SAR 34 GCC - USD 9
11-E-commerce website	**www.wysada.com/ae_en/**
Acceptance of COD	Yes
Visibility on the website	Yes. It is shown on the bottom of the homepage
Used logo/statement	Dollar paper icon was used to refer to acceptance of COD 
Clarity of related terms and condition	It stated clear policy with regard COD payment inside and outside UAE. For example, • For cash on delivery, an amount of AED 30 will be added. Nothing will be added to credit card payments • For cash on delivery, an amount of JOD 6 will be added. Nothing will be added to credit card payments • Delivery to the rest of the World: Only credit card payments are accepted.
12-E-commerce website	**www.wantitbuyit.com/**
Acceptance of COD	Yes
Visibility on the website	Yes. It is shown on the bottom of the homepage but it is hidden by the live chat window which might not be visible to the visitor.
Used logo/statement	Icon for cash exchange is used. In the following snapshot screen, the live chat window was closed so bar for the payment options is partially visible 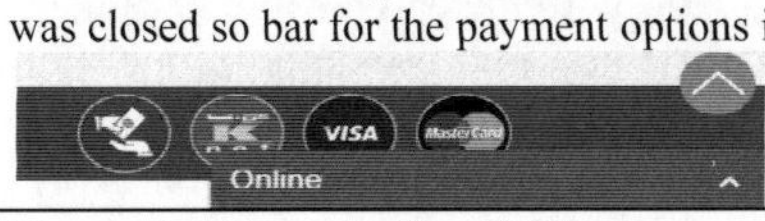
Clarity of related terms and condition	No certain rules regarding COD were mentioned.

4. RESULTS DISCUSSION AND IMPLICATIONS

This section discusses the results of the evaluation which are categorized into three main issues:

4.1 Acceptance of COD

Interestingly, we found all websites (n=12, 100%) accept payment by COD, and this provides evidence that this method is becoming popular and used by well-known websites in the Middle East region. The reviewed websites offer this option besides the traditional e-payment methods which might give them advantage over other websites that did not offer it. For this reason, among many others, these websites perhaps become popular in the region. This might motivate other e-commerce websites that have not yet provided this method of payment to consider this option. Thus, these companies might increase their sales as they can reach to more segments of the customers including those who are concerned about credit card security and privacy, and those who do not have credit card or simply would not prefer using it for online payment. For future research, it will interesting to find out for each website the percentage of sales made through different payment methods and identify if COD has high or low percentage compared to credit card or PayPal or prepaid card, for example. Such information will enable other companies to make proper decision with regard selecting/adopting more feasible payment method for e-commerce transaction. In addition, e-commerce companies need to study the costs of adoption this payment method as there are costs associated with it particularly if a customer decided not to buy an item when delivered. So, if the costs of offering the service are higher than the expected sales that will increase by targeting certain customers, it might not be feasible to accept it. Finally, it is important to mention that none of the websites offered only COD payment method. This means that it should be complementing other options but not completely replacing other e-payment options, as there are customers who prefer e-payment methods as they are more convenient for them.

4.2 Visibility and Logo/Image Design

The findings revealed that there is no consistency for the icon/image used to indicate acceptance of this payment method. It was found that some websites post statement or logo that explicitly indicates that they accept COD. However, some websites did not mention that on the homepage and the option was shown only when we selected item to checkout (see for example website #4& 5). Also, it was found that websites used different logos that reflect the concept of COD, for example website #10 used dollar sign while website # 11 used Dollar paper notes while others used just icon or button that has the phrase "Cash on delivery" (see for example website # 6, 8 & 10). In contrast to logos used for COD payment mode, there is standard logo used for other e-payment methods like MasterCard/Visa Card and PayPal. Some websites showed clearly the COD sign on the top of homepage (see for example website # 1 & 10). They also post it separately without showing other mode of payment while it is shown with other methods of payment at the bottom. This indicates that those websites (showed it on the top corner and at the bottom) want to attract the customers' attention to this mode of payment to encourage them to stay browsing the website and purchase. However, majority of the websites (8 out of 10, 2 did not show on the homepage) posted this on the bottom of the homepage which was not clearly visible as sometimes the visitor need to scroll down too long homepage (online catalog with many items) to see this option of payments while in one case the sign for this option was hidden by the popup live chat window. In other websites this option was not visible until the visitor decides to buy something when item is select for checkout (see for example website #4 & 5).

Since COD payment method becomes widely accepted by many e-commerce websites as shown by the results of the surveyed websites, a standard special logo could be created for this method of payment and added to the homepage of the website. This will increase it is acceptance as the standard logo increase awareness of this payment method. We suggest that paper note that reflects the accepted currency in particular country (local currency) or global currency like dollar or euro can be used. Yet, some symbols are not known for many customers that they refer to COD payment mode. A new third party companies might also be created that take care of the process of delivery and cash collection. These companies might have their own logo that becomes known to both customer and e-commerce website so they can trust them (i.e. third parties) for this purpose. For e-commerce website designers need to post the logo in a visible place on the homepage to attract the customers' attention. Future research might investigate if the design of the logo (for COD) and its location on the website have positive influence on customer's decision to buy from the website using this payment method.

4.3 COD Terms and Conditions

It was found that very limited number of websites that accept COD for international/foreign purchases; delivery is usually limited by geographical location within the country. An exception might be if the e-commerce company has several offices as the case with website #1, for example, where in other countries that can handle the delivery and cash collection. However, some websites offer this service in the multiple countries in the region (see for example website #10 & 11) by adding extra charge for that and this was explicitly indicated in these websites. Some websites did not provide any details or rules related to COD payment method (see for example website # 3 & 7) while others just mentioned that there are charges for this service. Obviously, e-commerce companies might charge an extra fee for the delivery and cash collection. It is also important to note that many specialized shipping companies only offer deliveries, so the cash collection process is not available. In this context, e-commerce companies might require its staff to carry out both activities: delivery and payment. We found that only one websites out of the twelve surveyed websites provided information with regard the return policy. It indicates that there is no cash refund for returned items purchased using COD; customers will be provided an online voucher with the same value which can be redeemed online (see for example website #5). In case of using COD payment, a customer might order item and he might not buy it when it is delivered so the companies might lose money for delivery that did not produce successful sale. Therefore, e-commerce companies might add extra charge to cover that cost. Finally, to increase transparency and increase the acceptance of this method, e-commerce websites need to provide clear and explicit policy and rules with regard using this payment method, for example Will the customer have to pay charges if s/he did not like the product at the moment of the delivery. Will the customer have to pay additional charge for the payment using COD even if he purchased the product? Will the COD is accepted only for item delivery inside the country or is also accepted for international delivery? Also, which categories of products that are accepted using this mode of payment? Are there any restrictions with regard the amount of purchased items (as it is made by cash)? All of these issues need to be clarified.

5. CONCLUSION

This paper is considered unique because it is the first research paper to the author's knowledge that addresses the COD payment method for e-commerce transactions. It evaluated most popular e-commerce websites in the Middle East region with regard the level of acceptance and related rules and conditions. It provided guidelines for e-commerce companies in two directions: 1) e-commerce websites that did not provide this payment method by showing them through evidences that there is high level of acceptance of this method by most popular website so they can consider this option which enable them to reach to more customers and thus increases their sales. 2) For those e-commerce companies that have already accepted this payment method, they need to provide more clearer polices and rules with regard using this payment method to avoid any confusion or failure that make it more worse than e-payment methods. This research also provides guidelines to them, particularly, the designers/contents managers of the website to use attractive reflective logo for COD concept, and post it in appropriate location on the homepage to attract the customers' attention.

In terms of research limitations, this study used only twelve websites for evaluation. The goal was not counting the number of reviewed websites per se, rather to consider some representative sample popular websites. Therefore, if additional 12 websites also added to the list (in section 3), it might be found that there are some websites that do not accept COD. In other words, this research does not aim to claim that COD is used by all e-commerce websites in the Middle East region but the results of evaluating the selected websites revealed by chance that all (n=12, 100% of the surveyed websites) accept this payment method.

Finally, COD could be the good option for certain customers and e-commerce websites in specific contexts, but it should be offered along with other e-payment methods. If the same study was conducted for selected most popular websites in other contexts/regions (e.g. North America, or Europe), the results might be different as the concept of COD might not be common on these regions. Thus, future research might be conducted to address this issue and support in generalizing the research results, or showing contradictions with the existing results

REFERENCES

Barkhordari, M. et al., 2017. Factors influencing adoption of e-payment systems: an empirical study on Iranian customers. *Information Systems and e-Business Management*, Vol. 1.

Bolt, W., Humphrey, D., and Uittenbogaard, R., 2005. The effect of transaction pricing on the adoption of electronic payments: a cross-country comparison. Working paper, Federal Reserve Bank of Philadelphia.

Copenhagen Economics, 2013. *E-commerce and delivery:* A study of the state of play of EU parcel markets with particular emphasis on e-commerce, European Commission, DG Internal Market and Services.

Daştan, İ., Gürler, C., 2016. Factors affecting the adoption of mobile payment systems: An empirical analysis. *Emerging Markets Journal*, Vol. 6, No. 1.

Ernst & Young, 2013. Rebirth of e-Commerce in India. Ernst & Young LLP Published in India. http://www.ey.com/Publication/vwLUAssets/Rebirth_of_eCommerce_in_India/%24FILE/EY_RE-BIRTH_OF_ECOMMERCE.pdf Accessed 28 December 2016.

Fmeextensions, 2016. TOP 25 Ecommerce Sites in Middle East & UAE Loved By Shoppers, https://www.fmeextensions.ae/blog/ecommerce-sites-uae-middle-east-dubai/ Accessed 10th December 2016.

Garry, 2016. Top 100 Ecommerce Online Shopping websites in UAE, Middle East, GCC: A Complete Listhttp://imapro.in/web/online-shopping-websites-in-uae-everything-you-want-to-know-about-e-commerce/ Accessed 10th December 2016.

Go-Gulf, 2015. Most Popular E-commerce Sites of the Middle East http://www.go-gulf.ae/blog/ecommerce-sites-middle-east/ Accessed 10th December 2016.

Hamid, N., & Cheng, A., 2013. A Risk Perception Analysis on the use of Electronic Payment Systems by Young Adult. *WSEAS Transactions on Information Science and Applications*, Vol. 10, No. 1, pp 26-35.

Hamid, T., 2014. Cash on delivery the biggest obstacle to e-commerce in UAE and region, http://www.thenational.ae/blogs/plugged-in/cash-on-delivery-the-biggest-obstacle-to-e-commerce-in-uae-and-region, Accessed 28 December 2016.

International Finance Corporation, 2014. E- and M-Commerce and Payment Sector Development in Vietnam http://www.ifc.org/wps/wcm/connect/67a0740047f652aab0d3f5299ede9589/EMcommerce.pdf?MOD=AJPERES Accessed 28 December 2016.

Kelkar, N., 2014. Top 4 Ecommerce Websites of Kuwait & Middle East. http://www.groundreport.com/top-4-ecommerce-websites-of-kuwait-middle-east/ Accessed 10th December 2016.

Kim, C. et al., 2010. An empirical study of customers' perceptions of security and trust in e-payment systems. *Electronic Commerce Research and Applications*, Vol. 9, No. 1, pp 84-95.

Lee, Z., Yu, H., & Ku, P., 2001. An analysis and comparison of different types of electronic payment systems. *Management of Engineering and Technology*, Vol. 2, pp 38-45.

Lim, B., Lee, H., & Kurning, S., 2007. Exploring the reasons for a failure of electronic payment systems: A case study of an Australian company. *Journal of Research and Practice in Information Technology*, Vol. 39, No. 4, pp 231-243.

Nair, A., 2016. Will CoD kill the Indian e-commerce star? https://yourstory.com/2016/04/cod-kill-indian-e-commerce/ Accessed 28 December 2016.

Ozkan, S., Bindusara, G., & Hackney, R.., 2010. Facilitating the adoption of e-payment system: Theoretical constructs and empirical analysis. *Journal of Enterprise Information Management*, Vol. 23, No. 3, pp 305-325.

Rouibah, K. 2015. Electronic Payment Systems Use and Satisfaction in an Arabic Country: Evidence from Kuwait. *Issues in Information Systems*, Vol. 16, No. II, pp 149-160.

LITERATURE ON WEBSITE EVALUATION IN HEALTH SECTOR

Demetrios Sarantis[1] and Delfina Sá Soares[1,2]
[1]*United Nations University – Operating Unit on Policy-Driven Electronic Governance*
Campus de Couros, Rua Vila Flor 166, 4810-445 Guimarães, Portugal
[2]*University of Minho – Department of Information Systems – ALGORITMI Center*
Campus de Azurém, Azurém, 4800-058 Guimarães, Portugal

ABSTRACT

A critical element in the evolution of health sector services provided through the internet is the development of appropriate websites that adequately serve the patients' needs. Hospitals, in order to deliver superior online services must first understand and then satisfy users' expectations. Health sector website assessment is built on identifying underlying dimensions, and conceptualizing relative metrics. Research and practitioner interest in health sector website assessment has considerably risen in recent years. In this article aspects of relative academic studies in health sector website assessment are reviewed and a holistic health sector websites' assessment framework is proposed, defining criteria and their relative indicators.

KEYWORDS

eGovernment, eHealth, Assessment Framework

1. INTRODUCTION

With patients taking over more responsibility for their own health care decisions, web is an appropriate media to facilitate information exchange between patients and health-services providers (Huerta, et al. 2014). Increasingly, hospital websites are beginning to operate as extension of hospital services, offering access to a range of information and applications (Leonardi, et al. 2007).

Health sector institutions' websites evaluation contribute to maximize the exploitation of invested resources by organizations in the development of user-perceived quality websites. Evaluation on websites related to medical health has recently become a hot topic in the studies of health informatics and information management. Reviewing relative literature, it can be found that there are several studies related to evaluation on health-sector websites, each one assessing a variety of elements. But there is not yet an unequivocal definition of the concept of health sector website quality and the discourse about health sector institutions websites' quality evaluation remains open (Moreno, et al. 2010).

The overarching aim of the present study is to review and analyse existing literature research efforts in the area of hospital website assessment and based on the extracted results, to propose an assessment framework that can integrate the identified aspects.

This paper is organized in five sections. The second section introduces the methodology applied, while section three reviews and analyses existing website quality assessment efforts in health sector. Section four illustrates the proposed health sector website assessment framework. Finally, section five presents conclusions and future perspectives of this work regarding further steps that can be taken.

2. METHODOLOGY

In our literature review we selected to conduct an exploratory study approach since it helps to acquire insight into the available literature by identifying the conceptual content of the field and by contributing to theory development towards formulating our conceptual framework (Shields and Tajalli, 2006). The research methodology contains three phases.

Material Collection. In the present study, six well-known academic online databases, Science Direct, EB-SCOHost, Google Scholar, Web of Science, Scopus and Wiley Online Library were selected to search for relevant studies. The literature search was carried out in article titles and abstracts from 2000 to February 2017. The search for related publications was mainly conducted as a structured keyword search.

Content Analysis. Content analysis was based on exploratory study of the selected articles carried out using systematic check techniques, on existing health sector web presence assessment studies. This type of research was chosen because it can provide significant insight into a given situation, facilitating the identification and structuring of new problems.

Framework Concepts. In designing the assessment framework, the following steps have been followed: a. Gleaning the main assessment elements from the selected literature. b. Propose framework's main assessment criteria. c. Allocate the identified elements of content analysis to the proposed criteria. d. Propose indicators to assess each criterion.

3. LITERATURE REVIEW

Apart from research concerning general approaches of website evaluation and evaluation on websites subjected to commerce, government and education, there are several studies focusing on quality assessment of health-sector organisations' websites. In this section, we review the existing literature on latter ones.

Llinás et al. (2008) evaluate and compare the user-orientation of Spanish, American and British hospital websites. In their descriptive study, they evaluate websites according to readability, accessibility and the quality of information provided. Lewiecki et al. (2006) develop and evaluate measurement tools to determine the quality of osteoporosis websites for patients. They use indicators in the categories of content, credibility, navigability, currency, and readability. Moreno et al. (2010) present a qualitative and user-oriented methodology for assessing quality of health-related websites based on a 2-tuple fuzzy linguistic approach. To identify the quality criteria set, a qualitative research has been carried out using the focus groups technique. According to the qualitative research results they define five quality dimensions, credibility, content, usability, external links and interactivity services. Huerta et al. (2014) and Huerta et al. (2016) assess the web presence of hospitals and their health systems based on five dimensions, accessibility, content, marketing, technology, and usability. Tsai and Chai (2005) developed an evaluation questionnaire for nursing websites covering overall impression, download and switch speed, accessibility and convenience, web page content, and compatibility with common browsers. Randeree and Rao (2004) consider the following factors for evaluating health sector websites: access/usability, audience, accuracy, timeliness, content, authority, and security. Guardiola-Wanden-Berghe et al. (2012) conducted an observational, descriptive and cross-sectional study carried out using systematic check techniques, on assessment of documentary and content quality assessment of eating disorder websites. Rezniczek et al. (2015) evaluate the quality of websites of Obstetrics and Gynecology departments in German-speaking countries using Google search rank, technical aspects, navigation and content as objective criteria. Maifredi et al. (2010) explored the characteristics of the contents and the user-orientation of Italian hospital websites. The analysis considered Italian hospitals with a working website assessing technical characteristics, hospital information and facilities, medical services, interactive on-line services and external activities. Bilsel et al. (2006) present a quality evaluation model which consists of seven major e-service quality dimensions, including tangibles, reliability, responsiveness, confidence, empathy, quality of information, and integration of communication issues of websites. Moslehifar et al. (2016) study focus in four different categories such as general information, accessibility of websites, functionality of websites, and facilities information provided in websites. Patsioura et al. (2009) proposed framework focuses on three main criteria, information, communication and electronic services. Norum (2001) evaluates the quality of Norwegian cancer hospitals' Websites according to general information, hospital details and technical aspects. Calvo (2014) assesses the quality and describe characteristics of websites of large Spanish hospitals evaluating the global quality, accessibility, usability, interactivity, updating, quality model and information. Liu et al. (2011), focus on the evaluation of quality of hospital websites in China using a pre-defined objective criterion based on content, function, design, and management & usage. Garcıa-Lacalle et al. (2011) determine which factors have an influence on website adoption and level of development over time. The used checklist includes elements such as general information, contacting information, web linkage, quality of care, information for patients, information about resources and performance, site navigation and usability, health information, services provided to professionals and facilitating transactions. Gruca & Wakefield (2004) evaluate the status of US hospital websites examining the following features: electronic documents, providing decision aids, linkages to partners, building trust via external verification, facilitating transactions, multiparty targeting, self-service information and discussion forums. The study conducted by Mira et al. (2006) on the readability and accessibility of Spanish hospital websites concludes that they need to be more patient oriented because the websites visited did not fulfil even half of the readability and accessibility attributes required by widely used standards. Mancini et al. (2005) found that the enforcement of accessibility regulations has helped to significantly improve hospital website accessibility in Italy.

4. ASSESSMENT FRAMEWORK

Based on the analysis of the above evaluation studies, we propose four fundamental health sector website assessment criteria – Content, Technology, Services and Participation – which cover the whole spectrum of the identified assessment elements of our literature review.

Table 1 classifies the identified assessment elements found in literature into each of the four proposed assessment criteria.

Table 1. Significant Identified Elements Assigned to the Proposed Criteria

Study	Content	Technology	Services	Participation
(Huerta, et al. 2014)	Content	Technology, Accessibility, Usability	-	Marketing
(Moreno, et al. 2010)	Content, Credibility	Usability, External Links	-	Interactivity Services
(Llinás, et al. 2008)	Address/Contact, General Information, Services, Patient Information, Research and Teaching	Page Features, Page Layout, Page Update, Technical Features	-	Patient Interaction, Media
(Lewiecki, et al. 2006)	Content, Credibility, Timeliness	Navigability, Readability,	-	-
(Huerta, et al. 2016)	Content	Technology, Accessibility, Usability	-	Marketing
(Tsai and Chai, 2005)	Overall Impression, Content	Download and Switch Speed, Accessibility and Convenience, Browser Compatibility	-	Interactivity Services
(Randeree and Rao, 2004)	Accuracy, Authority, Content, Timeliness	Accessibility and Usability, Audience, Security and Privacy	-	-
(Guardiola-Wanden-Berghe, et al. 2012)	Content, Document Features	-	-	-
(Rezniczek, et al. 2015)	Content	Navigation, Technical Aspects	-	Google Search Rank
(Maifredi, et al. 2010)	Hospital Information and Facilities, Hospitalization and Medical Services, External Activities	Technical Aspects	Appointments	Forum
(Bilsel, et al. 2006)	Reliability, Empathy, Quality of Information	Tangibles, Responsiveness, Assurance	Integration of communication	-
(Moslehifar, et al. 2016)	General Information Characteristics, Functionality Characteristics, Facilities Characteristics	Accessibility Characteristics	-	-
(Patsioura, et al. 2009)	Information Gathering	-	Communication & Transaction	-
(Norum, 2001)	General Information, Hospital Information	Technical Aspects	-	-
(Calvo-Calvo, 2014)	Presented Information, Updating the Contents, Quality References, Information for the Professionals, Supplier Information	Accessibility, Usability	Interactivity and Relationship with Users	-
(Liu, al. 2011)	Function, Content, Design	Management & Usage	-	-
(García-Lacalle, et al. 2011)	General Information, Contacting Information, Web Linkage, Quality of Care, Information for Patients, Information about Resources and Performance	Site Navigation and Usability	-	Health Information, Services Provided to Professionals, Facilitating Transactions

Study	Content	Technology	Services	Participation
(Gruca and Wakefield, 2004)	Electronic documents, Providing Decision Aids, Linkages to Partners, Building Trust via External Verification		Facilitating Transactions	Multiparty Targeting, Self-Service Information, Discussion Forums
(Mira, et al. 2006)	-	Readability, Accessibility	-	-
(Mancini, et al. 2005)	-	Accessibility	-	-

Health sector website evaluators must be able to clearly identify whether specific goals or targets have been met and where adaptations to institution's website strategy appear to be necessary. Progress toward achieving health institutions web presence goals can be tracked by selecting specific indicators that correspond and evaluate each of these criteria (Table 2). The performance indicators enable measurement of progress towards the achievement of the key objectives for each criterion, which in turn permits the ongoing evaluation of success in implementing the hospital's website aimed strategy.

Table 2. Criteria and Indicators Allocated to Each of Them

Content	Technology	Services	Participation
• Hospital Information	• Navigability	• Administration Procedures	• Community Interaction
• Quality Metrics	• Accessibility	• Appointments	• Media
• Organisational Structure and Medical Information	• Usability/Readability	• Patient Care	• Advertising/Marketing
• Patient Information	• Credibility		
• Research and Teaching	• Privacy/Security		

4.1 Content

Content criterion, evaluates the presence of information relevant to the user. It evaluates the quality, availability, relevancy, completeness and concise representation of specific information that it is expected to be provided in a health's sector institution website. Thereinafter the proposed indicators are analysed.

Hospital Information

Most of the hospitals provide general health information (Guardiola-Wanden-Berghe, et al. 2012), (Liu, al. 2011). Hospital designation and logo on the home page are usually included in the home page (Rezniczek, et al. 2015), (Moslehifar, et al. 2016), (Liu, al. 2011), (Gruca and Wakefield, 2004). Almost all sites include static information such as a general phone number for the hospital, fax number, postal address, e-mail address, VAT number, a map or directions to the hospital, parking information, transportation in-formation and a history of the institution (Llinás, et al. 2008), (Maifredi, et al. 2010), (Bilsel, et al. 2006), (Patsioura, et al. 2009), (Norum, 2001), (García-Lacalle, et al. 2011), (Gruca and Wakefield, 2004). Additional elements are illustration of complementary services (press, cafeteria, Wi-Fi, telephone etc.), phone directory of the institution and emergency information (Norum, 2001). Few take advantage of the available technology to provide a virtual tour of their facilities (Llinás, et al. 2008).

Quality Metrics

Public reporting of hospital quality data, empowers patients, referring physicians, and purchasers of health care with the information needed to make informed decisions regarding their care (Gruca and Wakefield, 2004). It also encourages hospitals and physicians to participate in continuous performance improvement by creating a healthy and competitive environment for better patient outcomes. Consequently, more and more hospitals are considering reporting their organizational quality metrics on their websites. Quality elements include the waiting list, the number of available beds, the admissions number report, the nosocomial infection rate, the inpatient mortality rate and the surgical mortality rate (Moslehifar, et al. 2016), (Norum, 2001), (Calvo-Calvo, 2014), (García-Lacalle, et al. 2011).

Organisational Structure and Medical Information

The organisation chart depicts institution's structure, it defines the hierarchy and the different roles that are involved (Llinás, et al. 2008). Essential information is the list of clinical services available at the hospital, the list of outpatient hospital services available (consultation, diagnostic services), the list of departments or units providing patient services, their relative working hours, their locations and their contact details (Llinás, et al. 2008), (Randeree and Rao, 2004), (Rezniczek, et al. 2015), (Maifredi, et al. 2010), (Bilsel, et al. 2006), (Moslehifar, et al. 2016), (Patsioura, et al. 2009), (Norum, 2001), (Liu, al. 2011), (García-Lacalle, et al. 2011).

For potential patients, an electronic version of doctors printed directory is essential (Liu, al. 2011). Apart from the list of employed doctors, sites should include doctor's phone number, email address, picture, education/certification and relative practice information (Lewiecki, et al. 2006), (Maifredi, et al. 2010), (Liu, al. 2011), (García-Lacalle, et al. 2011), (Gruca and Wakefield, 2004).

In this section health-disease specific information and relative treatment information is included (García-Lacalle, et al. 2011). It should also be provided the possibility to read online or to download health-care booklets and a medical glossary (Maifredi, et al. 2010).

Patient Information

A clear description of patient's rights and obligations is essential. Information that should be adequately addressed is the related indications for hospital admission and discharge (Llinás, et al. 2008), (Maifredi, et al. 2010), (García-Lacalle, et al. 2011). It also provides information for visitors [5]. Details of how to pay prescription charges, about private consultations/services and fees and information for foreigners is provided in this section (Moslehifar, et al. 2016).

Research and Teaching

Health institutions that have a teaching mission, include in their website, information about graduate medical education in general and information for medical students, undergraduate or postgraduate courses that are held at the hospital, schedule of activities that take place at the hospital (courses, workshops and conferences), scientific studies that the hospital promotes or is involved in and publications of the hospital itself (Llinás, et al. 2008), (Gruca and Wakefield, 2004).

The ability of hospital's website to provide relative information about the library presence, address, working hours, publications catalogue and available services (reading, loans, copies) is important (Llinás, et al. 2008), (Randeree and Rao, 2004).

4.2 Technology

This criterion appears to be a mixture of, mainly technical, items that relates to easy navigation, website quality, visual appeal, functionality and reliability. The technology criterion is related to how the content and services are assembled and made avail-able on a website. Technology criterion is analysed in the following indicators.

Navigability

Navigability indicator examines the easiness that the user finds the required piece of information by moving through the website. Elements that are evaluated include effective use of hyperlinks and the degree to which the interface helps the user orient himself within the website (Moreno, et al. 2010), (Llinás, et al. 2008), (Lewiecki, et al. 2006), (Huerta, et al. 2016), (Randeree and Rao, 2004), (Maifredi, et al. 2010), (Moslehifar, et al. 2016).

Accessibility

Accessibility indicator refers to the practice of removing barriers that prevent inter-action with, or access to website, by people with disabilities or people with restricted computer literacy (Huerta, et al. 2014), (Llinás, et al. 2008), (Huerta, et al. 2016), (Moslehifar, et al. 2016), (Calvo-Calvo, 2014). Elements that should be addressed include semantically meaningful HTML tags, textual equivalents provided for images, links named meaningfully, text and images that are large or enlargeable, flashing effects which are avoided or made optional, content that is written in plain language, compliance with WCAG W3C guide-lines, compatibility with different browsers and access from various devices (Huerta, et al. 2014), (Moreno, et al. 2010), (Llinás, et al. 2008), (Tsai and Chai, 2005), (Rezniczek, et al. 2015).

Usability/Readability

Usability indicator evaluates the ease of use of the website. Information should be presented concisely, without ambiguity and each item should be placed in the appropriate area (Lewiecki, et al. 2006), (Tsai and Chai, 2005), (Bilsel, et al. 2006). Some of the common aspects of usability are simplicity, consistency, familiarity, clarity and relevancy (Moreno, et al. 2010), (Tsai and Chai, 2005), (Bilsel, et al. 2006), (García-Lacalle, et al. 2011). For prospective and current patients to effectively use the information available at a hospital's website, they must have a search tool (Llinás, et al. 2008), (Tsai and Chai, 2005), (Maifredi, et al. 2010), (Moslehifar, et al. 2016), (Norum, 2001). Other essential features include website map, content in foreign languages, quick load time, graphics that open conveniently, website pages that can be printed, individual sub-pages that have specific and meaningful titles (Huerta, et al. 2014), (Llinás, et al. 2008),

(Lewiecki, et al. 2006), (Huerta, et al. 2016), (Tsai and Chai, 2005), (Randeree and Rao, 2004), (Maifredi, et al. 2010), (Moslehifar, et al. 2016), (Calvo-Calvo, 2014).

Credibility

Because of the critical role of hospital websites in human's health, credibility indicator is critical. Elements that should be evaluated include author and date of the provided information and the text quality which should be grammatically and spelling correct (Huerta, et al. 2014), (Moreno, et al. 2010), (Huerta, et al. 2016), (Randeree and Rao, 2004). Interest conflict declaration, date of last website update, HON (Health on the Net) foundation code certification, webmaster characteristics and sources and references should be clearly listed (Moreno, et al. 2010), (Llinás, et al. 2008), (Lewiecki, et al. 2006), (Tsai and Chai, 2005), (Randeree and Rao, 2004), (Guardiola-Wanden-Berghe, et al. 2012), (Bilsel, et al. 2006), (Patsioura, et al. 2009).

Privacy/Security

Health sector website privacy holds profound implications since service delivery impacts human life, legality and social policy. Related information presentation and dissemination has raised privacy concerns among both consumers and providers. A privacy policy describing the website's information practices should be easily accessible on the site (Bilsel, et al. 2006). Issues regarding patient confidentiality, copyright notice and terms of use, must be specifically addressed to become widely available (Randeree and Rao, 2004), (Liu, al. 2011).

Security management tools and usage is an important part of the website. Other elements included in this indicator are general disclaimers, ownership of the site and provision of a secure website using encryption techniques (e.g. HTTPS) (Moreno, et al. 2010).

4.3 Services

The trend towards creating individual patient profiles personalising the provided electronic services can bring many benefits to both hospital and patient. Personalised content can be provided during interactions with all users and this might improve loyalty to a particular hospital.

Administration Procedures

Health institutions can use online forms or provide standardised documents for downloading and uploading, to their users (Llinás, et al. 2008), (García-Lacalle, et al. 2011). Hospital websites are expected to facilitate interaction between visitors and the hospital staff (Patsioura, et al. 2009), (Calvo-Calvo, 2014). In order to achieve cost savings and streamline the treatment, hospitals allow visitors to submit e-mail requests for general health information (Moreno, et al. 2010), (Llinás, et al. 2008), (Calvo-Calvo, 2014), (García-Lacalle, et al. 2011), (Gruca and Wakefield, 2004). Some of them provide the capability for referring doctors to use e-mail referral forms or furthermore enable interactive communication applications (Calvo-Calvo, 2014).

Appointments

Translating visitor's interest in a hospital into action is one of the most important purposes of a hospital website. Online appointments and user membership registration are functions that should be included (Moslehifar, et al. 2016), (Liu, al. 2011). Some hospitals enable their customers to interactively schedule appointments via web forms or via e-mail (Maifredi, et al. 2010), (Gruca and Wakefield, 2004). Some websites include a printable checklist of items to bring to the hospital in the appointment (Gruca and Wakefield, 2004).

Patient Care

Features evaluated in this indicator provide an important link between patients and hospitals. Supporting professional practice, asynchronous communication between the patient and the physician is implemented through email or through web-based message exchange systems (Tsai and Chai, 2005), (Bilsel, et al. 2006). Some hospitals offer real-time chat sessions between doctors and patients, providing in this way the opportunity to the patient to pose follow-up questions (Liu, al. 2011). Through their websites, hospitals provide access to patient's medical records system that creates and maintains all patient data electronically (Randeree and Rao, 2004).

4.4 Participation

Participation criterion is used to describe the interaction between hospital, patients and online communities on the web. Online communities often involve members to provide content to the website and contribute in some way. Examples of such include forums, complaints forms, interaction with the media and hospital's marketing activities. Hospital sites can host patient support groups, interact with community organisations and become a portal for physician organisations and private medical offices.

Community Interaction

Hospital websites are aim principally to communicate with existing or prospective patients. Each patient has unique needs based on her health conditions. If hospitals can effectively meet patients' widely varying information needs by using internet technology rather than more personnel, they further their twin goals of better health for patients and higher efficiency (Moslehifar, et al. 2016). One such technology is a threaded discussion forum (e.g. diseases, allergies, treatments etc.) where visitors can post questions, and receive answers that other visitors may also access easily (Moreno, et al. 2010), (Tsai and Chai, 2005), (Maifredi, et al. 2010), (García-Lacalle, et al. 2011), (Gruca and Wakefield, 2004). They often use these tools to build a community of users to strengthen the relationship with their potential and current patients (Bilsel, et al. 2006), (Liu, al. 2011).

Media

Many hospitals exploit the immediacy of the web to report current news about the institution, press releases and internal announcements (Llinás, et al. 2008), (Moslehifar, et al. 2016), (Calvo-Calvo, 2014). In addition to general health information, many hospitals also inform the community about health events (Moslehifar, et al. 2016), (Gruca and Wakefield, 2004).

Marketing/Advertising

A hospital's website is one of its public faces (Watson, et al. 2000). Some hospitals use their websites to promote their work, and keep in touch with the different types of stakeholders (Guardiola-Wanden-Berghe, et al. 2012), (Moslehifar, et al. 2016), (Calvo-Calvo, 2014), (García-Lacalle, et al. 2011). Hospitals can use their website to expand the reach of their medical practices to anyone with Internet access and advertise the international availability of their services (Huerta, et al. 2014), (Huerta, et al. 2016), (Rezniczek, et al. 2015).

Website sponsors and investors should be also clearly disclosed and possible advertising material should be differentiated form other content (Lewiecki, et al. 2006). Social media applications can be included in this category (Facebook, Twitter, LinkedIn etc.) (Moslehifar, et al. 2016). Hospital websites can be a convenient way for health care providers to analytically inform patients of their liability regarding insurance issues (Moslehifar, et al. 2016).

5. CONCLUSIONS AND FUTURE WORK

A health-sector organisation's website has to be an integral part of the operating practices of the institution. Our review of related research has shown that hospital website assessment process can be based in four criteria, content, technical, services and participation.

The framework could help hospital management, health sector officials and website managers to understand causal links that show ''how'' and ''where'' a website is consistent with its strategy. This study should also be of interest to technology practitioners and researchers, as the findings shed light on the further development of performance measurements for hospital websites.

The assessment framework needs further development. Next step of our research will be to determine specific metrics and relative weights for each indicator in order to implement a concrete assessment instrument for health sector institutions web presence. Hospital websites assessment instrument, apart for health institutions' managers, will allow patients to search for hospitals and compare them based on their performance on various quality measures.

In terms of practical application, we plan to use it in Portuguese hospital's website assessment and discuss the results with hospitals' management and health sector authorities. This will complement views expressed in individual discussions and group workshops, to assess practical acceptability in a better way.

ACKNOWLEDGEMENTS

This paper is a result of the project "SmartEGOV: Harnessing EGOV for Smart Governance (Foundations, methods, Tools) / NORTE-01-0145-FEDER-000037", supported by Norte Portugal Regional Operational Programme (NORTE 2020), under the PORTUGAL 2020 Partnership Agreement, through the European Regional Development Fund (EFDR).

REFERENCES

Bilsel R.U. et al, 2006. A fuzzy preference? Ranking model for a quality evaluation of hospital web sites, International Journal of Intelligent Systems, Vol. 21, No. 11, pp 1181-1197.

Calvo-Calvo, M.A., 2014. Quality and characteristics of websites of large Spanish hospitals, Revista Espanola de Documentacion Cientifica, Vol. 37, No.1.

García-Lacalle J. et al, 2011. The unpromising quality and evolution of Spanish public hospital web sites, Online Information Review, Vol. 35. No.1, pp. 86-112.

Gruca T.S. and Wakefield D.S., 2004. Hospital web sites: Promise and progress, Journal of Business research, Vol. 57, No.9, pp 1021-1025.

Guardiola-Wanden-Berghe R. et al, 2012. Quality assessment of the Website for Eating Disorders: a systematic review of a pending challenge, Ciencia & Saude Coletiva, Vol. 17, No. 9, pp 2489-2497.

T.R. et al, 2014. Hospital website rankings in the United States: expanding benchmarks and standards for effective consumer engagement, Journal of medical Internet research, Vol. 16, No. 2.

Huerta T.R. et al, 2016. An Evaluation and Ranking of Children's Hospital Websites in the United States, Journal of Medical Internet Research, Vol. 18, No. 8.

Leonardi M.J. et al, 2007. Publicly available hospital comparison web sites: determination of useful, valid, and appropriate information for comparing surgical quality, Archives of surgery, Vol 14, No.2, pp 863-869.

Lewiecki E.M. et al, 2006. Assessment of osteoporosis-website quality, Osteoporosis international, Vol. 17, No. 5, pp 741-752.

Liu, X. et al, 2011. The quality and characteristics of leading general hospitals' Websites in China, Journal of medical systems, Vol. 35, No.6, pp 1553-1562.

Llinás G. et al, 2008. A Comparison of Websites from Spanish, American and British Hospitals, Methods Inf Med 47, pp 124-130.

Mancini C. et al, 2005. Health information in Italian public health websites: moving from inaccessibility to accessibility, Health Information & Libraries Journal, Vol. 22, No. 4, pp 276-285.

Maifredi G.et al, 2010. Italian hospitals on the web: a cross-sectional analysis of official websites, BMC medical informatics and decision making, Vol. 10, No. 1, pp 17.

Mira J.J. et al, 2006. Quality of websites in Spanish public hospitals, Medical Informatics and the Internet in Medicine, Vol. 31, No. 1, pp 23-44.

Moreno J.M. et al, 2010. A quality evaluation methodology for health-related websites based on a 2-tuple fuzzy linguistic approach, Soft Computing, Vol. 14, No. 8, pp 887-897.

Moslehifar M.A. et al, 2016. Assessing the quality of trust features on website content of top hospitals for medical tourism consumers, Malaysian Journal of Communication, Vol. 2, No. 1, pp 469-489.

Norum, J., 2001. Evaluation of Norwegian cancer hospitals' Web sites and explorative survey among cancer patients on their use of the Internet, Journal of Medical Internet Research, Vol. 3, No. 4.

Patsioura F. et al, 2009. Evaluation of Greek Public Hospital Websites, In ICE-B - International Conference on e-Business, Proceedings, pp 223-229.

Randeree E. and Rao H.R., 2004. E-health and assurance: curing hospital websites, International Journal of Electronic Healthcare, Vol. 1, No.1, pp 33-46.

Rezniczek G.A. et al, 2015. Quality of websites of obstetrics and gynecology departments: a cross-sectional study, BMC Pregnancy & Childbirth, Vol. 15, No. 1, pp 103.

Shields P.M. and Tajalli H, 2006. Intermediate theory: The missing link in successful student scholarship, Journal of Public Affairs Education, Vol. 12, No. 3, pp 313-334.

Tsai S.L. and Chai S.K., 2005. Developing and validating a nursing website evaluation questionnaire, Journal of Advanced Nursing, Vol. 49, No. 4, pp 406-413.

Watson R.T. et al, 2000. Integrated internet marketing, Communications of the ACM, Vol. 43, No. 6, pp. 97-102.

FACTORS AFFECTING ERP IMPLEMENTATION: CASE STUDIES FROM ORGANIZATIONS IN DEVELOPING COUNTRY

Paweena Wanchai
Department of Computer Science, Faculty of Science, Khon Kaen University, Khon Kaen, Thailand

ABSTRACT

Enterprise resource planning (ERP) systems have become one of the largest IT investments in recent years. Previous research reports unusually high failure in ERP projects, especially in developing countries. The aim of this study is to extend our understanding of ERP implementation in organizations in Thailand by identifying technological factors that affecting ERP implementation. Longitudinal case studies were undertaken to understand the implementation of ERP system. Data was collected by conducting in-depth interviews at various levels of the subject organizations, by observation and by examining their archived records when available. The result reveals that technological factors including strategic role of IT, BPR and customization, IT readiness, system integration, and data conversion and system testing deserve more attention during the implementation of ERP projects. Some actions are also recommended that can help bring troubled ERP projects under control.

KEYWORDS

ERP System, ERP Implementation, Critical Success Factors, Technological Factors, Case Study, Developing Country

1. INTRODUCTION

Today, organizations in Thailand are facing increasingly keen competition in the marketplace, their survivals are under challenge. Therefore, many organizations recognize the importance of introducing an enterprise resources planning (ERP) system to facilitate their management and improve their competiveness. By introducing this cross-functional software system, organizations can improve their productivity, customer service and at the same time lowering costs and inventories. ERP systems hold the promise of providing companies with greater competitive advantages (Davenport, 2000; Tsai, Lee, Shen, & Lin, 2012). Despite of its increasing adoption, the failure rate of ERP implementation is very high in developing countries (Asemi & Jazi, 2010; Hawking, 2007; Liang, Xue, Boulton, & Byrd, 2004; Martinsons, 2004; Sun, Ni, & Lam, 2015; Zhu, Li, Wang, & Chen, 2010). Previous research points out that companies encountered many unexpected problems and even failures when trying to apply ERP to improve their business processes and management, as ERP systems are extremely complex and difficult to implement. Previous research also revealed that the structure and processes embedded in an ERP system reflect Western cultures, it might not be appropriate in developing context due to cultural differences between developing and the West countries (Asemi & Jazi, 2010; Hawking, 2007; Liang et al., 2004; Martinsons, 2004; Sun et al., 2015; Zhu et al., 2010). Therefore, organizations who adopt these systems often find that ERP systems do not fit their practices.

The large difference between the ERP systems implementation success rate in developed and developing Asian countries produces a need for research examining generic and unique factors that affect ERP system implementation in developing countries. However, most of ERP studies have been conducted in Western countries' context, and little research has been studied in developing countries' context. Nowadays, more and more companies in Thailand adopt ERP systems to facilitate their business processes and operations. Previous research reported that organizations in Thailand lagged behind other developed countries in introducing advanced technologies and were found to have low technological capabilities (Intarakumnerd, Chairatana, & Tangchitpiboon, 2002). However, there is very limited research investigating factors affecting ERP system implementation in Thailand. In addressing this research gap, the aim of this study is to focus on the topic in Thai environment and unveil the difficulties in implementation of ERP with an emphasis on technological context.

2. LITERATURE REVIEW

ERP solutions began as a system for material requirements planning (MRP) in the 1990s focused on inventory and materials and evolved to extend business activities to more departments throughout the enterprise. The early 2000s ushered in ERP systems that provided greater collaboration between stakeholders with improved integration, enhanced customer relationship offerings, and optimized supply chain productivity. Advanced technology and Internet services spurred the evolution of ERP systems in the late 2000s with alternative technology offerings including hosted platforms and subscription-based Software as a Service in which organizations transfer the ERP technological infrastructure to third-party providers as a means of reducing technology costs and maintenance (Shaul & Tauber, 2013). As ERP systems evolved, the research focus evolved to keep the pace of knowledge consistent with the pace of ERP change. Early ERP researchers focused highly on factors involved in the planning and implementation stages with a particular interest in the strategic dimensions of ERP implementations. By the early 2000s with increased integration and ERP global expansion, researchers shifted their concentration to cultural issues, best practice and geographical conflicts. As the ERP market grew in the late 2000s to include small-enterprises, public sector organizations, higher education, and a variety of other markets, researchers progressed to include studies investigating and comparing factors between different organization types across all phases to understand ERP issues in specific contexts (Shaul & Tauber, 2013).

Both practitioners and academicians have conducted many discussions and studies on the ERP phenomenon during the past two decades. Regarding of this ERP phenomenon, many practitioners argue that ERP system is not suitable for organization in developing countries because of differences in economic systems, culture and business processes between Western developed countries and developing countries (Asemi & Jazi, 2010; Avison & Malaurent, 2007; Huang & Palvia, 2001; Kouki, Poulin, & Pellerin, 2010). In academics, scholars also conducted ERP studies in developing countries, they tried to provide insights for practitioners to know how to develop and implement ERP systems for developing countries companies, these studies include success factors of ERP implementation (Seng Woo, 2007; Shanks et al., 2000), failure stories of ERP implementation (Dwivedi et al., 2015; Liang et al., 2004), and ERP implementation outcomes (Martinsons, 2004). Previous ERP researchers focused highly on factors involved in cultural issues, management issues, best practice and geographical conflicts including language, top management support, project management, change management, training, business process reengineering (BPR) and human resource problem, with less emphasis on the technological factors (Avison & Malaurent, 2007; Dezdar, 2012; Liang et al., 2004; Martinsons, 2004; Sia & Soh, 2007; Upadhyay, Jahanyan, & Dan, 2011).With rapidly changing ERP markets, increased globalization, advanced technology, and organizational differences, one can appreciate the nuances and conflicting conclusions of ERP factors and their significance to project outcomes.

3. METHODOLOGY

Multiple case studies method was used in this research because of the opportunity to collect and gain in-depth knowledge and rich data relating to the phenomenon in its natural setting (Yin, 2009). Case study research is appropriate and commonly used in ERP research (Azevedo, Romão, & Rebelo, 2012). Data collection took place from 2013 until 2016 during pre-implementation, implementation and post-implementation stages. The usefulness of longitudinal research for triangulation as it allows repeat observations to increase the understanding of the research setting. Multiple sources of evidence were used, mainly in-depth interviews, observations and textual material. Triangulation of data was conducted to strengthen the research study, increase the reliability of the research, minimize any data bias and evaluation of findings data (Patton, 2005; Yin, 2009). The in-depth interviews were conducted with a variety of key informants, including users from different departments, members of the top management, functional area representatives, information technology (IT) professionals and ERP consultants. The interviews lasted between one and three hours each. Direct observations of the ERP work practices were also conducted. This included system monitoring related to accounting, management control, sales and distribution, materials management and project system processes. In addition, archival documents were used, including meeting minutes, training documents, and project reports. One-on-one interviews were supplemented by focused interviews where possible. The in-depth interviews were conducted with 75 participants: 25 interviews at each organization. NVivo software was used to collect and support analysis of the data gathered from the case studies. NVivo software is a product that can help researchers manage and analyze data (Rodik & Primorac, 2015). Data were analyzed within cases and across cases.

4. CASE STUDIES

Three ERP system implementations case studies are examined. One case represents situations where implementations were headed for failure but then resurrected. Two cases represent failed implementations.

4.1 Company Alpha

In order to keep up with this growth and development, Alpha began to seek a system that could meet its customers' increasing demands, while at the same time remaining productive as the business expands. In 2013, the company decided to implement a global ERP template based on SAP R/3. The ERP system focused on five modules with a strong financial flavor. These are finance, control, sales and distribution, materials management, and project structure. This ERP system was seen as the functional solution to be deployed among all the company units. Alpha undertook extensive BPR concurrently with the implementation of SAP as its new ERP software system. The project started with a workshop on process orientation that was presented to all the organization's executives and senior managers by a world leading expert on process re-engineering. The organization also instituted IT center of support for ERP systems at the headquarters where new modules were piloted and tested before being introduced throughout the organization. The IT center also developed in-house training programs that were extended when the system was upgraded or a new module was introduced. They provided a 24-7 helpdesk in order to help users with any problems they encountered. The ERP system was purposefully not customized, as that was considered costly, making subsequent upgrades difficult. However, after the ERP system go-live, some degree of customization, especially regarding reporting functionalities, was allowed. Changes to the project scope were considered, but only on the basis of tradeoffs against time, cost, and business impact. After the ERP system go-live, most of users rapidly became overwhelmed by its complexity. Data conversion was initially lacking in quality and problems with invoices occurred. This was corrected and the final implementation was successful.

4.2 Company Beta

In 2013, Beta started to implement ERP packaged solution (based on SAP R/3 software) such that the company business processes could be properly coordinated across multiple functions. The organization, however, continued to use some legacy systems such as finance and accounting system and the human resource management system. Beta employees offered the explanation that managing Thai human resource data related to legal requirements, tax, and benefit practices that were complex and unique. They further argued that local software better supported all the needs of standard reports. After the ERP system go-live, operational and functional problems arose almost immediately and did not subside. The reasons that the ERP system did not function as planned were directly attributed to problems with the system's implementation. The organization faced several problems in institutionalizing the ERP system. The organization also took several months to improve the system configuration and their IT infrastructure after going live. The legacy and ERP systems had to run in parallel when functional problems with the new system arose. Even after technical stability was achieved, the system was not understood very well by the end users. Many users continued using the old system. This resulted in a number of data issues. The main complaint was about system complexity and inflexibility as well as the lack of fit of the new processes with the system. The organization reported that the cancellation and eventual restarting of the ERP system implementation project delayed the project's completion by almost two years.

4.3 Company Gamma

Before Gamma implementing ERP system, most business transactions were conducted through paper-based processes and a number of legacy systems in their offices. ERP system was considered as a solution when management found it difficult to maintain the legacy systems after many modifications and the departure of key staffs in the IT department. The implementation started in early 2014. However, after the system go-live, some legacy system was used in parallel with SAP, as data from the legacy systems were still being used in some areas. Almost immediately at the end of implementing ERP, problems with basic system functionality began to occur. Participants also mentioned that when the organizations changed their existing business processes to fit with ERP systems, such standardization of business processes made employees' work processes more rigid and inflexible. ERP systems made work processes rigid by restricting the ways employees performed their tasks and by enforcing certain information and resource requirements. The sequence of activities and information/resource requirements could not be altered or circumvented during the execution of the work processes. Consequently, users believed that elements of their work processes could not be modified during execution. Most users preferred the ERP system to be customized to suit their familiar work patterns. Additional to the complexity of the ERP system, double data entry procedure was an important barrier to the acceptance of the system. Participants also complained that the reporting functionality of the SAP system was quite poor. This is because the system offered a set of standard reports which did not support the needs of the users. The organization faced the challenges of integrating various legacy systems with ERP system. Overall, the implementation of ERP at Gamma was a challenging process. The organization experienced with a delayed, over budget, and out-of-control implementation project.

Table 1 provides a summary of contextual conditions in each company.

Table1. A Summary of Contextual Conditions in Each Company

Company	Industry	Role of ERP	Role of IT department
Alpha	Food	Both operational and strategic roles Business process redesign to simplify and standardize processes	Use IT department as facilitator of the process of ERP implementation Adequate IT spending level
Beta	Home appliance manufacturer	Reduce time, cost and streamline operations Replacement of legacy systems	ERP implementation was very high reliance on external consultant Low IT spending level
Gamma	Pharmaceutical	To achieve operational efficiency Replacement of in-house legacy systems	ERP implementation was very high reliance on external consultant Low IT spending level

5. ANALYSIS AND DISCUSSION

The case study analysis reveals that strategic role of IT, BPR and customization, IT readiness, system integration, and data conversion and system testing are factors that affect ERP implementations. Each of the factors will be discussed in the following subsections.

5.1 Strategic Role of IT

IT departments play different roles in different organizations. The strategic role of IT within an organization is found to significantly impact the ERP system implementation. The strategic role of IT is composed of two concepts: strategic IT planning and the importance IT plays in the overall corporate strategy. Strategic IT planning is seen as being able to consistently meet the demands of the business through the use of information systems and technology. A strong competence in strategic IT planning will ensure that IT goals are aligned with the overall business goals. However, the creation of the IT strategic plan should be viewed with importance by the organization if it is to gain competitive advantage through the plan's execution. This research finds that in organizations in which IT plays a strategic role, top management might be more sensitive to strategic opportunities that can be achieved through the use of ERP system. In organizations in which IT plays a strategic role, IT units are more aggressive in seeking and trying out new ideas, technologies, and management practices. This evidence suggests that the organization that plan to use ERP system for strategic purposes have more effective ERP management processes than those that use ERP system to improve operational efficiency. Those firms that use ERP system strategically will be more inclined to recognize the advantages of using the ERP software features and functionality for competitive gain. Once the IT organization is in a position to advocate for an ERP project, the project should be more likely to take place.

5.2 BPR and Customization

The Western developed ERP systems, which have been developed from MRP systems and manufacturing resources planning (MRP II) systems, are manufacturing centric and emphasize on planning and feed forward control. They are characterized as being formalized, centralized and high addicted to the rules and procedures with which companies can achieve high efficiency by doing the things in a right way. Even though ERP vendors believe they have the most efficient modules with sufficient best practices, organizations sometimes place more trust in their own processes. The organizations find that ERP systems do not always satisfy all of their requirements. Sometimes business processes are so unique that they need to be preserved. This is also reflected by the users and ERP consultants in the interviews and they reported that companies usually prefer to use the system to automate current processes rather than following the changed processes defined by the ERP systems. The study reveals that, typically, the organizations need to customize ERP systems to satisfy their needs. Therefore, they ask vendors to make changes of functionality to fit their requirements. In some cases, organizations request some special functions, which are not included in vendors' products. Adding functionality can help organizations to develop functionality absent in the ERP software. Amending reports or displays is often needed. Adding new reports is another common ERP customization. To fill the gaps between a desired system and the current vendor system, or to gain competency in the market, most organizations will customize vendors' ERP systems during initial implementation or upgrades. The level of customization varies across organizations. Some large companies chose to customize more to keep their own best practices that give them competitive advantage.

The findings point out the importance of reorganizing the business processes to align to the implementation of the logical system, in order to gain tangible benefits. Customization is usually associated with increased implementation costs, longer implementation time, and inconvenient maintenance and upgrades from vendors. Therefore, most organizations should minimize customizations due to reasons of costs, time, and shortage of professional personnel. Customization should only be requested when essential or when the competitive advantage derived from using non-standard processing can be clearly demonstrated. In other words, organizations should try to adopt the processes and options built into the ERP, rather than seeking to modify the ERP to fit the particular business practices. Thus, it is recommended that customization adheres to the standardized specifications that the software supports. High customizations increased application complexity that lengthened project schedules and increased costs, which negatively affected the on time and on budget measurement of project success. In order to have a successful ERP implementation, the organization must pay close attention to the business processes, and how those processes align with the ERP system. By not recognizing the importance of BPR and how those processes support the software configuration, it may lead to ERP system implementation failure.

5.3 IT Readiness

IT readiness is referred to as the degree to which a firm prepares the environment and workforce to accept and configure new technology. It is imperative to assess the IT readiness of an organization, including their skills and infrastructure. IT skills refer to an IT staff's ability to configure and maintain information systems to support a business. Strong technical expertise and training availability have been found as essential for organizations to improve their core competencies. Organizations with a higher level of technical expertise and infrastructure can be expected to master the technical aspects of business and contribute more to firm performance than firms with a lower level of technical expertise and infrastructure. During the early stages of ERP implementation, organizations should initiate actions like (i) training their employees on the technical aspects of new technology, (ii) informing users about possible changes in business processes and/or job descriptions caused by the technology, and (iii) providing around-the-clock technological support.

Organization training and presence of help desks and technical support teams motivates users to accept the technology and enable new users to gain experience with and learn about the technology. Similarly, extensive communication about the new system not only guides potential users, gathers information, and reduces uncertainty, but it also significantly influences system acceptance and subsequent use. Technical IT skills are necessary beyond the time of initial installation; post-installation support is generally requisite to refine and adjust specific system attributes on a constant basis. Since ERP systems operate in a dynamic business environment, they must adapt to changes in the strategic and operational focus of the firm. The ERP project manager and team members should not only be technologically competent, but also understand the business requirements of the firm. During the chartering phase, a project leader's expertise is especially critical. If project leaders do not know what to do at certain decision-making points, it creates a significant problem. The skills and knowledge of the project team during the implementation phase is important in understanding the expertise of consultants in areas where team members lack knowledge. After the installation of an ERP system, IT staff should be able to solve any problems without the help of consultants.

The capability of ERP systems is largely dependent on the information technology, as well as the architectural design and options that are available in the implementation process. This is because the architectural design for every company may differ, depending on the industry and the size of the company. This process involves the search for a framework that assesses the gaps between architecture requirements and current IT environments to develop implementation strategies. This study proposes that in providing an architectural design for ERP systems, the following considerations must be incorporated: (1) network infrastructure; (2) server platform; (3) database management system; (4) data ownership; (5) client platform; (6) Web technology; (7) prerequisite user skills; and (8) IT capacity. This research finds that many enterprise architecture efforts have failed because management often views ERP system implementation as a stand-alone project, unwilling to invest in enterprise infrastructure. Thus, while successful ERP system implementation is often determined by business and organizational changes, architectural choices deserve thorough consideration during the system procurement phase, because the selection of ERP systems have technical and nontechnical impacts on the enterprise as well as the success of the ERP implementation.

5.4 System Integration

The analysis reveals that enhancing system integration both within the firms and enterprises and between suppliers and customers is important factor for ERP implementation. System integration is referred to as the degree to which an organization achieves unity in organizational subsystems by harmonizing different departments, modules, software, and legacy systems. ERP system cannot do everything a company needs. Companies may have to use other specialized software products that best meet their unique needs. These products have to be integrated along with all the homegrown systems with the ERP suite. It is to embrace both a set of physical factors and information flows that span the value chain. The organization possessing higher levels of integration tends to have higher performance. Internal integration results from a common integrated database and the implementation of common processes across divisions and regions. Typical common processes included in ERP systems are order entry, order processing, and warehouse management. Such commonality offers the capability to merge processes and provide major customers with a common and consistent interface with the firm. The benefits of an ERP system are limited unless it is seamlessly integrated with other information systems.

There are many challenges in ERP integration in organizations: seamlessly integrating with various functional ERP modules, integrating with other business software applications, integrating with legacy systems, and integrating the ERP system with suppliers. First of all, for a successful ERP integration, ERP module integration is imperative. ERP software is made up of many software modules. Each ERP software module imitates a major functional area of an organization. Common ERP modules consist of modules for product planning, purchasing from suppliers, inventory control, manufacturing, product distribution, sales order tracking, finance, accounting, marketing, and human resources. Secondly, integration with other business software applications is very important. E-business practice is the combination of strategies, technologies, and processes to electronically coordinate both internal and external business processes and to manage enterprise-wide resources, such as customer relationship management (CRM), supply chain management (SCM) and business intelligence (BI). To maximize the benefits of the ERP system, firms should tightly integrate the system with other internal and external business software. Using standardized data definitions and codes that are shared with other information systems is very important. Third, integration with legacy systems is also an important factor in ERP integration. Organizations have gathered huge amounts of data over the years, using legacy systems. The data in legacy systems are crucial to the survival, operations, and growth of organizations. In ERP projects, existing legacy systems have to be carefully defined and evaluated to determine the nature and scale of problems that an organization may encounter during implementation. It is important that an adequate infrastructure should be planned for so that it becomes reliably available and well in time. This research suggests that if organizational legacy systems are very complex, then the amount of technical and organizational changes required is likely to be high, and vice versa. Therefore, organizations should have a clear understanding of the existing legacy environment and the technological aspects involved in the ERP system. Fourth, integrating an ERP system with the suppliers using communication protocols and standards is also another considerable issue in ERP system integration.

5.5 Data Conversion and System Testing

A fundamental requirement for ERP system effectiveness is the availability and timeliness of accurate data. The cases evidences suggest that data problems can cause serious implementation delays, and as such, the management of data entering the ERP system represents a critical issue throughout the implementation process. Data conversion is defined as the conversion of existing data from legacy systems to the ERP system. This effort often involves translating or amalgamating existing data to conform to the specifications required by the ERP system. Within the company, the challenge lies in finding the proper data to load into the system and converting all those disparate data structures into a single, consistent format. Conversion can be an overwhelming process, especially if companies do not understand what needs to be included in the new systems and what needs to be omitted. In addition, interfaces with other internal and external systems require the ability to handle complex data sources and legacy data types.

System testing is defined as a set of tasks designed to assure that the ERP system is functioning as desired. It includes testing the software, hardware, network, processes, and procedures associated with the ERP system. Testing may be accomplished on both a modular and total system level. It should include testing of all types of potential situations, ensuring that the results produced in the test environment match those expected to occur. The thoroughness of the effort requires that consideration be given to tradeoffs made between testing each and every possible case, time available for testing, people and system resources available for testing, and the risk associated with the failure to detect flaws in the system due to testing omissions.

6. CONCLUSION

In this paper, an attempt has been made to identify some Thai-specific difficulties in the ERP implementation process. The results suggest the technological factors affecting the implementation of ERP system including strategic role of IT, BPR and customization, IT readiness, system integration, and data conversion and system testing. While a large number of businesses have already jumped on board by implementing ERP, organizations need to be careful since this technology may not be the perfect tool for all on account of its complexity and high cost. It is important for companies to be aware of certain critical issues before implementing any ERP package. Careful consideration of these critical factors will ensure a smooth rollout and realization of full benefits of the ERP solution. The findings of this research are also helpful in the following way for Western vendors to localize their systems for Thai organization. Western ERP vendors should realize and accept the facts that Thai management and work practices are far different from that of the Western world. Most of the Thai companies cannot catch up with the standardized best practices embedded in their ERP systems. Western ERP vendors should consider how to make their ERP packages more flexible in terms of the embedded processes while keeping the sophisticated functionalities in manufacturing and supply chain management. Western ERP vendors should also improve their finance and accounting functions to meet the requirement of local culture and laws. This study found that there are some companies who are using Western ERP systems; they are at the same time using finance and accounting software. This to some extent implies that the finance and accounting functions are still not able to satisfy the requirement of their clients. Therefore, Western ERP vendors also need to take these into consideration when localizing their systems. As with all research, this study has some limitations that may serve as the springboard for further research. This research investigated ERP system implementation in Thailand; one avenue for future research would be to examine the robustness of the findings across industries and countries. This study focuses on technological factors, other factors that could possibly affect ERP implementation have not been considered in this research. A further examination of the factors that influence ERP system implementation would facilitate further understanding of this complex process. It is also important to analyze the relationship between factors and performance, for both individuals and organizations, to provide additional insights into the downstream implications of the ERP system implementation.

REFERENCES

Asemi, A., & Jazi, M. D. (2010). A comparative study of critical success factors (CSFs) in implementation of ERP in developed and developing countries. *International Journal, 2*(5), 99-110.

Avison, D., & Malaurent, J. (2007). Impact of cultural differences: A case study of ERP introduction in China. *International Journal of Information Management, 27*(5), 368-374.

Azevedo, P. S., Romão, M., & Rebelo, E. (2012). Advantages, limitations and solutions in the use of ERP systems (Enterprise Resource Planning)–A case study in the hospitality industry. *Procedia Technology, 5*, 264-272.

Davenport, T. H. (2000). *Mission critical: Realizing the promise of enterprise systems*. Boston, MA: Harvard Business School Press.

Dezdar, S. (2012). Strategic and tactical factors for successful ERP projects: insights from an Asian country. *Management Research Review, 35*(11), 1070-1087.

Dwivedi, Y. K., Wastell, D., Laumer, S., Henriksen, H. Z., Myers, M. D., Bunker, D., ... Srivastava, S. C. (2015). Research on information systems failures and successes: Status update and future directions. *Information Systems Frontiers, 17*(1), 143-157.

Hawking, P. (2007). Implementing ERP systems globally: Challenges and lessons learned for Asian countries. *Journal of Business Systems Governance and Ethics, 2*(1), 21-32.

Huang, Z., & Palvia, P. (2001). ERP implementation issues in advanced and developing countries. *Business Process Management Journal, 7*(3), 276 - 284.

Intarakumnerd, P., Chairatana, P.-a., & Tangchitpiboon, T. (2002). National innovation system in less successful developing countries: the case of Thailand. *Research Policy, 31*(8), 1445-1457.

Kouki, R., Poulin, D., & Pellerin, R. (2010). The impact of contextual factors on ERP assimilation: Exploratory findings from a developed and a developing country. *Journal of Global Information Technology Management, 13*(1), 28-55.

Liang, H., Xue, Y., Boulton, W. R., & Byrd, T. A. (2004). Why Western vendors don't dominate China's ERP market. *Communications of the ACM, 47*(7), 69-72.

Martinsons, M. G. (2004). ERP in China: One package, two profiles. *Communications of the ACM, 47*(7), 65-68.

Patton, M. Q. (2005). *Qualitative research*: Wiley Online Library.

Rodik, P., & Primorac, J. (2015). To Use or Not to Use: Computer-Assisted Qualitative Data Analysis Software Usage among Early-Career Sociologists in Croatia Symposium conducted at the meeting of the Forum Qualitative Sozialforschung/Forum: Qualitative Social Research

Seng Woo, H. (2007). Critical success factors for implementing ERP: the case of a Chinese electronics manufacturer. *Journal of manufacturing technology management, 18*(4), 431-442.

Shanks, G., Parr, A., Hu, B., Corbitt, B., Thanasankit, T., & Seddon, P. (2000). Differences in critical success factors in ERP systems implementation in Australia and China: a cultural analysis. *ECIS 2000 Proceedings*, 53.

Shaul, L., & Tauber, D. (2013). Critical success factors in enterprise resource planning systems: Review of the last decade. *ACM Computing Surveys (CSUR), 45*(4), 55.

Sia, S. K., & Soh, C. (2007). An assessment of package organisation misalignment: Institutional and ontological structures. *European Journal of Information Systems, 16*(5), 568-583.

Sun, H., Ni, W., & Lam, R. (2015). A step-by-step performance assessment and improvement method for ERP implementation: Action case studies in Chinese companies. *Computers in Industry, 68*, 40-52.

Tsai, W.-H., Lee, P.-L., Shen, Y.-S., & Lin, H.-L. (2012). A comprehensive study of the relationship between enterprise resource planning selection criteria and enterprise resource planning system success. *Information & Management, 49*(1), 36-46.

Upadhyay, P., Jahanyan, S., & Dan, P. K. (2011). Factors influencing ERP implementation in Indian manufacturing organisations: A study of micro, small and medium-scale enterprises. *Journal of Enterprise Information Management, 24*(2), 130-145.

Yin, R. K. (2009). *Case study research: Design and methods* (4th ed.). Los Angeles, CA: Sage.

Zhu, Y., Li, Y., Wang, W., & Chen, J. (2010). What leads to post-implementation success of ERP? An empirical study of the Chinese retail industry. *International Journal of Information Management, 30*(3), 265-276.

HUMAN RESOURCE INFORMATION SYSTEMS ADOPTION AND USE IN A UNIVERSITIY ENVIRONMENT

Mampilo M. Phahlane[1] and Raymond M. Kekwaletswe[2]
[1]*University of South Africa, South Africa, Johannesburg*
[2]*University of the Witwatersrand, South Africa, Johannesburg*

ABSTRACT

The paper examines the adoption and use of human resources information system (HRIS) in a university environment. Universities are acknowledged as unique and yet there is a lack of empirical research that is carried out in such environments, specific to HRIS adoption and use. To this point, the technology organization and environment (TOE) framework was used as a lens to analyze how HRIS was adopted and used. An interpretive, case study of a South African university informed the conceptualization of a framework for how HRIS may be adopted and used sensitive to an African university context. This paper posits that for HRIS adoption and use to be relevant and appropriate there has to be a consideration for environmental context in which the university operates, national and university culture, varied stakeholders, national and university's contextualized strategy and mandate.

KEYWORDS

HR Environment, HRIS Adoption, HRIS Use, University

1. INTRODUCTION

Organizations depend on the performance of their human capital to survive (Lippert and Swiercz, 2005).The management of human resources (HR) information is essential to the 21st century human resources department in any organization (Troshani et al., 2011). To become effective and efficient, organizations are relying on human resource information system (HRIS) to assist them in managing HR information; universities in South Africa have adopted and are using HR systems for such purposes.

HRIS have great value in organizations; HR activities could be automated using HRIS (Tansley et al., 2001; Strohmeier, 2007; Bondarouk et al., 2009) by providing electronic based HR for all employees whenever they need it (Ulrich, 1997), therefore setting up the HR department to be fully automated (Hussain et al., 2007). This in turn minimises errors that are associated with manual work.

Waring and Skoumpopoulou (2012) have expressed the lack of understanding for enterprise wide systems such as HRIS in universities, they further assert that research that stems from the higher education sector indicates that many universities do not understand the nature of such technologies and their unintended outcomes as a result of their adoption and use, moreover the complex nature of universities adds to this challenge. This lack of understanding about the interaction of complex information systems and organizations has led to organizations not getting value for their investment.

To address this challenge, the paper addresses this question: *What defines a university's HR environment?* That is to explore a university's environment in which HRIS is adopted and used; this understanding is significant as an environment influences the adoption of an IS and how it is subsequently used. Strohmeier (2007) posits that researchers need to understand the context in which the practitioner works, along with the relationships between the actors affected, the firm's strategies and activities, and the technologies implemented before attempting to determine its consequences and ways to improve HR performance. Hence the importance of understanding a university's HR environment as a place where employees work and interact with each other, where strategies are conceptualized and implemented and technologies like HRIS are adopted and used. Further, the paper makes another contribution by proposing a framework for HRIS adoption and use in a university based on the environment.

The rest of the paper is organised as follows; HRIS adoption and use in organizations is discussed, followed by a discussion on higher education sector in South Africa, a case story of university investigated, the methodology adopted follows, then an analysis of the findings, discussions about the findings and the last discussion is the relevant conclusions.

2. HRIS ADOPTION AND USE IN HIGHER EDUCATION INSTITUTIONS

HRIS can be defined as an amalgamation of computer software and hardware, organisational procedures, policies, data and people essential to direct the HR function (Kassim et al., 2012). Human resources (HR) are key assets in any organisation (Troshani et al., 2011), to manage HR effectively, almost all the organisations have a human resource management (HRM) department with some form of automation afforded by HRIS.

HRIS is used at all levels in organizations; at a functional level it keeps track of employee's personal and function based information (Harris and Desimone, 1995). The system can help with administrative efficiency which means information will be processed faster, improved employee communication, lower HR costs, greater information accuracy and overall HR productivity improvements (Wiblen et al., 2010). At a strategic level HRIS can change the way in which organizations are managed and improve organizational performance (Katou and Budhwar, 2006). Strategic value from HRIS could be derived by designing and implementing policies and practices that ensure that human assets contribute towards realising organizational goals. Data generated by HRIS could also assist with decision making through HR planning by forecasting workforce demands and therefore a quicker response time to changing competitive landscapes (Lippert and Swiercz, 2005). Further, the regulatory nature of HR means HRIS could assist with meeting some of the regulatory requirements set (Hendrickson, 2004).

HRIS literature on adoption and use in institutions of higher learning has been growing; Samkarpad (2013) investigated individual and group adoption of HRIS in universities and colleges in India. Altarawneh and Al-Shqairat (2010) investigated the adoption of HRIS by Jordanian public universities on how the system is used, some of the benefits and challenges users face when engaging with the system.

HRIS use studies in higher education include the work of Bamel et al. (2014) who surveyed teaching staff's perception about functions, benefits and barriers of HRIS use in India's public universities. Chugh (2014)'s conceptual paper explores the use of HRIS in the Australian higher education sector. Kumar et al. (2015)'s study was based at public universities in Fiji and explored factors such as usefulness, satisfaction and ease of use to test the usability of HRIS by university employees.

This next section discusses the theoretical framework that was used as a lens to studying HRIS adoption and use in a university environment.

3. THEORETICAL FRAMEWORK

Identifying contingency variables is one of the ways of studying IS adoption and use in organizations, these variables often explain adoption and use outcomes in organizations and are categorized into technology, organizational and environment (Tornatzky and Klein, 1982; Troshani et al., 2011). Technology adoption and it's use is considered a complex and context sensitive undertaking, so it's important to understand the context in which the technology will be implemented in, and there's a call in TOE literature to extent this understanding to include HRIS context (Lipper and Swiercz, 2005; Teo et al., 2007).

The technology context is focused on technology influencing the adoption decision (Yang et al., 2007). The decision is usually based on the benefits and gains a potential technology could have for the adopting organization.

The organizational context, describes the organization in terms of characteristics such as size, scope, structure that could inhibit or enable the adoption process (Oliveira and Martins, 2010). Enablers of technology adoption include better change management, top management support, communication, training and a high degree of centralization; inhibitors to adoption include IS complexity, compatibility and legacy systems (Premkumar and Ramamurthy, 1995; Rogers, 2004; Chong and Ooi, 2008). For this study, the organizational context is about understanding the HR environment where the HRIS was adopted and is currently used in a university.

The environmental context is the industry in which the organization conducts its business in; these include competitors and government regulation (Tornatzky et al., 1990). Organizational, technological and environmental factors present opportunities or inhibitors of technology adoption and use in organizations; hence the importance of this framework as a lens for analyzing HRIS adoption and use, as it focuses on the environment in which the organization conducts business in. The section that follows describes the context in which the university operates from.

4. HIGHER EDUCATION SECTOR IN SOUTH AFRICA

According to the council of higher education report (CHE, 2014) universities play an important role in society and can be considered social institutions that produce the people who collectively act as catalysts for social change and necessary skills for the sustainability and growth of any economy. Because of their social and economic importance; they are subject to many forces – social, political and economic, whether international or local – to which they are slowly responsive to, and simultaneously they lead the way to imagining and enacting new futures.

According to a report released by Council of Higher Education (CHE, 2014) as of 2011, South African contact Universities had over 600 000 students, and just above 65 000 staff members with the University of South Africa a distance education provider with just above 300 000 students.

Universities are under increasing pressure as the student population continues to grow rapidly (HESA report, 2011). This growth in turn puts added load on the personnel in such institutions. The added pressure also means universities have to attract and retain skilled, knowledgeable people to address the demand. Higher education South Africa (HESA report, 2014) details some major characteristics of higher education in South Africa and are summarised as:

Student access, opportunity and success: Expansion and greater equity, low participation, high attrition and low completion rates

The number of university students was just above 1 million in 2014, almost double the student population in 1993. As student access to universities increase; there should also be a focus on improving student performance and quality of education.

Research and postgraduate education: expansion and greater equity, low participation and graduations, and possible stasis

Postgraduate student enrolment and research output remain low in relation to national economic and development needs. An impediment to improving the situation is the fact that only 34% of academics have doctoral degrees which is a necessity for quality research and supervision.

Epistemological transformation: critical issue yet poor progress

Social inclusion and exclusion in SA higher education extends well beyond the issues of institutional and academic culture; it's also about engaging in epistemological and ontological issue associated with teaching and learning, curriculum reform and pedagogical practice.

Securing the next generations of academics: strong consensus, clear development programme

The substantive growth of the student population in higher education and the establishment of new universities mean that a larger academic force is required. This coupled with the challenge of transforming the historical social composition through redress and equity. This could be achieved by ensuring there's an agreement and commitment to transformation objectives, clear plans on how that will be carried out.

The higher education institutional landscape: de facto differentiation and diversity yet not fully settled policy

The previous made up of the higher education landscape meant differentiation which was accompanied by a set of conditions related to academic programmes, knowledge production, staff qualifications, student access, opportunities and quality, infrastructure, funding and geographical location which are mostly urban. With the aim of having institutions of higher learning needed to meet the goals of a transformed higher education system.

The challenge of funding of Higher Education

The increased student enrolment means an added pressure to resources in higher education, currently; government is the biggest funder of higher education in South Africa, followed by tuition fees and another third stream income (donations, research grants etc.). The department of higher education and training (DHET) as a government department is the biggest funder of universities and other institutions of public higher education in South Africa, the department spent 26 Billion Rands in 2013, up from 11 Billion Rands in 2013. Besides funding higher education; the department acts as a regulator and an accreditation body for universities, therefore becoming one of the most relevant stakeholders in universities.

These characteristics of higher education in South Africa influence how universities conduct themselves, the decisions taken by management and how employees go about their daily tasks; all these make what universities are in South Africa and have a significant influence on how HRIS is adopted and used.

5. CASE DESCRIPTION

The paper is about a university in South Africa; the University of the Witwatersrand and it considers itself a "research intensive university located in the heart of Johannesburg, a dynamic metropolitan, world-class African city with over 33 000 students, with a third as postgraduates". The university has over 6500 staff members; with 4 700 as academics, with slightly over 1700 who are full time and over 300 internationals. Admin and support staff are just above 1500 and other staff just above 350 (Wits annual report, 2015:5).

Besides generating wealth, allocating resources and using business systems to support the university; the environment is further characterized by scholarship and intellectual leadership skills which are no longer sufficient for running higher education institutions. Efficient management is more important with technology supporting students and staff alike. These are some of the environmental considerations for the strategic objectives of the university, with most relying on technology to enable some of these activities. So it is imperative to understand the environment in which the HRIS was adopted and is used into.

6. METHODOLOGY

HRIS at Wits University was implemented as part of an enterprise resource planning (ERP) system and an Oracle ERP was chosen for this purpose. The adoption happened in 2005 just after the merger of some higher institutions in South Africa, although Wits University did not merge with any institution; there were a lot of changes in the higher education environment that influenced how things will happen moving forward. Oracle provides a software base that looks at the entire organization, finance, HR, payroll, a student system as well within the university and replaced some legacy systems that were in use but not integrated.

The research is interpretive by nature which guided the research design and methodology. A case study strategy of a South African university was adopted using interviews, documents and observations as data collection techniques. Theoretical purposive sampling of top management, middle management and HR personnel were sampled specifically for their knowledge and experiences of HRIS adoption and use within the university; top management defines policies that define the HR department, middle management enforce the policies and HR personnel are operational employees who are in the HR department. Interviews were analyzed using thematic analysis and documents analyzed using content analysis.

7. ANALYSIS AND INTERPRETATION OF FINDINGS

A number of themes emerged from the analysis of the interviews conducted; these themes are indicative of the type of environment in which HRIS was implemented and used into. The interviews were transcribed, analyzed and presented by with a participant's quote and its interpretation.

7.1 Complex Environment (Different Types of Employees)

A university is a complex environment as expressed by one of the participants. Despite the complexity nature of the environment; the university must still find a way to work around such complexities so as to continue with the order of the day.

"*the university context is very complex because we've got visiting professors, permanents, temporaries, sessionals, joint staff between departments, there's a lot of different person types, all of those people have to be loaded on the HR system*"

The statement above references the type of employees that exist in the university and how these will have to be accommodated; visiting professors, permanents, sessionals (who work during certain periods of the academic calendar), joint staff between departments etc. This type of differences influence the way HR does things and that in turn defines how HRIS must accommodate the differences.

"*And people always ask is why there are so many administrators and few academics, shouldn't it be the other way around? But some of these administrators provide academic support. In order for you to be an academic you need the support. And that's how the system in terms of budget, subsidy is set up and that's how we're set up because DHET can raise concerns to say, there's too many people in these areas. So there's intelligence around that sort of reporting and the data that comes out of the HR side.*"

HR in universities is set up in a way that there's more support staff and few academics; although Wits University is set up that there are more academics, the number of permanent academics is far lower than that of permanent admin staff. This is of concern as a university needs more teaching staff than support staff, but the argument is that academic staff needs support staff to complete their academic duties. This setup is approved and verified by the department of higher education and training (DHET), who are the major funders and regulators of higher education in South Africa.

7.2 HR as a Point of Truth

The importance of HR within the university is highlighted by the statement that HR is a point of truth or the heart of the system. The statement cements the fact that in order for the university to move forward, precautions must be taken in ensuring that employees are well taken care of.

"*HR is regarded as a point of truth; the heart of the system, if you look at any financial statement, the biggest cost component is your staff always*"

The statement above describes how important HR is in the university as a heart or point of truth, where it all begins and ends. From HR personnel who ensure that the right people are recruited and timeously to the academics who ensure that academic activity takes place and management who make the necessary strategic decisions.

7.3 HR as Culture Specific

National culture often influences organizational culture, because of the regulatory nature of HR it means laws and regulations passed at national level influence how organizations conduct their HR. Often regulations and laws are enforced and universities have no choice but to follow as there's always consequences for noncompliance.

"*...HR is culture specific, and if for instance in SA you have so many laws that govern labor relations, that has become a culture from which HR progresses...forgetting that the laws of the country might also be inhibiting... investors do not have the confidence in our labor law system*"

The country's labor laws dictate how organizations, including universities, conduct HR and that becomes the HR culture as a result, and this means it's difficult for HR to grow from any other point because of the constant changes in labor regulations and laws and compliance to these laws.

7.4 HR as Legal Compliance

Compliance is important as it's about following labor laws and regulations of the country, other compliances include information on Tax, compensation and benefits compliance. This ensures that employees are protected from misuse and conditions of service are adhered to by the employee.

"...the traditional role had been to ensure that there's legal compliance because everybody is employed according to some law, ranging from immigration to labor law, conditions of service, there needs to be compliance so that you have a peaceful workplace"

Because of labour laws in place to protect employees in the county, HR and HR systems assist in making sure that there are procedures and rules are followed when hiring and dismissing employees in universities and other HR related activities while in employment.

8. DISCUSSION

Despite the insufficient literature describing university contexts where information systems such as HRIS are adopted and used; Bollou and Ngwenyama (2008) discuss the importance of ICT within an African context and how ICT investments have been prioritized over other pressing human needs. To this point, it is imperative to understand contexts in which such investments are adopted and used into. Wits University is a complex environment with its own history and ways of doing things; such organizational characteristics should always be accommodated when planning to adopt information systems such as HRIS. HR as a point of truth or the heart of the system is about the view that HR is the center of it all or it could be interpreted that the HR system is at the heart of the ERP in the university, feeding information into the other university systems; where it all starts.

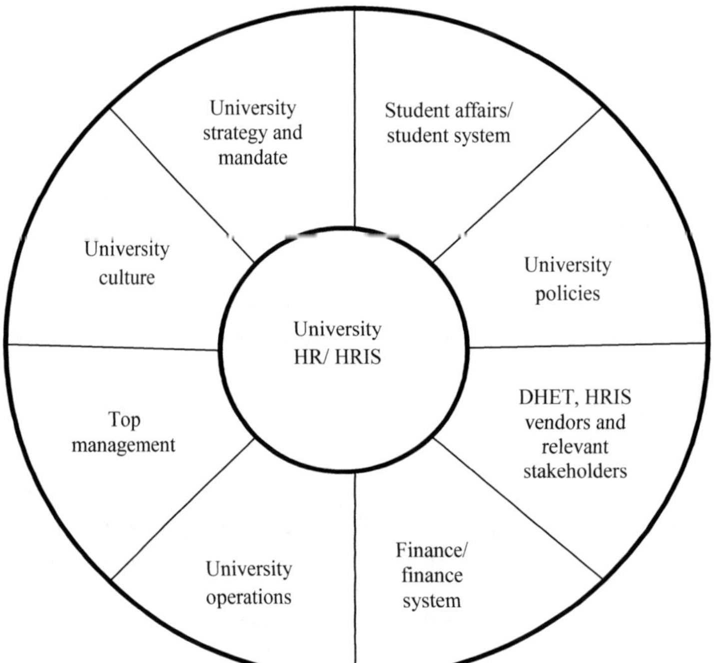

Figure 1. Framework for HRIS Adoption and Use in a University Environment

Figure 1 depicts a framework for HRIS adoption and use in a university environment and highlights HR or HRIS as the heart of the system or the point of truth at the centre of the entire university ERP. HRIS or HR environment is influenced by policies that the university modifies or creates; these could be HR, ICT or other university policies. The student system at undergraduate level keeps track of academic employees and the modules that they're linked to with the students registered in that module and at postgraduate level the system keeps track of supervisors and their students, often communicating things that are happening at the university. The university strategy is about ensuring HRIS enables the university's strategies and mandates; that is, HR personnel, decision makers and overall university staff to assist in realizing those objectives. The university culture is influenced by the national culture, because HR is culture specific, the university has its norms and values that influence how its employees behave. Top management decision bodies in universities are often made up of council and its members; the decisions that they take have a bearing on the HRIS adoption and use. University operations and how the university conducts its business and how they interact with other stakeholders such as DHET, HRIS vendors etc., influence HRIS adoption and use decisions.

9. CONCLUSION

Within the university HR or HRIS is acknowledged as a point of truth or the heart or the center of the ERP; this shapes the environment in which it is adopted and used in. The environment is acknowledged to be influenced by internal and external variables; internal variable include university policies, ICT related matters, the university goals and objectives, management decisions and culture. Externally, stakeholders such as DHET, HR professional bodies and labor laws influence HR within universities. HR environment in universities is geared more towards compliance and for reporting to funders such as DHET. When adopting and using systems such HRIS top management must be aware of the universities' unique nature. The suggested framework on HRIS adoption and use in university environments takes cognizant of environmental variables in a South African university.

The themes identified in this research can be further examined in the context of another higher education institution in other countries or South Africa. Additionally each of the themes identified can be explored in more detail or more contextual variables added to understand higher educational HR environments or the empirical findings interpreted differently.

REFERENCES

Altarawneh, I., & Al-Shqairat, Z. (2010). Human resource information systems in Jordanian universities. *International Journal of Business and Management*, *5*(10), 113.

Bamel, N., Kumar Bamel, U., Sahay, V., & Thite, M. (2014). Usage, benefits and barriers of human resource information system in universities. *VINE: The journal of information and knowledge management systems*, *44*(4), 519-536.

Bondarouk, T.V., Ruel, H.J.M., & Van Der Heijden, B. (2009). E-HRM effectiveness in a public sector organization: a multi-stakeholder perspective. *International Journal of Human Resource Management*, 20(3), 578-590

Bollou, F., & Ngwenyama, O. (2008). Are ICT investments paying off in Africa? An analysis of total factor productivity in six West African countries from 1995 to 2002. *Information Technology for Development*, *14*(4), 294-307.

Chong, A. Y-L, & Ooi, K. B. (2008). Adoption of interorganizational system standards in supply chains: an empirical analysis of RosettaNet standards. *Industrial Management & Data Systems*, *108*(4), 529-547.

Chugh, R. (2014). Role of human resource information systems in an educational organization. *Journal of Advanced Management Science Vol*, *2*(2).

Council of Higher Education, (2014). Annual report. Available online at http://www.che.ac.za/sites/default/files/publications/CHE%20Annual%20Report%202015_16.pdf. Accessed 20 October 2016

Harris, D. M. & Desimone, R. L. (1995). *Human resource development*. TX: Dryden Press, Forth Worth.

Higher Education South Africa (HESA). (2011). *A generation of growth: Proposal for a national programme to develop the next generation of academics for South African higher education*. Available online http://www.hesa.org.za/sites/hesa.org.za/files/2011-%20HESA%20Building%20the%20Next%20Generation%20of%20Academics.pdf. Accessed 22 October 2014

Higher Education South Africa. (2014). South African *Higher education in the 20th years of democracy: context, achievements and key challenges*. Available online at http://www.dhet.gov.za/summit/Docs/2010Docs/HESA_Portfolio%20Committee%20Presentation_5%20March%202014_Final%20(1).pdf. Accessed 14 May 2015.

Hussain., Z., Wallace, J., Cornelius N.(2007). The use and impact of human resource information systems on human resource management professionals. Information and Management, 44, 74-89

Kassim, N.M.D., Ramayah, T., & Kurnia, S. (2012). Antecedents and outcomes of human resource information systems use. *International Journal of Productivity and Performance Management*, 61(6), 603-623

Katou, A. A., & Budhwar, P. S. (2006). Human resource management systems and organizational performance: a test of a mediating model in the Greek manufacturing context. *The international journal of human resource management*, *17*(7), 1223-1253.

Kumar, B. A., Kumar, I., & Hussein, S. (2015). Usability Study of Online Human Resource Information Systems at Fiji National University: A Case Study. *Asian Journal of Information Technology*, *14*(1), 42-48.

Lippert, S. K., & Swiercz, P. M. (2005). Human resource information systems (HRIS) and technology trust. *Journal of information science*, *31*(5), 340-353.

Oliveira, T., & Martins, M. F. (2010, September). Information technology adoption models at firm level: review of literature. In *European Conference on Information Management and Evaluation* (p. 312). Academic Conferences International Limited.

Premkumar, G., & Ramamurthy, K. (1995). The role of interorganizational and organizational factors on the decision mode for adoption of interorganizational systems. *Decision sciences*, *26*(3), 303-336.

Rogers, E. M. (2004). A prospective and retrospective look at the diffusion model. *Journal of health communication*, *9*(S1), 13-19.

Samkarpad, S. (2013). Status of Human Resource Information Systems (HRIS) in Universities and Affiliated Colleges in Hyderabad. *IUP Journal of Organizational Behavior*, *12*(2), 20.

Strohmeier, S. (2007). Research in e-HRM: Review and implications. Human Resource Management Review, 17 (1), 19-37

Tansley, C., Newell, S., & Williams, H. (2001). Effecting HRM-style practices through an integrated human resource information system: An e-greenfield site?. *Personnel Review*, *30*(3), 351-371.

Teo, T. S., Lim, G. S., & Fedric, S. A. (2007). The adoption and diffusion of human resources information systems in Singapore. *Asia Pacific Journal of Human Resources*, *45*(1), 44-62.

Tornatzky, L. G., Fleischer, M., & Chakrabarti, A. K. (1990). *Processes of technological innovation*. Lexington Books.

Tornatzky, L. G., & Klein, K. J. (1982). Innovation characteristics and innovation adoption-implementation: A meta-analysis of findings. *IEEE Transactions on engineering management*, (1), 28-45.

Troshani, I., Jerram, C., & Rao Hill, S. (2011). Exploring the public sector adoption of HRIS. *Industrial Management & Data Systems*, *111*(3), 470-488.

Ulrich, D. (1997). Human Resource Champions: The next agenda for adding value and delivery results. *Harvard Business School Press, Boston*, 24.

Waring, T., & Skoumpopoulou, D. (2012). An enterprise resource planning system innovation and its influence on organisational culture: a case study in higher education. *Prometheus*, *30*(4), 427-447.

Wiblen, S., Dery, K., & Grant, D. (2010). Transitioning From a Proprietary to Vanilla HRIS: The Resulting Implications for Talent. *Proceedings of the 3rd European Academic Workshop on Electronic Human Resource Management*, Bamberg, Germany, May 20-21.

Wits annual report (2015). Available online at https://www.wits.ac.za/media/wits-university/students/academic-matters/documents/2015%20Ann%20Report%20Online%20Version.pdf. Accessed 15 November 2016

Yang, H. K., Lee, S. M., & Lee, S. G. (2007). Adoption of information and communication technology: impact of technology types, organization resources and management style. *Industrial Management & Data Systems*,*107*(9), 1257-1275.

A MODEL FOR MEASURING THE IMPACT OF ENTERPRISE RESOURCE PLANNING (ERP) SYSTEMS ON ORGANIZATIONAL PERFORMANCE

Paweena Wanchai
Department of Computer Science, Faculty of Science, Khon Kaen University, Khon Kaen, Thailand

ABSTRACT

Enterprise resource planning (ERP) systems are believed to produce operational improvements and sustained competitive advantage. However, multiple studies reveal contradictory results as to whether such expected benefits have materialized. The aim of this research is to propose a theoretically well-grounded method for measuring the long term impact, and benefits from ERP systems implementation. The theory and the method are discussed and tested in the context of organizations in Thailand. This research leverages three fundamental specifications for the examination of impacts as follows: performance ratios, labor productivity (production function), and stock market valuation (Tobin's Q). Financial data were extracted for one year prior ERP systems implementation, and four years post-implementation, for a total of five years of financial data. The analysis suggests that 1) ERP systems do not have a significant effect on firm performance even after four years of implementation and 2) the specific modules implemented do not make a substantial difference to firm performance either. This study adds value to the knowledge base by helping understand the impact that ERP systems have on organizational performance.

KEYWORDS

ERP System, ERP Implementation, Business Performance, Organizational Performance, Developing Country

1. INTRODUCTION

The goal of ERP implementation is to enhance organizational effectiveness and to produce operational improvements. ERP systems have been viewed as effective information technology (IT) investments having the potential to optimize the contribution of profit maximization factors in organizations. Despite the huge costs associated with ERP implementation and use, empirical evidence supporting the view that investments in ERP systems enhance firm performance has been elusive. The academic research focusing on the relationship between ERP systems as large scale enterprise-wide IT systems and firm performance produce mixed findings (Nicolaou, 2004, Hunton et al., 2003, Matolcsy et al., 2005, Dwivedi et al., 2009, Ahmed and Ayman, 2011, Velcu, 2007, Hitt and DJ Wu, 2002). Some studies have indicated a positive impact from ERP investments while other studies have shown a negative impact. The mechanisms through which ERP systems impact productivity and hence profitability, appear to remain least understood. Implementing ERP systems is a large and complex undertaking. ERP systems take considerable time to implement and, depending on the scale and complexity of a business, might take from three to five years (Nicolaou, 2004). Studies on the impact of ERP investments also indicate a two-to-five year delay in seeing benefits and suggest measuring benefits after three years (Nicolaou, 2004, Poston and Grabski, 2001). Moreover, the platform nature of ERP systems which suggests that while base ERP systems can provide an integration of internal systems, it may not provide benefits unless customized and business specific add-on modules are implemented. Some modules, such as those for finance and accounting, are adopted by almost all organizations. In some cases, organizations choose not to implement a module because they already have a system or proprietary software for that particular role. Previous research notes that the scope of ERP systems affects its implementation (Nicolaou, 2004). However, ERP scope has not been researched heavily and needs further exploration.

How to evaluate the value of ERP systems to an organization becomes a critical issue, especially given the increasingly important role of ERP systems in today's business world. In order to assess more accurately the impact of ERP investments on organizations, it is also necessary to employ proper measures for various variables over a long period. Other questions include: How long does it take for ERP systems spending to lead to performance improvement? Answers to these questions can facilitate an understanding of the true value of ERP systems and help managers to reap the full benefits of such investments. The goal of this study is to propose a theoretically well-grounded method for measuring the long term impact and benefits from ERP systems. The theory and the method are discussed and tested in the context of organizations in Thailand. The main research questions for this study are:

1. How do ERP implementation and use affect the long-term performance of an organization?
2. How does the scope of ERP implementation affect performance of an organization?

2. LITERATURE REVIEW

Impact of ERP systems on organizational performance

Even though ERP systems have been widely used for decades, there remains lack of research on the impact of ERP systems on organizational performance. The inconsistencies observed among various studies investigating the relationship between ERP investments and organizational performance have been attributed to variation in methods, measures used in the investigates and levels of analysis (Morris, 2011, Ahmed and Ayman, 2011, Annamalai and Ramayah, 2011, Madapusi and D'Souza, 2012, Hwang and Min, 2013, Tenhiälä and Helkiö, 2015, Shen et al., 2016, Galy and Sauceda, 2014, Egdair et al., 2015). Some studies report a positive impact from ERP system implementation while other studies report a negative impact (Cao et al., 2013, Zhu et al., 2010). Such studies utilized various theories and methods for data collection and analysis including productions functions, economic theories and traditional accounting models. Still others have used survey data or field studies to assess operational and intangible gains, including user satisfaction (Dwivedi et al., 2009, Velcu, 2007, Ahmed and Ayman, 2011). Unfortunately, much of this research was executed without a strong underlying theory. Such limitation for lack of a strong theoretical base undermined the results, and highlighted the need to utilize a strong theoretical development and a rigorous research design (Grabski et al., 2011).

Performance measurement

A diversity of methods, drawing from different theories, informed prior work on assessing benefits due to IT investments. Some of these studies have used traditional financial performance measures such as return on sales (ROS), return on assets (ROA), return on investments (ROI), cost of goods sold over sales (CGSS), and a production function to assess the impact of IT investments (Bharadwaj, 2000, Short et al., 2007, Bhatt and Grover, 2005). ROA and ROI measured return on invested capital. ROS measured profitability; CGSS measured cost. Researchers have also made the case for the use of market or value-based measures and have argued that these measures are better indicators of firm performance than the financial or accounting measures. The most popular measures in this category are stock market returns, earnings per share, and Tobin's Q. Tobin's Q is defined as the ratio of the market value of the firm and the replacement value of the firm's assets (book value). Various methods have been proposed for calculating Tobin's Q. Chung and Pruitt (1994) proposed a method, which computes an approximation of the theoretically more accurate Tobin's Q values, by using readily available basic financial and accounting data, which is computed with the formula in (1).

$$\text{Tobin's Q} = \frac{(MVE+PS+DEBT)}{TA} \quad (1)$$

Where:
MVE = (Closing price of share at the end of fiscal year) * (Common shares outstanding)
PS = Liquidating value of the firm's outstanding preferred stock
DEBT = (Current liabilities - Current assets) + (Book value of inventories) + (Long term debt)
TA = Book value of total assets

Overall, the current literature uses different notions of value, ignores the long run versus short run issues in measurement, and the fundamentally platform and option creating nature of ERP-type investments. This research employs multiple measures of performance, namely, ROA, ROI, ROS, CGSS, labor productivity, and Tobin's Q, in a longitudinal analysis. Multiple measures offer the advantages of data triangulation that include the reduction of measurement errors and improved construct validity. By employing a longitudinal data analysis format, this research focuses on changes in performance while abstracting from the absolute level of performance, thus controlling time invariant errors.

3. THEORETICAL FRAMEWORK AND HYPOTHESES

The research model for this study is presented below, in Figure 1, and shows the proposed theoretical framework for this study, including relationships. The framework includes independent and dependent variables. Dependent variables were affected by two independent variables, which correspond to ERP implementation, and ERP modules implemented.

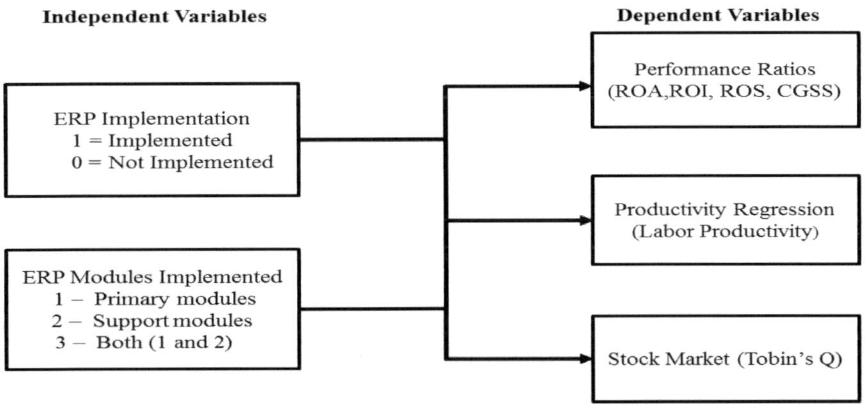

Figure 1. Schematic Diagram for the Research Model

Independent variables

The first independent variable, ERP implementation, represented the segregation of enterprises that have implemented ERP, from the ones that did not implemented an ERP solution. The second independent variable, ERP modules implemented, classified enterprises base on the type of modules implemented. The ERP modules implemented variable utilized three categories, to characterize enterprises base on modules that are put into service as follows: 1) implemented primary modules only which support supply chain activities, and include all modules with the exception of human resources and financials modules, 2) implemented support modules only, which are the ones for human resources and financials, and 3) implemented all modules including primary and support modules. Degree or scope of implementation for this study depends on whether primary or support modules were implemented. In this study, performance of organizations that have implemented primary modules, support modules, and both primary and support modules were compared. For this research, ERP implementation status has a nominal scale. Either an organization has implemented ERP system, which is considered a value of 1, or otherwise, which is considered a value of 0. ERP scope also has a nominal scale as either an organization has implemented primary modules only, which is considered level 1, support modules only, which is level 2, or both primary and support modules, which is level 3.

Dependent variables

This study utilized various performance measures, which were characterized by ratios based on input from the financial statement of each organization in scope. The first dependent variables in this study represented financial performance and included ROA, ROI, ROS, and CGSS. The second dependent variable revolved around productivity, specifically labor productivity (LP), and represented how productive employees were in the event of ERP implementation for the enterprise, and it was calculated by dividing total sales by the number of employees. High ratio indicates more productivity per employee. ERP implementation is expected to increase the LP ratio; hence, improved employee productivity would be expected. Finally the last dependent variable was the stock market valuation which offered a practical long term view of the productivity variable discussed above; the expectation was to experience significant increases in market valuation as a result of ERP implementation. Stock market valuation was interpreted as the future gains and the mitigation of all ERP implementation risks. Such computation, for stock market valuation took the form of the Tobin's Q ratio, market value / book value, where high ratios showed high market rewards. Table 1 below delivers summary for definitions for the measurement variables in scope for this research.

Table 1. Summary - Performance Measurement Variables

Performance Variables	Definitions
Return on Asset (ROA)	Net income, divided by total assets, multiplied by 100
Return on Investments(ROI)	Net income, divided by total invested capital, multiplied by 100
Return on Sales (ROS)	Net income, divided by net sales, multiplied by 100
Cost of Goods Sold divided by Sales (CGSS)	All costs directly allocated by the company to production, divided by net sales, multiplied by 100
Labor Productivity (LP)	Sales , divided by number of employees
Tobin's Q	(MVE+PS+DEBT)/TA

Hypotheses

As discussed in the previous section, the two independent variables, which include ERP implementation status and ERP scope, contribute to organizational performance. In this section, two hypotheses based on the foregoing discussion are stated. In assessing the impact of ERP implementations on organizational performance, it was assumed that the direct impact of ERP systems, which includes data and process integration and streamlining of operations, would eventually influence an organization's financial performance. Based on the theoretical framework proposal for this study, organizations that have implemented ERP systems should exhibit improved performance from ERP implementation; specifically, organizations that implemented ERP systems should differentiate on the productivity improvements from ERP implementation (Hitt et. al 2002). Hence, it was expected to see improvements in performance on organizations that implemented ERP systems, and the first hypothesis for this study was as follows:

H1: ERP implementation affects organizational performance positively when measured by financial performance ratios analysis, productivity regressions, and stock market valuation.

Previous researches revealed that the scope of ERP systems highly affects its implement (Hitt and DJ Wu, 2002). Nicolaou (2004) noted that firms that enabled support modules only (i.e. financials and human resources), had better performance when compare to those that enabled only primary modules (i.e. all other modules) as indicated by the performance ratios for cost of goods sold over sales. Additionally, the study by Nicolaou (2004) exhibited lower performance for firms that adopted primary and support modules, when compared to ones that implemented support modules only, as indicated by the performance ratio for return on assets. Clearly, as indicated by previous research, ERP modules implemented has a significant impact on performance. Hence, the second hypothesis was as follows:

H2: The scope of ERP modules implemented has impact on organizational performance for organizations that have implemented ERP.

4. RESEARCH METHODOLOGY

This study followed Hitt et al. (2002), for formulas and estimated regression of multiple financial performance ratios, and used the general estimation equation below for productivity of ERP systems.

$$\log(\text{performance ratio numerator}) = \text{intercept} + \log(\text{performance ratio denominator}) + \text{adoption variables} + \text{year controls} + \text{industry controls} + \varepsilon$$

For the estimation regression exercise, this study compared multiple performance ratios to capture different characteristic of organizational performance. Furthermore, the study took into account dummy variables to capture transitory, economy-wide shocks that would impact organizational performance. Additionally, the study also controlled for industry to remove deviation on performance ratios, due to industry specific eccentric characteristics. The primary advantage of using such financial performance ratio analysis was the ability to capture multiple aspects to assess organizational performance. On the other hand, the primary disadvantage was that such model specification lacks a sound theoretical approach; hence, should be infer as a correlation, and not estimations of a strong econometric model. To negate such limitation, this study used two other approaches: productivity regression and Tobin's Q analysis.

Productivity regressions follow the fundamental theory production function, and such theory assumes firms have a production process defined by a functional form of f(*), and such function relates outputs to the capital (value added, which is sales minus materials, designated as VA) and labor input variables (capital, K; labor, L). The Cobb-Douglas function is the commonly used functional form for the production function (Hitt and DJ Wu, 2002). In such equation, the intercept variable in a log-log regression has a unique rationalization, and is fundamentally a ratio of output to an index of inputs an organization would consume. Furthermore, to capture disparity in performance, other variables can be included to the Cobb-Douglas production function equation, in its log-log form whose coefficients represent productivity differences as a percentage, and yields the following estimation equation for productivity regressions.

$$\log VA = \text{intercept} + \text{adoption variable} + a_1 \log K + a_2 \log L + \text{year controls} + \text{industry controls} + \varepsilon$$

ERP implementation, would translate into value added; hence, informed investors would estimate such value, and the stock market will reflect such valuation as a result of ERP systems. Furthermore such investor valuation would include intangible benefits from ERP implementation, otherwise not capture using the production function approach, and one could argue that such approach for market value would better represent the total benefit of ERP systems. This research used the Tobin's Q analysis to capture such investor valuation, and adopts a simplified equation to correlate the market value of the organization, to the assets in use. Additionally, the general Tobin's Q equation form for this study included variables to represent shifts in market value as a result of ERP systems, to include time and industry dummy variables, as indicated in the equation below.

$$\log(\text{market value}) = \text{intercept} + \text{adoption variable} + a_1 \log(\text{book value}) + a_2 \text{ IT capital} + \text{years dummies} + \text{industry dummies} + \varepsilon$$

All three approaches for analysis, in scope for this research, represented the benefits organizations would realize, over a wide variety of sample organizations. Hence, one would have to assume, that not all implementation projects were successful, and others would surpass expectations. Consequently, the results represent an average across multiple sample organizations, and one should be conscious about variances for individual firms, as the results represent the sample average value only. The sample was 20 organizations in Thailand that implemented ERP systems. Financial performance indicators were extracted from the COMPUSTAT database and Datastream database, one year prior to ERP implementation, and four years after implementation, for a total of five years of financial data.

5. HYPOTHESIS TESTING AND RESULTS

The first statistical model will test for the impact of ERP implementation on firm performance as measured by financial ratios after controlling for other variables. The specific functional form to be used is as follows:

$$(R_t - R_0) = \beta_0 + \beta \text{ Module Type} + \varepsilon, \text{ where}$$

R_t = Ratio at time t, R_0 = ratio one year prior to ERP implementation, and Module type refers to the type of modules installed.

The specification examines the relationship between change in the value of a financial ratio at time t ($R_t - R_0$) and the type of module implemented at t=0. Module type is a categorical variable and is coded as -1 for primary modules, 0 for support modules and 1 for all modules. For each ratio, the regression is repeated for 4 years past the date of implementation (i.e., using change in R_1, R_2, R_3 and R_4 with respect to R_0). This allows one to conclude whether the change in ratio in period t is explained by the module type. Thus, it tests the hypothesis that ERP implementation leads to benefit realization some years after implementation.

A consistent procedure was designed for examining several financial ratios of interest. In the first step, a specific financial ratio was chosen for analysis. In a second step, the descriptive statistics for the ratio were examined and observations falling outside +/- three standard deviations were removed from analysis, since they could be potential outliers. Third, a regression was performed for changes in ratio for each year compared to the base year (i.e., R_4-R_0, R_3-R_0, R_2-R_0 and R_1-R_0) with the module type as a dependent variable.

Illustration using performance ratios

The analysis was using performance ratios include ROA, ROI, ROS and CGSS as the dependent variable. Descriptive statistics were presented for the final sample of 20 organizations in Table 2 below. The estimated models were presented in Table 3.

Table 2. Descriptive Statistics for Performance Ratios as Performance Indicator (N=20)

	Mean	Median	Std. Deviation	Minimum	Maximum
ROA_Year_0	1.065	3.622	8.294	-31.807	32.416
ROA_Year_1	-0. 961	3.094	10.911	-36.358	14.674
ROA_Year_2	-1.356	4.320	17.270	-23.455	36.761
ROA_Year_3	0.539	5.319	21.467	-16.210	43.121
ROA_Year_4	0.785	3.727	15.741	-42.583	51.928
ROI _Year_0	2.089	7.501	14.272	-34.642	74.345
ROI _Year_1	1.078	6.575	16.828	-33.813	117.937
ROI _Year_2	-1.656	5.419	21.467	-54.200	33.114
ROI _Year_3	1.533	11.716	16.610	-23.527	53.286
ROI _Year_4	1.940	13.232	61.346	-84.410	71.516
ROS_Year_0	2.897	3.908	11.616	-28.482	48.364
ROS_Year_1	-1.886	3.473	26.429	-82.417	35.468
ROS_Year_2	1.789	72.174	7.924	-52.937	53.436
ROS_Year_3	2.868	5.894	25.590	-139.329	44.168
ROS_Year_4	2.105	3.831	14.246	-57.101	52.822
CGSS _ Year_0	61.547	67.212	18.236	8.258	93.585
CGSS _ Year_1	56.595	60.831	23.456	2.129	95.183
CGSS _ Year_2	53.734	62.539	19.426	12.584	192.877
CGSS _ Year_3	48.283	56.741	24.365	6.018	261.892
CGSS _ Year_4	61.943	63.231	26.023	5.653	139.401

Table 3. Summary with Performance Ratios as Performance Indicator (N=20)

Model	Coefficient for MODULE	p-value	Adjusted R^2
ROA_Y1-Y0 = f(MODULES)	0.018	.72	.03
ROA_Y2-Y0 = f(MODULES)	0.051	.38	.01
ROA_Y3-Y0 = f(MODULES)	0.016	.74	.04
ROA_Y4-Y0 = f(MODULES)	-0.004	.93	.02
ROI _Y1-Y0 = f(MODULES)	-1.471	.52	.03
ROI _Y2-Y0 = f(MODULES)	-7.633	.34	.00
ROI _Y3-Y0 = f(MODULES)	-4.872	.33	.00
ROI _Y4-Y0 = f(MODULES)	4.156	.30	.01
ROS_Y1-Y0 = f(MODULES)	5.628	.16	.03
ROS_Y2-Y0 = f(MODULES)	1.265	.24	.03
ROS_Y3-Y0 = f(MODULES)	1.696	.23	.00
ROS_Y4-Y0 = f(MODULES)	1.265	.73	.01
CGSS _Y1-Y0 = f(MODULES)	3.995	.72	.00
CGSS _Y2-Y0 = f(MODULES)	2.662	.81	.01
CGSS _Y3-Y0 = f(MODULES)	2.939	.97	.00
CGSS _Y4-Y0 = f(MODULES)	2.739	.87	.00

The above table suggests that, when performance ratios were used as performance indicators, ERP implementation did not have a significant effect on performance improvement for the organizations even after four years of implementation. Very low adjusted R-squared suggests that module variable explains almost no variation in performance ratios change.

Analysis using labor productivity (LP) ratio

Analysis was repeated using LP ratio as the dependent variable. Descriptive statistics were presented for the final sample of 20 organizations in Table 4 below. The estimated models were presented in Table 5.

Table 4. Descriptive Statistics for LP Performance Indicator (N=20)

	Mean	Median	Std. Deviation	Minimum	Maximum
LP_Year_0	186.213	121.561	116.312	96.312	221.302
LP_Year_1	95.862	81.624	62.301	46.181	147.234
LP_Year_2	116.314	183.356	157.162	64.974	279.657
LP_Year_3	104.276	153.473	213.354	51.626	320.318
LP_Year_4	192.302	201.152	329.651	, 87.238	310.871

Table 5. Summary with Labor Productivity as Performance Indicator (N=20)

Model	Coefficient for MODULE	p-value	Adjusted R^2
LP_Y1-Y0 = f(MODULES)	-67.438	.51	.02
LP_Y2-Y0 = f(MODULES)	-24.795	.76	.04
LP_Y3-Y0 = f(MODULES)	21.863	.74	.06
LP_Y4-Y0 = f(MODULES)	9.972	.89	.01

The above table suggests that, when labor productivity was used as a performance indicator, ERP implementation had no significant effect on labor productivity. Very low adjusted R-squared also suggests that module variable explains almost no variation in labor productivity change.

Analysis using Tobin's Q ratio

The analysis was repeated using Tobin's Q ratio as the dependent variable. Tobin's Q is defined as the ratio of market value over book value. Descriptive statistics were presented for the final sample of 20 organizations in Table 6 below. The estimated models were presented in Table 7.

Table 6. Descriptive Statistics for Tobin's Q Performance Indicator (N=20)

	Mean	Median	Std. Deviation	Minimum	Maximum
Tobin's Q _Year_0	5.246	3.142	20.521	-16.802	53.232
Tobin's Q _Year_1	2.375	2.521	12.234	-33.670	18.394
Tobin's Q _Year_2	-3.312	2.597	28.106	-84.452	17.619
Tobin's Q _Year_3	-1.319	-2.873	17.652	-72.233	19.355
Tobin's Q _Year_4	4.278	3.923	9.204	-3.029	49.773

Table 7. Summary with Tobin's Q as Performance Indicator (N=20)

Model	Coefficient for MODULE	p-value	Adjusted R^2
Tobin's Q _Y1-Y0 = f(MODULES)	-1.457	.43	.03
Tobin's Q _Y2-Y0 = f(MODULES)	-6.532	.33	.00
Tobin's Q _Y3-Y0 = f(MODULES)	-3.239	.34	.00
Tobin's Q _Y4-Y0 = f(MODULES)	3.122	.30	.01

The above table suggests that, when Tobin's Q was used as a performance indicator, ERP implementation did not have a significant effect on stock market even after four years of implementation. Very low adjusted R-squared suggests that module variable explains almost no variation in Tobin's q change.

The results suggested that the first hypothesis, relating ERP implementation, was not supported as organizations would not exhibit significantly improved performance. Analysis also suggested that the second hypothesis was not supported as implementation of ERP modules did not have a significant effect on any performance measure over a four year period following implementation.

6. CONCLUSIONS

Applying a sound theoretical methodology, this study adds value to the knowledge based by helping comprehend the impact that ERP systems have on organizational performance. To answer the research questions, regressions were executed to depict the ratio change, against the modules implemented. The results revealed that ERP implementation did not affect financial performance of an organization significantly when measured over a four-year post implementation period. Regression analysis was executed to determine the impact of module type implemented. For this exercise, the ratio change was regressed against the module type, which provided the information to determine changes in the ratios as it would have been explained by the module type. The results showed that module selection during ERP implementation did not have a significant effect on financial performance for ERP adopters over a four-year post adoption period. The results from this research contrast to some previous work on ERP which suggests an improvement in a performance measure and similar to other work which did not find a change in performance measure (Cao et al., 2013, Zhu et al., 2010).

There are a number of implications for this research to research and practice. Prior ERP investments studies have inconsistently reported mixed findings on ERP investments and organizational performance, with some arguing for the lack of an appreciable impact on ERP investments and business performance. A number of researchers have consequently called for research that investigates the effect of ERP investments on organizational performance. Research findings from this study, in addition to helping in furthering understanding the role of ERP investments in organizational performance, also justifies the need for ERP investments, and can guide managers while making ERP investment decisions.

The sample selection for this study included only organizations in Thailand. There could be a limitation factor for biased results; as it is only a subset of the entire population of organization that implemented ERP systems. As a result, this limitation would have an impact for the generalizability for the study, since the sample only included a subset of the population. Also, other variables that could have an impact on ERP implementation were not taken into consideration. Variables excluded for this study included organizational context, external microeconomic factors, knowledge of ERP users, training, IT support, quality and size of ERP implemented, vendor quality support, and organizational change management variables, and would need to be addressed in future studies.

REFERENCES

Ahmed, A. and Ayman, M. 2011. The Effect of ERP System Implementation on Business Performance: An Exploratory Case-Study. *Communications of the IBIMA*.

Annamalai, C. and Ramayah, T. 2011. Enterprise resource planning (ERP) benefits survey of Indian manufacturing firms: An empirical analysis of SAP versus Oracle package. *Business Process Management Journal,* 17, 495-509.

Bharadwaj, A. S. 2000. A resource-based perspective on information technology capability and firm performance: an empirical investigation. *MIS Quarterly*, 169-196.

Bhatt, G. D. and Grover, V. 2005. Types of information technology capabilities and their role in competitive advantage: An empirical study. *Journal of Management Information Systems,* 22, 253-277.

Cao, J., Nicolaou, A. I. and Bhattacharya, S. 2013. A longitudinal examination of enterprise resource planning system post-implementation enhancements. *Journal of information systems,* 27, 13-39.

Chung, K. H. and Pruitt, S. W. 1994. A simple approximation of Tobin's q. *Financial management*, 70-74.

Dwivedi, Y. K., Papazafeiropoulo, A. and ESTEVES, J. 2009. A benefits realisation road-map framework for ERP usage in small and medium-sized enterprises. *Journal of Enterprise Information Management,* 22, 25-35.

Egdair, I. M., Rajemi, M. F. and Nadarajan, S. 2015. Technology Factors, ERP System and Organization Performance in Developing Countries. *International Journal of Supply Chain Management,* 4.

Galy, E. and Sauceda, M. J. 2014. Post-implementation practices of ERP systems and their relationship to financial performance. *Information & Management,* 51, 310-319.

Grabski, S. V., LeecH, S. A. and Schmidt, P. J. 2011. A review of ERP research: A future agenda for accounting information systems. *Journal of information systems,* 25, 37-78.

Hitt, L. M. and Wu, D.J, X. Z. 2002. Investment in enterprise resource planning: Business impact and productivity measures. *Journal of Management Information Systems,* 19, 71-98.

Hunton, J. E., Lippincott, B. and RecK, J. L. 2003. Enterprise resource planning systems: comparing firm performance of adopters and nonadopters. *International Journal of Accounting Information Systems,* 4, 165-184.

HwanG, W. and Min, H. 2013. Assessing the impact of ERP on supplier performance. *Industrial Management & Data Systems,* 113, 1025-1047.

Madapusi, A. and D'souza, D. 2012. The influence of ERP system implementation on the operational performance of an organization. *International Journal of Information Management,* 32, 24-34.

Matolcsy, Z. P., Booth, P. and Wieder, B. 2005. Economic benefits of enterprise resource planning systems: some empirical evidence. *Accounting & Finance,* 45, 439-456.

Morris, J. J. 2011. Measuring the impact of enterprise resource planning (ERP) systems on shareholder value. *Review of Business Information Systems (RBIS),* 15.

Nicolaou, A. I. 2004. Firm performance effects in relation to the implementation and use of enterprise resource planning systems. *Journal of information systems,* 18, 79-105.

Poston, R. and Grabski, S. 2001. Financial impacts of enterprise resource planning implementations. *International Journal of Accounting Information Systems,* 2, 271-294.

Shen, Y.-C., Chen, P.-S. and Wang, C.-H. 2016. A study of enterprise resource planning (ERP) system performance measurement using the quantitative balanced scorecard approach. *Computers in Industry,* 75, 127-139.

Short, J. C., Ketchen, D. J., Palmer, T. B. and Hult, G. T. M. 2007. Firm, strategic group, and industry influences on performance. *Strategic Management Journal,* 28, 147-167.

Tenhiälä, A. and Helkiö, P. 2015. Performance effects of using an ERP system for manufacturing planning and control under dynamic market requirements. *Journal of Operations Management,* 36, 147-164.

Velcu, O. 2007. Exploring the effects of ERP systems on organizational performance: Evidence from Finnish companies. *Industrial Management & Data Systems,* 107, 1316-1334.

Zhu, Y., Li, Y., Wang, W. and Chen, J. 2010. What leads to post-implementation success of ERP? An empirical study of the Chinese retail industry. *International Journal of Information Management,* 30, 265-276.

A NEW TOOL OF INVESTMENT ANALYSIS FOR THE DECISION SUPPORT INFORMATION SYSTEM

Yelena Buturlakina
D. Serikbayev East Kazakhstan State Technical University, Ust-Kamenogorsk, the Republic of Kazakhstan

ABSTRACT

This paper deals with a new tool of investment analysis based on prediction of the problem of insufficient funding arising during the implementation phase of investment projects. The numerical results were obtained and compared with the help of artificial neural networks, Kohonen maps, decision trees, and logistic regression. The resulting model allows to identify correctly about 70-80% of the outcomes. The tool developed has been implemented within a decision support system using multi-agent approach and used for the analysis of small hydroelectric plants projects.

KEYWORDS

Decision Making/Process, Decision Support Systems, Forecasting, Risk

1. INTRODUCTION

For investment projects, evaluation is the first and the most important component of the business endeavor. No one can answer with certainty what will happen tomorrow, next week or next year. Moreover, decision makers often must consider much longer time periods. Investors often risk considerable financial resources and thus a desire to minimize this risk is easily understood. Evaluation of investment projects includes the following tasks:

- Evaluation of the financial feasibility of the project;
- Assessment of profitability;
- Identification of boundary conditions for the effective implementation of the project;
- Risk assessment and sustainability of the project.

A variety of standard methodologies and guidelines has been developed for the solution of these problems. However, modern computational tools allow us to apply mathematical modeling techniques for more specific problems. In our study the effectiveness of a variety of analytical techniques is examined to determine the most effective approach for each particular case.

The task is to predict the occurrence of "Lack of funding" problem. According to reports on the implementation of investment projects supported by state funding in the Republic of Kazakhstan, this problem is the most commonly encountered. In case of stable prediction results a new method of investment analysis can be developed and implemented within the decision support system for small and medium-sized businesses.

2. BACKGROUND

In particular, mathematical models are widely used to determine the effectiveness of scientific research, country risk, credit scoring, bankruptcy prediction, stock prices, etc., and can perform well. Therefore, many researchers are applying these methods to solve specific problems, for example, Andriosopoulos et al. (2012) consider the probability of share repurchases, which they believe is an important indicator of company activity and the prospects for its bankruptcy.

The data mining techniques are widely used in a variety of economic research projects. For example, in the above-mentioned paper (Andriosopoulos et al., 2012), the authors used a logistic regression; Psillaki et al. (2010) using the same tool assessed the credit risk of a company on the basis of its activities. Petkova et al. (2011) use logistic regression to prove the relationship between the business reputation of a firm and its willingness to introduce new "clean" technologies.

The structure and learning algorithms of artificial neural networks can vary significantly and, therefore, normally, several different models of neural networks are compared in order to select the most effective ones. Khashman (2010) compares the performance of neural networks with a different number of layers for the assessment of internal credit risk. The Kohonen Self-Organizing Maps (SOM), which is a special type of neural networks, are used by Nakaoka et al. (2005) and Lukyanitsa et al. (2009) for stock price prediction as well as creation of a portfolio with minimal risk. Another example is an assessment of the quality of collective investment decisions (Pham et al., 2011). Chen et al. (2010) use a classification based on Kohonen networks to predict the behavior of companies in terms of their financial activity. Fioretti (2004) studies the investment behavior of companies of different sizes, based on a model built using self-organizing maps.

Decision trees are another popular tool much used for the analysis of investment projects. For example, Pendharkar (2010) defined the effectiveness of IT projects by means of decision trees, Tan et al. (2010) and Munoz et al. (2011) use them to analyze energy production and wind turbines, respectively. Gonzalez-Carrasco et al. (2012) have developed software, based on fuzzy decision trees, to evaluate the credit risks of bank borrowers.

3. PROBLEM FORMULATION

In this study a database of investment projects being implemented in the regions of the Republic of Kazakhstan and funded from the state budget is being used. This database contains information about the title of the project, its timing, the responsible authorities, the projects' costs, the region and the branch of the industry, as well as problems encountered during the implementation of the project. By the time of writing this paper there were 157 available investment projects on the site. The following problems were noted:

- Lack of funding
- Organizational issues
- Lack of infrastructure
- Land purchase
- Lack of resources
- No market
- Other

A project can face several problems (up to 3). There is a description of each problem and proposed measures to address it.

The research aims to create a tool of investment planning, which would allow prediction of the probability of a problem occurrence based on external information about the project. Because only the information about the projects implemented in the Republic of Kazakhstan is used, the resulting financial instrument can be applied for projects planned only in the regions of the Republic of Kazakhstan. However, the procedure used is universal, and can be adapted to any country, if there is the necessary information.

The study is based on the hypothesis that there is a relationship between external indicators of the investment project, ("costs", "region" and "industry branch") and problems during the implementation of the project. If such a relationship is established, the resulting mathematical model will be primarily useful for potential investors. Knowledge up front that the probability of a problem is significantly high, allows the required measures to avoid it to be implemented at the first stage of planning. Also problem patterns can be identified and used to find out and eliminate its cause.

4. PROBLEM SOLUTION

4.1 Data Analysis Techniques

4.1.1 Logistic Regression

Lu et al. (2012) describes logistic regression as the most appropriate tool to determine the relationship between a categorical variable and one or more categorical or continuous variables.

$$y = F(x_1, x_2, \ldots, x_n)$$

Logistic regression differs from common regression by its output values, whose range does not exceed 0 to 1 and can be interpreted as the probability of a particular outcome.

$$P\{x|y\} = \sigma\ (y <x,\omega>),\ y \in Y,$$

where σ is a sigmoid function

$$\sigma(z) = \frac{1}{1+e^{-z}}.$$

In general, if the predicted value is less than 0.5, the result is treated as 0, otherwise as 1. This threshold is also used in this study; the error of identification was set to 0.05.

Since the input signals "Branch" and "Region" are discrete, their normalization has been made and, therefore, each value of the signal corresponds to the factor of the model. Calculated regression coefficients are shown in Table 1.

Table 1. Calculated Logistic Regression Coefficients

Branch		Region	
Agribusiness and food industry	0	Akmola oblast	0
Mining and metallurgical industry	0.0216	Aktobe oblast	-0.6422
Space activities	0.3172	Almaty oblast	-0.0641
Light industry	0.3388	Almaty Sity	-0.6764
Engineering	-0.102	Astana Sity	0.1513
Oil and gas industry	-0.0804	Atyrau oblast	-0.4609
Petrochemistry	0.2152	East Kazakhstan oblast	0.0871
Other	0.2368	Jambyl oblast	-0.5252
Construction industry	0.8841	West-Kazakhstan oblast	0.0153
Transport infrastructure	0.9057	Karaganda oblast	-0.597
Tourism and Sports	1.2014	Kostanay oblast	-0.0489
Pharmaceutics	1.2229	Kyzylorda oblast	-0.6611
Chemical industry	0.7821	Mangistau oblast	0.1665
Energetics	0.8037	Pavlodar oblast	-0.4457
		North-Kazakhstan oblast	0.1023
		South-Kazakhstan oblast	-0.5099

Constant coefficient is equal to -0.41 and “costs” coefficient is 0.0007.

4.1.2 Kohonen Self-Organizing Maps

Chen et al. [10] reported that from 1980, when the first Kohonen self-organizing maps were introduced, to 2000 over 4,300 studies were performed with them. Kohonen [17] defined the Self Organizing Maps as a neural network model that implements a competitive learning strategy. The main difference of self-organizing maps from other clustering methods is the fact that they do not require any additional information about the data. This study uses a field of 16 by 12 hexagonal cells; the error of identification is 0.05.

4.1.3 Decision Trees

A decision tree is a block diagram that uses a branching method to illustrate every possible outcome of a decision. An automatic construction algorithm, which allows two options of branching, was used in the study. The accuracy of detection was chosen here as a priority over the tree compactness. This method was originally designed for categorical data. In the case of continuous input the data are converted into categorical data. For example, in the present case the following rule was obtained: «If the project costs are less than 0,045 billion tenge, the project will likely face the problem «Lack of funding». Thus, the continuous value of the "project costs" was divided into two categorical values, namely, "more than 0,045 billion tenge" and "less than 0,045 billion tenge."

4.1.4 Artificial Neural Networks

Artificial neural networks with back-propagation are the most commonly used and the most carefully crafted forms of neural networks. Jiang [18] showed that 80-90% of the studies involving neural networks use this type.

This study employs a back-propagation neural network of a two-layer perceptron with the sigmoid activation function, nine neurons in the input layer, and a detection error of 0.05. An increase in the number of input layers or neurons did not show any improvement in neural network performance and, thus, the simplest structure has been chosen.

4.2 Methodology

Normally, in such classification studies large sets of training and testing data are used. As the number of projects available for the analysis is not very large, most of the data (141 projects) were used for training (90%), since even a slight increase in the training set (10%) could significantly improve the outcome for some methods. The projects in the training set are selected in order, starting from the beginning of the table. The software allows one to select the data in a random order, but the training set must contain all possible values of the categorical variables while a random selection cannot guarantee it. In addition, the training and test sets should be of similar nature in order to compare the effectiveness of different methods accurately. The remaining 16 (10%) projects were used to test the models.

4.3 Short Description of the Projects Used

Most of the projects are concerned with design, construction, modernization and reconstruction of various civil and industrial structures such as schools, water and gas pipelines, factories, all located within the Republic of Kazakhstan. The projects' costs range from 0.03 billion tenge (100,000 USD) for "The introduction of a drip irrigation in field crop cultivation and the construction of a potato storage" project, to 925 billion tenge (3,000,000 USD) for "The construction of an integrated petrochemical complex" one.

The most common problems encountered during the implementation phase "Lack of funding", "Lack of infrastructure" and "Organizational issues" were selected for the analysis. The projects that required the analysis are labeled as "True", and those without the problem as "False". Input parameters for all the methods are "the project costs" (continuous type), "the oblast" (categorical type) and "the branch" (categorical type).

5. NUMERICAL RESULTS

The problem studied was "Lack of funding" since it is the most commonly encountered one. In fact, 71 (45%) of the projects faced it. Moreover, it is only a problem encountered in 57 projects, while the other 14 projects have additional problems above it. The results of classification are shown in the Table 2.

Table 2. "Lack of Funding" Classification Results

Method	Classification results							
	Historical data (141 projects)				Test data (16 projects)			
	TT[a]	*FF*[b]	*TF*[c]	*FT*[d]	*TT*	*FF*	*TF*	*FT*
Logistic regression	29	61	34	17	2	9	5	0
Kohonen maps	44	71	19	7	5	8	2	1
Neural networks	38	70	25	8	4	8	3	1
Decision tree	16	76	46	2	3	9	4	0

a. TT - true classified true values
b. FF - true classified false values
c. TF - misclassified true values (the error of the 1st type)
d. FT - misclassified false values (the error of the 2nd type)

The diagram in Figure 1 shows the quality of the test sets classification by each of the methods.

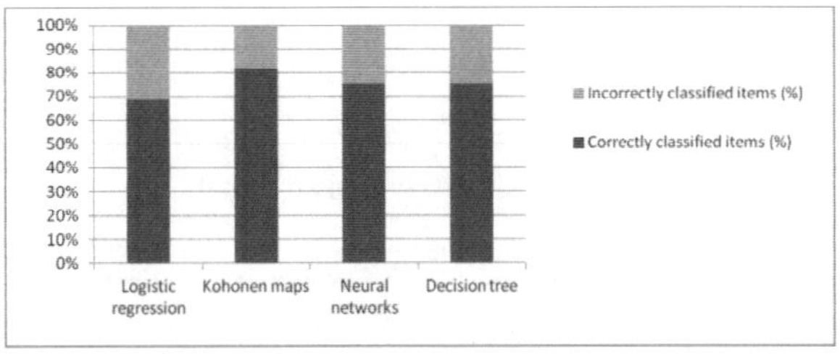

Figure 1. "Lack of Funding" Classification Quality

As may be seen, all the methods show good classification accuracy, - from 70 to 80% of cases were classified correctly. However, besides the proportion of correctly classified items, the selectivity and sensitivity of the method must also be considered. All the methods tend to classify elements as false, that is, the number of incorrectly classified false values is smaller than the number of incorrectly classified true values. However, such an approach can be dangerous in terms of the risk prediction because it is more important to recognize the likelihood of a risk situation and take preventive measures than to deal with the consequences of unrecognized risk. Therefore, in this case sensitivity is an important classification criterion. Methods, if possible, were tuned to maximum sensitivity, for example, the threshold at which the element should be classified as true was lowered.

The Table 2 shows that "Kohonen maps" demonstrate the best sensitivity for the training and the test sets.

6. APPLICATION OF THE RESULTS

Demonstrated results allow to use the classification methods considered in "Lack of funding" problem forecasting for investment projects in the Republic of Kazakhstan. The most useful tool, despite the worst result of the classification, is the method of logistic regression, since it allows to calculate a probability of the problem occurrence. Knowing this probability, the investor can make their own conclusion and make the decision. For example, if the value of the risk to 45% of situation will be evaluated by binary methods as risk-free, however, the likelihood of the problem is still very high and requires more attention. In this case, it is recommended to take into account the results of all considered methods. The decision logic is presented in Figure 2.

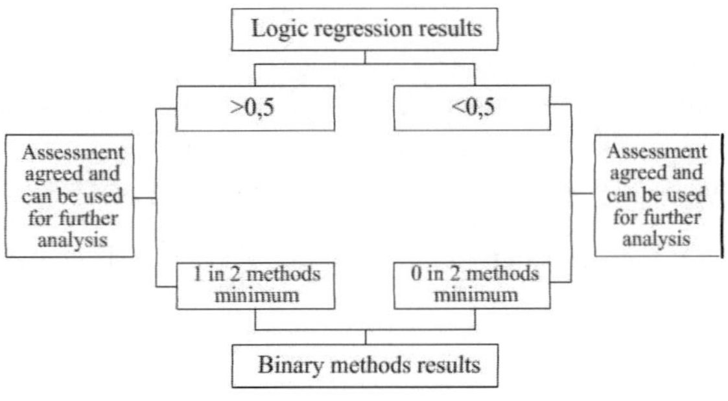

Figure 2. The Decision Logic

This decision logic has been used for assessment of investment projects of small hydro power plants.

The calculation of "Lack of funding" problem probability, i.e. the result of logistic regression, was performed using the following formulas based on the coefficients calculated (Table 1). For all project "Branch" factor is the same and equal to 0.8037, which corresponds to the "Energetic". Thus, the formula for calculating the parameter z in the formula of sigmoid function for the projects in Almaty oblast is the following:

$$z= -0,4192+0,0007*x_1+0,8037*1-0,0641*1,$$

where x_1 is project costs (thousand dollars).

For projects in Zhambyl oblast:

$$z= -0,4192+0,0007*x_1+0,8037*1-0,5252*1.$$

For projects in South Kazakhstan oblast:

$$z= -0,4192+0,0007*x_1+0,8037*1-0,5099*1.$$

For projects of East Kazakhstan region:

$$z= -0,4192+0,0007*x_1+0,8037*1-0,087*1.$$

For a project in Akmola oblast:

$$z= -0,4192+0,0007*x_1+0,8037*1.$$

The initial data of analysis and results of classification are in table 3.

Table 3. The Initial Data and The Classification Results

	Initial data				Forecast			
№	Title	Oblast	Project cost (thous. dollars)	NPV (thous. dollars)	Kohonen Maps	Decision Tree	Neural Network	Logistic Regression
1	Bartorgayskaya	Almaty	20000	64795,95	1	1	1	0,582
2	Bodrevskaya	Almaty	80000	109446,71	1	1	1	0,593
3	Kerbulak	Almaty	100000	2544308,98	1	0	1	0,597
4	Kerbulak 277	Almaty	100000	76054,28	1	0	1	0,597
5	Kyzylkungey	Almaty	181950	118487,69	1	0	1	0,610
6	Maynakskaya	Almaty	120000	586540,67	1	0	1	0,600
7	Toktyshak	Almaty	37000	340265,60	1	0	1	0,586
8	WPP	Akmola	550000	1069167,59	1	1	1	0,685
9	Aksu	Almaty	300000	6083610,20	1	0	1	0,631
10	Aktogay	Almaty	106250	3833298,64	1	0	1	0,598
11	Aktogay 2	Almaty	237500	6103018,18	1	0	1	0,620
12	Aksay	Zhambyl	75000	2360744,01	1	1	1	0,478
13	Balykchy	South Kazakhstan	200000	4310191,72	0	0	1	0,505
14	Vannovsky	South Kazakhstan	75000	1826109,01	0	1	1	0,482
15	Georgievskaya	Zhambyl	187500	8006640,62	1	0	1	0,498
16	Dzhabagly	South Kazakhstan	125000	3650102,09	0	0	1	0,562
17	Kamenskaya	Zhambyl	162500	4489255,54	1	0	1	0,494
18	Karakastekskaya	Almaty	50000	1122708,10	1	0	1	0,588
19	Lugovskaya	Zhambyl	56300	1440296,82	1	1	1	0,475
20	Panfilovskaya	Almaty	100000	1733941,92	1	0	1	0,597
21	Sarytogayskaya	Almaty	87500	1308028,82	1	1	1	0,595
22	Tekesskaya	Almaty	187500	4314531,73	1	0	1	0,612
23	Turgusunsky	East Kazakhstan	106300	3154488,40	0	0	1	0,634

"1" in the table is the forecast of a positive outcome, i.e. "Lack of funding" is inevitable, "0" - a negative outcome - "Lack of funding" is not expected. As it is seen in the forecast columns the most of risk assessments are agreed. Assessments of highlighted projects are not agreed, but in most cases differences in the forecasts do not exceed the statistical error. In general, for such projects risk assessment is carried out by rounding to the maximum, i.e. "Lack of funding" is more likely occurs than not , because from the point of view of investment analysis, the risk of an adverse situation should better be exaggerated rather than downplayed.

Forecasting other problems with an existing training set of projects is not available; however, the result can be improved by increased number of observations. The remaining issues contained in the database are very rare, and their prognosis also required increased number of observations with "true" outcome.

7. SHORT DESCRIPTION OF THE DECISION SUPPORT SYSTEM ARCHITECTURE

An information system based on the multi-agent architecture is the most acceptable for the implementation of the methods described above (Figure 3). A multi-agent system is a system formed by multiple interacting intelligent agents. An intelligent agent is a program able to independently carry out tasks specified by the user, for long periods of time. In given decision support system intelligent tracking agents perform database monitoring and providing updating of mathematical models in case of new data available.

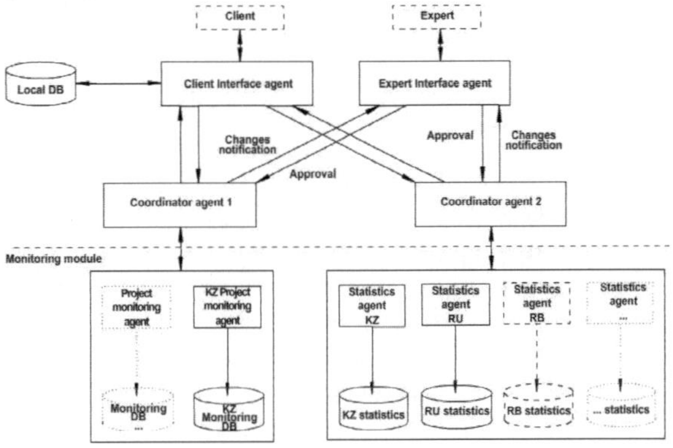

Figure 3. The Decision Support System Architecture

"Client" is a decision support system user – businessman, decision maker or investor interested in investment project assessment. The tool developed is available for the Client through web-based interface of "Client Interface agent".

"Monitoring module" contains "KZ Project monitoring agent" – a monitoring agent observing the database of investment projects. As soon as new data have been added to the database monitoring agent downloads them and sends to "Coordinator agent 1". The algorithm of the further process is shown in Figure 4.

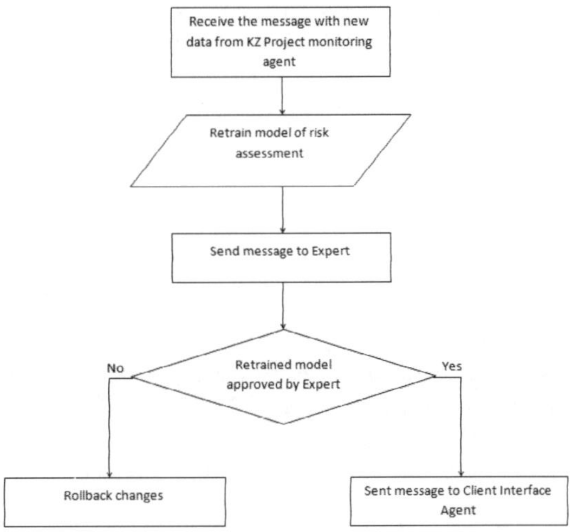

Figure 4. The Flowchart or Retraining Algorithm

As long as new information sources have been created new monitoring agents can be added to "Monitoring module".

8. CONCLUSION

The above study shows the high efficiency of Data Mining methods for predicting the risk of "Lack of funding" problem during the implementation of investment projects in the Republic of Kazakhstan. It can be affirmed that there are some factors that influence the occurrence of this problems depending on the project costs, region and industry type. Despite the small amount of training set the results obtained are stable for all the analysis techniques. So the method developed can be used as an additional tool for investment analysis. A predicted high level of risk for small hydroelectric plants projects will attract the investors' attention and make them to plan the projects cash flows more carefully. The wide range of users interested in projects risk assessment can access the tool via web-interface of the decision support system.

REFERENCES

Andriosopoulos, D.G., Pasiouras, F. and Zopounidis, C., 2012. An application of multicriteria decision aid models in the prediction of open market share repurchases. *Omega,* Vol. 40, No. 6, pp. 882-890.

Chen, J., Huang, C. and Chen, A., 2010. Applying self-organizing mapping neural network for discovery market behavior of equity fund. *Wseas transactions on information science and applications,* Vol. 7, No. 2, pp. 230-240.

Fioretti, G., 2004. The investment acceleration principle revisited by means of a neural network. *Neural Computing & Applications,* Vol. 13, No. 1, pp. 16-23.

Gonzalez-Carrasco, I., Colomo-Palacios, R., Lopez-Cuadrado, J.L., Garci´a-Crespo, A. and Ruiz-Mezcua, B., 2012. A private banking multi-investment portfolio advisor. *Information Sciences,* Vol. 206, pp. 63-82.

Jiang, H. and Ruan, J., 2010. Investment Risks Assessment on High-tech Projects Based on Analytic Hierarchy Process and BP Neural Network. *Journal of networks,* Vol. 5, No. 4, pp. 393-402.

Khashman, A., 2010. Neural networks for credit risk evaluation: Investigation of different neural models and learning schemes. *Expert Systems with Applications,* Vol. 37, No. 9, pp. 6233-6239.

Kohonen, T., 2001. *Self-Organizing Maps.* Springer-Verlag, New York, USA.

Lu,Y. and Karpova, E., 2012. An Investigation of Chinese Textile Firms' R&D Performance. *Clothing and Textiles Research Journal,* Vol. 30, No. 3, pp. 217-231.

Lukyanitsa, A.A., Nosov, S.V. and Shishkin, A.G., 2009. Risk minimization with self-organizing maps for mutual fund investment. *Proceedings of IEEE Congress on Evolutionary Computation*, pp. 2361-2365.

Munoz, J.I., Contreras, J., Caamano, J. and Correia, P.F., 2011. A decision-making tool for project investments based on real options: the case of wind power generation. *Annals of Operations Research,* Vol. 186, No. 1, pp. 465-490.

Nakaoka, I., Tani, K., Hoshino, Y. and Kamei, K., 2005. A portfolio selection by SOM and an asset allocation of risk/nonrisk assets by fuzzy reasoning using the selected brands. *Proceedings of International Conference on Systems, Man and Cybernetics*, Vol. 3, pp. 2769-2774.

Pendharkar, P.C., 2010. Valuing interdependent multi-stage IT investments: A real options approach. *European Journal of Operational Research,* Vol. 201, No. 3, pp. 847-859.

Petkova, A.P., Wadhwa, A., Yao, X. and Jain, S., 2011. Being first or making a difference? A study of U.S. venture capital investments into the "clean" energy sector. *Frontiers of Entrepreneurship Research,* Vol. 31, No. 2, pp. 49-61.

Pham, H.V., Tran, K.D., Thang, C., Cooper, E.W. and Kamei, K., 2011. Human reasoning awareness quantified by self-organizing map using collaborative decision making for multiple investment models. *Proceedings of International Conference on Complex, Intelligent and Software Intensive Systems,* pp. 101-108.

Psillaki, M., Tsolas, I.E. and Margaritis, D., 2010. Evaluation of credit risk based on firm performance. *European Journal of Operational Research,* Vol. 201, No. 3, pp. 873-881.

Tan, B., Anderson, E.G., Dyer, J.S. and Parker, G.G., 2010. Evaluating system dynamics models of risky projects using decision trees: alternative energy projects as an illustrative example. *System Dynamics Review,* Vol. 26, No. 1, pp. 1-17.

AN EXPERT SYSTEM APPROACH FOR THE SELECTION OF CLOUD SERVICE DELIVERY AND DEPLOYMENT MODELS

Mustafa I. M. Eid, Ibrahim M. Al-Jabri and Mohammed Sadiq Sohail
King Fahd University of Petroleum & Minerals
Dhahran, Saudi Arabia

ABSTRACT

The pervasive and expanding interest of many organizations worldwide in adopting cloud technology affirms its effectiveness in terms of cost and time. However, one of the challenging decisions facing management in adopting cloud services is what combinations of cloud service delivery (SaaS, PaaS, or, IaaS) and deployment models (Private, Public, Hybrid, or Community) to take on. A literature review found a lack of research work addressing this selection decision problem. To fill the research gap, the paper proposes an expert system approach for reaching a managerial decision on the right combination of service delivery and deployment models for a business firm to adopt. The paper proposes a rule-based expert system prototype, which provides advice based on criteria that utilize a set of relevant key characteristics of the cloud service delivery and deployment models. Then it evaluates the system prototype. Lastly, the paper will conclude with a discussion of the research results, its practical implications, limitations, and further research directions.

KEYWORDS

Expert systems, cloud service models, cloud deployment models, cloud computing adoption, cloud computing management, characteristics of cloud computing models

1. INTRODUCTION

Recent statistics on the cloud computing technology market growth are surging. A very recent survey on cloud computing trends (Weins, 2016), informs that private cloud adoption increased from 63 percent in 2015 to 77 percent, driving hybrid cloud adoption up from 58 percent to 71 percent year-over-year. The survey concludes that hybrid cloud adoption is increasing as both cloud users and cloud providers mature. Cloud computing represents a shift of computing paradigm with a move towards outsourcing of computing resources with characteristics like on-demand self-service, expendable resource scalability, zero up-front investment, and measured services (Catteddu & Hogben, 2009; Azadegan &Teich, 2010). It has provided an attractive alternative for many businesses in terms of cost saving in establishing and maintaining IT resources. In addition, managing software licensing and upgradation to meet the continuously growing computing demands are complex and costly as well. However, the cloud computing industry offers businesses a number of different adoption scenarios. Therefore, businesses face a number of challenging decision-making issues in their endeavor to adopt cloud computing to support their business processes and operations. For example, which of the cloud service delivery models from available options (SaaS, PaaS, or IaaS) is best to adopt? In addition, which deployment model amongst the common models (Private, Public, Hybrid, or Community) suits their organizational conditions and fulfills their business information needs and budget requirements? Answering these decision questions is not simple and requires the consideration of the relevant decision factors, which in turn generates multiple decision scenarios simultaneously.

A review of existing literature revealed a lack of research work in addressing the above two questions pertaining to managerial decision making of cloud computing adoption. Thus, the objectives of this paper is to fill the research gap by proposing an expert system prototype and evaluates its effectiveness to support management in addressing the above mentioned two selection decisions for managing the adoption of cloud computing. Section 1 provides a literature review focused on cloud computing models and the characteristics of service delivery and deployment models. In, addition, this section will provide an overview of the relevant decision making approaches including expert system and multi-criteria decision analysis. Section 2 describes the research methodology. Next, section 3 describes a proposed expert system to support the selection decision of cloud service delivery and deployment models. Section 4 evaluates the proposed expert system. Section 5 discusses the results. Being the first paper to propose the expert system approach, this research will provide new insights into managing cloud-computing adoption. In addition, it will extend our understanding of managing the adoption of cloud computing. Lastly, section 6 will conclude the paper.

2. LITERATURE REVIEW

2.1 Cloud Computing

In an era of information and globalization, immense computing power is required to generate business intelligence and competitive gains (Liu & Orban, 2008). Nonetheless, operating a private data center and managing software licensing and upgradation to meet ever-increasing computing demand is complex, and costly as well. It promises to provide a solution in the form of on-demand computing, swift deployment, little required maintenance, fewer IT staff and; hence, lower cost. The study by Al-Jabri (2014) found that higher awareness of cloud computing leads to higher adoption. Such captivating promises have made this technology a primary academic, research, IT, and business media topic over the last few years (Preston, 2011).

2.2 NIST Definition of Cloud Computing

Both academics and industry have tried to define cloud computing technology but no unified definition has been adopted so far. For example, Buyya (2009) defined cloud computing as "parallel and distributed computing built upon collection of dynamically provisioned interconnected and virtualized computers. They are presented as one or more unified computing resource based on service level agreements established through negotiation between the service provider and consumers." Kramer (2012) defined it as "a new computing paradigm, which changes the purchasing, maintenance and disposal process of IT by providing on-demand procurement of a dynamic basket of IT resources. These resources are hosted in specialized data centers and can be purchased and scaled over the Internet, on-demand and location independently." The most widely acknowledged definition of cloud computing in literature is the one presented by NIST. NIST defines cloud computing as ''A model for enabling convenient, on-demand network access to a shared pool of configurable computing resources (e.g. networks, servers, storage, applications, and services) that can be rapidly provisioned and released with minimal management effort or service provider interaction", Mell and Grance (2011). Furthermore, NIST pronounced five common characteristics for cloud computing, including On-demand self-service, broad network access, resource pooling, rapid elasticity, and measured service. It also defined three standard service delivery models and four deployment models. The service deliver models are Software as a Service (SaaS), Platform as a Service (PaaS), and Infrastructure as a Service (IaaS). The deployment models are Private cloud, Public cloud, Hybrid cloud, and Community cloud.

2.3 Decision Support for Managing Cloud Computing

As cloud computing technology use became more popular during the last decade, researchers started to pay more attention to the managerial decision-making issues faced by organizations interested to adopt cloud computing. The research by Conway and Curry (2013) addressed the management of cloud computing adoption from a lifecycle approach perspective. They developed a lifecycle model for managing cloud-computing adoption. Also, Marks & Lozano (2010) proposed an adoption lifecycle model for guiding management during the stages of planning for, and the implementation of, cloud computing in organizations. In addition, Hill, et al. (2013) emphasized the importance of strategic planning for cloud computing adoption in the context of information systems strategy as it provides a road map for all aspects of managing the adoption of cloud computing in organizations. Strategic planning for cloud computing is concerned with aligning cloud investment with business needs to improve business competitive advantage. The research by Whaiduzzaman, et al. (2014) focused on addressing the service selection for cloud computing using the multi-criteria decision-making (MCDM) approach. They described the multi-criteria decision analysis (MCDA) types and characteristics and compared several methods by synthesizing and reviewing the existing literature. The selection decision for cloud services and their deployment by organizations requires the consideration of a number of related conflicting factors that represent characteristics of cloud services and relevant organizational conditions. Usually, decision makers face such multi-criteria decision problems. In such multiple criteria decision situations, a compromise has to be made because in most real-world situations, no single alternative satisfies all criteria but one alternative may be better in terms of some of the criteria while other alternatives may outperform it, if judged based on the remaining criteria Rehman, et al. (2012).

Existing research work on the amalgamation of expert systems technology with cloud computing has not been even. That is, existing research work has focused more on utilizing cloud computing technology to support the delivery of expert system applications as cloud services, than on using expert system approach to support management decisions of cloud technology adoption. For example, Al-Ghamdi, et al. (2011) proposed an expert system to determine diabetes treatment based on cloud computing platforms. Rajesh Kumar, et al. (2013) proposed an expert system software as a service to support security of medical diagnosis information access; and Gagliordi (2015) developed a cloud-based architecture to support the delivery of mobile intelligent tutoring/learning systems. On the other hand, Zheng, et al. (2013) proposed an expert system for the evaluation of commercial cloud services. They built their expert system based on accumulating and organizing existing evaluation experiences of commercial cloud services in a knowledge base. The expert system aims to make previous evaluation experiences conveniently reusable and sustainable. Based on the customer's computing requirements, this expert system provides suggestions on the evaluation metrics and analytic modeling to utilize ranging from cost-benefits analysis to selection of cloud provider. Our literature review found a lack of research work on the use of an expert system approach to support management decisions on selecting the right cloud service delivery and deployment models. To fill this research gap, our paper proposes an expert system to support management decisions with respect to adopting the right cloud service delivery and deployment models, while satisfying organizational conditions and computing requirements.

2.4 Key Characteristics of Cloud Service Delivery and Deployment Models

For an organization to decide what type of cloud service delivery to adopt, it needs to be aware of the relevant key characteristics of service delivery models. In Table 1, we define five key characteristics that we believe to be most relevant to the selection of a delivery service model among the three alternative cloud service models (SaaS, PaaS, and IaaS).

Table 1. Key Characteristics Relevant to Selecting Cloud Service Models

Characteristic	Description	Reference
Service functionality	The function of the provided cloud service. For example, software, system development, data storage, web hosting, or server	Saripalli & Pingali, 2011
Cost of service	Service price and payment terms	Garg, 2013; Godse & Mulik, 2009
Service adaptability to business needs	The degree of flexibility the firm will have with changing the cloud service workflow to suit a firm innovated business process	Saripalli & Pingali, 2011
Available IT skills	Availability of organizational staff IT skills	De Borja, 2013; Layo, 2013
Service setup time	Setup/installation time taken for the client to start using service	Saripalli & Pingali, 2011

The cloud deployment models represent alternative options for deploying the selected cloud service model. For an organization to decide what type of cloud deployment model to adopt, it also needs to be aware of the relevant characteristics of cloud deployment models. In Table 2, we define four key characteristics that we believe are most relevant to the selection of a cloud deployment model among the four alternative cloud deployment models.

Table 2. Key Characteristics Relevant to Selecting Cloud Deployment Models

Characteristic	Description	Reference
Cost of cloud deployment	a. Initial capital cost plus b. Additional operating cost	Saripalli & Pingali, 2011; Williams, 2012
Privacy and security of data	Security level of the used service and client data maintained by the cloud deployment model. This includes: a. Degree of confidentiality of data maintained by the cloud deployment model b. Data integrity (data accuracy and recovery) c. Level of audibility d. Access control	Garg, 2013; Güner & Sneiders, 2014; Morgan & Conboy, 2013; Sun, et al. (2014)
Control of service and/or data	a. Location of Client's data storage (client's local server or cloud server) a. Manageability b. Ease of monitoring the service c. Autonomy (degree of political control or ownership the firm will exercise on the cloud service)	Güner & Sneiders, 2014; Morgan & Conboy, 2013;
Level of Industry Integration	level of integration between an organization and its suppliers, business partners, or collaborators	Mell & Grance, 2011; Metha, 2012

3. METHODOLOGY

When an organization has already decided to adopt cloud computing, it then needs to make two further decisions. (1) what service delivery model and what cloud deployment model to choose or adopt (for example, Public SaaS, Public PaaS, Private SaaS, Hybrid SaaS, Public IaaS, Hybrid IaaS, Community IaaS, etc.) and (2) to select the right service and provider from a set of alternative services and service providers. Therefore, two logical steps are involved in making adoption decisions. First, an organization will need to determine the service delivery and deployment models to adopt. Second, it will then need to select the best service provider who is capable of delivering the desired service and its deployment from the available set of alternative providers. This study focuses on developing an expert system which assists management to make the first decision in deciding on the best combination of service delivery and deployment models. To achieve this end, our research methodology consists of two steps:

- Develop an expert system prototype for the selection of cloud service delivery and deployment models
- Evaluate the proposed expert system

An expert system is a knowledge-based system that imitates human intelligence abilities in making decisions or solving problems in a well-defined problem domain of human expertise such as medical diagnosis, solving auto mechanical problems, or advising on financial loan applications. The concepts and theory of expert systems constitute a well-recognized branch of the artificial intelligence field of study. An expert system is defined by Jackson (1998) as a computer system that emulates the decision-making ability of a human expert. It is commonly agreed that an expert system should have three main components, namely knowledge base, inference engine, and user interface. The first step in the development of expert systems involves understanding and structuring or representing human knowledge/expertise of the desired problem domain. The second step is developing the inference engine and user interface. Developers build expert system components in different ways. Depending on the nature and complexity of the desired expert system, developers build them in different ways. One way is to build expert systems using an expert system shell. Other ways that are more time consuming use a logical programming language such as Prolog, ADA, and LISP, or using other programming languages such as C, C#, or PASCAL. An example of an expert system shell is the Java Expert System Shell (JESS), Friedman-Hill (2001).

As previously mentioned above, in order to construct the knowledge base of an expert system, developers will need to structure the knowledge domain of human expertise using one of the knowledge representation methods. Representing the knowledge of a human expert in a specific and well-defined domain depends on the nature of knowledge. One of the oldest and most common methods of representing knowledge and reasoning is rule-based. Other methods of representing and inferring human knowledge include case-based reasoning, fuzzy logic, and neural networks. The research by Grosan & Abraham (2011) defined the rule-based expert (production) system as a system that represent knowledge in terms of a set of rules that tells what to do or what to conclude in different situations. In what follows, we describe the desired expert system we developed to support management with reaching a decision on the best combination of cloud service and deployment models. We shall in this paper name our expert system as the Cloud Adoption Management (CAM) expert system.

4. A PROPOSED EXPERT SYSTEM

The authors follow the lifecycle model of expert system development offered by O'keefe & Lee (1990), which integrates verification and validation into the systems development process. This model follows the evolutionary spiral model of software systems development methodology proposed by Boehm (1988), which involves system prototyping. The development process of the expert system prototype includes four stages:

1. Requirements Analysis
2. Knowledge Acquisition
3. Prototyping
4. Implementation and maintenance

We designed the decision-making process based on the expert system approach, in two phases. We adopted the previously defined key characteristics in Tables 1 and 2, to develop two sets of four factors criteria that represent organizational conditions. In phase 1, in order to select the most suitable service delivery model for an organization, the decision maker user will enter the scale values for the four factors that represent their organizational conditions. Then, the system will provide a suggested service delivery model (SaaS, PaaS, or IaaS) and one alternative if any exist. Similarly, in phase 2, in order to select the most suitable cloud deployment model for an organization the decision maker user will enter scale values for the four organizational conditions that apply to the selection of the cloud deployment model. Then the system will provide a suggested cloud deployment model (Private, Public, Hybrid, and Community) and one alternative if any exist. However, the proposed system design allows the end user to adjust the system suggested service delivery or deployment models in a natural way. That is by having a number of trials, which can be saved in the system database for later reference by the decision maker end user. In addition, since the two criteria applied in each phase are independent, the selection decision for both the service delivery model and deployment model may be reached simultaneously or independently. However, the way we designed the expert system advisor page in our proposed expert system prototype (as explained further on), drive the end user to perform phase 1 first then phase 2. The two phases of the decision making process supported by our expert system are:

Phase 1: select the service delivery model

Phase 2: select the cloud deployment model

We constructed our expert system knowledge base by formulating the rules of expertise of the knowledge domain of selecting cloud service delivery and deployment models. We define the knowledge domain under investigation as the set of rules of expertise used for the selection of the right type of cloud service delivery and deployment model that best suit an organization interested in adopting cloud computing. As mentioned earlier, the decision of selecting the right combination of service delivery and deployment models depends on weighing a criterion that includes a number of relevant and conflicting factors. We needed to develop the desired criteria ourselves since a unified criteria used by human experts in the field of IT management does not exist, nor it is found in the existing cloud adoption management literature. Therefore, we developed two sets of criteria. The first criteria set, for the selection of service delivery model, consists of four factors drawn from the key characteristics previously defined in Table 1 above. The following four factor criteria along with their defined three-scale measure represent organizational conditions relevant to the selection of the service delivery model:

1 Available Budget for Cloud Service (ABCS) delivery model: *available budget for hiring a particular service delivery model (SaaS, PaaS, or IaaS)*. Three scale values are: Low (Limited funds available), Medium (Adequate funds available), and High (Abundant funds available).

2 Required Level of Service Adaptability (RLSA): *the level of service delivery model flexibility with respect to changing user requirements, and needs of the organization adopting cloud computing*. Three scale values are: Low (little change needed in the required software), Medium (moderate change needed in the required software), and High (much change needed in the required software).

3 Available IT Skills (AITS) in an organization: *degree of IT skills availability in the organization adopting cloud computing*. Three scale values are: Low (Available with low IT skill level), Medium (Available with moderate IT skill level), and High (Available with high IT skill level).

4 Urgency of Needed Cloud Service (UNCS): *degree of urgency of needed cloud service*. Low (16 - 30 working days, not urgent), Medium (6 -15 working days, moderately urgent), and High (1- 5 working days, urgent).

The second criteria set, for the selection of service deployment model (public, private, hybrid, and community), consists of four factors drawn from the key characteristics previously defined in Table 2 above. The following four factor criteria along with their defined three-scale measure represent organizational conditions relevant to the selection of the cloud deployment model:

1 Available Budget for Service Deployment (ABSD) model: *available additional budget for deploying a particular service delivery model:* public, private, hybrid, or community. Three scale values are: Low (Limited funds available), Medium (Adequate funds available), and High (Abundant funds available).

2 Required Level of Data Privacy and Security (RLDPS): *level of data privacy and security, needed by the organization adopting cloud computing*. Three scale values are: Low (little need for data privacy and security), Medium (moderate need for data privacy and security), and High (much need for data privacy and security).

3 Required level of user control (RLUC): *degree of control to manage a particular cloud service needed by the organization adopting cloud computing*. Three scale values are: Low (little need for managing the service by the user), Medium (moderate need for managing the service by the user), and High (much need for managing the service by the user).

4 Level of industry integration (LII): *level of integration with business partners, needed by the organization adopting cloud computing*. Three scale values are: Low (little integration with business partners), Medium (medium integration with business partners), and High (high integration with business partners).

We used the first criteria to define the rules of expertise for the selection of the service delivery model for a required service type. We used the second criteria to define the rules of expertise for the selection of the service deployment model for a required service type. However, before developing an appropriate set of rules of expertise of the knowledge domain, we first chosen six types of common required services (RS) for which a decision of the appropriate service delivery and deployment models is needed. The chosen six types of required services are:

1 Readymade software (RMS): standard software such as email system, payroll application, ERP system, etc.

2 Custom built software (CBS): any software with nonstandard requirements that an organization wishes to build. For example, a decision support system to support customer services.

3 Web hosting (WH): hosting and maintaining an organizational website.

4 Data storage (DS): storage of any kind of organizational data for backup and recovery, archiving, document management, etc.

5 Computer server (CS): a computer network server used for storing and running databases, websites, mail, or web business applications.

6 Computer network (CN): a computer network used for establishing an intranet and/or extranet to run applications that support organizational business processes.

According to Merritt (2004), it is possible in certain cases to fit logical relationships (rules of expertise) into a database, if one can structure these relationships in a tabular format. In an effort to develop the desired expert system for managing the adoption of cloud computing, we could formulate 486 rules of expertise, each rule determining the type of service delivery model to suit a single hypothetical organizational case scenario. Each hypothetical case scenario consists of a set of conditions/requirements representing a certain organizational situation at a certain point in time. In addition, we could formulate 486 rules of expertise each rule determining the type of service deployment model to suit a single organizational case scenario. As a result, we created two relational database tables to encode the rules of expertise of the knowledge domain that we articulated based on the aforementioned four factor criteria for each of the two phases of the designed decision making process. Thus, the first decision table used in Phase 1 of the decision making process, includes all possible case scenarios of organizations with assumed conditions (in terms of scale values of the four factors for selecting the service delivery model), and the suggested service delivery models. Table 3 includes a sample of the case scenarios entered in the first decision table.

The second decision table, used in Phase 2 of the decision making process, includes all possible case scenarios of organizations with assumed conditions (in terms of scale values of the four factors for selecting the service deployment model), and the suggested service deployment models. Table 4 includes a sample of the case scenarios entered in the second decision table. These two decision tables represent the knowledge base of our expert system for selecting the best combination of service delivery and deployment models for an organization intending to adopt cloud computing.

Table 3. A Sample of Case Scenarios with Associated Decisions for Selecting Service Delivery Models

Case #	RS	ABCS	RLSA	AITS	UNCS	Suggested service delivery model	Alternate service delivery model
1	RMS	Low	Low	Low	Low	SaaS	
2	RMS	Low	Low	Low	Medium	SaaS	
3	RMS	Low	Low	Low	High	SaaS	
4	RMS	Low	Low	Medium	Low	SaaS	PaaS
5	RMS	Low	Low	Medium	Medium	SaaS	

Table 4. A Sample of Case Scenarios with Associated Decisions for Selecting Cloud Deployment Models

Case #	RS	ABSD	RLDPS	RLUC	LII	Suggested service deployment model	Alternate service deployment model
1	RMS	Low	Low	Low	Low	Public	
2	RMS	Low	Low	Low	Medium	Public	Community
3	RMS	Low	Low	Low	High	Community	
4	RMS	Low	Low	Medium	Low	Public	Private
5	RMS	Low	Low	Medium	Medium	Public	Community

The purpose of the proposed expert system prototype is to demonstrate the feasibility of the proposed solution to handle the selection decision problem under investigation. The system prototyping step involves selecting the right tool for building the proposed expert system solution and then building the expert system prototype. Following that comes the evaluation of the prototype capability in handling the aforementioned selection decisions of managing cloud computing adoption. In what follows, the paper describes the proposed system prototype in terms of its development environment and the Graphical User Interface (GUI).

The authors used the C# programming language supported by the MS Visual Studio.net (2014 version) environment to build the system. The proposed system is web-based. The reason for this choice, is that the rules are organized in a relational database structure and the logic of inference engine and the design of the GUI are both simple to program. The system GUI consists of six pages. The homepage has a standard menu bar, which appears in all system pages. The menu bar has six options:

1. "Service Delivery" option lists all 486 case scenarios for selecting service delivery models, criteria values, and decisions, from the knowledge base.
2. "Service Deployment" option lists all 486 case scenarios for selecting service deployment models, criteria values, and decisions, from the knowledge base.
3. "Users" option lists existing user accounts and create new accounts and/or edit/delete existing ones.
4. "User Selection Trials" option has two functions. This is the only page used by the decision maker end user, which acts as the expert system advisor page.
5. "Delivery Upload" option allows the authors to upload new case scenarios to the system knowledge base. The authors created all 486 possible case scenarios with their selected service delivery models, in an MS Excel file and then imported them using this option. Using this option, the authors can add more case scenarios for selecting service delivery models for additional service types.

6. "Deployment Upload" option allows the authors to upload new case scenarios to the system knowledge base. The authors created all 486 possible case scenarios with their selected service deployment models, in an MS Excel file, then imported them using this option. Using this option, the authors can add more case scenarios for selecting service deployment models for additional service types.

5. EVALUATION OF THE PROPOSED EXPERT SYSTEM

In order to prove the value of the proposed CAM expert system for selecting the best service delivery and deployment models that suit an organization circumstances and requirements, it is necessary to evaluate its effectiveness, based on certain criteria. According to Suen, et al. (1990), the evaluation should focus on three critical issues, verification, validation, and measuring performance of the proposed system prototype. Methods of evaluating expert systems performance (or effectiveness) are discussed by Suen, et al. (1990). The authors encouraged using formal methods similar to methods used for the same purpose in software engineering for evaluating expert systems, including verification and validation, as well as applying appropriate performance metrics. Verification is concerned with internal consistency of the expert system that is verifying completeness and correctness of the knowledge base and inference engine. Validation, on the other hand, is concerned with validating the external behavior of an expert system that validates the correctness of responses (given advice) of the expert system during its use. Measuring expert system performance is concerned with the size of the knowledge base in terms of rules and facts, response time, cost, and difficulty of problems that an expert system is capable of solving. For the verification part, the authors manually verified the completeness and correctness of all stored case scenarios and associated selection decisions. In addition, they checked the correctness of the inference engine design and implementation. For measuring the expert system performance, the authors used the system thoroughly to ensure good response time and its ability to deal with any real world organizational case scenario. They found the system response time to be very satisfactory and adequate to the task of dealing with any real case scenario.

To perform the validation part, the authors validated the proposed system using a group of nine human experts in IT management. All selected human experts had long experience in managing software development projects and/or software evaluation and selection. To maintain objectivity, the nine invited experts are not involved in the development of the expert system (O'keefe & Lee, 1990). The authors conducted a focus group workshop for this purpose. We approached the validation issue by measuring the convergence or extent of agreement between the proposed system prototype advice and the human expert advice. The authors drew 40 case scenarios from the expert system knowledge base and presented them, in a unified templates to the participating human experts. To maintain objective validation of the expert system, the chosen test cases were a mix of average to moderately difficult (O'keefe & Lee, 1990).

5.1 Data Analysis

To validate our expert system, we need to apply the right statistical test, which is quantitative in nature. According to O'keefe & Lee (1990), a good method to measure consistency of responses of an expert system performance compared to human experts is the Kappa statistic proposed by Cohen (1960). Next, we will apply the cosistency analysis using the Kappa statistic. Basically, Kappa statistic or Coefficient measures agreement between two raters of a single category, the expert system in our case, (Cohen, 1960). We calculated Kappa in two steps. First, for the selection decision of the three service delivery models (SaaS, PaaS, and IaaS) and for each of the six type of services included in the knowledge base. Secondly, for the selection decision of the four service deployment models (Public, Private, Hybrid, and Community) and for each of the six type of services. For each of the participating expert users and types of required services, we calculated Kappa Coefficient as follow:

$K = Po - Pe / 1 - Pe$,

Where Po is the overall proportion of observed agreement between raters (in our case the expert system response and human expert response to solving a test case), and Pe is the overall proportion of expected chance agreement. The calculated K Coefficient value will be between 0 and 1. The more K is closer to 1, is the greater agreement between the raters, and the closer to 0, the agreement diminishes. The following example in Table 5 illustrates how we calculated the K Coefficient for validating the selection of service delivery models rated by the expert system and expert user #2. The numbers in the intersection cells represent percentage of agreement or disagreemnet between system selection and expert user selection. For example the number 0.25 represents percentage of agreement of SaaS models, but the number 0.125 represents percentage of disagreement.

Table 5. Calculation of K Coefficient for the Selection of Service Delivery Model for the RMS Required Service Type

Expert User #2				
	SaaS	PaaS	IaaS	Total
SaaS	0.25	0	0	0.25
PaaS	0.125	0.625	0	0.75
IaaS	0	0	0	0
Total	0.375	0.625	0	1

Po = 0.25 + 0.625 + 0 = 0.875
Pe = (0.375 * 0.25) + (0.625 * 0.75) + (0 * 0) = 0.632
K = (0.875 – 0.562) / (1-0.562) = 0.714

Next, we calculated the K Coefficients for each of the participating users. Table 6 below shows all K Coefficient values for the selection of service delivery and deployment models, for all expert users, and the average K for all expert users. The overall K Coefficients of all expert users are 0.69 and 0.77 respectively, which are closer to 1. This indicates that the proposed expert system performs at a good satisfactory level, for selecting the service delivery and deployment models for the RMS service type. Then, we calculated the overall K Coefficient values for the rest of five service types, for which case scenarios are included in the knowledge base. Table 7 shows the claculated K Coefficient values for all service types and for the selection of both service delivery and deployment models.

Table 6. K Coefficients for the Selection of Service Delivery and Deployment Models for the RMS Required Service Type

Expert User	**K**	**Expert User**	**K**
User #2	0.714	User #2	0.680
User #3	0.750	User #3	0.828
User #4	0.647	User #4	0.797
User #5	0.746	User #5	0.795
User #6	0.746	User #6	0.807
User #7	0.613	User #7	0.792
User #8	0.726	User #8	0.723
User #9	0.673	User #9	0.714
User #10	0.625	User #10	0.81
Overall K Coefficient for all users	0.69	Overall K Coefficient for all users	0.77

Table 7. Overall K Coefficients for All Service Types

Service type	**Overall K Coefficient for service delivery model selection**	**Overall K Coefficient for service deployment model selection**
RMS	0.69	0.77
CBS	0.7	0.8
WH	0.75	0.76
DS	0.92	0.84
CS	1	0.71
CN	1	0.84
Overall K for all service types	0.84	0.79

6. DISCUSSION

The paper proposed an expert system prototype to support management decision in selecting cloud service delivery and deployment models. In a bid to evaluate the proposed system effectiveness, we performed three tasks as per the evaluation guidelines of given by O'keefe & Lee (1990). First, we verified the correctness and completeness of the formulated rules, which are stored in the expert system knowledge base. The rules are formulated based on two sets of criteria for the selection of service delivery models and service deployment models. In addition, we verified the correctness of the inference engine logic. Secondly, we validated the degree of correctness of responses given by the expert system by a group of nine human expert (IT management decision makers) elicited during a one-day focus group workshop. The nine experts provided their responses in terms of agreement or non-agreement with the expert system suggested models. Then, we conducted the data analysis using Kappa Coefficient analysis, suggested by Cohen (1960), on the collected data. The findings of the data analysis show that the overall K Coefficients for nine participating expert users, for all service types, and for both the service delivery and service deployment model selection are 0.84 and 0.79 respectively. The calculated K Coefficients being closer to the value 1, indicate that the proposed expert system's advice is very close to the human experts' advice. Thus, it can be deduced that our expert system performs well, but it is hard though to claim that our proposed expert system performance completely matches the performance of human experts in this problem domain. However, the proposed expert system leverages managers' experience in cloud computing and intuition to guide them to make faster and satisficing decisions with respect to the selection of service delivery and deployment models that best suit their organizational conditions and requirements. In addition, this is the first paper in the body of knowledge of managing cloud computing adoption apply the expert system approach to provide a decision support solution to the selection problem of service delivery and deployment models. Therefore, from this perspective, this paper represents an original research contribution, extending the body of knowledge of managing cloud computing adoption. However, due to the fact there exists no similar expert system or decision support system that tackles the same problem domain, it is not possible to compare the merits of the proposed expert system with other similar decision support systems.

7. CONCLUSION

Based on an extensive review of cloud computing literature, the paper identified two sets of criteria for the selection of service delivery and service deployment models. Each set of criteria consists of four key factors based on which a selection decision can be taken. Then, based on the criteria, the authors formulated all possible case scenarios and associated rules to reach the selection decision on the choice of cloud service delivery and deployment models. Each case scenario represents one set of hypothetical organizational conditions and requirements with the associated selection decision. All possible case scenarios are stored in a knowledge base and a program logic is developed as an inference engine along with a graphical user interface to support management end user in making the selection decision. Therefore, the paper proposed an expert system approach to support decision making regarding what type of service delivery and deployment models an organization should adopt. It applied for the first time an expert system approach to support decision making regarding cloud computing adoption, and more specifically the choice of service delivery and deployment models thereof. The main advantage of the proposed expert system is that it is easier to use and apply by management as it is based on intuition. It is more practical and less time consuming compared to other methods of decision making, such as the multi-criteria decision making method, which can be applied to reach the same desired decision. In addition, being the first time the expert system approach used to handle the research decision problem, represents an original research contribution to the body of knowledge in the fields of expert systems and decision support systems

The results of the validation data analysis are promising in that the expert system derived advice on selection decisions is very close to the human expert advice, which indicates the appropriateness of the expert system approach to support management decisions of cloud computing adoption. With respect to the limitations of the proposed approach, one that deserves mentioning here is that the scale values of (Low, Medium, and High) of the criteria factors entered by the authors or the end user decision maker are subjective. That is very much depends on the end user's judgment and evaluation. However, the proposed expert system prototype provides the "user trials' function, which allows end users to create and save in the expert system database, as many trials as they wish, whereby they can change scale values of the criteria factors more than once. In addition, saved user trials in the system database allow users to perform what if analysis and to refer back to their trials and select the best representative trial for their organizational scenario. Another limitation is that the current version of the proposed expert system prototype does not provide explanation of its suggested selection decisions. Thus, future research work may be focused on adding an explanation component to it. Moreover, further research may be carried out in developing a multi-criteria decision making method to tackle the same problem domain and compare its results with the results of our proposed expert system approach.

ACKNOWLEDGEMENT

This project was funded by the National Plan for Science, Technology, and Innovation (MAARIFAH) – King Abdulaziz City for Science & Technology through the Science & Technology Unit at King Fahd University of Petroleum & Minerals – Kingdom of Saudi Arabia, award number (14-INF83-04).

REFERENCES

Al-Jabri, I. M., 2014. The perceptions of adopters and non-adopters of cloud computing: application of Technology-Organization-Environment framework. Proceedings of the Fourteenth International Conference on Electronic Business, ICEB2014, December 8-12, Taipei, pp. 250-257.

Azadegan, A. and Teich, J., (2010). Effective benchmarking of innovation adoptions: A theoretical framework for e-procurement technologies. *International Journal of Benchmarking*, Vol. 17, No. 4, pp 472–490.

Boehm, B. W., 1988. A spiral model of software development and enhancement. *IEEE Computer*, May, 61-72.

Buyya, R., Yeoa, C. S., Venugopala, S., Broberg, J., and Brandic, I., 2009. Cloud computing and emerging IT platforms: Vision, hype, and reality for delivering computing as the 5th utility. *Future Generation Computer Systems*, Vol. 25, No. 6, pp 599–616.

Catteddu, D. and Hogben, G., 2009. Cloud computing risk assessment. *European Network and Information Security Agency (ENISA)*, pp 583-592.

Cohen, J. (1960). A cofficent of agreement for nominal scales. *Educationa and Psychological Measuremnts,* Vol. 20, pp 37-47.

Conway, G. and Curry, E., 2013. The IVI Cloud Computing Life Cycle. In Ivanov, I. I., Sinderen, M., Leymann, F., and Shan, T. (Editors). Communications in Computer and Information Sciences, Vol. 367, No. 1, pp 183-199, Springer, Heidelberg.

De Borja, F., 2013. Cloud Computing Skills Required for IT Employees. *Cloud Times*, February 2013. http://cloudtimes.org/2013/02/06/cloud-computing-skills-required-for-it-employees/ (Accessed May 2015)

Gagliordi, N., 2015. Enterprise software spend to reach $620 billion in 2015: Forrester. *ZDNet*. Available at: http://www.zdnet.com/article/enterprise-software-spend-to-reach-620-billion-in-2015-forrester/.

Garg, S. K., Versteeg, S., and Buyya, R.. (2013). A framework for ranking of cloud computing services. *Future Generations Computer Systems Journal*, Vol. 29, No. 4, pp 1012-1023.

Godse, M. and Mulik, S., 2009. An Approach for Selecting Software-as-a-Service (SaaS) Product. *IEEE International Conference on Cloud Computing*, Bangalore, pp. 155-158.

Grosan, C. and Abraham, A. (2011). Intelligent Systems: *A Modern Approach.* Intelligent Systems Reference Library, Volume 17. Springer, ISBN 978-3-642-21003-7.

Güner, E. O. and Sneiders, E., 2014. CLOUD COMPUTING ADOPTION FACTORS IN TURKISH LARGE SCALE ENTERPRISES. PACIS 2014. Available at http://www.pacis-net.org/file/2014/1845.pdf (accessed May 2016)

Friedman-Hill, E. J. (2001). JESS, the expert system shell for Java platform. Sandia National Laboratories, Version 6.

Jackson, P., 1998. *Introduction to Expert Systems* (3 ed.), Addison Wesley, ISBN 978-0-201-87686-4.

Kramer, F., 2012. Musings on the cloud - A customer oriented concept formation on cloud computing with respect to SME. *European, Mediterranean & Middle Eastern Conference on Information Systems EMCIS2012*, June 7-8, Munich, Germany.

Layo, I., 2013. Future of Cloud Computing Projects and Skills Competency Analysis. *Cloud Times*, November 2013. http://cloudtimes.org/2013/11/19/future-of-cloud-computing-projects-and-skills-competency-analysis/

Liu, H. and Orban, D. (2008). Gridbatch: Cloud computing for large-scale data-intensive batch applications. *Eighth IEEE International Symposium on Cluster Computing and the Grid Conference.*

Marks, E. A. and Lozano, B., 2010. *Executive's Guide to Cloud Computing*. John Wiley & Sons Inc., 2010, Hoboken, New Jersey.

Mell, P. and Grance, T., 2011. *The NIST Definition of Cloud Computing*, National Institute of Standards and Technology (NIST). US Department of Commerce. Special Publication 800-145.

Merritt, D., 2004. Best Practices for Rule-Based Application Development. The Microsoft Corporation Architecture Journal, January 20014. https://msdn.microsoft.com/en-us/library/aa480020.aspx

Metha, N., 2012. Cloud Deployment Models-Read the Important Differences. *Cloud Tweaks*, 2 July 2012. http://cloudtweaks.com/2012/07/4-primary-cloud-deployment-models/

Morgan, L. and Conboy, K, 2013. Factors Affecting the Adoption of Cloud Computing: An Exploratory Study, *Proceedings of the 21st European Conference on Information Systems (ECIS2013).*

O'keefe, R. M. and Lee, S. (1990). An Integrative Model of Expert System Verification & Validation. *Expert Systems with Applications*, Vol. 1, No. 1, pp 231-236, .

Preston, R., 2011. Top 10 CIO Priorities. *Information Week.* Available at: http://www.informationweek.com/news/globalcio/interviews/231901248 (Accessed October 25, 2011).

Rehman, Z., Hussain, O. K., and Hussain, F. K., 2012. IaaS Cloud Selection using MCDM Methods. *The Ninth IEEE International Conference on e-Business Engineering (ICEBE 2012)*, pp. 246-251.

Saripalli, P. and Pingali, G., 2011. MADMAC: Multiple Attribute Decision Methodology for Adoption of Clouds. *IEEE 4th International Conference on Cloud Computing.*

Suen, C. Y., Grogono, P. D., and Shinghal, R., 1990. Verifying, Validating, and Meauring Performance of Expert Systems. *Expert Systems with Applications*, Vol/ 1, No. 1, pp 93-102.

Sun, L., Dong, H., Hussain, F. K., Hussain, O. K., and Chang, E., 2014. Cloud service selection: State-of-the-art and future research directions. *Journal of Network and Computer Applications*, Vol. 45, No. 1, pp 134-150.

Weins, K., (2016). Cloud Computing Trends: 2016 State of the Clod Survey. *RightScale website*, posted on 09 February, 2016. http://www.rightscale.com/blog/cloud-industry-insights/cloud-computing-trends-2016-state-cloud-survey

Whaiduzzaman, M., Gani, A., Anuar, N. B., Shiraz, M., Haque, M. N., and Haque, I. T., 2014. Cloud Service Selection Using Multi-criteria Decision Analysis. *The Scientific World Journal*, Vol. 1, Article ID 459375, pp 1-10.

Williams, B. (2012). *The Economics of Cloud Computing: An Overview For Decision Makers*. Network Business series, Cisco Press.

DESIGNING AN AGILE SCRUM TEAM FORMATION MODEL

Mazni Omar and Noor Liza Ahmad Khasasi
Human-Centered Computing Research Lab
School of Computing, Universiti Utara Malaysia
06010 UUM Sintok, Kedah, Malaysia

ABSTRACT

Scrum is one of the agile software development methodologies that have been accepted widely by software engineering (SE) community. This is because agile principles that emphasize on rapid development process, which enables quality software to be delivered on time and within budget. Successful agile scrum project depends on the high-performance of team members that assigned to a specific software project. Therefore, when the right team member assigned to the right project, it will boost the effectiveness and performance of team. To date, the team formation of Scrum team is based on project manager's experience. This has led to difficulty in managing Scrum project due to inconsistency of decision making and conflict among team members. Thus, this study aims to propose an Agile Scrum team formation model by matching personality behavioural and skill sets (technical and soft skills) criteria with project's complexity. The proposed model was further validated using a case study. Results demonstrate that the proposed model is able to help the management to form and select the right Agile Scrum Product team to work on the right IT software development project. The outcome of this study contributes to the significant criteria to select team members based on the complexity of the software project and serves as a practical contribution towards forming high performance Agile Scrum team.

KEYWORDS

Agile, Scrum, project management, team formation, personality, skillsets

1. INTRODUCTION

Scrum is a people-centric development method that enables people to respond effectively toward rapidly changing and highly emergent requirements. It has been claimed to be the most widely used methodology among software practitioners (Cohn, 2010; Scrum Alliance, 2014), as it ensures well-verified working software that can be delivered on time. In addition, Scrum focuses on project management and requirements management phase, which are critical in software development stage. The key element of a successful Scrum project is depending on the high performance of the Agile Scrum team assigned to the project (Cohn, 2010).

Agile Scrum team is a self-organizing and cross-function team; work as a close-knit team to complete the work that has been promised to be delivered for each sprint. The role and responsibility of each team member is clearly defined by Scrum team roles of Scrum Master, Product Owner, and the Development team. The development team comprises of not more than 9 people working exclusively on a project at one time. Forming a high performing Agile Scrum team is a challenge as it requires a combination of high level of individual and team autonomy (Hoda and Murugesan, 2016; Moe, Dingsøyr, and Dybå, 2008), thus, a dynamic team member is highly needed.

Historically, Agile Scrum team formation was largely dependent on project managers' experience (Zaraket, Olleik, and Yassine, 2013; Andre, Baldoquin, and Acuna, 2011; Cohn, 2010). This has led to difficulty in managing Scrum projects due to inconsistency in the decision making when it came to determining the team composition. According to the extant studies in this field, in order to form high-performing teams, personality assessments and profiling techniques should be used in the selection process (Zaraket et al., 2013; Donsbach et al., 2009).This strategy helps the manager to closely match team members' skill sets with the IT software development project requirements, which should be weighted in order or preference and importance for the company and/or client. Personality assessment is used to assess the team members' behavioural traits to ensure their higher compatibility, while profiling is used to match the formed Agile Scrum team with the particular IT software development project (Zaraket et al., 2013; Donsbach et al., 2009). Thus, this study proposed an Agile Scrum Team Formation (AGTEF) Model to realize the team formation requirements.

This paper is organized as follows. A review of literature regarding personality behaviour, skillsets and software requirements project are introduced in Section 2. Then, the proposed Agile Scrum team formation model is explained in Section 3, followed by model evaluation Section 4. Results and discussion are discussed in Section 5 and conclusion and recommendation are drawn in Section 6.

2. REVIEW OF LITERATURE

This section discusses the input parameters –personality behaviour, skillsets, and project requirements that are used to construct the AGTEF model.

2.1 Personality Behaviour

Personality compatibility within an Agile Scrum team is important to overcome team issues. This is because the right combination of compatible members encourages team positive attitudes (Licorish and MacDonnel, 2015; Howard and Rogers, 2011). One of the popular tools to measure personality behaviour is DISC. DISC is a proven reliable and valid behaviour assessment, which used to help people better understand how they approach their task in work environment (Licorish and MacDonnel, 2015). It is a better choice compared to Myer-Briggs Type Indicator (MBTI) due to its simplicity, measures individual's behaviour for specific environment, and not too personal where result can be shared publicly (DiscProfile, 2015).

DISC measures fundamental behavioural of (1) *dominance* – degree to which an individual seeks to control his or her environment which relating to control, power and assertiveness, (2) *influence* – degree to which an individual seeks social interaction with other people which relating to social situation and communication, (3) *steadiness* – degree to which an individual seeks consistency and stability in his or her environment which relating to patience, persistence, and thoughtfulness, and (4) *conscientiousness* – degree to which an individual seeks to confirm to formal rules and structure which relating to structure and organization (DiscProfile, 2015). It is only relatively recent development that is being applied to achieve greater team dynamism on Agile Scrum teams (Howard and Rogers, 2011) yet to be fully embraced by the SE field. Table 1 shows the communication strategies to be applied for specific behaviour type (Howard and Rogers, 2011).

Table 1. Strategies for Communicating (Howard and Rogers, 2011)

Behaviour Type	Strategies for Communicating
Dominator	Get to the point; be clear; be specific; be brief; present an overview with facts; provide alternatives and talk about results.
Influencer	Be friendly; talk; ask questions; stay on the topic; be open; talk feelings; and have fun.
Supporter	Allow time to warm up; be part of a team; present new ideas gently; be agreeable; suggest outcomes; and draw out opinions.
Critical Thinker (person with conscientiousness)	Be serious; be prepared; be organized; present details; present pros and cons; give solid evidence; allow time for questions; ask questions; and give options for decisions.

The proposed model adopts DISC to measure individual's behavioural personality trait specifically for workplace. This is to enable other team members to understand the right approach to deal with each other and to ensure smooth gelling process of the formed Agile Scrum team. It is important for each team member to know each other behaviour traits in order to understand and to accept why a person reach and behave the way they do.

2.2 Skillsets

Hard skills are particular, teachable and measurable abilities that are essential to complete one job or role in workplace. Hard skill is required to ensure on time deliverable of quality software product to the stakeholders. Programming language, spoken and written language, database knowledge, domain or expert area, scrum role experience, scrum hour experience, number of sprints involved, and experience in past projects are being considered in designing the AGTEF model (Gupta and Suma, 2013; Zaraket et al., 2013; Henry, 2013; McCuller, 2012; Cohn, 2010; Prabhakaran, 2010).

Soft skill is required to ensure smoothness and acceleration of communication process. Team effectiveness and high performance is directly supported by soft skills like communication skills, management skills, thinking skills, teamwork skills, leadership skills, creative skills, facilitation skills, analytical skills, people skills, interpersonal skills and planning skills (Gilal et al., 2016; Licorish and MacDonnell, 2015; Hidding and Nicholas, 2014; Gupta and Suma, 2013; PMBOK, 2013; Uikey and Suman, 2012; Capretz and Ahmed, 2010; Prabhakaran, 2010).

2.3 Project Requirements

Selection of projects and the allocation of team members to work on the project based on technical skills have been proven to maximize profit for software companies (Zaraket et al., 2013). Software project requirements included for this study are adopted from various resources of Software Design Document (SDD) templates of IEEE Recommended Practice for Software Design Description, non-Scrum and Scrum Project Management Body of Knowledge (PMBOK). Software design is a process by which software project requirements are translated into a representative of software components.

Project introduction, purpose, system overview, design constraints, project reference, database design, hardware architecture, hardware detail design, software architecture, software detail design, system security and integrity controls, and user stories are the project requirements used for Agile Scrum Team (Hidding and Nicholas , 2014; PMBOK, 2013; Uikey and Suman, 2012; Wallace, Keil and Rai, 2004; Jiang and Klein, 2000).

3. PROPOSED MODEL

The AGTEF model is constructed with one big complex process. To simplify the complex model, the complete AGTEF model process are divided into four (4) sub-processes which are; 1) Individual/Candidate Data Gathering sub-process, 2) IT Software Development Project Data Gathering sub-process, 3) Team Formation and IT Software Development Project Matching sub-process, and finally 4) Team Performance Level Prediction sub-process as illustrated in Figure 1.

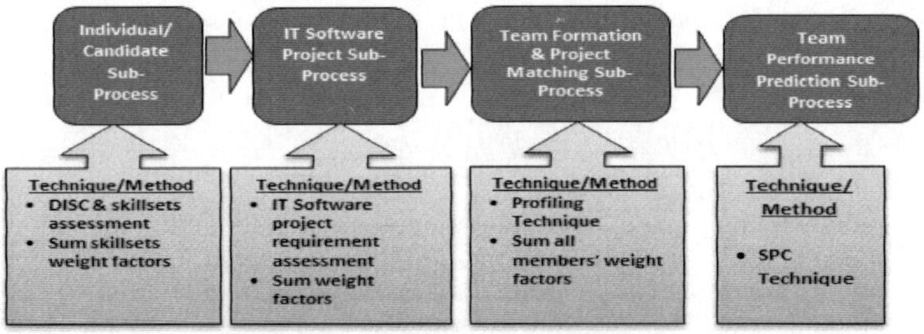

Figure 1. The AGTEF process model

3.1 Individual/Candidate Data Gathering Sub-Process

Individual/Candidate Data Gathering sub-process comprises of data gathering activity catered to collect individual information of DISC behaviour trait, hard skills proficiency level, soft skills proficiency level, and other supporting information required to support the AGTEF model. First, candidates are required to take DISC assessment to get to know and understand their own blend of DISC behaviour traits. This assessment was designed follows the free DISC assessment method recommended by (Howard and Rogers, 2011). Once the assessment is completed, individual's DISC's result is calculated and explained briefly.

Simultaneously, managers of each candidate are required to fill in candidates' hard skills and soft skills proficiency level information. These hard skills and soft skills proficiency are based on the manager's evaluation based on their own judgment and assumption. Each selected skillsets of hard skills and soft skills were assigned a three-scale rating of beginner, intermediary, and advanced. Rating beginner is assigned with weighting 1, intermediary as weighting 2 while advanced with weighting 3. The three-scale rating and weighting were recommended by the researchers for easier calculation. The average of all the skillset are then calculated to get the candidate's total weighting as illustrated in the following Table 2.

Table 2. Skillsets' proficiency weighting

Weighting	Proficiency Level
1	Beginner
2	Intermediary
3	Advanced

The combination data from both hard skills and soft skills proficiency levels are then calculated as average to get the total individual weighting. All these collected information are saved into an individual/candidate database to be retrieved and consumed by Team Formation and IT Software Development Project Matching sub-process whenever required.

3.2 IT Software Development Project Data Gathering Sub-Process

In the IT Software Development Project Data Gathering sub-process, management group or the project manager groups are required to input the pre-defined information required in order to process the AGTEF model. These requirements were selected and adapted from various resources of Software Design Document (SDD) templates of IEEE Recommended Practice for Software Design Description, non-Scrum and Scrum Project Management Body of Knowledge (PMBOK) as explained in Section 2.

The collected information is then calculated to get the IT software development project weighting. The IT software development project weighting is assigned by calculating whether the difference between the company's estimate duration to complete the project with what had been projected by the customer. This weighting was also proposed by the researchers for easier estimation level of IT project difficulty. If the completion estimation is less from the customer's projection, a weighting of 1 to be assigned, weighting 2 is for same projection while a weighting 3 for IT software development project that require more than customer's deadline to be completed as show in Table 3.

Table 3. IT Software Development Project's Weighting

Weighting	Condition
1	Company's estimation of completion < Customer's deadline
2	Company's estimation of completion = Customer's deadline
3	Company's estimation of completion > Customer's deadline

To end the IT Software Development Project Data Gathering sub-process, all the collected information are saved into a project database to be retrieved and consumed by the Team Formation and IT Software Development Project Matching sub-process whenever required.

3.3 Team Formation and IT Software Development Project Matching Sub-Process

Team Formation and IT Software Development Project Matching sub-process is activated whenever the management group decided to form team to work on an IT software development project. Hard skills proficiency and previous role of a candidate are used as the main parameters in profiling for the right candidate to be assigned to a project which ultimately to form a team.

At first the AGTEF model will look for Scrum Masters based on their experience, hard skills proficiency and availability from the candidate database. Temporary teams will be created based on the number of returned Scrum Master along with the information of their corresponding DISC result and individual weighting. For example; if there are four available Scrum Masters, then four temporary teams of Team 1, Team 2, Team 3 and Team 4 will be created as illustrated in Figure 2.

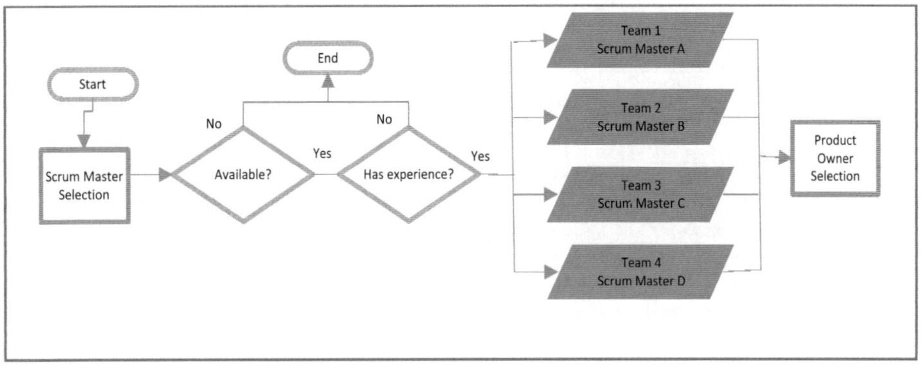

Figure 2. AGTEF's Scrum Master Selection Flow

Next, the AGTEF model will look for Product Owners. Similar to the query used to search for Scrum Masters, the Product Owner's experience, hard skills proficiency and availability are also required. Again, the AGTEF model will look for the returned number of Product Owner then assign one to each of the newly created teams in previous activity of Scrum Master selection, whilst matching the Product Owner's behaviour trait with Scrum Master's behaviour trait compatibility. If the number of Product Owner is less than the number of previously created teams, the team without Product Owner will be discarded as shown in the following Figure 3.

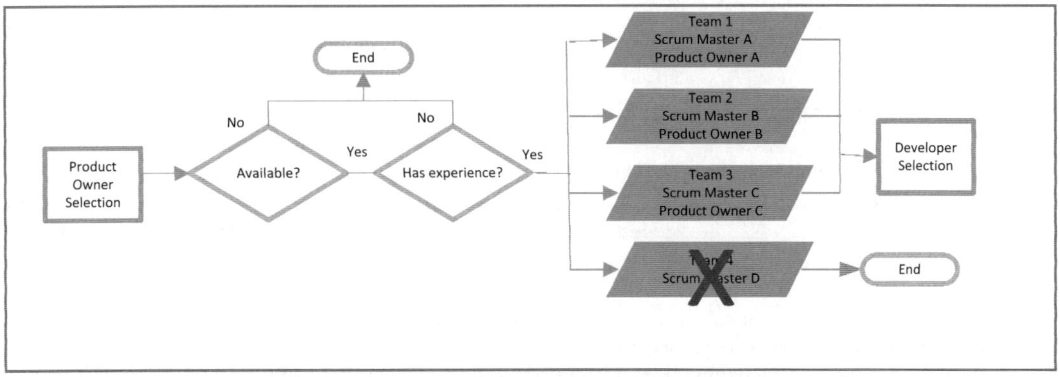

Figure 3. AGTEF's Product Owner Selection Flow

Teams with one Scrum Master and one Product Owner each will be used for the next activity of Developer selection. The AGTEF model will assign a group of developers depending on the required number of developers and specialized roles stated in IT software development project requirement. Specialized roles that are being considered by AGTEF model are DB Specialist, UI Designer, technical writer, and developers as explained earlier in Section 2. The following Figure 4 illustrated the flow used to accomplish Developer Selection activity.

If the project requires full time DB Specialist involvement, the AGTEF model will look for available DB Specialists with the required experience and hard skills proficiency. Same logic applies for UI Designer and technical writer if full time involvement is required to complete the IT software development project. Finally, developers including testers will be queried out according to their availability, experience and hard skills proficiency.

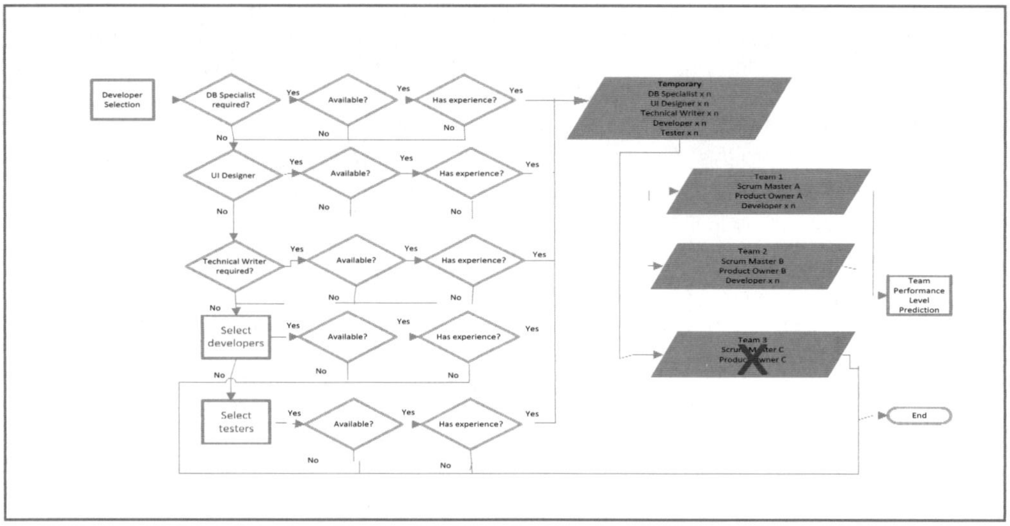

Figure 4. AGTEF's Developer Selection Flow

All the results of these queries will be kept in temporary candidate pool. Then, the AGTEF model will randomly assign selected candidates from the temporary candidate pool to the created teams from previous activities (refer to Figure 4) whilst matching the compatibility of behaviour trait of each team members where of a mix of unique traits is much recommended (Howard and Rogers, 2011).

Once a team is formed and proposed to work on a project, the team total weighting of the whole team is calculated based on the average of all team members' personal weighting. Multiple teams may be proposed by the AGTEF model depending on the availability of candidates to work on the project. The proposed teams and their respective team total weightings values are then to be carried forward to the next sub-process which is to predict the high performance level of each formed and proposed team.

3.4 Team Performance Level Prediction Sub-Process

The final sub-process to complete the AGTEF model process is the Team Performance Level Prediction sub-process. This sub-process is required to predict the performance level of the proposed teams. Parameters used by the sub-process are the processed and calculated values of team weightings and IT software development project weighting supplied from the previous sub-processes. Finally, management team needs to select and assign a team from the multiple teams formed and proposed by the AGTEF model to actually work on the IT software development project. It is up to the management team's discretion to make the final judgment in assigning the team to work on a particular project.

In this sub-process, a combination of Statistical Process Control (SPC) technique and the velocity planning method (Cohn, 2010) are used by the predictor agent. SPC is a quality control method applied to monitor and control a process through statistical analysis. Monitoring and controlling a process ensures that it operates at its full potential. Control level of SPC lower limit and upper limit values are calculated by AGTEF model from the IT software development project weighting. Velocity planning method asserts ± 10% range values are to be used for a known team working in a known domain and technologies while ± 50% range values are to be used if all factors are unknown.

The parameters used for this prediction process are each proposed team's weighting and IT software development project's weighting. First, SPC upper limit and lower limit values from the IT software development project's weighting are calculated. Then, the AGTEF model will plot prediction graph to show in overall where each proposed team is located in between the values of IT software development project's weighting, SPC's upper limit and SPC's lower limit. Higher position of the team in the prediction graph indicated higher performance level predicted from the team.

From the previous Team Formation and IT Software Development Project sub-process, two teams of Team 1 and Team 2 are being proposed by the AGTEF model for final selection. Consider the domain and technologies to work on are not known, a +50% from IT software development project weighting will be used for SPC upper limit value while -50% value of IT software development project weighting is to be used for SPC lower limit value. Plotted prediction graph is as illustrated in the following Figure 5.

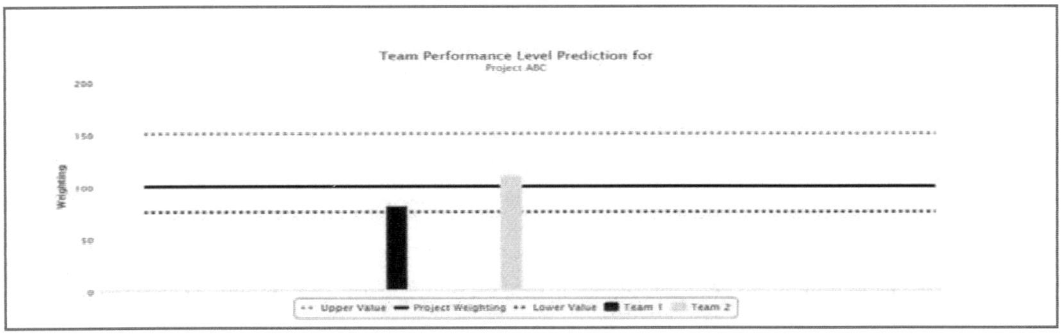

Figure 5. AGTEF's Team Performance Level Prediction Graph

The management group then will make the final decision on the team to work on an IT software development project based on the proposed teams and team performance prediction supplied by the AGTEF model. Once the management has assigned the team to work on a project, the team members of the selected team availability status will become not available. This action is required to make sure none of the team members of the selected team to work on other project at the same time.

4. MODEL EVALUATION

A case study was conducted to validate the proposed AGTEF model. This approach was appropriate for model evaluation, as the study participants comprised of individuals qualified in the related field, allowing them to provide meaningful contribution to the study. In particular, they were asked to reflect on research outputs and impacts of pre and post implementation of the AGTEF model in the selected workplace (Miller et al., 2014; Levinson and Librizzi, 2013). The AGTEF model was applied at a well-known corporation practicing Scrum methodology in delivering IT software development projects. The selected company has about five years of experience in Scrum, with a few certified Scrum members on the board. Prior to commencing the case study, the researchers contacted one of the senior company employees to obtain permission to contact the relevant staff members and conduct research at their premises.

The case study sample comprised of 20 employees, who were chosen based on their current job scope, role, and contribution to previous IT software development projects completed for the company. After the AGTEF prototype with logon credential was updated for each selected participants for future use, a briefing was conducted to explain their involvement in the study, the research objectives, the AGTEF model, the DISC personality behavioural traits, and the expected case study outcomes. Providing an explanation on the DISC personality behavioural traits was required to ensure that the participants understand the DISC personality behavioural concepts. It also allowed them to use the acquired knowledge to handle others according to their respective DISC personality behaviour traits. Each participant was also given a hyperlink to access the AGTEF's DISC assessment tool and was given one week to complete the assessment. During this period, the reporting manager of each selected participant was interviewed, allowing the researchers to obtain information on the subordinate's hard and soft skills, as this was one of the criteria applied by the

AGTEF model. The AGTEF skillset proficiency database was updated accordingly, based on the inputs from the participants' reporting managers. In addition, the company's IT Business Application Manager was asked to select two similar IT software development projects, one of which was to be completed by a team proposed by the AGTEF's model, while a manually selected team worked on the other.

In the second week of the case study, the AGTEF's IT software development project requirements were completed using the data pertaining to the selected IT software development project chosen in the previous week. The company's IT Business Application Manager was asked to select seven team members, including the Scrum Master and Product Owner, to work on a project during one working week. In addition, the AGTEF model was used to propose and form a cross-functional Agile Scrum Product teams for the IT software development project. However, the IT Business Application Manager was allowed to revise the team composition as necessary. One IT software development project was given to the selected Agile Scrum Product team. As noted above, another 7-member team, including a Scrum Master and a Product Owner, was formed manually by the IT Business Application Manager and was given another project, similar to the one assigned to the Agile Scrum Product team. Both teams had five working days to complete the project.

The researchers observed the teams as they worked on their respective projects, focusing on their personal interactions, team effectiveness, and the performance level. They also sought feedback from the IT Business Application Manager. Team performance was measured based on the members' ability to conduct effective meetings, communicate well as a group, allow all opinions to be heard, come to consensus or reach a decision, maintain clear focus, show respect to all team members, put personal agendas on hold, and collaborate with others. Further metrics included full participation from all members, clear roles and assignments, willingness to share, style diversity, greater commitment to the team, customer satisfaction and acceptance, efficient decision making, friendly environment, listening, and shared leadership leadership (Parida et al., 2015; Mealiea and Baltazar, 2005; Abran and Buglione, 2003). The entire case study was completed in two weeks.

5. RESULTS AND DISCUSSION

Both team observations and personal interviews revealed that the newly formed cross-functional Agile Scrum Team Formation executed the project much more successfully relative to the manually selected team. The former was particularly effective in holding brainstorming sessions, as every member actively participated in the discussions, which tended to be dominated by a few highly assertive members in the second case. In addition, in the Agile Scrum Product team, tasks were assigned based on the members' skillset proficiency provided by the AGTEF model, while the other team assigned tasks based on the basic assumption that each member should be able to fulfil his/her duties. Although both teams managed to deliver their respective IT software development projects on time, functionality and quality of the project delivered by the Agile Scrum Product team was higher compared to that delivered by the other team. The following Table 4 summarized the observation made.

Table 4. Case Study Results

Observation Point	AGTEF Model	Manual Selected Team
Fully cross-functional	Yes	No
Team gelling process	Fast	Moderate
Brainstorming session	Smooth – all participated	Smooth – ideas only from few members
Task assignment	Based on skillset proficiency result	Based on assumption
Project delivered on time	Yes	Yes
Acceptance of quality and functionality of delivered project	High	Acceptable
Runs effective meetings	Yes	No
Communicates well as a group	Yes	No
Allows all opinions to be heard	Yes	Sometimes
Comes to consensus or decision	Fast	Moderate
Clear focus	Yes	Yes
Respect among team members	Yes	Sometimes

Observation Point	AGTEF Model	Manual Selected Team
Personal agenda put on hold	Yes	Moderate
Collaboration within the team	Good	Good
Full participation from all members	Yes	Sometimes
Clear roles and assignments	Yes	No
Willingness to share	Yes	Yes
Style diversity	Yes	No
Greater commitment to the team	Yes	No
Faster decision making	Yes	No
Friendly environment	Yes	Cordial
Listening	Yes	No
Shared leadership	Yes	Yes

Thus, it can be deduced from the evaluation process that the AGTEF model is able to assist the management and staff members in forming the best Agile Scrum Product team to work on a particular IT software development project. By applying the DISC personality behavioural traits, the team members were able to understand the team dynamics. They anticipated each other's reactions and exhibited more tolerance toward each other. Given that the overall performance level of the Agile Scrum Product team formed by the AGTEF model was superior to that of the manually selected team, the model effectiveness was demonstrated in the case study.

6. CONCLUSION AND RECOMMENDATIONS

With this proposed model, it is hoped that this study can help organization to form highly effective Agile Scrum team. Moreover, this study also highlights the importance of assembling correct team members to deliver high quality working software on time by taking into consideration of each team member's individual personality behaviour and skillset (hard-skills and soft-skills) and software project complexity. The development of team formation model specifically for Scrum IT software development project serves as a practical contribution towards forming high performing team. The complete mapping process of the AGTEF model and the weighting used for the AGTEF model also are major contribution of this study.

Several issues or threats to validity must be considered in conducting this study. The main threat to the validity of this study is that the evaluation of the model in the form of a case study was carried out in a very short time for a simple project delivered in one sprint. Thus, a single case study may not be generalized. More evaluation needs to be carried out in order to observe the team behaviour processes and team results for a longer period with complex project and thus, corroborate the research findings. Nevertheless, in order to reduce potential biasness during the observation, the discussions with the manager were made and each team's progress was closely monitored by them. Accordingly, this study represents a first step toward achieving cross-functional Agile Scrum Product team formation through the use of systematic model approach.

ACKNOWLEDGEMENT

The authors wish to thank the Ministry of Education Malaysia for funding this study under Fundamental Research Grant Scheme (FRGS), S/O project code: 12818.

REFERENCES

Abran, A., and Buglione, L., 2003. A multidimensional performance model for consolidating balanced scorecards. *In Advances in Engineering Software*, Vol. 34, No. 6, pp. 339-349.

Andre, M., Baldoquin, M. G., and Acuna, S. T., 2011. Formal model for assigning human resources to teams in software projects. *In Information and Software Technology,* Vol. 53, No. 3, pp. 259-275.

Capretz, L. F., and Ahmed, F. 2010. Making sense of software development and personality types. *IT professional*, Vol. 12, No. 1, pp. 6-13.

Cohn, M., 2010. *Succeesing with Agile: Software Development using Scrum.* Pearson Education, Inc., Boston, USA.

DiscProfile, What is DiSC®? (2015) *The DiSC personality test explained,* [Online]. Available at: https://www.discprofile.com/what-is-disc/overview/ [Accessed January 15, 2016].

Donsbach, et al., 2009. *Team Composition Optimization:The Team Optimal Profile System (TOPS).* KS: United States Army Research Institute for the Behavioral and Social Sciences.

Gilal, A, R., Jaafar, J., Omar, M., Basri, S., and Waqas, A., 2016. A rule-based model for software development team composition: Team leader role with personality types and gender classification. *In Information and Software Technology*, Vol. 74, pp. 105-113.

Gupta, S., and V, Suma., 2013. Empirical Study on Selection of Team Members for Software Projects – Data Mining Approach. *In International Journal of Computer Science and Informatics,* Vol. 3, No. 2, pp. 2231 –5292.

Henry, T. R., 2013. Creating Effective Student Groups: An Introduction to groupformation.org. *Proceeding of the 44th ACM Technical Symposium on Computer Science Education (SIGCSE)*, Colorado, USA, pp. 645 – 650.

Hidding, G.J. and Nicholas, J.M., 2014. Reducing I.T. Project Management Failures: Early Empirical Results. *IEEE Proceedings of The 47th Hawaii International Conference on System Sciences (HICSS)*, Hawaii, USA, pp. 4305-4314.

Hoda R., and Murugesan, L.K., 2016. Multi-level agile project management challenges: A self-organizing team perspective. *In Journal of Systems and Software*, Vol. 117, pp. 245-257.

Howard, K., and Rogers, B., 2011. *Individuals and Interaction: An Agile Guide.* Pearson Education, Inc., Boston, USA.

Jiang, J. and Klein, G., 2000. Software Development Risks to Project Effectiveness. *In Journal of Systems and Software,* Vol. 52, No. 1, pp. 3-10.

Licorish, SA., and MacDonell, S.G., 2015. Communication and personality profiles of global software developers. *In Information and Software Technology*, Vol. 64, pp. 113-131.

Levinson, H., and Librizzi, R., 2013. *Using Software Development Tools and Practices in Acquisition* (No. CMU/SEI-2013-TN-017). Carnegie-Mellon Univ. Pittsburgh Software Engineering Inst.

McCuller, P. 2012. *How to Recruit and Hire Great Software Engineers: Building a Crack Development Team.* Apress Berkely, CA, USA.

Mealiea, L., & Baltazar, R., 2005. A strategic guide for building effective teams. *In Public Personnel Management*, Vol. 34, No. 2, pp. 141-160.

Miller W.E. et al., 2014. *Agile Software Teams: How They Engage with Systems Engineering on DoD Acquisition Programs* (No. CMU/SEI-2014-TN-013). Carnegie-Mellon Univ. Pittsburgh Software Engineering Inst.

Moe, N. B., Dingsøyr, T., and Dybå, T., 2008. Understanding Self-organizing Teams in Agile Software Development. *IEEE Proceedings of the 19th Australian Conference on Software Engineering,* Perth, Australia, pp. 76-85.

Parida, A., Kumar, U., Galar, D., and Stenström, C. 2015. Performance measurement and management for maintenance: a literature review. *In Journal of Quality in Maintenance Engineering*, Vol. 21 No. 1, pp. 2-33.

Prabhakaran, P. 2010. *Skills for Scrum Agile Teams*. [Online]. Available at :http://www.infoq.com/articles/ skills-for-scrum-agile-teams. [Accessed January 15, 2016].

A Guide to the Project Management Body of Knowledge (PMBOK® Guide)—Fifth Edition, 2013, Project Management Institute (PMI).

Scrum Alliance. 2014. *Core Scrum,* [Online]. Available at: https://www.scrumalliance.org/why-scrum/ core-scrum-values-roles [Accessed January 15, 2016].

Uikey, N. and Suman, U., 2012. An empirical study to design an effective agile project management framework. *ACM Proceedings of the CUBE International Information Technology Conference (CUBE '12),* Pune, India, pp. 385-390.

Wallace. L. Keil. M. and Rai.A., 2004. Understanding software project risk: a cluster analysis. *In Information & Management*, Vol. 42, No. 1, pp. 115-12.

Zaraket F. A., Olleik, M., and Yassine, A. A., 2013. Skill-based Framework for Optimal Software Project Selection and Resource Allocation. *In European Journal of operational Research,* Vol. 2, No. 1, pp. 308-318.

SPEEDING UP TIME-TO-MARKET OF IT INVESTMENTS

Mark van der Pas
European Center for Digital Transformation, Maastricht University
Tongersestraat 53, Maastricht, The Netherlands

ABSTRACT

Speed is important as it helps organisations realising goals earlier and outperforming competition. In this paper we study drivers for time-to-market based on a ten year natural experiment in a large, IT intensive, commercial organisation. It is shown that the amount of projects and the cost per project are correlated positively to time-to-market. Furthermore different incentive structures hold clear influence on time-to-market; changing them has shown to be a good instrument to accelerate.

KEYWORDS

Information Technology; Information Management; Incentives; Time-To-Market, Stage-Gated Process

1. INTRODUCTION

It takes effort and time to turn an idea into a launched IT investment. This time is called time-to-market or Speed-to-Market (comp. McNally et al. 2011, Feng et al. 2012) and is an important concept in new product development since speed can provide first mover advantage or the advantages of a fast follower (Rasmusen and Yoon 2012). Economic consequences of being late to market can be significant and include higher development and manufacturing cost, lower profit margin and lower market value (Hendricks and Singhal 1997 and 2008). A fast time-to-market is positively associated to the success of new products (Chen et al. 2005, McNally et al. 2011), or nonlinear for high uncertainty products (Chen et al. 2012).

Benefits of a fast time-to-market not only apply for revenue generating new products but also for investments reducing costs. In general the latter also hold advantages in case the savings materialise quickly and the project team is needed for a shorter period (comp. Pass and Ronen 2014). Furthermore a shorter time-to-market improves quality due to faster feedback cycles, pushes motivation since the work leads to a fast result and reduces risks due to new circumstances such as the availability of new technologies (comp. Reinertsen 2009). On top the longer a project runs the more the scope of a project can change. This so called requirements creep (Verhoef 2003) holds an average monthly growth rate of 1,1% (Jones 2000). Reducing the time-to-market reduces this requirements creep and its involved costs. Given these considerations it can be understood that time-to-market has become a management priority (Luftman et al. 2013).

Time-to-market can be measured using stage-gated processes where specific tasks are grouped into phases (Gee 1978, Griffin 1993, Kessler and Chakrabarti 1996). Chopping up work into packages and allocating them to phases can be traced back to the 15th century where the architect of the Santa Maria del Fiore in Florence divided his project into six steps (Chao and Ishii 2005). Over decades several models for stage-gated processes have been designed; these are not only applied for building cathedrals but also for creating chemical plants, building airplanes and creating new products. The models differ over the start point, end point, amount of phases and split of work packages between those phases. Several models start from the creation of an idea (Ali et al. 1995); alternative starting points are 'project start' or 'analysing the requirements' (Pass and Ronen 2014). Where some processes end with a 'launch' phase (Ali et al. 1995 and Baker and Bourne 2014), others include the 'life cycle' (e.g. Desouza et al. 2009). The process could even be extended to comprise the 'decommissioning' of the asset (Furneaux and Wade 2011). Between the start and end point multiple phases like 'develop concept', 'scoping', 'requirements definition', 'determine feasibility', 'build business case', 'product design', 'development', 'implementation', 'testing and validation' and 'production' are defined (Gee 1978, Griffin 1993, Cooper 2001, Reinertsen 2009). Decision points separating the phases are known as 'gates', 'milestones' and 'tollgates' (Cooper 2001, Chao and Ishii 2005) and determine whether a project migrates into the next stage or is terminated. Monitoring these decisions creates transparency on a lot of topics such as the amount of ideas captured, the number of launches in a certain timeframe and the amount of projects being executed at the same time. The decisions can also be used to calculate time-to-market. Subtracting the launch date e.g. from the starting date of the feasibility phase creates transparency on time-to-market (comp. Kessler and Chakrabarti 1996).

More and more products contain significant IT components or are even completely IT based such as mobile apps, online payment systems, on-demand streaming media and blockchain based currencies. Software development lifecycles (e.g. Balaji and Sundararajan Murugaiyan 2012) also apply stage-gated processes regularly (e.g. Vavpotic and Bajec 2009, Guntamukkala et al. 2006). An early example comes from Royce who detailed in 1970 the basic activities of 'analysis' and 'coding' into an eight step waterfall. Later more enhanced processes like Merise (e.g. Fitzgerald 1998) and System Analysis and Design, Structured System Analysis and Design Method (e.g. Ramakrishnan 2012) where defined and recently work is split up using scrum and agile techniques (Pass and Ronen 2014). This area is so extensive that it initiated several meta studies and models were developed to select an adequate process (Khan and Suyfan Beg 2013 and Siau and Ross 2011).

This paper works from a portfolio of stage-gated decisions for IT investments and its research question is: what drives the optimisation of time-to-market in a stage-gated environment? The work is important for better understanding and managing efforts to accelerate. This effort is presented in the following sections, commencing with a discussion of our theoretical foundations and the associated hypotheses. We then outline our research method and present our results. Finally, we conclude with a discussion of the research, its limitations, and its significance for research and practice.

2. THEORY AND HYPOTHESES

Time-to-market can be influenced by several factors such as the legacy IT infrastructure, capabilities, governance, experience and education level. Also the industry and even the structure of the stage-gated process can influence time-to-market. In this research we focus on three topics to better understand their impact on time-to-market: first the amount of projects running at the same time, second the size of the project budget and third the incentive structure.

Executing too many projects at the same time is a recurring complaint in the industry (Zika-Viktorsson et al. 2006, De Reyck 2005). An oversized portfolio (Blichfeldt and Eskerod 2008) is not only very common it also triggers 'multitasking' which is seen as one of the core competencies for managing multiple projects (Patanakul and Milosevic 2008 and Aaltonen 2006). Multitasking can reduce time-to-market (e.g. Robinson and Richards 2009, Pass and Ronen 2014) as can easily be illustrated over two projects (comp. Anavi-Isakow and Golany 2003). The first project, project *a*, has a time-to-market of t_a and the second project (*b*) of t_b. The average time-to-market when *b* is executed after finishing *a* is:

$$(t_a + t_a + t_b) / 2 = t_a + 0.5\ t_b$$

The average time-to-market in a multitasking case, where project *a* is first semi-finished, after that half of project *b* is delivered, then *a* is fully completed and finally *b* is finalised, is:

$$(0.5\ t_a + 0.5\ t_b + 0.5\ t_a + 0.5\ t_a + 0.5\ t_b + 0.5\ t_a + 0.5\ t_b) / 2 = t_a + 0.75\ t_b$$

Whilst t_b is a positive figure the average time-to-market in the first situation is faster than in the multi tasking alternative (assuming that reordering the projects does not change t_a nor t_b). On top additional time is lost due to switching activities (Rubinstein et al. 2001) and due to correcting the failures resulting from task switching (Gilbert and Shallice 2002, Monsell 2003). A higher work in progress also increases queues in the system which will increase leadtime and variability (Reinertsen 2009). This leads to the conclusion that executing more projects at the same time decelerates time-to-market given existing resources. In case the resources can be scaled then this effect can be mitigated; but since it is an on-going complaint of IT managers we nevertheless expect time-to-market to slow down with an increasing amount of projects.

H1. The amount of projects is correlated positively with time-to-market.

In the second hypothesis we shift our attention from the amount of projects to the average project cost. The basic assumption is that the higher the project cost, the more work needs to be done which will prolong time-to-market (comp. Lavazza et al. 2013). So if project *a* from the H1 example holds less budget than project *b* then we would expect $t_a < t_b$. Verhoef (2002) even defined a benchmark confirming a relationship between function points (Garmus and Herron 2001) and time-to-market: the project duration equals the amount of function points to the power 0.32. Although this seems plausible there are at least three reasons to doubt this. First cost of commercial of the shelf software can form a significant part of an IT investment. The fees charged for this software is only partially determined by the initial cost to create the software whilst this fixed cost can be reimbursed over all paying customers. Nevertheless the actual price of the software does not need to correlate to this cost calculation as it can be determined by other factors (such as the profit targets of the supplier and the benefits for the customer). This model further is expected to accelerate time-to-market since the software is already created when it is purchased (Schulz 2000 and Julian et al. 2011). Second a relation between the project cost and the amount of work is assumed. This relationship is not always present and can often not be validated due to the absence of a unity on the amount of IT delivered like function points. When the amount of function points is known, then the project cost can be calculated by multiplying them with the cost per function point. In daily praxis the appliance of function points for this purpose is limited as measuring function points is costly (Lavazza et al. 2013) and only a few organisations are using them (e.g. Bok and Raman 2000). The absence of these units limits organisations' capabilities to monitor the relationship between cost and amount of work and for that the relationship of cost to time-to-market as defined by Verhoef. Third project cost can be increased with the purpose of speeding up time-to-market, this can be done over additional staff and by minimising procedures like skipping negotiation time in the purchase processes. Verhoefs' power function makes clear that speeding up time-to-market can be costly as the efficiency of software creation reduces exponentially (comp. McNally et al. 2011). But when executed successfully it would lead to both higher project costs as well as faster time-to-market. Despite these considerations we expect time-to-market to be related to the average project cost.

H2. The cost of a project is correlated positively with time-to-market.

The incentive structure is the third and final parameter studied in this paper. IT supported incentives have shown to generate disproportionate productivity gains (Aral 2012) and in daily praxis numerous incentives have been created for IT. Examples for the latter are the availability of the IT-infrastructure, the amount and impact of IT-security breaches and the customer satisfaction of the IT-helpdesk. In this study we focus on three time-to-market related incentives for the IT investment portfolio: plan accuracy, efficiency and impact. These three are described in the next sections.

Plan accuracy, or delivering projects according to the planned cost, time and quality, has been an important topic in IT for decades (Atkinson 1999, The Standish Group 2004 and Flyvbjerg and Budzier 2011). It is so meaningful that project managers have turned plan accuracy into a de facto 'honor code'; they do not want their projects to be late nor to overrun budget. Plan accuracy is valued by organisations too, since numerous project managers and their management are rewarded monetarily for compliance. These plan accuracy incentives are focussed on e.g. the percentage of projects delivered on time and in budget or the forecast to actual ratio (e.g. Eveleens et al. 2012). Alternatively the EQF (Estimated Forecast Quality), a more advanced time weighted approach calculating the difference between the forecasts and the actuals, can be used to measure plan accuracy (DeMarco 1982).

Besides plan accuracy organisations also hold an interest in efficiency. The speed of execution and the cost to produce software are the key concepts for efficiency. Optimal efficiency is defined as 'technical efficiency' and measured over the distance between the maximum output of the available resources and the actual output (Shao and Lin 2002). Where plan accuracy can be calculated over simple performance indicators, measuring efficiency is more challenging since the maximum output is a theoretical concept normally unknown in IT and the usage of function points is limited in daily praxis. But efficiency incentives can be focussed on lowering the cost per function point and also on, especially relevant for this study, speeding up time-to-market. The latter can be calculated more easily using the timestamps of stage-gate decisions.

The impact of an IT investment is the effect of that investment. The impact can be financial such as cash, Internal Rate of Return (IRR) or Net Present Value (NPV) (e.g. Van der Pas and Furneaux 2015) but can also be on customer experience such as Net Promoter Score (Reichheld 2003) and the Customer Effort Score (Dixon et al. 2010) or on compliance to new legislation. An example for an impact incentive is to maximise the total delivered NPV of the IT investment portfolio.

The three incentives, plan accuracy, efficiency and impact can push for contradictory decisions. Improving efficiency can reduce the portfolio impact and plan accuracy can be optimised at the cost of efficiency. These conflicting effects are described in the next two sections.

Prioritising efficiency can reduce impact and vice versa. This can be illustrated over the sequence of executing projects where optimising time-to-market can require a different queueing discipline than maximising impact. Again we use the two projects from Hypothesis 1 to illustrate this. In case project *a* holds a shorter time-to-market than project *b*, then the average time-to-market is improved by first executing *a* and then *b*. So if t_a is shorter than t_b then:

$$t_a + 0.5\ t_b < t_b + 0.5\ t_a$$

The overall impact of the portfolio can also be optimised over the row order of the investments. If project *b* is executed after project *a* then the total NPV of the portfolio using a discount rate of *i* equals:

$$NPV_a + NPV_b / (1+ i)^{t(a)}$$

To maximise the total impact the projects should be prioritised based on the combination of NPV, time-to-market and discount rate. Project *b* should be started before project *a* if:

$$NPV_b + NPV_a / (1+ i)^{t(b)} > NPV_a + NPV_b / (1+ i)^{t(a)}$$

This is also correct when $t_a < t_b$ (assuming that reordering the projects does not change the input variables). We conclude that the optimal queueing discipline depends on the chosen incentives.

Some activities to optimise plan accuracy reduce efficiency. A project leader could consider improving plan accuracy by including more risks into the estimation. If he expects that a task can normally be done in two days then he could plan three or perhaps even more days to protect himself for schedule overrun. This extra time is reserved for unexpected additional complexity, requirements creep or for the non-compliance of preconditions such as required input not being delivered on time or with the right quality. It also protects, besides tons of other reasons, against non-availability of important expertise holders, or resources like testing environments being reprioritised. Adding additional contingency is well accepted; the lack of it is even considered as one of the reasons for overruns (Flyvbjerg et al. 2003). This strong focus on plan accuracy could go at the cost of efficiency in case the task is delivered in three days whilst only two days were needed. This is not unlikely due to the new plan of three days, because of procrastination problems (Ariely and Wertenbroch 2002) and since delivering in two days would indicate an inaccurate plan. So in case contingencies are planned that do not occur and the plan is nevertheless consumed completely, then plan accuracy is optimised at the cost of efficiency.

Due to the absence of efficiency units for a lot of organisations, the limited availability of impact KPIs and the strong pressure on plan accuracy we expect that plan accuracy is optimised at the cost of fast impact focused time-to-market. Changing the incentive structure towards efficiency and impact will change the queueing discipline as well as the tons of small decisions (so not only a few big ones) that optimise efficiency or impact. This leads to hypothesis 3 where we expect that the time-to-market is influenced by the incentive structure. Plan accuracy based incentive structures will hold the slowest time-to-market; the fastest time-to-market is expected for an efficiency based incentive structure. Hypothesis 3 is defined as:

H3. Time-to-market is correlated with the existing incentive structure.

3. METHOD

The hypotheses are tested using data from a natural experiment. The data was offered by a large commercial organisation and cover a time span of 10 years (March 2004 – April 2014) and more than $1bn investments. The organisation used a gated process and calculated the time-to-market from the start of the feasibility phase until the (commercial) launch of the asset. There was a high process discipline, which was also enforced by their portfolio management tool using a workflow to approve or reject gates. The gated process was updated with minor changes over the 10 years, but the related milestones nor the division of work over the stages changed.

In this study we focus on projects that benefit from a fast time-to-market and excluded investments that should not be speeded up such as 47 legal projects with a prescribed launch date as the only instrument to improve their time-to-market is a late project start which could add unnecessary risks and cost. We excluded these projects and the cancelled projects, that never got launched, from the study and used a remaining data set of 1595 launched projects. The average project cost in the data set were 579k. Whereas 88% of the projects held a budget of less than $1m, 185 projects held a larger budget. The 17 projects with a budget over $10m consumed 29% of the total investment.

The organisation used three incentive structures in the ten-year time-period. Up to 2007 the involved management and staff was incentivised for plan accuracy; projects needed to be delivered on time and in budget. The target was to keep the amount of projects with a budget overrun of more than 10% below a predefined percentage of projects. That percentage increased over the years due to the good performance against this plan accuracy target. From 2007 up to 2011 the incentive was on delivering value fast, a combination of impact (NPV) and efficiency (time-to-market). This was measured with a formula that weighted the time-to-market of the delivered project with their NPV; the time-to-market of a high NPV project was weighted stronger in to the incentive than the time-to-market of a lower NPV project. The organisation accomplished to outperform this target and it was raised every year because of that performance. As from 2011 none of the three incentive structures were applied; the incentives of IT staff and management were not related to plan accuracy nor to the efficiency or the impact of the IT investments. The projects are allocated to the period in which they are launched; this is consistent to the incentives of organisation in this study.

4. RESULTS

The goals that were set through the incentives showed an improved performance over the years. Plan accuracy improved year on year during the time the incentive on plan accuracy was active. The organisation achieved a relatively high plan accuracy with a median EQF of 6.0. This EQF is a blended value made up out of an unprecedented median EQF of 10.3 for cost optimisation projects and a median EQF of 4.7 for new product development projects (Eveleens et al. 2012). The higher uncertainty of new products as compared to optimising existing and known processes could explain the difference in EQF between these two categories. Also the new target, the combination of value and time-to-market, showed a year on year improvement as it was incentivised as from 2007. Although the longitudinal development was positive the absolute performance could not be compared since no benchmarks are known to the author.

The hypotheses were tested with regression analyses combining categorical and continuous predictors. The categorical predictors are needed for H3 and were combined with dummy coding with reference groups on incentives.

H1 and H2 are tested with a Pearson's product-moment correlation and both are significant (***). The project budget explains 12% of the proportionate variance in time-to-market ($R^2 = 0.12$). The explaining power of the amount of projects is much lower; less than 1% of the proportionate variance. A model combining both predictors in a multiple regression is significantly better than both models with single predictors (* as compared to the model used for H1 on the amount of projects and *** as compared to the model using project budget). The combination of project budget and amount of projects explains 12% of the time-to-market variance.

In H3 the three incentive structures were tested as categorical predictors for the dependent variable time-to-market in a regression analysis. The three categories differ significantly (***) and the average time-to-market dropped with 30% when switching from plan accuracy to the combined efficiency and impact incentive. This improvement in time-to-market can be based on dropping the plan accuracy incentive as the latter can be optimised at the cost of time-to-market as well as on the work done by IT management and staff to improve the performance against the new target. The actual time-to-market in the absence of an incentive was 7% below the time-to-market with the efficiency and impact incentive. Since the amount of projects reduced with 3% and the average project cost reduced even with 34% the expected time-to-market would have accelerated faster in case the incentive was remained.

Combining the three variables into one model improves the prediction of time-to-market. Overall 15,4% (R^2) of the variance in time-to-market can be explained by the variables project cost, amount of projects at the same time and incentive structure.

5. CONCLUSION

Time-to-market is an important performance indicator for the process of developing new products as well as cost optimisation IT investments. A faster time-to-market enables the benefits to hit the profit and loss statement of a company earlier and helps to outperform competition.

Practitioners aiming to improve the performance of their IT investment portfolio can use the results of this study to determine the goals they want to accomplish with their portfolio as well as the usage of the three instruments (project cost, work in progress and incentive) to improve their goal accomplishment. Overall the 10 years natural experiment showed an improvement of more than 40% on time-to-market, which was, amongst others, driven by the amount of projects running at the same time (work in progress), the average project cost and the incentive structure. Impressive was the change from plan accuracy to a combined impact and efficiency incentive, which was accompanied by an improvement of 31%.

Further research on time-to-market of IT investments could be focused on benchmarking both time-to-market performance as well as the impact of IT investments. This would allow organisations to compare their performance in these arena's with other organisations and is expected to be relevant since large differences in time-to-market have been seen in daily praxis by the author. A second topic for future research could be on the IT investments that do not use a stage gated approach. Especially agile development is gaining attention and although the duration of a sprint does not really express the time-to-market of an IT investment, the time it takes for a described idea to be available for (new) customers or internal staff to benefit from the process improvements could be used as a proxy.

REFERENCES

Aaltonen, P., 2010. *Co-selection in R&D Project Portfolio Management: Theory and Evidence*. PhD thesis. Helsinki University.

Ali, A.A. et al, 1995. Product innovativeness and entry strategy: Impact on cycle time and break-even time. *Journal of Product Innovation Management,* Vol. 12, No. 1,pp 54-69.

Anavi-Isakow, S. and B. Golany, 2003. Managing multi-project environments through constant work-in-process. *International Journal of Project Management,* Vol. 21, No. 6,pp 9-18.

Aral, S. et al, 2012. Three-way complementarities: performance pay, human resource analytics, and information technology. *Management Science,* Vol. 58, No. 5,pp 913-931.

Ariely, D. and K. Wertenbroch, 2002. Procrastination, deadlines and performance: self-control by precommitment. *American Psychology Society,* Vol. 13, No. 3,pp 219-224.

Atkinson, R., 1999. Project management: cost, time and quality, two best guesses and a phenomenon, its time to accept other success criteria. *International Journal of Project Management,* Vol. 17, No. 6,pp 337-342.

Baker, M and M. Bourne, 2014. A governance framework for the Idea-to-Launch process. *Research-Technology Management,* Vol. 57, No. 1,pp. 42–48.

Balaji, S. and M. Sundararajan Murugaiyan, 2012. Waterfall versus V-Model versus Agile: a comparative study on SDLC. *International Journal of Information Technology and Business Management,* Vol. 2, No. 1,pp 26-30.

Blichfeldt, B.S. and P. Eskerod, 2008. Project portfolio management - There's more to it than management enacts. *International Journal of Project Management,* Vol. 26, No. 6,pp 357–365.

Bok, H.S. and K.S. Raman, 2000. Software engineering productivity measurement using function points: a case study. *Journal of Information Technology,* Vol. 15,pp 79–90.

Chao, L.P. and K. Ishii, 2005. Design process error proofing, benchmarking gate and phased review life-cycle models. Presented at IDETC/CIE 2005, Long Beach, CA, USA, September 24-28.

Chen, J. et al, 2005. The impacts of speed-to-market on new product success: the moderating effects of uncertainty. *IEEE transactions on engineering management,* Vol. 52, No. 2,pp 199-212.

Chen, J. et al, 2012. New product development speed: too much of a good thing? *Journal of Product Innovation,* Vol. 29, No. 2,pp 288-303.

Cooper, R.G., 2001. *Winning at new products: accelerating the process from idea to launch*. Cambridge Massachusetts: Perseus publishing.

DeMarco, T., 1982. *Controlling Software Projects*, Yourdon Press, Prentice Hall.

Desouza, K. et al, 2009. Crafting organizational innovation processes. *Innovation: Management, Policy & Practice,* Vol. 11, No. 1,pp 6-33.

Dixon, M., K. et al, 2010. Stop Trying to Delight Your Customers. *Harvard Business Review,* Vol. 88, No. 7/8, pp 116-122.

Eveleens, J.L., et al, 2012. Quantifying forecast quality of IT business value. *Science of Computer Programming,* Vol. 77, No. 3,pp 314-354.

Feng, T. et al, 2012. Customer orientation for decreasing time-to-market of new products: IT implementation as a complementary asset. *Industrial Marketing Management,* Vol. 41, No. 6,pp 929-939.

Fitzgerald, B., 1998. An empirical investigation into the adoption of systems development methodologies. *Information & Management,* Vol. 34, No. 6,pp 317-328.

Flyvbjerg, B. et al, 2003, *Megaprojects and risk. An anatomy of ambition*, Cambridge University Press, Cambridge, UK.

Flyvbjerg, B. and A. Budzier, 2011. Why your IT project may be riskier than you think. *Harvard Business Review,* Vol. 89, No. 9,pp 23-25.

Furneaux, B. and M. Wade, 2011. An exploration of organizational level information systems discontinuance intentions. *MIS Quarterly,* Vol. 35, No. 3,pp 573-598.

Garmus, D. and D. Herron, 2001. *Function Point Analysis -- measurement practices for successful software projects*. Addison-Wesley, Boston, USA.

Gee, S., 1978. Factors affecting the innovation time-period. *Research Management*, Vol. 21, No. 1,pp 37-42.

Gilbert, S.J. and T. Shallice, 2002. Task-Switching: a PDP model. *Cognitive Psychology*, Vol. 44,pp 297-337.

Griffin, A., 1993. Metrics for measuring product development cycle time. *Journal of Product Innovation Management,* Vol. 10, No. 2,pp 112–25.

Guntamukkala, V. et al, 2006. An empirical study of selecting software development life cycle models. *Human Systems Management,* Vol. 25, No. 4,pp 265-278.

Hendricks, K.B. and V.R. Singhal, 1997. Delays in new product introductions and the market value of the firm, the consequences of being late to market. *Management Science, Vol.* 43, No. 4,pp 422-436.

Hendricks, K.B. and V.R. Singhal, 2008. The effect of product Introduction delays on operating performance. *Management Science,* Vol. 54, No. 5,pp 878-892.

Jones, C., 2000. *Software assessments, benchmarks, and best practices*, Information Technology Series, Addison-Wesley.

Julian, C. et al, 2011. Commercial-Off-The-Shelf selection process. *Engineering Management Journal,* Vol. 23, No. 2, pp 63-71.

Khan, P.M. and M.M. Suyfan Beg, 2013. Extended Decision Support Matrix for Selection of SDLC-Models on Traditional and Agile Software Development Projects. *International Journal of Software Engineering Research & Practices,* Vol. 3, No. 1,pp 1-8.

Kessler, E. H. and A. K. Chakrabarti, 1996. Innovation speed: A conceptual model of context, antecedents, and outcomes. *Academy of Management Review,* Vol. 21, No. 4,pp 1143–1191.

Lavazza, L. et al, 2013. Towards a simplified definition of function points. *Information and Software Technology,* Vol. 55,pp 1796-1809.

Luftman, J. et al, 2013. Key information technology and management issues 2012-2013: an international study. *Journal of Information Technology,* Vol. 28, No. 4,pp 354-366.

McNally, R.C. et al, 2011. New Product Development processes and new product profitability: exploring the mediating role of speed to market and product quality. *Journal of Product Innovation,* Vol. 28, No. 1, pp 63-77.

Monsell, S., 2003. Task switching. *Trends in cognitive sciences,* Vol. 7, No. 3, pp 134-140.

Pass, S. and B. Ronen, 2014. Reducing the software value gap. *Communications of the ACM,* Vol. 57, No. 5,pp 80-87.

Pas, van der M. and B. Furneaux, 2015. Improving the Predictability of IT investment Business Value. *European Conference on Information Systems 2015*, paper 190, http://aisel.aisnet.org/ecis2015_cr/190/

Patanakul, P. and D. Milosevic, 2008. A competency model for effectiveness in managing multiple projects. *The Journal of High Technology Management Research,* Vol. 18, No. 2,pp 118-131.

Ramakrishnan, S., 2012. System Analysis and Design. *Information Technology & Software Engineering,* December 2012.

Rasmussen, E. and Y.R. Yoon, 2012. First versus second mover advantage with information asymmetry about the profitability of new markets. *The journal of industrial economics,* Vol. 15, No. 3,pp 375-405.

Reichheld, F.F., 2003. The one number you need. *Harvard Business Review,* Vol. 81, No. 12,pp 46-54.

Reyck, de B. et al, 2005. The impact of project portfolio management on information technology projects. *International Journal of Project Management,* Vol. 23, No. 6,pp 524–537.

Robinson, H. and R. Richards, 2009. An introduction to critical chance project management. *AACE International Transactions* PS.S03.1-11.

Royce, W.W., 1970. Managing the development of large software systems: concepts and techniques. In: *Proceedings of the 9th International Conference on Software Engineering*, Monterey, CA: 328–338.

Rubinstein, J.S. et al, 2001. Executive control of cognitive process in task switching. *Journal of Experimental Psychology: Human Perception and Performance*, Vol. 27, No. 4,pp 763–797.

Schulz, A.P. et al, 2000. Development and integration of winning technologies as key to competitive advantage. *Systems Engineering,* Vol. 3, No. 4,pp180-211.

Shao, B. M. and W. T. Lin, 2002. Technical efficiency analysis of information technology investments: a two-stage empirical investigation. *Information Systems Journal,* Vol. 21, No. 5,pp 249-268.

Siau, K. and M. Ross, 2011. Evaluation techniques for systems analysis and design modelling methods – a review and comparative analysis. *Information & Management,* Vol. 39, No. 5,pp 391-401.

The Standish Group, 2004. *Chaos demographics, third quarter research report*, The Standish Group.

Vavpotic, D. and M. Bajec, 2009. An approach for concurrent evaluation of technical and social aspects of software development methodologies. *Information and Software Technology,* Vol 51,pp 528–545

Verhoef, C., 2002. Quantitative IT Portfolio Management. *Science of Computer Programming,* Vol. 45, No. 1, pp 1-96.

Verhoef, C., 2003. *Quantifying the value of IT investments*, Vrije Universiteit Amsterdam, Amsterdam, Netherlands.

Zika-Viktorsson, A. et al, 2006. Project overload: An exploratory study of work and management in multi-project settings. *International Journal of Project Management,* Vol. 24, No. 6,pp 385-394.

RFID TECHNOLOGY ADOPTION IN KUWAIT

Kamel Rouibah and Lama A. M. Aljaljouli
College of Business Administration, Kuwait University, Shuwaikh Campus, 13055 Kuwait

ABSTRACT

RFID is a new technology that has received widespread use over the last decade. This study focuses on giving an overview of this technology as well as investigating factors that affect the intention to adopt this technology in an Arab country by using a mixed approach of data collection (quantitative and qualitative). The qualitative study shows some fields of its application as well as its advantages and potential obstacles toward its spread in Kuwait. Quantitative approach focused on a sample of 144 participants and the qualitative approach involves interviewing an expert in RFID. Main results reveal that RFID is in its early stages of adoption and is applied in very narrow fields (hospitals, banks and supermarkets) and is still not widely spread in Kuwait. In addition, the results reveal four important factors that may affect the intention to adopt RFID in Kuwait. These factors are relative advantage, complexity, trust, and privacy and security. However, this study did not test the direct paths from the four exogenous variables to the intention to use RIFD. Results of this study are important to advance the theory and practice of RFID in developing countries.

KEYWORDS

RFID Adoption, Bar Code, Diffusion of Innovation, Relative Advantage, Complexity, Trust, Privacy and Security

1. INTRODUCTION

RFID stands for the Radio Frequency Identification. It is the substitution of the Universal Product Code bar codes developed in the 1970s, and uses radio waves instead of light waves to read a tag. RFID is categorized as one of the ten competitors' technologies in the 21th century. This technology allows tracking people and objects without a line of sight. RFID has different applications in many fields including supply chains, human identity verifications, healthcare, construction industry, timing system in athletic stadiums, vehicle environment, disaster evacuation response, automobile immobilizers, animal tracking, payment systems, automatic toll collection, and inventory management (Nambiar 2009; Rouibah et al., 2011). The market of this technology is promising. The market was estimated at $8.8 billion in 2013, $9.5 billion in 2014 and $10.1 billion in 2015, and expected to reach $13.2 billion in 2020. This market includes tags, readers and software/services for RFID cards (Das and Harrop 2006). This study aims to give an overview of this technology in term of its definition, history, components system and how it works, the main difference between RFID and bar code technology, as well its different applications. This study also aims to explore factors that affect the use of this technology in Kuwait, which is an Arab country; based on the Theory of Diffusion of Innovation, using a mixed research approach that combines a qualitative and quantitative data collection.

2. BACKGROUND OF RFID

2.1. Definition of RFID

RFID is one technology among a variety of other automatic identification technologies that are used to recognize and track objects or people including bar codes systems, biometrics systems, smart cards, near field communication technologies and optical characters recognitions. RFID uses the wireless electromagnetic fields to transfer data from the tag to the reader. RFID uses Electronic Product Code (EPC) number to identify objects or humans. EPC is a unique number that identifies a specific object, which was developed by the Auto-ID center and is presently managed by EPCglobalEPC. The EPC number is stored on an RFID tag. The tag carries minimum information about the object. Additional and required data can be obtained from the network database that stores related information about the objects. This will result in simplifying the RFID tag as much as possible, and making the price of the tag very cheap. It is expected that that RFID technology will spread widely and quickly to different industries; making it a replacement for the bar code technology (Harrison 2004).

2.2. History of RFID

The roots of RFID technology goes back to 1940 during the Second World War. The German, Japanese, American and British armies were all using radar to caution their men of approaching enemy planes. The first active Identify Friend or Foe (IFF) system, similar to RFID concept, was developed by the British, and was used during the Second World War in order to solve the problem of identifying planes and distinguishing them from those of the enemies. In 1948 Harry Stockman published a paper called "*Communication by Means of Reflected Power*" which built the basics for RFID technology. In the 1950s and 1960s many laboratory experiments have been conducted to discover how radio frequency could be used to identify objects from distant places. In 1970s, Los Alamos National Laboratory was asked by the Energy Department to develop a system for tracking nuclear materials. The scientists suggested putting a tag in the trucks and readers at the gates of protected amenities. The reader transmitted radio frequency waves and let the tag respond with an ID and communicate additional data. In the 1980s, companies started using RFID tags as alternatives for barcodes. Companies started advertising for anti-theft systems that used radio frequency waves to determine whether an item had been paid. In 1990s, RFID saw the boom of its development. And from year 2000 till date RFID has been widely applied in different areas and its products increasingly became an important part in people's daily life (Sun and Jiang 2013) including animal tracking (Rouibah et al., 2011) and document management (Rouibah and Al-Zanki 2013).

2.3. Components of RFID System and how it Works

RFID system operates using the radio spectrum and consists of four components: tags, readers, middleware, and application software system.

Tag contains very small semiconductor chips and a very small antenna. The chip has a unique Electronic Product Code (EPC). The antenna performs the communication between the tags and the readers. There are different kinds of tags: active tags and passive tags. *Passive tags* receive their power from the electromagnetic energy transmitted from the reader itself. They are readable up to a surface of 2.5 square m However *active tags* operate in a longer range, and use power from an internal source like a battery. Table 1 shows the differences between *passive tags* and *active tags*.

Table 1. Differences between Passive Tags and Active Tags (Sun and Jiang 2013)

Passive tags	Active tags
Use electromagnetic energy transmitted from the reader	Use the power from an internal source like a battery
Short range	Long range
Low data transmission rates	High data transmission rates
Can read a few tags at once	Can read many tags at once
Small in size	Large size
Require no infield maintenance	Require infield maintenance
Easy manufacturing	Difficult manufacturing
Low cost	High cost

The *Reader* receives information from the tag and transmits it to the computer system for processing and identification. *Middleware* sits between the RFID reader and the application software system, and facilitate data communication between the reader and the system. *RFID Software* application represents the most critical part of an RFID system. It operates the process by controlling the reader to read and write information from the tags, and manage the collected data. The application software sends commands and accepts warnings. As an example, RFID identifies an animal and sends a command to the reader to identify it as a sheep, when the reader receives any information, it will send a warning to the application that this animal belongs to person X who claims he is the owner and not person Y. In this way the application software can manage livestock easily and immediately and allows settling of conflicts between animal breeders. To operate the RFID system with efficiency, the tag must receive a signal with certain strength from the reader and the reader must be sensitive enough to capture the weak response from the tag, so the tag and the reader can be coupled in one of two ways.

2.4 Comparison between RFID and Bar Code Technologies

White et al., (2007) made a comparison between Barcodes and RFID, which are considered two technologies of automatic identification and data capture. They are used as both automatic identification and tracking technologies of objects and people. The major difference between barcodes and RFID is the line-of-sight. *First*, while barcodes must pass through an optical laser or any imaging technology to be scanned, RFID uses the radio waves. Therefore tags can be read if it is within range of a reader without a line-of-sight. *Second*, unlike barcodes that identify only manufacturer and product, and not the unique item, RFID tag gives a unique item level identification based on EPC, and more data can be known upon request about a certain item including its position. For example, the barcode on one grape juice carton is the same as any other carton. Accordingly, it will be impossible to identify which bottle has the first expiration date, but using RFID tag, each bottle will have a unique code that tracks such information about it (White et al., 2007). Table 2 shows the differences between *bar code tags* and *RFID Tags*.

Table 2. Advantages of Bar Code Tags vs. RFID Tags (White et al., 2007)

Criteria of comparison	Barcode tags	RFID tags
Human capital /read data	Read manually by a human, once at time	Read automatically and more than one tag at time
Line of sight	Require a line of sight	Do not require a line of sight
Durability	Low	High
Security	Low	High
Event Stimulation	Cannot be used to stimulate special events (like do openings, alarms)	Can be used to stimulate special events (like door openings, alarms)
Ability for updating	Stored data cannot be updated	Stored data can be updated
Cases in damaging	Ease to damage and cannot be read when damaged	Hard to be damaged

3. LITERATURE REVIEW ABOUT RFID

3.1 A Subset of RFID Studies Adoption

Many studies focused on different issues related to RFID adoption. And the number of published articles increased considerably between 1990 and 2017. The literature review carried out by White et al., (2007) showed that the number of published studies reached nine thousand by 2005 from almost zero in 1990s. Since the number is increasing this study only reviews a subset of these studies.

Garfinkel et al. (2005) focused on the privacy and security issues facing RFID technology, discussed privacy risks and threats, and suggested solutions to improve these two issues for RFID systems. Authors also discussed RFID deployment and potential applications. They discussed how this technology will spread widely in the next years.

Hennig et al., (2005) focused on the privacy and security issues for the RFID system and how to overcome these two challenges. The authors mentioned that tracking without knowledge, by means of hidden tags or readers directly clashes with the privacy regulations. Moreover, people might change their actions when they believe their information is recorded and tracked. This directly conflicts with human rights. For example in one branch of Wal-Mart (in the USA) there have been tests with RFID in customer space without telling them photos were automatically taken of customers in the process of buying a certain product, triggered by embedded RFID tags upon leaving the shelf. Hennig et al., (2005) discussed the check lists that already existed for the privacy enhancing concepts and suggested one check list to help in this direction.

None of these concepts are able to address all privacy issues relevant to the RFID system. There are still some misconceptions regarding privacy and data protection.

Fuhrer and Guinard (2006) focused on implementing RFID system in the healthcare and pharmaceutical settings. RFID system will facilitate the work of doctors, nurses, and other medical staff. It will also make patients more comfortable by reducing the medical errors (wrong medicine or diagnoses). On the other hand, authors mentioned that there are some problems that must be solved before the healthcare community can fully embrace the RFID technology. Furthermore, the consequences and side-effects of radio waves on the exposed humans need to be clarified before expecting a widespread use of this technology in these two fields. Also, privacy and security must be insured while using this system in the healthcare environment.

Nath et al., (2006) discussed the significance of RFID in the market, and explained four major RFID applications for this promising technology: (i) *Static RFID readers* can be implemented in rented cars, planes and luggage labels and help to track them instantly and efficiently. In healthcare industry tags could be used to reduce medical problems like wrong medicine or dosage form. (ii) *Mobile readers* embedded in mobile phones can be used to read information from tags on products to give full information about them as well as for electronic payments. Also, embedded tags in packages can improve the postal work. (iii) *RFID for actuation,* this is the case of using this technology in hotels, where customers can use embedded tags in their mobile phones in order to execute routine tasks such as automatic check in, check out, payments as well as providing customers with service they like. An illustrating example consists for a customer using his mobile phone as a smart key to access his room. (iv) *Incorporating sensor technologies based RFID* represents an important and promising field of applications where attached RFID sensors to human bodies can give information about stress, weather resistance, blood pressure, heart rhythm etc. As a result, medical practitioners (e.g. physicians, doctors, nurses) may now more quickly get information about their patients especially in emergency cases (e.g. road accidents).

White et al., (2007) address a comparison between RFID and bar coding technologies. Authors also discussed different applications of RFID technology in some major retailer companies in their supply chains, as the case of Tesco, Marks and Spencer, Wal-Mart, and Prada. To reduce the literature review we cite only the case of Wal-Mart that necessitates its top 100 suppliers to now implement RFID tags on all products carried into their storehouses. White et al., (2007) also conducted a study at Marks and Spencer in which they compared advantages of RFID technology over bar code. Marks and Spencer had implemented RFID system within its refrigerated food distribution chain, to replace the existing barcode system that had been in use for many years. Twenty five employees had been fully trained on both bar-code system and RFID scanning equipment. Results revealed that RFID is faster and reliable in conducting operations than bar codes. In fact, the difference between the times taken to perform the operation using RFID was in average 9.67 seconds (SD = 3.0134), while it is 24.48 seconds (SD = 3.6858) with the barcode scanning system. This supports the view that RFID can increase the productivity, and lower product search times compared to bar coding.

Nambiar (2009) conducted a literature review on RFID applications in term of studies that focused on identification, monitoring, authentication and alerting based RFID. He also studied the privacy and security issues related to this technology and how to overcome these two challenges. He also studied some of the RFID applications such as its use in the supply chains and healthcare fields.

Chatfield et al. (2010) discussed the RFID applications for e-governments. According to the authors RFID has many applications which can be used in disasters like earthquakes, and volcanos. But these applications are not studied effectively by the e-government. Natural disasters have many economic and social impacts on the affected communities. These effects can be reduced by using RFID systems. The Japanese government's RFID promotion policy considers RFID deployment not only for supply chain management context, but also to address societal issues such as disaster prevention and environment protection. Chatfield et al. (2010) dicussed how e-government research priorities need to build regional disaster preparedness, as an integral part of their e-government development policy.

Sun et al., (2013) discussed the importance of the RFID system in the construction field, and how to benefit from this technology. Different applications for RFID technology in the construction industry were discussed including: construction time and schedule management, construction quality management, construction supply chain management, construction safe management, construction document management and construction waste management

Woellik et al., (2014) conducted an experiment that has been done to compare RFID system in track fields with the light barriers. Measurements show an average error compared to light barrier less than 0.04 second. In case of wearing more than one transponder across the body the average error will be less than 0.02 second. As a result, timing during training can be easier by using RFID system, because the measured times are 20-60 seconds close to the results given by official timing systems. These results can be stored and used as a data base for the coach to evaluate each trainer and improve his/her performance.

3.2 Applications of RFID

Applications of RFID are growing very fast and are used to track every thing from objects, to people to animals. These applications are appearing in many fields and areas of our daily life, such as the following : Use of RFID timing system to track players, record their performance during play, and analyze their training performance in athletic stadium (Woelliket al., 2014); use of RFID technologies in hospitals for patient identification, tracking new born babes, blood tracking and making sure that the right blood batch is given to the right patient, tracking equipment, avoiding their theft and ease the work of doctors, nurses, and other medical staff (Fuhrer and Guinard 2006); use of RFID in supply chains to increase productivity, minimizing loss, and reduce of human errors (Wamba, 2008); use of RFID for evacuation response during crisis and disasters by rapidly locating the places for different categories of people (e.g. old, children, disabled people and high value assets in order to minimize losses (Chatfield et al., 2010), RFID for livestock animals and to reduce the manipulation of state subsidies (see Rouibah et al., 2011), document and file management (Rouibah and Al-Zanki 2013).

3.3 Research Model Based Theory of Diffusion of Innovation

Diverse theories were used to study new IT technologies adoption, including Technology Adoption Models and its variation, Theory of Reasoned Action, Theory of Planned Behavior and Diffusion of Innovation Theory (DOI). DOI is one of the oldest in social science theories. It originated in communication to explain how, over time, a new technology, idea or product gains spreads through a social system. The end result of this diffusion is that people, as part of a social system, adopt a new IT idea, behavior, or product. Adoption means that a person does something differently from what they do previously (i.e., purchase or use a new product, acquire and perform a new behavior, etc.). The key to adoption is that the user must see the artifact (here RFID) as a new or an innovative product. There are five main factors that influence adoption of such innovation: (i) Relative advantage refers to the degree to which an innovation is seen as better than the idea, program, or product it replaces; (ii) Compatibility refers to how consistent the innovation is with the values, experiences, and needs of the potential adopters; (iii) Complexity refers to how difficult the innovation is to understand and/or be used; (iv) Triability refers to the extent to which the innovation can be tested or experimented with before a commitment to adopt is made. (v) Observability refers to the extent to which the innovation provides tangible results.

This is a preliminary study that aims to study factors that affect intention to use or not to use the RFID in Kuwait. Among existing theories, this study uses, for this first phase, two main factors from DOI (relative advantage and complexity), which are similar to the main constructs in TAM (see Rouibah and Hamdy 2009). In addition, two additional factors (trust and privacy & security) derived from the literature review were added (Rouibah et al., 2016) since these two factors are getting more attention from the research community. The four factors are hypothesized to influence users' intention to adopt RFID.

4. RESEARCH METHODOLOGY

To investigate factors that affect RFID adoption in Kuwait we used mixed approach that combines qualitative and quantitative data collection.

4.1 Sample and Procedure of Data Collection

Unlike previous studies, this study targets different fields as areas of potential applications and adoption in Kuwait, including hospitals, supermarkets, banks, libraries, commercial shops and hypermarket. Target participants are those working in these fields. A questionnaire was developed that included two parts: demographic data and questions related to the factors in the research model. Because we reused item constructs from past studies, this questionnaire was written in English and then translated to Arabic language by following established procedures (Lowry et al., 2011) by the first researcher who is fluent in both English and Arabic. Then two additional professors ensure the fit of the translation and repeated until it converged. We also pre-tested the instrument with 15 undergraduate students from MIS course at a public business school. The final version of the questionnaire was distributed using the three social media networks (whatsApp, Facebook, and Instagram) and by emails. Each distributed questionnaire was accompanied with a letter that describes what RFID is and its potentials for businesses. Each questionnaire item was scored on a five-point Likert-type scale (ranging from strongly disagree to strongly agree). 200 respondents participated, however, only 144 answers were completed.

4.2 Construct Measurements

Items constructs used in this study were inspired from other researchers and adapted for the purpose of this study: relative advantages (Fuhrer and Guinard 2006; Nambiar 2009; Woellik et al., 2014), *complexity* (Tsai et al., (2010), Trust (Garfinkel et al., 2005; Hennig et al., 2005; Honarzade and Anari 2013), privacy and security (Fuhrer and Guinard 2006; Data Privacy and Integrity Advisory Committee 2006; Sini et al., 2009), and intention to adopt (Venkatesh and Davis (2000).

5. DATA ANALYSIS AND RESULTS

5.1 Demographic Data and Behavior of Respondents With Regards to RFID

Data analysis shows that 51 % of the respondents were male against 49% for women. The majority of respondents (48.7 %) are young since their ages are less than 29, followed by those between 30 and 39 years (31.9%), and those more than 40 years (19.4%). Most participants are not aware of the existence of RFID and had never heard about it before this study (55%) against 45% who had already heard about it.

5.2 Descriptive Data

Collected data was analyzed using SPSS 22. The following table provides descriptive data in terms of the mean and standard deviation (SD) for the four factors that are hypothesized to influence the intention to use RFID. From this table we can see that the means for the 5 *items of trust* construct vary from 3.03 to 4.41, with the standard deviations varying from 0.69 to 1.1, which are far from the neutral cut point (2.5). The means for the 3 items of *privacy and security* construct vary from 3.74 to 4.35 with the standard deviations varying from 0.74 to 1.04, which are also far larger than the neutral cut point. The means for the 3 items of *relative advantage* construct vary from 3.79 to 3.88 with the standard deviations varying from 0.81 to 0.86, which are also far larger than the neutral cut point. Finally, the means for the 2 items of *complexity* construct vary from 3.53 to 3.71; with the standard deviations varying from 0.81 to 0.82. These results show that the respondents agree and strongly agree with the major items in the research instruments, and their answers are close since the standard deviation values are very small.

Table 3. Demographic Data for the Research Model Constructs

Construct	Item construct	Mean	SD
Trust (T)	T1: I trust giving each child to wear a bracelet with an embedded RFID tag t track the children every-where within a certain area in the stores of Kuwait	4.41	0.69
	T2: I trust RFID tags, but should be destroyed at checkouts or points of sale after sale	4.01	0.91
	T3: I am aware of identity theft caused by RFID	3.80	0.84
	T4: I like to visit hotels and trust those that provide their special customers with an embedded RFID tag in their mobile phones to get special treatments	3.47	1.06
	T5: I don't trust and shop from a store that I knew used RFID technology.	3.03	1.10
Privacy and Securit (PS)	PS1: RFID bracelet can secure newborn children in hospitals from being exchanged or theft	4.35	0.77

	PS2: Transferring medical records data onto RFID wristbands for patients is good idea	4.08	0.74
	PS3: RFID chipped passports are a good way to store personal details.	3.74	1.04
Relative Advantage (RA)	RA1: RFID technology is helpful in allowing an organization to remain competitive (applying RFID technology in hospitals, supply chains, hotels, shopping centers, etc.)	3.88	0.81
	RA2: Using RFID in athletic stadiums can improve the players' performance by tracking them during the play, so each player can have a full record of accurate performance.	3.80	0.86
	RA3: RFID tags on medicines' bottles can help to combat counterfeiting, but patients should be aware about these tags	3.79	0.82
Complexity (C)	C1: It is easy to understand and use RFID technology	3.71	0.81
	C2: RFID tracking is a safe technology (for eyes, children, pregnant women, etc.)	3.53	0.82

5.3 Toward the Validation of the Research Model

Since we reused and customized previous items based on IT related studies, and in order to validate the research model, we first conducted the factor analysis using Varimax with Kaiser Normalization as the extraction method. Results reveal the existence of four distinct factors, which accounted for 58.80 per cent of the variance in collected data. After applying factor analysis, we found out that these questions can be loaded on 4 factors with mostly different items than those used. The items which were taken from previous studies got different names in this study because of different contexts and cultures where they were applied.

Table 4. Results of the Factor Analysis Based on the Rotated Component Matrix

Items and their label	**Component**			
	1: Relative advantages	**2: Trust**	**3: Security & privacy**	**4. Complexity**
T2: I trust RFID tags, but should be destroyed at checkouts or points of sale after sale			.792	
T3: I am aware of identity theft caused by RFID			.681	
T1: I trust giving each child wear a bracelet with an embedded RFID tag to track the children every-where within a certain area in the stores of Kuwait		.666		
PS1: Transferring medical records data onto RFID wristbands for patients is a good idea		.679		
PS2: RFID bracelet can secure newborn children in hospitals from being exchanged or theft		.808		
T4: I like to visit hotels and trust those that provide their special customers with an embedded RFID tag in their mobile phones to get special treatments	.713			
PS3: RFID chipped passports are a good way to store personal details	.566			
RA1: RFID technology is helpful in allowing an organization to remain competitive (applying RFID technology in hospitals, supply chains, hotels, shopping centers, etc.)	.776			
RA2:U sing RFID in athletic stadiums can improve the players' performance by tracking them during the play, so each player can have a full record of accurate performance	.659			
RA3: RFID tags on medicines' bottles can help to combat counterfeiting, but patients should be aware about these tags	.688			
C1: It is easy to understand and use RFID technology	.471			
T2: I trust RFID tags, but should be destroyed at checkouts or points of sale				.840
C2: RFID tracking is a safe technology (for eyes, children, pregnant women, etc.)				.462

5.4 Qualitative Data Collection

This study also employs a qualitative approach where authors interviewed an expert of RFID, who works as a Senior Electrical Engineer at Option One Consultants. Interview questions were centered on the following questions: Where are the RFID systems applied in Kuwait? He answered "*RFID is a new technology applied in hospitals, banks, libraries, commercial shops and hypermarkets*". As for the driving forces that push toward RFID adoption and applications, he answered "*In hospitals RFIDs are used to control the staff for quality assurance, to monitor the location of equipment, especially medical equipment and computers since RFID is currently applied in two local hospitals (Al Seif Hospital and Royal Hayatt hospital)*". He also added that "*in banks RFIDs are used to monitor keys for safety boxes. This is the case of the National Bank of Kuwait, a well-known and reputable bank in the Arab world. In hypermarkets RFIDs are used to monitor cashier safety box after finishing the working hours. In libraries RFIDs are used only to control the locations of books in bookshelves and not in to ease the borrowing process of "self-check in/out, check-in out services, and shelf management*". With regard to what types of tags (active or passive) are used in Kuwait, and why, he answered: "*In hospitals both tags are used. Active tags are used by doctors to communicate with other staff, but these are costly. Passive tags are not expensive and widely used for normal staff (such as nurses) and for equipment*". With regards to the total cost ownership to install RFID systems, he clarified that "*In hospitals; it costs around 0.5 to 1.0% of the total project cost if both active and passive tags are used; however it is 0.35% if only passive tag systems are selected to be used for limited areas*". To the question "Do you think people and employees are ready and will accept RFID for tracking purposes, he answered "*Yes, people in Kuwait are ready and will not object to its use since this technology has several advantages including ease of use, and facilitate their work, monitor the needed persons, and add more safety to their valued resources*". As to the obstacles and problems that inhibit its acceptance, he commented "*there are technical and human related problems. As for technicality, RFID requires investment in IT infrastructure including availability of servers, network coverage area for each tag when having concrete walls, as well as needed frequent operations and maintenance efforts*". As for human obstacles, he commented "*RFID needs caution during use. Good use and avoidance of water while wearing a bracelet with an embedded tag are necessary steps towards ensuring sustainability of their use*".

6. CONCLUSION

RFID is a new developing technology that is getting widespread use. This technology is becoming widely used in different fields to track people, objects and animals. This study has two contributions. *First*, unlike previous studies in western contexts (Europe, USA, and Australia), this study focused on RFID in an Arab country, a developing country, not well known by western researchers. *Second*, it used a mixed approach of data collection (quantitative and qualitative) and found that RFID is adopted in very limited fields (hospitals, banks, libraries and supermarkets). This study suffers from two general limitations: *First*, the qualitative study sheds more light on RFID applications and its uses; it focused however on interviewing only one expert. *Second*, the quantitative study developed a model based on DOI, conducted factor analysis related to the research model, however, the paths analyses and hypotheses validation were not tested. As future directions, this study encourages the pursuit of data analysis based on structural equation modelling tools (such as Amos or LISREL), as well as expanding the scope of the study to include more factors that may influence RFID use and continuous use including cost, ease of the setting up, top management support, skills set available, and the availability of the necessary IT infrastructure.

REFERENCES

Aghdasi F., 2010. Research Trends in RFID Technology. Interim: Interdisciplinary Journal, Vol. 6, No 1, pp. 68 - 82

Chatfield A., Wamba, S.F., and Hirokazu T., 2010. E-Government challenge in disaster evacuation response: the role of RFID technology in building safe and secure local communities. *43rd Hawaii International Conferences on System Sciences (HICSS)* (pp. 81-91). Hawaii: Research Online.

Das M.R., and Harrop D.P (2006). RFID Forecasts, Players & Opportunities (2006-2016) web., http://www.idtechex.com/research/reports/rfid_forecasts_players_and_opportunities_2006_2016_000137.asp

Data Privacy and Integrity Advisory Committee 2006. *The Use of RFID for Human Identity Verification*, December 6, 2006. Retrieved November 11, 2013, from The Department of Homeland Security: http://www.dhs.gov/xlibrary/assets/privacy/privacy_advcom_12-2006_rpt_RFID.pdf

Fuhrer P., and Guinard D., 2006. Building a Smart Hospital using RFID technologies. *1st European Conference on e-Health (ECEH06)*, pp. 3-12), Switzerland.

Garfinkel S., Juels A., and Papp R., 2005. RFID Privacy: An Overview of Problems and Proposed Solutions. *Radio Frequency Identification,* pp. 34-43.

Harrison M., 2004. EPC Information Service Data Model and Queries. *Auto-ID Centre* 3-19.

Hennig E., Ladkin B., Sieker B., 2005. Privacy Enhancing Technology Concepts for RFID Technology Scrutinized. Germany, University of Bielefeld, Germany, RVS Group.

Honarzade M., and Anari M., 2013. RFID: A Tool for Achieving Competitive Privilege in Hotel Industry. *Reef Resources Assessment and Management Technical Paper* no 38, pp. 326-333

Lowry, P. B., Cao, J. and Everard, A., 2011. Privacy concerns versus desire for interpersonal awareness in driving the use of self-disclosure technologies: The case of instant messaging in two cultures," *Journal of Management Information Systems,* Vol. 27, pp. 165-204

Nambiar N., 2009. RFID Technology: A Review of its Applications. *Proceedings of the World Congress on Engineering and Computer Science* no 2, pp. 2-7. San Francisco: California State University

Nath B., Reynolds F., and Want R., 2006. *RFID Technology and Applications.* Guest Editors' Introduction, January-March, 22-24.

Rouibah K, and Al-Zanki K., 2013. RFID For Document Management: Assessment of Scenarios Implementation: An Arab case study. *International Conference on Information Resources Management (Conf-IRM) Conference Theme*: Managing IT in a Consumerized IT world Natal, Brazil, 22-24 May, 2013; web: http://www.conf-irm2013.org/callforpapers.html

Rouibah K. and Al Ateeqi , and Rouibah S., 2011. Does the Introduction of RFID Technology Improve Livestock Subsidy Management in Kuwait? A Success Story from an Arab Country. Journal of Cases in Information Technology, Vol. 13, No. 1 pp. 15-36

Rouibah K., and Hamdy, H., 2009. Factors Affecting Information Communication Technologies Usage and Satisfaction: Perspective From Instant Messaging in Kuwait. *Journal of Global Information Management,* Vol. 17, No 2; April/June 2, pp. 1-29

Rouibah K., Lowry P., and Hwang Y., 2016. The effects of perceived enjoyment and perceived risks on trust formation and intentions to use online payment systems: New perspectives from an Arab country. *Electronic Commerce Research and Application,* no 19, pp. 33–43

Sini E., Locatelli P., Restifo N., and Torresani M., 2009. Healthcare Professionals Identification at regional and local level: an RFID integrated scenario based on synergic experiences. *European Journal of ePractice* no 6, pp. 1-11.

Sun C., and Jiang F., 2013. Research on RFID Applications in Construction Industry. *Journal of Networks* no 8, pp. 1221-1228.

Tsai C., Lee, M., and Wu CH. C, 2010. Determinants of RFID adoption intention: Evidence from Taiwanese retail chains. *Information & Management* no 47, pp. 255-261.

Venkatesh V. and Davis F.D., 2000. A theoretical extension of the technology acceptance model: Four longitudinal field. *Management science,* No 46, pp. 186-204

Wamba F.B., 2008. Enhancing Information Flow in a Retail Supply Chain Using RFID and the EPC Network: A Proof-of-Concept Approach. *Journal of Theoretical and Applied Electronic Commerce Research* no 3, pp. 92-105.

White G., Gardiner G., Prabhakar G.P., and Abd Razak A., 2007. A comparison of barcoding and RFID technologies in practice. Journal of Information. *Information Technology and Organizations* no 2, pp. 119-132.

Woellik H., Mueller A., and Herriger J., 2014. Permanent RFID Timing System in a Track and Field Athletic Stadium for Training and Analyzing Purposes. *The 2014th Conference of the International Sports Engineering Association*, pp. 203-207; Klagenfurt, Germany

Wyld D., 2005. RFID: The Right Frequency for Government. Louisiana: IBM Center for the Business of Government.

Short Papers

ANALYSIS OF THE NIKKEI 225 INDEX AND FUTURE PREDICTION

David Ramamonjisoa and Yoshiki Sato
Iwate Prefectural University, 152-52 Sugo Takizawa Iwate Japan

ABSTRACT

In this paper, we present the result of our experiment on analyzing the Nikkei 225 index past data and prediction based on rules we have discovered and developed. We collected all Nikkei 225 index past data on daily average closing prices. We applied several technical analyses on the time series Nikkei 225 data. Technical analysis examples are simple moving average (SMA), regression, ARIMA models and seasonal return rates. Our analysis correlates to the most important moves in the past data and other indicator such as foreign exchange rate. Through the observations of those technical analyses, we discovered some patterns and designed rules that can be applied to forecast short or long term prices. Our first results are presented and we conclude with some forecasts data.

KEYWORDS

Nikkei 225 Index, ARIMA, Time Series Analysis, Regression Analysis, Rule Based System

1. INTRODUCTION

Stock market forecasting is an interesting problem in artificial intelligence where the goal is to make profit in the investment based on available resources and rules. In emerging and developed countries, stocks are the driver of the economy to grow and to maintain the country private industry or company to run. Forecasting the stock price is based on fundamental and/or technical analysis. Dow theory is an example of technical analysis based on Dow Jones Industrial Average index. The weak Efficient Market Hypothesis (weak EMH) postulates that the stock market is unpredictable based on publicly available information and past data. Meanwhile, the increasing exponentially of algorithmic trading in the market has changed the situation and created some more efficient market with less loss comparing to human traders only. This was demonstrated by the early research on trading rules with moving averages by Brock et al. (1992) and charting patterns such as head-and-shoulder or inverse head-and-shoulder by Lo et al. (2000). We focus our study to the Nikkei 225 index and technical analysis in order to develop an intelligent agent trader in the future.

In this paper, we present the result of our experiment on analyzing the Nikkei 225 index past data and prediction based on rules we have discovered and developed. We collected all Nikkei 225 index past data on daily average closing prices. We applied several technical analyses on the time series Nikkei 225 data. Our analyses are simple moving average (SMA), regression, ARIMA models and seasonal return rates. Our analysis is focused only on past daily average closing data. Through the observations of those technical analyses, we discovered some patterns and designed rules that can be applied to forecast short or long term prices. Our first results are presented and we conclude with some forecasts data.

2. THE NIKKEI 225

The Japanese Stock Market is the world's second largest because of the government policies of liberalizing capital transactions with other countries and democratization of stock ownership. The 225 companies listed on the First Section of the Tokyo Stock Exchange are forming the Japanese Stock Market. Those 225 listed companies stocks are updated in real-time and are published by the Nihon Keizai Shinbun. They are called Nikkei 225 Average or for short Nikkei225. The Nikkei225 is an economic indicator for the country and surveyed by the government and the central bank of Japan for their monetary policy, financial stability and growth target. The Tokyo Stock Exchange has another indicator called TOPIX (Tokyo stock Price Index) representing all listed companies and the entire market performance but it is hard to follow. The Nikkei225 is the equivalent of the Dow Jones Industrial Average in New York Stock Exchange. The chart in Figure 1 shows the yearly returns of the Nikkei225 from 1997 to 2015. We can observe the loss effect -41% caused by the financial crisis during 2008, -18% loss on March 2011 disaster and the high return +57% during the financial easing by the central bank of Japan during 2012 until the end of 2016. The year 2016 is flat to +0.42% of return rate.

The highest value in the last 30 years is 38915.87 yen on 29th December 1989, the lowest price in the last 30 years is 7054.98 yen on March 10, 2009, and the average value in the last 30 years is 16844 yen.

The question is now concerning the current policy from the Central Bank of Japan, the government policies and changes in US economics on Asia. Will the negative interest rates, treasuries yield curve controls and inflation target 2 percent growth adopted by the central bank and new economic policies make the positive or negative return of the Nikkei225 for the next 5 years?

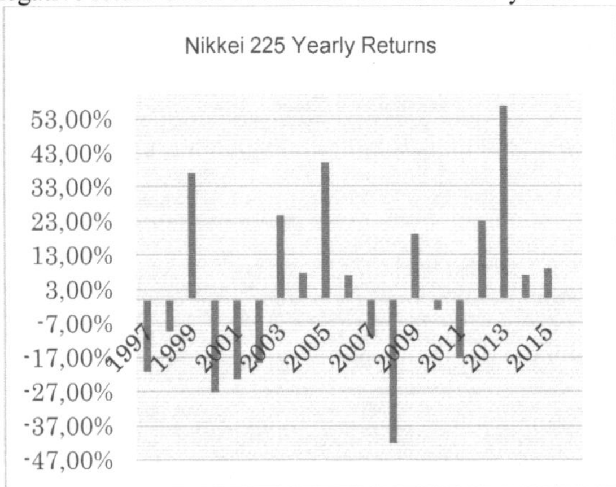

Figure 1. Returns of the Nikkei 225 from 1997 to 2016

Figure 2. Death cross and golden crosses for Nikkei 225

3. MOVING AVERAGE LINE ANALYSIS

The NIKKEI 225 is a "univariate time series." Given a sequence of the daily price Nikkei data $\{S_t\}_{t=1}^{N}$, the n-moving average is a new sequence $\{MA_t\}_{t=n}^{N+n-1}$ defined from the S_t by taking the arithmetic mean of subsequences of n terms (Ruey S. Tsay, 2005).

$$MA_{t+n} = \frac{1}{n}\sum_{j=t}^{t+n-1} S_j, \quad (3.1)$$

$MA_{t+50} = \frac{1}{50}\sum_{j=t}^{t+50-1} S_j = \frac{1}{50}(S_t + S_{t+1} + \cdots + S_{t+49})$ is the 50 days moving average of the Nikkei 225.

We will obtain a sequence $\{MA_t\}_{t=50}^{N+50-1} = \{MA_{50}, MA_{51}, \ldots, MA_{N+49}\}$.

The moving average line is simply the average closing price of the Nikkei 225 and shows the lagging price with time $t - n$. It smoothes out the daily price volatility to indicate actual trend and absorb the unusually high and unusually low closes during the n specified period. In real situation, n is set to 10-day, 25-day, 50-day, 75-day, 100-day, or 200-day. They are used as signals to sell or buy the stock when the daily chart crosses those average lines. When a faster moving average line crosses a slower moving average line, the signals are known by the traders as stronger. Traders called them "death cross" or "golden cross." The classical death cross is the intersection of a 50-day moving average line and a 200-day moving average line in the down trends as shown in the figure 2. The classical golden cross is the intersection of a 50-day moving average line and a 200-day moving average line in the up trends as shown in the figure 2. We can use a *n1*-day moving average line and *n2*-day moving average line to find other death cross and golden cross depending on the forecast period. For example, n1 = 25 and n2 = 75 can give much more crosses than the classical ones and we can use for short term trade. n1=100 and n2 = 200 is an example for a long term forecast trade with few crosses.

After a golden cross, when the trend line persists to the up trends for a long period (more than a year), traders call them a bull trend. For example, the period after golden cross at end of the year 2012 is a bull trend until August 2015. In the contrary, after a death cross, when the trend line persists to the down trends for a long period (more than a year), traders call them a bear trend. For example, the period after the death cross at the end of the year 2007 during the Lehman Brothers bankrupty and bubble burst of the financial market. The great depression during 1929 is comparable to those bear trends in 2007 where the world market crashes simultaneously and the result lasted for years created the real economy slowdown, decreasing growth domestic products and the ending of the gold standard. During the period of 2007 to 2017, there were several recessions where the GDP contracted for consecutive years. The bull trend during 2012 is the result of the financial easing by the bank of Japan and developed countries to relieve the disaster during March 2011. The interest rate of the central bank is negative in Japan and nearly 0% for the federal reserve bank of US for facilitating the lending and reviving the economy.

4. REGRESSION MODEL AND ARIMA MODEL

4.1 Regression Model

We use a simple linear regression model to study the relationship between the Nikkei 225 and the forex exchange currency US dollar/Yen rate. The explanatory variable is the currency rate. The linear function to fit the data is as below.

$$y = \beta_1 x + \beta_0 \qquad (4.1)$$

y is the Nikkei 225 and x is the USD/Yen rate during the past 10 years.

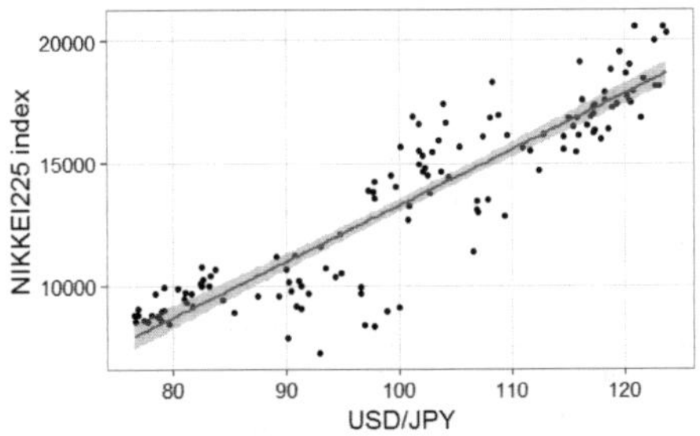

Figure 3. Nikkei 225 and USD/Yen Pair Trend

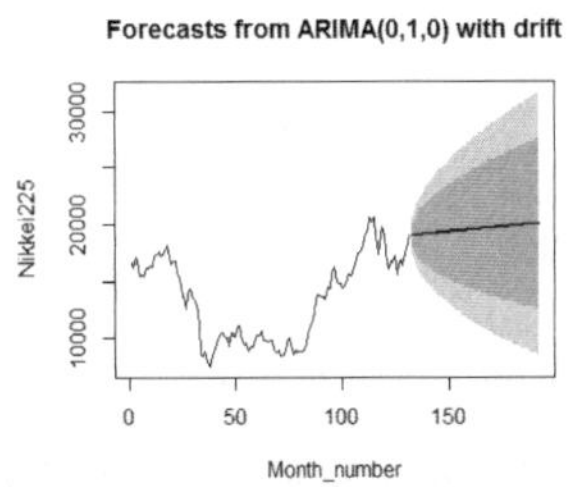

Figure 4. Forecast from Arima Model

In the figure 3, we obtain the fitted model on those data. Strong yen and weak dollar has a correlation to low Nikkei 225 price and weak yen and strong dollar gives a high Nikkei 225 price. All data points on Nikkei 225 above 20000 in figure 3 correspond to a rate over 120. Similarly, the majority of data points corresponds to a rate below 80 is having a Nikkei 225 below 10000. The Nikkei 225 is composed of corporate companies depending heavily on currency rate for export or import goods. The effect of the weaker yen is a good signal for stock uptrend and inflation on economy. Japan has struggled deflation for more than 30 years since the bubble burst of the Nikkei 225 in December 1989. Beside the central bank policy, the government has raised tax on goods twice since then to increase the public spending. The first tax hike was after the Hanshin earthquake in 1996 and the second was after the Tohoku earthquake and tsunami in 2012. The government has also intervened to foreign exchange market directly to stabilize the market and create some trend reversals (Dominguez, 2006).

4.2 ARIMA Model

ARIMA models are, in theory, the most general class of models for forecasting a time series which can be made to be "stationary" by differencing (if necessary), perhaps in conjunction with nonlinear transformations such as logging or deflating (if necessary). A random variable that is a time series is stationary if its statistical properties are all constant over time. A stationary series has no trend, its variations around its mean have a constant amplitude, and it wiggles in a consistent fashion, i.e., its short-term random time patterns always look the same in a statistical sense. The latter condition means that its autocorrelations (correlations with its own prior deviations from the mean) remain constant over time, or equivalently, that its power spectrum remains constant over time. A random variable of this form can be viewed (as usual) as a combination of signal and noise, and the signal (if one is apparent) could be a pattern of fast or slow mean reversion, or sinusoidal oscillation, or rapid alternation in sign, and it could also have a seasonal component. An ARIMA model can be viewed as a "filter" that tries to separate the signal from the noise, and the signal is then extrapolated into the future to obtain forecasts.

The procedure for making the ARIMA model is as follows (Schmueli and Lichtendahl, 2016):

- Make correlograms (ACF and PACF). PACF will indicate AR terms and ACF will show MA terms.
- Fit the model. Find the residuals and do diagnostic tests. If the residuals are autocorrelated, then fitted model is good. Otherwise, repeat the same process.
- Use the fitted model for the forecasting purpose.

The ARIMA forecasting equation for a stationary time series is a linear (i.e., regression-type) equation in which the predictors consist of lags of the dependent variable and/or lags of the forecast errors.

Let $\{S_{t+1}, S_{t+2}, \dots S_{t+n}\}$ a time series with a size n, we can express the value of S_{t+n} with the other values and an error ϵ_t

$$S_{t+n} = \beta_0 + \beta_1 S_{t+n-1} + \cdots + \beta_n S_t + \epsilon_t \quad (4.2.1)$$

the mean is

$$\mu_t = E[S_t] = \mu = \text{constant} \quad 1 \leq t \leq n \quad (4.2.2)$$

We applied the ARIMA model to the Nikkei 225. We forecast 4 years ahead since 2016. Figure 4 shows the forecast result with the ARIMA model as p=0, d=1, q=0. The blue line is the mean projected until 2020, the area around in blue is the coverage (lower and upper bound) of one standard deviation and grey area is the coverage of two standard deviations. The Nikkei 225 is not a stationary series so the best fit model is the random walk ARIMA(0,1,0).

$$\widehat{S_t} = \mu + S_{t-1} + \epsilon_t \quad (4.2.3)$$

We can observe with the figure 4 that it is very difficult for the Nikkei 225 index to overcome the price of 20000 yen for long time with the past 20 years data analysis only.

5. SEASONAL MONTHLY RETURN RATES

Our motivation to find some patterns in the seasonal monthly return rates comes from the paper by Ben Jacobson and Cherry Zhang (Ben Jacobson and Cherry Zhang, 2014). These authors have studied worldwide stock market historical data to produce seasonal monthly return rates and concluded that the well-known seasonal effect such as "Sell in May and Go away" (May through October) is a general pattern for over 300 years in all stock prices except of an island in Indian Ocean.

We studied the monthly seasonal return rate of the Nikkei 225 for the past 20 years. We obtained the histograms in figure 5. The Nikkei 225 does follow the general pattern of stock market as negative or neutral return from May until October. The negative return on January is also well understood as January effect and the result of the Christmas and New Year holidays. The chart shows the 10 years and 20 years monthly return rates. June and July have different opposite outcome that we consider neutral in June and negative return in July. August has the most negative return rate because it represents the holiday season during the summer in Japan. November and December are generally very profitable months.

6. RULE BASED SYSTEM FOR ANALYSIS AND PREDICTIONS

For optimizing the analysis and prediction, we have combined all the technical analyses in a rule based system. We examine each scenario possible on combination of the uptrend or downtrend, death crosses or golden crosses, positive or negative seasonal period, ARIMA forecast result, and regression results. For example, a rule on trend reversal is the presence of a cross in the moving average lines and change in trend line. Another rule example is about the foreign exchange USD/Yen value lower than 80 implying the Nikkei 225 to be lower than 10000 yen. When USD/Yen is greater than 120yen, a Nikkei 225 above 20000 yen or higher has a high probability to happen. Buying or selling signal for short term should refer to the seasonal returns such as summer selling and November buying. The Japanese economy is in good condition so the bull trend will continue based on our technical analysis, however it is still in its recovery period which can produce some corrections when the central bank or government changes policies according to some circumstances.

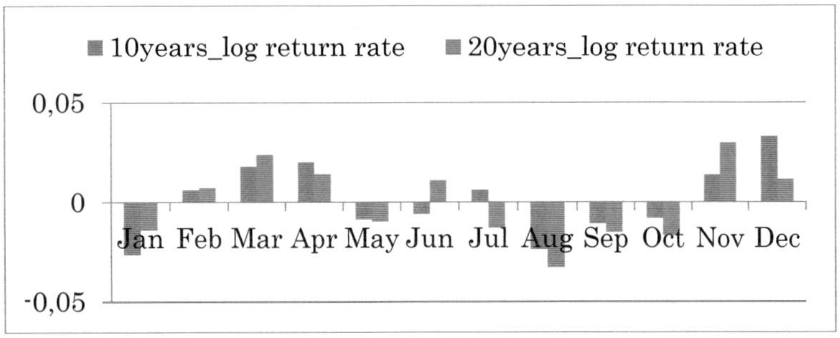

Figure 5. Seasonal Monthly Log Return Rates for Nikkei 225 Stock Index

7. CONCLUSION AND FUTURE WORKS

We presented different tools for analyzing the fluctuation of the time series data such as Nikkei 225 stock data. We introduced our rule based system for synthetizing the results of each tool and building a prediction system for estimating the future price of the stock for short term or long term.

For the future, combined machine learning techniques can be used to improve the accuracy such as in Patel J., et al. (2015), model dealing with volatilities and ARMA (Krishnalal, et al., (2010), Kumar, et al. (2012), Mantri, 2013, Leung et al., (2014), Seker et al., (2014). We will merge the result of the technical analyses to our fundamental analysis to build an intelligent agent forecaster and test to the real market in a society of agents.

REFERENCES

Book

Ruey S. Tsay 2005. *Analysis of financial time series*. John Wiley & Sons Publishers, New Jersey, USA.

Schmueli, G. and Lichtendahl, K.C., 2016. *Practical Time Series Forecasting with R*. Axelrod Schnall Publishers, USA.

Journal

Brock, W. et al. , 1992. Simple technical trading rules and the stochastic properties of stock returns, *Journal of Finance*, 157(5), pp 1731-1764.

Lo, A. et al., 2000. Foundations of Technical Analysis: Computational Algorithms, Statistical Inference, and Empirical Implementation, Journal of Finance, vol. LV, No 4, pp 1705-1765.

Dominguez K.M.E., 2006. When do central bank interventions influence intra-daily and longer-term exchange rate movements? *In Journal of International Money and Finance 25*, pp 1051-11071.

Patel J., et al. (2015). Predicting stock market index using fusion of machine learning techniques. *In Expert Systems with Applications*, Volume 42, Issue 4, Elsevier Publisher, pp 2162-2172.

Krishnalal G., et al. (2010). A New Text Mining Approach Based on HMM-SVM for Web News Classification. *In International Journal of Computer Applications* Volume 1, No. 19.

Kumar R. B., et al. (2012). Financial News Classification using SVM. *In International Journal of Scientific and Research Publications*, Volume 2, Issue 3.

Mantri J.K. (2013). Comparison between SVM and MLP in Predicting Stock Index Trends. *In International Journal of Science and Modern Engineering (IJISME)*, Volume-1, Issue-9.

Seker S.E., et al. (2014). Time Series Analysis on Stock Market for Text Mining Correlation of Economy News. *In International Journal of Social Sciences and Humanity Studies*, Vol.6, No.1.

Conference paper or contributed volume

Jacobsen, Ben and Zhang, Cherry Yi, The Halloween indicator, 'Sell in May and go Away': An Even Bigger Puzzle (October 1, 2014). Available at SSRN: https://ssrn.com/abstract=2154873 or http://dx.doi.org/10.2139/ssrn.2154873.

Leung C.K.S. et al. (2014). A Machine Learning Approach for Stock Price Prediction. *In proc. of the 18th International Database Engineering & Applications Symposium IDEAS'14*, pp. 274-277, ACM New York, USA, 2014.

THE BEST PRACTICE IN IMPLEMENTING ITIL SERVICE TRANSITION FOR SUCCESSFUL IT SERVICE PRODUCTION

Mohamed Basel Almourad, Mohammed Hussain and Feras Al-Obeidat
Zayed University, P. O. Box 19282, Dubai, UAE

ABSTRACT

The Information Technology Infrastructure Library (ITIL) is the de facto standard framework for providing guidance to IT service delivery and support processes. The ITIL framework has a life cycle of five stages covering the implementation of an IT service. Service transition is the last stage in a project lifecycle before the IT service goes live. This place in the lifecycle is critical, because the success of the project depends on the smooth transition into service operation. This exploratory research investigates the best practices of ITIL service transition stage implementation. IT experts from five case studies have been interviewed to identify challenges and have recommended the best practices that can be used for successful service transition implementation.

KEYWORDS

IT service management, ITIL, Service Transition, Best Practice

1. INTRODUCTION

The success of achieving most business goals of an organization depends directly on the capability of Information Technology (IT) support. IT Service Management (ITSM) refers to the implementation and management of quality IT services that meet the needs of the business. IT service management is performed by IT service providers through an appropriate mix of people, processes and IT (Van Bon & van Ver Veen, 2010). ITIL is a widely accepted approach to ITSM in the world. ITIL was originally developed in the late 1980s by Britain's Central Computer and Telecommunications Agency (CCTA), now known as the Office of Government Commerce (OGC). The last edition of ITIL V3 was published in 2011. It provides a more holistic perspective on the full life cycle of services, covering the entire IT organization and all supporting components needed to deliver services to the customer. Furthermore, ITIL V3 enables organizations to deliver appropriate services and continually ensure they are meeting business goals and delivering benefits. The ITIL V3 processes are currently detailed within five core publications that introduce five Service Lifecycle stages: Service Strategy, Service Design, Service Transition, Service Operation, and Continual Service Improvement.

2. MOTIVATION AND THE GOAL OF THIS RESEARCH

Many IT organizations find the implementation of ITIL complex (Pollard & Cater-Steel, 2009), difficult to implement (Pollard & Cater-Steel, 2009), and some failed completely (Rúben Filipe de Sousa & Mira da, 2010). Furthermore, empirical research in the IT service management domain is in its childhood (Conger, et al., 2008), lacks scientific discussions (Hochstein, et al., 2005) and has only just emerged (Iden & Langeland, 2010). The few studies that have been achieved on ITIL have are mainly focused on general implementation issues [8], ITIL critical success factors (Pollard & Cater-Steel, 2009), (Almourad & Johari, 2014), impact of cloud computing on ITIL (Almourad & Hussain, 2014) (Almourad & Hussain, 2014), or impact of ITIL implementation on business/IT alignment (De Haes & Van Grembergen, 2015). Many IT service personnel request further research to explore the best practices in implementation of each ITIL stages.

Service transition (ST) sits at the center of the ITIL lifecycle structure. Service design supplies its inputs, and service operation receives its outputs which are usable IT services. The ST is also responsible for ensuring that all aspects of a new or changed service are smoothly transitioned to the live environment or real world phase, with the minimum impact on the business as possible. ST helps manage risks and ensure stakeholder readiness for the new, changed or retired service. The core of ST is incorporated in seven processes (See section 4). When exploring the best practices of the above processes, necessary changes can be managed in the broader service environment. Further, ITIL experts can observe the big picture that allow us to make those changes with an awareness of their potential impact on the rest of your IT services, on the business, and on other factors.

3. RESEARCH METHODOLOGY

A qualitative research using case studies is used to identify the best practice of ITIL service transition implementation. We adopted a qualitative method, as this research is exploratory in nature. The case study method provides the opportunity to ask penetrating questions and to capture the participant's rich experiences and thoughts. A total of five case studies reflecting five different organizations are selected and case semi-structured interviews with ITIL personnel were conducted. The selected organizations from United Arab Emirates (UAE) have either fully or partly adopted ITIL. Due to commercial sensitivity of the information and comments, the actual names of the organizations can't be disclosed. The five cases are referred to throughout the case discussion as cases A-E. ITIL experts in these organizations were interviewed and questioned. The questionnaire contains two main parts: Part A, contains questions about the organization (i.e. size, nature, number of IT staff, etc.). Part B, contains questions about the best practice in implementing each process of the seven ITIL service transition processes. The questions in part B are used as a guide through the interviews. Other emerged questions and ideas during the interviews were also considered.

4. DISCUSSION AND FINDING

The interview's questionnaire outcome of the five case studies were analyzed to identify patterns and summarize the main characteristics of approach and to select quotations that are supportive of the patterns and themes identified across all cases (Creswell, 1998). The cross case analysis of the five organizations has generated important best practices that must be considered when implementing ITIL service transition processes. The impacts of every process are detailed and illustrated with quotations from the ITIL personnel who has been interviewed and questioned. The following sub sections give reminder of each of the seven ITIL service transition processes and the corresponding best practices founded.

4.1 Transition Planning and Support (TPS)

This process considers all aspects of a new or changed service design, makes plans for transition of a service into the live environment and coordinates required resources. Basically, TPS is a bridge that ensures such service requirements, which are formulated in Service Design Package (SDP), arrive into service operation.

The main output of TPS are plans. They cover different areas, e.g. change management plan, test plan and report, evaluation plan, release plan, deployment plan, schedule plan, financial plan. To successfully finalize the transition phase, it is important that the SDP contains entry and exit criteria as well as deliverables of each stage in new or changed service introduction (cases A, B, E). When organizations run several projects at the same time (cases A, C, D) TPS process is responsible for coordinating all the projects. Roles and responsibilities must be assigned for all activities. If there is contention, a schedule that meets the requirements of the stakeholders must be established. Also, the progress of a service change must be monitored. Measurements must be recorded during the service transition so such a measurement can be used to create reports, track the effects of a dynamic environment, and amend the transition plans as needed (B, C, E).

4.2 Change Management (CM)

The aim of this process is to understand and minimize risks and disruption while implementing IT changes. The process ensures that standardized methods and procedures are used for effective management of all changes.

All case reported that there is no change without risk and in certain cases a change may create further risk. The CM would evaluate all proposed changes and evaluate them for their benefits and risks, and also consider all impacts. Before deploying a change, it must be systematically tested. The deployment should include a back out plane. Cases B & D indicated the limitation of resources thus it is not feasible to accomplish all changes. The CM could prioritize the changes so that limited resources are allocated to the changes that produce greatest benefit or/and minimize risks based on the business need. One of the biggest challenges of change management process is challenging people's behavior to adapt the new or different service or product (cases A, C, E). People have a psychological need to feel safe and comfortable with changes to them and around them. Awareness and education plan must be deployed before accommodating the change. All stakeholders affected by the change must feel they are part of the process.

Appoint the right skill person for the role of CM to site within the Change Advisory Board (CAB) (Case B). Choosing the wrong individual to fill the CM position or not giving the appropriate level of authority can create major problems.

4.3 Service Asset and Configuration Management (SACM)

This process defines and controls the assets of services and infrastructure. In addition, assets could use various artifacts created during the service management such as policies, service level agreements and the service catalog. ITIL uses the term Configuration Item (CI) to refer to any asset type. SACM maintains one or more Configuration Management Database (CMDBs) to keep up to date information about every CIs.

All case stressed that CMDBs must be accurate and up to date. To achieve this goal, SACM relies heavily on the CM process to ensure that only authorized changes occur and that the results of this change are accurately recorded. SACM must create the right logical model of the IT infrastructure by utilizing the CMDBs. The model records the relationships and dependencies between CIs and the service assets. Both the model and the SMDBS forms the configuration management system (CMS). The relationships between CIs can be used by the CM process to illuminate risks and service impacts. Also, the model is crucial to problem & incident management, change & release management and planning operation; it will help reduce the risk of lengthy outages and service interruptions. The Problem Management processes utilizes the model to point the path from a failed CI to the service(s) it impacts. Cases (A, B, C) indicated that CIs should be defined at the right level of granularity. It is wise to plan CIs with a single, critical business service instead of dealing with the entire catalog at the outset. The wrong level of granularity with too much detail (generating extra work) or too little detail (inadequate control). Using a top-down approach with a service will show you just how much detail is needed to achieve the benefit. Cases (B, D, E) indicated that CMDBs must be always accurate and up to date. Moreover, the initial recording of the CI should be considered as a baseline so regular and ad-hoc configuration audit can be performed to check the consistency of CMS with the physical state of all assets. To achieve this goal, SACM relies heavily on the CM process to ensure that *only* authorized changes occur and that the results of change are accurately recorded. Further, SACM should maintain a secure storage where IT assets are locked. When an asset needs to be in a known working state the secure storage is a major component in a successful service continuity program. Master software libraries and copies of all developed software must be secured in Definitive Media Library (DML) (Cases A, C, D, E). A backup and restore policy must be developed for the DML. Only media from the DML is acceptable to use in releases.

4.4 Release and Deployment Management (RDM)

RDM is the process of determining, acquiring, releasing and deploying changes into an IT environment. The process is responsible for planning, scheduling and controlling the movement of releases to test, pre-production and production environments. In conjunction with the use of CM, RDM will enhance an organization's capabilities to develop, compile, reuse, distribute and rollback releases in accordance with defined policies that improve efficiency and reduce business disruption. Lack of effective RDM will contribute up to 80% of production incidents in large organizations with complex IT services (Spafford & Colville, 2013).

Cases (A, B, D, E) indicated that before the release goes to the live environment and also placed in the DML the release should be: Verified against the defined requirements; tested by Service Validation and Testing process (see section 4.5); documented in release documentation; and Placed in the Definitive Media Library (DML). (See section 4.3). Cases (A, C, D) stressed that the deployment of the release should be performed from the copy available in the DML to the live environment following an agreed plan and schedule. Cases (A & D) suggest adopting a version control because it has the ability to identify failures, easily roll back to a known state, and quickly deploy a change. The version control is required for everything including infrastructure and configuration code. Cases (A, B, C) pointed out that all required skills and knowledge must be transformed to Service Operation people so they can deliver, use, support, and maintain the service according to required warranties and service levels. Manual deployments, poor collaboration between teams, and a lack of control of the release process all lead to poor quality releases. To achieve higher levels of performance, organizations should adopt automation that provides high performance, better quality and speed.

4.5 Service Validation and Testing (SVT)

SVT ensures that deployed releases and the resulting services meet customer expectations, and to verify that IT operations is able to support the new service. SVT is concerned with reducing the life cycle costs of services and release packages by grabbing defects, wrong assumptions, and ignored design elements before they hit the production environment. SVT is the latest chance for confirming that the new or modified services meet strategy and design requirements and that the expected results will be achieved.

Service operation team is normally held accountable for any failures. Thus, rigorous test process based on Service Design Package should be put in place before moving a service into production. Results of the testing should be provided to the change evaluation process (section 4.6) to support a decision on whether to proceed with the new or changed service project. All cases reported that any service should be at least tested for both utility and warranty, however, additional types of tests that are performed also depend on the functionality of the service, For example: usability testing, agreement and regulation testing and operational readiness testing. All cases also agreed that tests of a service must be designed and carried out by personnel who have not been involved in any other design or development activities for this service. Cases (A, B. C) emphasized that the test environment must consider the predicted working environment for the period of its anticipated operation.

4.6 Change Evaluation (CE)

The aim of change evaluation is to provide uniform and structured methods of determining the performance of a change relating to the likely impact on the business, on any existing or proposed services and the current and future IT infrastructure.

Cases (A, B) emphasized the necessity for organizations to define what they consider being significant changes, and so decide which changes should use the CE process, and which can be evaluated as part of the CM process. Cases (A, B, C, D) suggested that stakeholder's expectations and requirements must be clearly understood. This will lead to better understanding of the *intended effect* of a change and the expected benefit of its implementation. This also applies to the *unintended effects* for a change which was unexpected or planned for. Deep discussion of these effects with stakeholders is essential so they can be taken into account and the full impact of a service change is understood. Cases (A, E) differentiated between predicted vs actual performance and risk. They suggested that evaluating must be conducted for the predicted performance and risks and also the actual performance and risks. Case A indicated that the change evaluation process should evaluates separate change phases prior to moving on to the next one. For example, (change evolution prior to planning, building, deployment and after deployment). All cases agreed that the result of the formal Change Evaluation is documented in a Change Evaluation Report, which is the main output of the CE process.

4.7 Knowledge Management (KM)

The KM process is responsible for sharing perspectives, ideas, experience and information, and for ensuring that these are available and reusable in the right place and at the right time. Knowledge evolves from data to wisdom using Data Information Knowledge Wisdom (DIKW) model. Data is just a set of facts, information is data within context, knowledge is information processed by human experience and understanding, and wisdom is when you can make informed decisions (Lacy & Macfarlane, 2011).

Case D describes knowledge as power when it is not presented within an organization, as otherwise there is a risk of falling into an endless loop of rediscovering the same thing again and again. The KM process enables informed decisions, and improves efficiency by reducing the need to rediscover knowledge. Cases (A, B, C, E) emphasized the necessity to construct the appropriate data model that is able to hold efficient information at appropriate level of granularity. Further they advised that both data and information must be periodically assessed for the usefulness. It is very important to identify any data and information that are no longer relevant or outdated to the organization's knowledge requirements. Archive the no longer relevant or obsolete data and information. All cases agreed about the necessity of forming and accumulating an effective KM system and they pointed out that this is a task of everybody. However, cases (D, E) raised an important point. In competitive environment people like to protect their knowledge, especially when there are rewards and recognition for doing so. One way to promote a knowledge sharing environment is to adopt a reward model for sharing. With a knowledge & wisdom sharing environment people grow, the organization grows, and management is able to make the wisest decisions possible

5. CONCLUSION

Service transition facilitates the implementation of a service that is designed to meet customer specifications and service strategy inputs. A key goal of service transition is to ensure that the expectations from the business are met. Effective service transition means the service is ready to move into operation with least risks, unintended negative impact, and knowledge management for all stakeholders. In this paper we explored the best practices and recommendations for implementing service transition seven processes. The best practices are drawn by interviewing key IT service manager personnel from five different organizations who have either fully or partially implemented ITIL in their organizations.

REFERENCES

Almourad, M. B. & Hussain, M., 2014. The Impact of Cloud Computing on ITIL Service Design Processes Authors. *International Journal of Information Technology & Computer Science.*

Almourad, M. B. & Hussain, M., 2014. The Impact of Cloud Computing on ITIL Service Strategy Processes. *International Journal of Computer and Communication Engineeri,* 3(5)

Almourad, M. B. & Johari, J., 2014. Resolution of Challenges That Are Facing Organizations before ITIL Implementation. *International Journal of Future Computer and Communication,* 3(3), pp. 210-215.

Conger, S., Winniford, M. & Erickson-Harris, L., 2008. *Service Management in Operations.* s.l., s.n.

Creswell, J., 1998. *Qualitative inquiry and research design: Choosing among five designs.* CA: Sage.

De Haes, S. & Van Grembergen, W., 2015. *IT governance structures, processes and relational mechanisms: Achieving IT/business alignment in a major Belgian financial group.* s.l., IEEE, pp. 237-237.

Hochstein, A., Tamm, G. & Brenner, W., 2005. *Service oriented IT management: benefit, cost and success factors.* Vancouver , s.n., p. 98.

Iden, J. & Langeland, L., 2010. Setting the stage for a successful ITIL adoption: A Delphi study of IT experts in the Norwegian armed forces. *Information systems management,* 27(2), pp. 103-112.

Pollard, C. & Cater-Steel, A., 2009. Justifications, Strategies, and Critical Success Factors in Successful ITIL Implementations in U.S. and Australian Companies: An Exploratory Study. *Information Systems Management,* Mar, 26(2), pp. 164-175.

Rúben Filipe de Sousa, S. & Mira da, M., 2010. *A Maturity Model for Implementing ITIL v3.*, IEEE Computer Society.

Shang, S. & Lin, S.-F., 2010. Barriers to Implementing ITIL-A Multi-Case Study on the Service-based Industry. *Contemporary Management Research,* 6(1).

Spafford, G. & Colville, R. J., 2013. *How IT Operations Can Set Up an Effective, Centralized Release Management Process." Gartner, June 3, 2013,* s.l.: Gartner.

Van Bon, J. & van Ver Veen, A., 2010. *Foundations of ITIL, Volume 3.* s.l.:Van Haren.

DETECTING SYSTEM INTRUSIONS BY USING BOTH LABELED AND UNLABELED DATA

Eric P. Jiang
Department of Computer Science, University of San Diego,
San Diego, United States of America

ABSTRACT

In this paper, we propose a semi-supervised learning approach, which is based on the well-known AdaBoost algorithm, for system intrusion detection. The approach uses only a small set of labeled training data to build up initial models of normal and anomalous system activity behaviors, and then it applies additional unlabeled audit data to further refine the behavior models. Experiments with the approach on a variant of the KDD Cup 99 data have shown that the proposed semi-supervised approach delivers a high detection rate while maintaining a very low false positive rate, and it represents a viable and competitive method for detecting system intrusions.

KEYWORDS

Data Mining, Intrusion Detection System, Data Preprocessing, Semi-Supervised Learning

1. INTRODUCTION

More people than ever before are using various Internet connected devices to conduct their daily activities in communications, information searching, entertainment and education, and all of these activities are heavily dependent on reliable and secure network connections. Unfortunately, hostile attacks on the underlying network infrastructure by malicious predators have never stopped and in fact, the number of reported attacks has been increased quite significantly. Such network or system attacks would have the potential for a devastating large-scale system failure, service interruption or the total unavailability of service (Saadawi & Jordan, 2011).

To help secure information systems and network infrastructure against intentional and potentially malicious threats, various network defense or security systems have been developed and employed. Conventional security approaches are the mechanisms designed in firewall, authentication tools, and computer servers that monitor, track and block viruses and other malicious activities. However, as network threats are constantly evolving, using these methods for detecting known attacks is not enough to protect users and networks. Higher-level tools are indeed needed to discover a broader range of embedded network and system intrusions and understand intrusion techniques used by attackers. An approach in this direction is to build intrusion detection systems.

In this paper, we propose a semi-supervised approach for system intrusion detection that aims to take advantages of both supervised and unsupervised learning methods. The approach is based on the well-known AdaBoost learning algorithm. Specifically, it first uses a small set of labeled training data to build initial profiles of normal and anomalous activity behaviors and then, in an iterative fashion, uses additional unlabeled system audit data to further refine the behavior profiles. Finally, it applies the refined profiles to new network instances and labels them either normal or abnormal based on their proximity to the profiles.

The rest of the paper is organized as follows. We provide some background and related research work in Section 2. We then present our proposed semi-supervised approach in detail in Section 3. In Section 4, we discuss our experimental setup with a variant of the KDD CUP dataset and provide the intrusion detection performance of the semi-supervised approach on the dataset. Finally we offer some future work and concluding remarks in Section 5.

2. RELATED WORK

Due to a growing number of system intrusions, many organizations have been implementing various software tools to deal with security breaches. Intrusion detection systems (IDS) are those that have recently gained a significant amount of interest in the IT community (Verwoerd & Hunt, 2002). Over the past two decades many IDS techniques have been proposed to model system usage behaviors and then use the modeled behaviors to classify new system usage events as normal or abnormal.

There two major paradigms for designing IDS and they are misuse detection and anomaly detection. Approaches used for misuse detection, also called signature detection, are developed specifically to recognize unique patterns or signatures of known intrusions and to predict and detect subsequent similar attempts. Over the years, many supervised machine-learning methods such as fuzzy rules (Abraham, Jani, Thomas & Han, 2007), neural networks (Cannady, 1998), support vector machines (Mukkamala, Janoski & Sung, 2002), genetic programming (Abraham, Grosan & Martin-Vide, 2007) and decision trees (Kruegel & Toth, 2003) have been used in misuse detection IDSs. Misuse detection systems are generally capable of detecting abnormal activities accurately and therefore carry low false positive rate. However, the systems cannot detect new types of intrusions. Approaches used for anomaly detection, on the other hand, are designed to profile normal system usage patterns and then detect possible intrusions based on their deviations from the profiled normal patterns. Anomaly detection systems can potentially detect unknown intrusions but, in comparison to misuse detection systems, they generally carry higher false positive rate and lower intrusion detection rate.

3. A SEMI-SUPERVISED APPROACH

In the last few years, there has been surging interest in developing semi-supervised learning models that are capable of learning from both labeled training samples and additional unlabeled data. The semi-supervised learning paradigm has been successfully used in many areas that include text classification (Jiang, 2012). Experiments have shown that using both labeled and unlabeled data in an appropriate semi-supervised learning setting can usually help enhance classification accuracy. Moreover, developing efficient semi-supervised IDSs is a practically meaningful task as, in a typical real-world information system environment, large amounts of unlabeled audit data are easily collected and accessible whereas manually labeled system usage data are usually very limited in supply.

We propose a semi-supervised approach for system intrusion detection. It uses both labeled and unlabeled training data for learning normal and abnormal system activity behaviors and then uses the learned behaviors to classify incoming system usage events. The approach involves an incremental learning procedure with a base classification algorithm. More specifically, given a set of labeled training data and a set of additional unlabeled data, the approach first applies the base algorithm on the labeled data to build an initial supervised model. Then, it uses the model to classify the unlabeled data and assign each instance from the data a classification confidence score, which can be expressed as a probability between zero and one. It then adds a portion of the newly labeled data with top confidence scores to the labeled data set to build subsequent supervised learning models. The process is repeated until some predefined stopping criteria are satisfied. The final classification model produced in the process is used to predict incoming system events and detect potential intrusions. The proposed semi-supervised approach for system intrusion detection is summarized in Figure 1.

We use the AdaBoost method (Freund, & Schapire, 1996) as our base classification algorithm in the semi-supervised learning approach. AdaBoost, or Adaptive Boosting, is a well-known ensemble machine learning method and it can be used in conjunction with other learning algorithms such as decision trees to improve classification performance. The method itself involves an iterative process that produces a sequence of classification models and in each step of the process, it builds a classification model that focuses more on the training samples that are misclassified by the previous model. This is accomplished by using an adaptive weighting scheme on the training data. Specifically, AdaBoost begins by assigning an equal weight to all training samples and it builds a classification model for the training set. The classification model error is calculated as the sum of the weights of the misclassified samples divided by the total weight of all training samples. This error is then used to update weights by

$$weight_{SAMPLE}(new) = weight_{SAMPLE}(old)\frac{error_{MODEL}}{1-error_{MODEL}}$$

for all correctly classified training samples, and there are no weight changes for misclassified samples. Once all sample weights are updated, they are normalized and this normalization step effectively increases the weight for misclassified samples and decreases that for correctly classified ones. The process is repeated for a number of times until some stopping criteria are reached and generates a sequence of classification models. The final classification output from AdaBoost is formed by a weighted majority vote of the models and the weight for the models is given by

$$weight_{MODEL} = \log \frac{1 - error_{MODEL}}{error_{MODEL}}$$

This weight scheme gives a high weight to a model that performs well on the training samples and gives a low weight to a model that performs poorly.

There are several advantages of using semi-supervised learning methods for system intrusion detection. Unlike supervised learning counterparts that typically require a sufficient amount of training data to deliver decent classification performance, our proposed semi-supervised approach requires only a small quantity of labeled samples to train the initial learning model. In a typical real-world network environment, labeled training data are expensive to obtain and the quantity of such data can be very limited. Unlike unsupervised methods that perform clustering just on unlabeled data, our approach utilizes additional unlabeled audit data in conjunction with the labeled samples and the incremental learning process, based on the AdaBoost models, helps further improve its overall classification accuracy.

Inputs: A set of labeled documents L and a set of unlabeled documents U
Output: A text classifier

- Build an initial AdaBoost classification model by L
- Loop
  - Apply the model to classify U
  - Assign each classified instance a classification confidence score
  - Select a portion of classified instances with top classification confidence scores L_{new}
  - Update L and U by $L = L \cup U$, $U = U - L_{new}$
  - Build a subsequent AdaBoost classification model by L
  - If the max iteration number is reached or the proportion of classified instances exceeds the threshold, then stop; otherwise repeat the loop.

Figure 1. The AdaBoost Based Semi-Supervised Learning Approach

4. EXPERIMENTS AND EXPIRICAL ANALYSIS

4.1 Dataset

As one of the very few publically accessible network or system intrusion datasets, the KDD Cup 1999 set (KDD-Cup, 1999) has been extensively used as a benchmark for analyzing and evaluating IDSs built by various pattern recognition and machine learning algorithms. However, there are some inherent problems with the KDD Cup dataset that have been reported in literature (Tavallaee, Bagheri, Lu & Ghorbani, 2009). One of the primary problems associated with the dataset is that it contains a large portion of duplicated records and it has about 78% and 75% duplicated records in its training and testing set, respectively. These extensively duplicated records can cause learning models to focus more on those frequent records and as a result of this, for instance, the overall intrusion detection performance of a learning model can be heavily influenced by its detection on one or multiple frequent testing instances. In order to address this and other issues, a modified variant of KDD CUP dataset, also called NSL-KDD, was proposed (Tavallaee, Bagheri, Lu & Ghorbani, 2009). The modified dataset removes all duplicated records in KDD CUP and in addition, by partitioning the remaining records into five groups that are based on their numbers of correctly predicted by several commonly used machine learning algorithms, it constructs the new (and more challenging) dataset by randomly sampling instances from the groups in such a way that the number of records selected from each group is inversely proportional to the percentage of records in the original groups. The NSL-KDD dataset was used in our experiments.

4.2 Experiment Setup

The formulated NSL-KDD training dataset has a total of 125,973 records and 41 features, and among them, 67,343 records are labeled as normal activity and 58,630 records as intrusion. For our experiments, we have done a number of pre-processing steps with the dataset. More specifically, we first took a few small random samples from the dataset with the sizes ranging from 200 and 450 and then examined the distributions on values of all its categorical features. Note that NSL-KDD, which is different from the original KDD-CUP, has only distinct records. We found that a number of its categorical features contain none or very few distinct values and therefore, they can be either not useful or carry very limited ability in modeling and predicting network behaviors. For this reason, we eliminated five features (namely, *land*, *urgent*, *num_shells*, *num_outbounds_cmds*, and *is_host_login*) from the dataset. In addition, from the remaining categorical features, we also found that some particular categories of the three features, *num_failed_log*in, *su_attempte*d and *num_access_files*, have only very few values in the entire dataset. We also cleaned this by removing a small number of the records from the set that correspond to these category values. The resulting dataset has 125,878 records and 37 features.

We used the preprocessed NSL-KDD training dataset for building a semi-supervised learning model to profile normal and abnormal network activity behaviors and then for analyzing and evaluating the prediction performance of the model. In our experiments, we first randomly sampled a small set from NSL-KDD as the labeled dataset to build the initial learning model in our semi-supervised approach. Then, we randomly selected another set from the remaining records as the additional unlabeled dataset, with the size being ten times of the labeled dataset, to augment the labeled samples in the iterative leaning process and to further improve network behavior profiles. Finally, we randomly sampled a set of testing data with a fixed size of 10,000 from the remaining records. This data selection process was repeatedly for ten times and we then calculated the averaged classification metrics as the measures of our classification performance.

4.3 Results and Analysis

There are a number of different performance measures that have been proposed for IDSs. Since intrusion detection is an imbalance classification problem and the normal data typically outnumber the intrusion data, the classical accuracy measure clearly is not a good choice. On the other hand, the intrusion detection rate and the false positive rate have been considered as the most popular indicators of IDS performance as they measure, for a given testing sample set, what percentage of intrusions the system is able to detect and how many incorrect classifications it makes in the process. Table I shows the detection rate and false positive rate of the proposed semi-supervised algorithm with the training data size ranging from 200 to 600, with an increment of 100.

From Table 1., we can provide a few observations. First, the experimental results indicate that our proposed semi-supervised learning approach can be very efficient in detecting various system intrusions. Using a good portion of additional unlabeled data to augment the training process, the semi-supervised method, Semi-AdaBoost, can be particularly effective in achieving a very low false positive rate while maintaining its good performance in intrusion detection. For instance, when we use only 300 labeled records in training, Semi-AdaBoost can deliver a very low false positive rate. In addition, Semi-AdaBoost demonstrates a sharp reduction in false positive rate when the size of the labeled training data changes from 200 to 300 and then a slow decrease as the size of the training data gets larger. For the detection rate, on the other hand, Semi-AdaBoost shows a relatively steady up trend for the size between 200 and 500 and then has a very gentle increase when the size becomes larger.

Secondly, in any real-world network environment, the amount of labeled intrusion records is often very scarce and hence, it might be very difficult to find a direct approach to modeling system intrusions accurately. A semi-supervised approach offers an alternative or indirect way to address the problem. It uses, in addition to the labeled data, additional unlabeled data that are usually collected and accessible in practice. Among the unlabeled data, a vast majority of them are normal system usage records and they can be used to further improve the system profile of normal usage activity. Therefore, as a direct positive consequence, they can help reduce the system's false positive rate. The increased accuracy of the normal profile should also help detect more system intrusions as a by-product.

Table1. Intrusion detection performance of Semi-AdaBoost

Labeled Training Data Size	Detection Rate	False Positive Rate
200	95.68%	1.98%
300	96.49%	0.57%
400	96.98%	0.57%
500	97.52%	0.36%
600	97.64%	0.31%

5. CONCLUSION AND FUTURE WORK

We have proposed a new semi-supervised learning approach for system intrusion detection. It is based on the well-known AdaBoost learning algorithm and requires a small set of labeled training data and utilizes a large amount of additional unlabeled data in an iterative learning process. The approach aims to use both labeled and unlabeled data in an integrated manner to achieve good performance in intrusion detection. The methodology behind the approach is practically meaningful as labeled data are usually available in a very limited quantify and unlabeled system audit data are abundant in supply. Experiments with a variant of the well-known KDD Cup 99 data have shown that the proposed semi-supervised approach represents a competitive method in detecting system intrusions and in particular, it is very effective in achieving a low false positive rate.

We would like to continue and expand this system intrusion detection research project in several directions. One direction is a further investigation of the possible optimal parameter setting with Semi-AdaBoost. For instance, we would like to find out what percentage of internally classified of unlabeled data should be used to augment the learning process and what impact it may have on system overall classification performance. Another area in which we want to explore is the choice of other base learning algorithms. In addition, we would like to conduct a thorough comparative study in intrusion detection efficiency that would include Semi-AdaBoost and several widely used supervised learning algorithms.

REFERENCES

Abraham, A., Jani, R., Thomas, J. & Han, S. Y. (2007). DSCIDS: Distributed softcomputing intrusion detection system. *Journal of Network and Computer Applications*, 30 (1), 381-398.

Abraham, A., Grosan, C. & Martin-Vide, C. (2007). Evolutionary design of intrusion detection programs. *International Journal of Network Security*, 4(3), 328-339.

Cannady, J. (1998). Aritificial neural networks for misuse detection. *Processdings of the 1998 National Information System Security Conference*, 443-456.

Freund, Y. & Schapire, R. E. (1996). Experiments with a new boosting algorithm. *Proceedings of the 13th International Conference in Machine Learning*, 148-156.

Jiang, E. P. (2012). Automatic text classification from labeled and unlabeled data. In Magdalena, et al. (Eds.), *Intelligent Data Analysis for Real-Life Applications: Theory and Practice*. Hershey, PA: IGI Global Publishing.

KDD-Cup: The International Knowledge Discovery and Data Mining Tools Competition Dataset. (1999). Retrieved from http://kdd.ics.uci.edu/datasets/ kddcup99/kddcup99.html.

Kruegel, C. & Toth, T. (2003). Using decision trees to improve signature-based intrusion detection models. *Proceedings of the 6th International Workshop on the Recnt Advances in Intrusion Detection,* 173-191.

Mukkamala, S., Janoski, G. & Sung, A. T. (2002). Intrusion detection using support vector machine. *Proceedings of Advanced Simulation Technologies Conference,* 178-183.

Saadawi, T. & Jordan, L. (Eds.) (2011). Cyber infrastructure protection. Retrieved from http://www.strategicstudiesinstitute.army.mil/pdffiles/pub1067.pdf.

Tavallaee, M., Bagheri, E., Lu, W. & Ghorbani, A. A. (2009). A detailed analysis of the KDD CUP 99 data set. *Proceedings of the 2009 IEEE Symposium on Computational Intelligence for Security and Defense Applications,* 53-58.

Verwoerd, T. & Hunt, R. (2002). Intrusion detection techniques and approaches. *Computer Communications*, 25, 1356-1365.

FRAMEWORK BASED ON STEM FOR THE DEVELOPMENT OF PROGRAMMING COMPETENCE: CASE STUDY OF MODELING OF PROBLEMS IN ENGINEERS TRAINING

Marcos Lévano[1], Andrea Albornoz[2], Gabriel Venegas[1]
[1]*Escuela de Ingeniería Informática*
[2]*Departamento de Lenguas*
Universidad Católica de Temuco
Av. Manuel Montt 56 Casilla 15-D, Temuco, Chile

ABSTRACT

The present work proposes a framework based on STEM for the teaching and learning of programming with scope in modeling the problem in basic engineering sciences. The methodology for the framework is implemented in the competency-based curriculum for the line of Software Engineering in the training of professionals for the Engineering Computer Science at Catholic University of Temuco (Chile). We propose a case study with the STEM approach, following the Bloom's taxonomy steps in the modeling of systems with the coupling of the respective technologies in Web 1.0, Web 2.0 and Web 3.0.

KEYWORDS

Framework, STEM, Programming, Bloom's Taxonomy, Modeling

1. INTRODUCTION

In XXI century, we are dedicated to create a society based on knowledge, in which competences of each person are focused on current technologies related to teaching and learning, and needed throughout life.
The new student generations are proactive and they need to leave a mark in their own style, codified according to social behavior. Big challenges are generated when we try to give answers to a society based on big scale knowledge, in different levels of formal or non-formal training. According to their own political systems, some countries in Latin America are making efforts to generate a kind of education that leads to the development of their nations, allowing to decrease socio-economic and cultural gaps.

The innovation on web technologies transferred information into production force from the unidirectional owners (Web 1.0) (Turcsányi-Szabó, 2012), to the vast amount of information shared with bidirectional users (web 2.0) (Ajjan & Hartshorne, 2008), ending in an attraction of information of the user (Web 3.0) (Kubilinskienė & Kurilovas, 2008; Bisol et al, 2015) facilitated by Artificial Intelligence when it provides an innovative, effective and potentially useful extraction of semantic information. The passive consumers are given information about new scenarios in which their contribution of information becomes an active producer (Turcsányi-Szabó, 2012).

As integrated approaches of science, technology, engineering, and mathematics (STEM) become more common (Moore et al, 2015), the necessity of developing effective strategies in theses interdisciplinary environments becomes more important. The integration of STEM (Karahan, Guzey & Moore, 2015) allows high levels of synergy in the science, technology, engineering, and mathematics disciplines making trainees have a real experience education.

This work aims to propose the formation of engineers focused on STEM with learning and teaching based on basic science problems and algorithmic abstraction for the use of computer programming tools supported by Web 1.0, 2.0 and 3.0 technologies.

The problem is formulated in the following way: How can we improve the formation of engineers with capacity of problem modeling in engineering science and make computational simulations by a STEM approach? To answer this research question we propose a framework with the STEM approach in which we develop a case study that covers three stages: modeling, discretization, and simulation centered on a knowledge society.

The expected result for this work is the framework proposing six steps such as modeling, interpretation of phenomenon to the model, application of modeling to the problem, decomposition of the parts of the result, discussion and critics of the solution and contextualization of the solution to another problem. In the results we associate Bloom's taxonomy (Anderson & Krathwohl, 2001) and Web technologies according the several technological means for support of the configurations of learning and teaching for the style of the trainee.

2. PROPOSAL OF FRAMEWORK WITH STEM APPROACH

The framework steps proposed are focused on STEM approach (science, technology, engineering, and mathematics) (table 1).

Table 1. STEM Approach Framework

STEM approach framework	**Bloom's taxonomy**	**Learning and teaching technologies**
Step 6: Contextualize the solution to another problem	Creation	Team work (Web 3.0)
Step 5: Discus and question the solution	Evaluation	personal learning networks (PLN), personal learning environments (PLE) (Web 2.0, Web 3.0)
Step 4: Decomposing the parts of the results	Analysis	personal learning environments (PLE) (Web 2.0)
Step 3: Application of the modeling to the problem	Application	Moodle (groups) (Web 2.0)
Step 2: Interpretation of the model's phenomenon	Comprehension	Information producers (Web 2.0)
Step 1: Modeling	Knowledge	Moodle (Web 1.0)

The framework covers 6 steps related to the Bloom's taxonomy and associates technology as a resource for learning and teaching development.

Step 1: modeling is the process in which the educator teaches to cultivate knowledge for modeling a problem and represent it with mathematical tools, algorithms and engineering.

Step 2: interpreting the phenomenon in the modeling is the process of comprehending the connection of cause and effect of the problem of the model referent to the system.

Step 3: application of the modeling to the problem is the process of applying tools to the representations of the system under study.

Step 4: decomposing the parts of the model is the process of decomposing and explaining why a model solves a problem.

Step 5: discussing and questioning the solution is the process of assessing the impact of the modeling to the problem in the solution and implications.

Step 6: contextualizing the solution to other problems is the process of creating new solutions to other problems or modify the modeling structure to find new solutions or unique solutions.

3. METHODOLOGY APPLICATION: CASE STUDY FOR MATHEMATICAL MODELING

3.1 Modeling and Discrete Models Simulation of Differential Equations Systems: Spring and Mass System

3.1.1 Modeling the System: Steps 1 and 2

In the system modeling we will be using high order differential equations, obtaining a lineal mathematical model of concentrated parameters, of a mechanical system of translational mechanical system of second order with components of mass and spring of second order. The model is simplified considering motions in just one plane and differential equation of the model is obtained applying physical laws. The analysis of this type of dynamic systems represented by this type of equations is very common in subjects like Physics and Differential Equations. The simple harmonic motion is a mass-spring system consisting of a mass *m* united to a spring fixed to a wall as shown if figure. It is supposed to be a motion without friction in the horizontal surface. The differential equation of the spring- mass is,

$\frac{d^2x}{d^2t} - \frac{kx}{m} = 0$ where, $w^2 = \frac{-k}{m}x$. How the equation was formulated: solving the equation. Second Newton's law postulates that the force applied on a body is directly proportional to the acceleration it acquires. Mathematically, $F = ma$

And as the acceleration is the second derivation of position with respect to time, we have, $F = m\frac{d^2x}{dt^2}$

In this way, this expression allows to obtain the equation of motion if we know the forces that act on the studies body. In the simplest version of the vibrational harmonic simple motion, the only force causing system oscillation is the form $F = -kx$

Replacing the equation of the Newton's second law, we obtain,

$$-kx = m\frac{d^2x}{dt^2} - - - - - - \rightarrow \frac{d^2x}{dt^2} = \frac{-k}{m}x$$

Algorithmic abstraction of the problem in Python programming language,

```
def f(t, x, v):
  return - k/m*x
def g (t, x, v):
  return v
```

Simplifying the differential equation obtained, we introduce a w constant which value is,

$w = \sqrt{\frac{k}{m}}$ thus, $\frac{d^2x}{dt^2} = -wx$

Technology for learning and teaching

a) Student focus: The focus is to receive knowledge based on a problem context, interacting with a learning management system (LMS). The teacher gives material to the students, so they have the work of learning by reading the learning guide.

The students then generate their own information by forming a teamwork support by Web 2.0 (Dabbagh & Reo, 2011) technologies, googleDocs and ShareLatex, thus, they become information producers.

b) Teacher focus: The focus is to produce information in the framework of basis for the students learning. Web 1.0 information with a Moodle platform (Dabbagh & Reo, 2011) has a role of promoting digital material, videos and backward lessons.

3.1.2 Discretization of the System, Steps 3 and 4

To solve the simulation and the first order differential equation and simulate that it resulted, we use the fourth order Runge Kutta algorithm, where by replacing the estimations we obtain,

$y_{k+1} = y_k + \frac{h}{6}(m_1 + 2m_2 + 2m_3 + m_4)$, where, $m_1 = f(t_k, y_k)$; $m_2 = f\left(t_k + \frac{h}{2}, y_k + m_1 h/2\right)$

$m_3 = f\left(t_k + \frac{h}{2}, y_k + m_2 h/2\right)$; $m_4 = f(t_k + h, y_k + m_3 h)$

Algorithmic abstraction of the problem in Python programming language,

```
while 1:
        rate(50)
        k1 = h*f( t, x, v)
        i1 = h*g( t, x, v)
        k2 = h*f( t+h/2, x + i1/2, v + k1/2)
        i2 = h*g( t+h/2, x + i1/2, v + k1/2)
        k3 = h*f( t + h/2, x + i2/2, v + k2/2)
        i3 = h*g( t + h/2, x + i2/2, v + k2/2)
        k4 = h*f( t + h, x + i3, v + k3)
        i4 = h*g( t + h, x + i3, v + k3)
        v = v + k1/6 + k2/3 + k3/3 + k4/6
        x = x + i1/6 + i2/3 + i3/3 + i4/6
```

Technology for learning and teaching

a) Student focus: It has as objective the algorithmic representation for modeling the problem, it is focused on putting into practice the implementations in a high-level programming language. The students generate their own personal learning environment (PLE) using blogger and websites.

b) Teacher focus: The focus is the following and feedback to validate finished products as a reviewer of the student's binnacle.

3.1.3 Simulation of the System, Steps 5 and 6

Spring-mass system with one mass and two masses (figures 1),

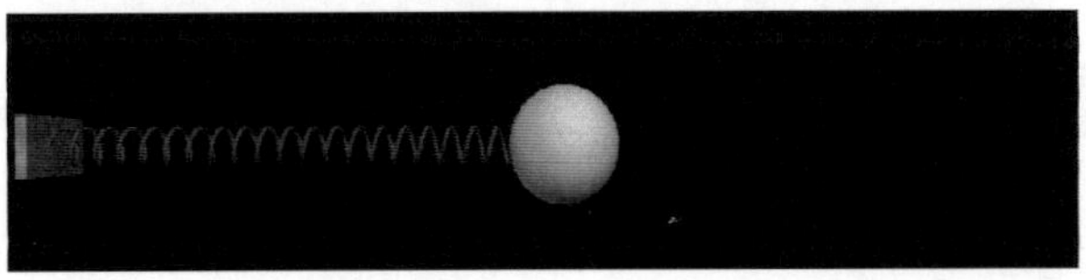

Figure 1. One Mass Spring System

Technology for learning and teaching

a) Student focus: It has the objective of assessing the model for the solved problem and making questions in different scenarios by working based on interpersonal teamwork, making papers, and discussing the process of the solution.

The technological means of the processes are that the student should make another modeling with another physical phenomenon.

b) Teachers focus: The teacher verifies the evaluation rubrics of the student progress in evaluating the solution of the problem. The teacher gives cases in which the students must be able to show their learning outcomes. Then they must contextualize the solution in other problems and solve them.

4. DISCUSSION AND RESULTS

Alignment and curriculum

The subjects that align the professional profile in the Engineering Computer Science program concern subjects of basic sciences and programming, where the modeling of problems by mathematical and algorithmic tools is the base of the engineer formation, with focus in achieving development specific competences of the career like "applied sciences of engineering" and "software development". The interrelation and integration of the subjects of the formative process is reached based on the multidisciplinary work with units of support in basic sciences and computer sciences.

In the development of general competences integrated with the subjects we can see the degree of levels as it develops in the curriculum of the Engineering Computer Science program.

5. CONCLUSIONS

The training involves high commitment and leads to face challenges by raising the levels of achieving cognitive development with tools to face problems solving in the different areas of engineering sciences.

The curriculum for the Engineering Computer Science program allows to develop educational innovations in order to validate the specific and general competences of the students towards the achievement of the university professional profile.

REFERENCES

Ajjan, H. and Hartshorne, R. (2008). Investigating faculty decisions to adopt Web 2.0 technologies: Theory and empirical tests. The Internet and Higher Education, 11(2), 71 80. [Online]. Available: http://www.sciencedirect.com/science/article/pii/S1096751608000225

Anderson, L. W. and Krathwohl, D. R., et al (Eds..) (2001) A Taxonomy for Learning, Teaching, and Assessing: A Revision of Bloom's Taxonomy of Educational Objectives. Allyn & Bacon. Boston, MA.

Bisol et al. 2015. Teacher education for inclusion: Can a virtual learning object help?. *Computers & Education* Vol. 85, pp. 203-210.

Dabbagh, N. and Reo, R. 2011. *Back to the future: Tracing the roots and learning affordances of social software*. In M. J. W. Lee, and C. McLoughlin (Eds.), Web 2.0-based e-learning: Applying social informatics for tertiary teaching. Hershey, PA: IGI Global.

Glancy, Aran W. and Moore, Tamara J., Theoretical Foundations for Effective STEM Learning Environments. (2013). Engineering Education Working Papers. Paper 1. http://docs.lib.purdue.edu/enewp/1

Kubilinskienė, S. and Kurilovas, E. 2008. Lithuanian Learning Objects Technical Evaluation Tool and its Application in Learning Object Metadata Repository. *In Informatics Education Contributing Across the Curriculum: Proceedings of the 3rd International Conference "Informatics in Secondary Schools – Evolution and Perspective"* (ISSEP-2008). Torun, Poland, pp. 147 – 158.

Karahan, E., Guzey, S.S., and Moore, T.J. 2014. Saving pelicans: A STEM integration unit. *Science Scope*, Vol. 38, No. 3, pp. 28-34.

Lévano A. Marcos & Herrera A. Oriel. 2012. Validation strategies of competences in a computer science curriculum. *International Conference of the Chilean Computer Science Society*, IEEE, pp. 9-11.

Moore, T.J., Doerr, H.M., Glancy, A.W., and Ntow, F.D. 2015. Modeling...What a concept! *Mathematics Teaching in the Middle School*, Vol. 20, No. 6, pp. 358-364.

Turcsányi-Szabó Márta. 2012. Aiming at Sustainable Innovation in Teacher Education – from Theory to Practice. Informatics in Education, 2012, Vol. 11, No. 1, pp. 115–130.

STUDENT-READINESS FOR USING MOBILE DEVICES: AN EMPIRICAL STUDY AT A UNIVERSITY IN SOUTH AFRICA

Kobus van Aswegen and Estelle Taylor
North-West University, Potchefstroom Campus, South Africa

ABSTRACT

The aim of this paper is to investigate student-readiness for mobile learning at a South-African University. Mobile learning is a rapidly expanding field of educational research and practice across schools, colleges, universities and the work place. The nature of learning should be changed by mobile devices and the networks and structures to which they connect people. Some researchers are of the opinion that there is not enough evidence to prove that mobile technology has either a positive or negative impact on learning and empirical studies showed that students' use and competency, with these technologies, varied considerably. This raises important questions about the readiness of learners. A questionnaire was distributed electronically to students, after completing a Computer and Information literacy module. It appears that the students will have sufficient skills to participate in a mobile learning course. The outcome, regarding students' blended learning readiness, was mainly positive, with only a few potential problem areas that have to be addressed. Students felt that mobile learning have some disadvantages such as the distraction factor, battery-life, note-taking and reliable internet access. Possible advantages mentioned by the students included mobility, access to different sources in one place, ease of use and saving paper and money.

KEYWORDS

Mobile Learning, Student-Readiness, Blended Learning

1. INTRODUCTION

The aim of this paper is to investigate student-readiness for mobile learning at a campus in South Africa. The paper starts with background, leading to the problem statement and aim of this paper. The next section is the literature review, followed by the methodology that was followed for this research. Finally, the results and the conclusion are discussed.

2. BACKGROUND AND PROBLEM STATEMENT

Mobile devices offer potential benefits which, until now, no single communicational tool had combined. The possibilities for application suggest that these can and should be used for the purposes of teaching and learning (Böck, 2012). Mobile learning is a rapidly expanding field of educational research and practice across schools, colleges, universities and in the workplace (Cook, 2010). According to Batista, Behar, and Passerino (2013), the role of formal education has been questioned and challenged as access to information increases. Cook (2010) agrees, stating that, in view of the increasing portability and functional convergence of technologies, as well as the reduction in their cost, and the cost of services available for them, mobile devices have become more and more central to the life-worlds of users.

Traxler (2013) writes that mobile technology is no longer something bolted on to our daily experiences but it is now built into our daily experiences. Mobiles are eroding ideas of time and physical place and the use of mobile devices challenge the notion that formal education is located in a specific place with knowledge distributed through specific channels by assigned individuals. According to Traxler (2012) formal education systems, delivering learning at specific locations and at specified times, are to an increasing extent, less well-aligned to the needs of our societies. Mobile devices have huge potential in enriching traditional interactions within the classroom, by bridging the gap between the classroom and the worlds of students (Pachler, Cook, & Bachmair, 2012). According to Traxler (2012) educational institutions are functioning in rapidly changing social contexts and spaces, and this is increasingly difficult if one takes into account the social impact of mobile devices. The use of mobile devices is forcing some educators to develop alternatives recognizing that people are now learning in an environment in which the transfer of knowledge is being supplemented with the understanding of where to find the knowledge that is needed (Traxler, 2012).

Mobiles have an influence on the way ideas, images, information and learning are produced, stored, distributed, delivered and consumed as mobiles enable everyone, including learners, to generate and transmit content for learning, not just passively store and consume it (Traxler, 2012); (Adami, 2012). The potential of mobile devices emphasizes the need for changes in the relationship between teachers and learners as well as learners and their peers (Pachler et al., 2012).

Digital media make the production of a variety of texts possible and these texts can be shared collectively and publicly distributed by means of interconnected spaces, to anyone with an interest in them. The use of these media has given rise to a variety of genres, for example, video blogs, texts, tweets, blogs, or the whole range of artefacts forwarded in social network platforms. This environment, in which often students seem to navigate and participate better than teachers, raises questions for those willing to keep pace with changes (Adami, 2012). According to Pachler et al. (2012) educational institutions need to give serious thought to how they plan for, support and integrate emergent technologies. By misappropriating mobile devices, one runs the risk of increasingly alienating young people from their formal education. Adami (2012) asks an important question, namely how educators can fill the gap between formal and informal contexts for learning. He also queries the role institutions for teaching and learning should play if they want to attempt to make some educational sense of these changes. According to Traxler (2013) research on mobile learning has demonstrated that mobile devices can deliver learning to people, communities and countries, where other educational interventions have been too expensive, difficult or demanding.

From the above it can be seen that the nature of learning is being, or should be, altered by mobile devices and the networks and structures to which they connect people. However, some researchers are of the opinion that there is not enough evidence to prove that technology has either a positive or negative impact on learning (Heinze & Procter, 2012). Jones (2013) refers to several different research studies on mobile learning and the most important of these results are: there were differences in students' technology adoption and use and there were digital divides between different kinds of students; there was not sufficient empirical evidence to support the claim that students' use of digital media had transformed the way in which they learn; there was no empirical evidence that there is a single new generation of young students entering Higher Education; students persistently reported that they preferred moderate use of Information and Communication Technologies (ICT) in their courses; empirical studies showed that students were not all equally competent with technologies and their patterns of use varied considerably. This is also reiterated by Corrin, Bennett, and Lockyer (2013) and their results demonstrated diversity in students' technology access, usage, confidence and adoption. Whilst some students made extensive use of technology across all the contexts of their life, others made limited use of technology for very specific purposes. Corrin et al. (2013) write: "*The digital natives claims assume that students' informal use of technology has equipped students with the digital literacy and skills necessary to tackle any technology offered in the classroom. In reality, a wide variance in technology confidence and ability has been found in this study as well as others. Students are different, with different learning styles and approaches*".

This raises important questions about the readiness of learners. When considering mobile devices for teaching and learning educators have to take into account that digital literacies, reflecting a different mindset from conventional literacies, are necessary to make use of the potentials and requirements of communication in this form (Böck, 2012). Taking the characteristics of mobile devices into account, it seems possible that the scope of action might be expanded for certain groups—through sensitive use of such devices, based on a profound understanding both of the social conditions of such groups and the affordances of the devices (Böck, 2012). Research on the digital divide clearly show that the relation of social factors and media usage is highly complex (Böck, 2012).

An interesting quote from Böck (2012) emphasizes this problem: "*Mobile learning assumes that learners are ready to enter into the demands of situations and tasks of learning under their own agency, to be active in their shaping of their own learning. But can we assume, unproblematically, that the necessary mindset, the specific attitudes and dispositions to learning are actually 'there', are characteristics of all learners?*"

It can be seen from literature that on the one hand there is much enthusiasm for mobile learning and its' advantages, on the other hand, there are questions about the results of mobile learning. Furthermore, there is research indicating that educators cannot assume that learners are ready, willing and able to participate in mobile learning. This brings us to the aim of this paper, namely to investigate student-readiness for mobile learning, at a campus in South Africa.

3. LITERATURE REVIEW ON MOBILE LEARNING

Pachler, Bachmair, and Cook (2009) explains that mobile learning is not about delivering content to mobile devices but, instead, about being able to operate successfully in, and across, new and ever changing contexts and learning spaces. Therefore, for them, mobile learning is not primarily about technology. According to Adami (2012) the following questions need to be addressed when considering mobile learning, taking into account the changing landscape and the influence of this on learners: should institutions for teaching and learning teach to select, transform, assemble and recontextualize information?; should schools consider further abilities which can support the required/developed ones, such as the ability to evaluate critically what is selected and to assess creatively the new possible contexts, re-contextualizations and re-significations?

According to Cook (2010) there are three phases of mobile learning:

The first phase focuses on what mobile devices (PDAs, pen tablets, laptops or smartphones) can achieve in an educational context for formal education and training. This phase makes productive use of the affordances of mobile technologies such as e-books, classroom response systems, handheld computers in classrooms, data logging devices and reusable learning objects. A focus on learning outside the classroom is a characteristic of the second phase of mobile learning. This can include field trips, museum visits, professional updating, bite-sized learning and personal learning organisers. The third phase is characterised by a focus on the mobility of the learner, the design or the appropriation of learning spaces and on informal learning and lifelong learning.

Challenges of mobile learning include the fact that the availability of communications infrastructure alone is not enough to support mobile learning. There is furthermore a need for well-designed learning systems; these systems should take into account both technical and pedagogical aspects of such forms of learning (Khan & Matskin, 2012). Other challenges include that the design processes related to mobile devices, inevitably involves designing for a 'match-box' sized, small interface. Issues include navigation over multiple platforms (i.e. different types of devices and operating systems), locating relevant information by providing usable navigation (through touch screens or buttons, etc.), structuring of a learning task to suit the affordances of the mobile device, and evaluating that scenario (Cook, 2010).

4. METHODOLOGY

The questionnaire was distributed electronically to first year students after completing a Computer and Information literacy module. It was completed by 1391 students. Both quantitative research was done as the researchers wanted to measure certain variables as well as understand students' own perceptions.

5. RESULTS

The questionnaire started off with questions on the background information and basic computer knowledge of the students. Of the 1391 respondents, 63.85% were female students and the rest male. The largest proportion (33%) of the respondents started using a computer on a regular basis between the ages of 10 and 14, and by the age of 17, just over 90% of the students were using a computer on a regular basis. What is still disconcerting, is that almost 10% of the students only started using a computer at university. More than 88% of the respondents use email on a regular basis. We also wanted to determine if there is a case for blended learning being delivered on tablet devices. More than 50% of students don't own tablets. Of the 43.8% of students that owns a tablet, 41% (<19% in terms of the total number of respondents) use it regularly.

Respondents were asked to what extent they agree to statements regarding their online skills. The results can be seen in table 1. It is clear that most students agree that they do have the necessary online skills, but there are, however, still some students who do not feel confident about their online skills.

Table 1. Online Skills of Students

Statement	Strongly Disagree	Somewhat Disagree	Somewhat Agree	Strongly Agree
I have the basic skills for finding my way around the Internet (e.g., using search engines, entering passwords)	7.05%	10.78%	22.36%	59.81%
I can send an email with a file attached	2.73%	4.17%	6.54%	86.56%
[I think that I would be comfortable using a computer several times a week to participate in a course.	5.97%	11.50%	25.95%	56.58%
I think that I would be able to communicate effectively with others using online technologies (e.g., email, chat)	4.17%	4.96%	12.94%	77.93%
I think that I would be able to schedule time to provide timely responses to other students and/or the instructor.	5.25%	26.60%	27.32%	40.83%

Respondents were asked to what extent they agree to statements regarding blended learing. They questionnaire provided them with a definition of blended learning and they had to respond to certain statements. See table 2 for these results.

Table 2. Blended Learning Readiness

Statement	No	Yes
I am comfortable and proficient at creating, saving, locating, and opening different types of files on a computer.	5.13%	94.87%
I have regular access to a reliable computer.	4.12%	95.88%
I have reliable access to a high-speed Internet connection (DSL, cable, dorm, etc.).	22.10%	77.90%
I know how to login and use the eFundi environment and access it regularly to check for new messages.	1.01%	98.99%
I have no problem retaining information if I read it.	9.70%	90.30%
I am comfortable using online discussion forums.	27.54%	72.46%
I am comfortable learning through individual reading and study.	7.52%	92.48%
I can learn from a variety of formats (lectures, videos, podcasts, online discussion/conferencing).	5.29%	94.71%
If I can't figure out something, I am comfortable asking my classmates or the instructor for help via email, discussion board, or chat.	12.70%	87.30%

From the results in table 2 it can be seen that most students feel that they have the skills needed for blended learning.

5.1 Interpretive Analysis of Open Questions

The interpretive analysis was done by coding the answers. The answers to every question were analysed and a code was assigned to each category found in the answers.

The first open question: "In your opinion what will be the biggest drawback of using a tablet for learning?"

A total of 967 students answered this question and the more frequented categories can be seen in table 3.

Table 3. Drawbacks of Using a Tablet for Learning

Category	Number of answers referring to this category
The distraction of other aspects such as social media and games is a problem.	214
Battery-life is too short.	140
Taking notes / making changes / summaries are difficult.	122
Internet access is not always available.	97
Some students prefer books.	88
The effect of the light on eyes is seen as a problem.	80
Screen size is too small.	78
The cost of the devices means that not everyone can own one.	55
Costs for data are high.	43
Students feel that there will be less personal interaction when using tablets.	23

Answers relating to the first category, namely the distraction of other aspects such as social media and games, were: "*I'm easily distracted. So I'll just play games on the tablet and won't study*" and "*I will not be able to focus*".

Some of the answers indicating a preference for books, and referencing to the problem with making notes were: "*You can't physically touch and hold the paper and make notes and highlight important points- I like to feel it in my hand"; "Ever since we began our educational life, we have been using books and textbooks and have accustomed to it. I personally would not be pleased with using e-textbooks because I am used to using the normal textbooks"; "People like me prefer learning material on paper as we make our own notes and just end up printing out the electronic material anyway"; "When I write I remember better. Thus I fear using a tablet for learning would jeopardise my learning skills".*

Students also expressed concern with important abilities diminishing: "*You lose the ability to make use of doing research in libraries as well as using paper and pen to summarize your work"; "You depend on it too much rather than critically thinking".*

The second open question: "In your opinion what will be the biggest advantage of using a tablet for learning?"

A total of 1010 students answered this question and the more frequented categories can be seen in table 4.

Table 4. Advantages of Using a Tablet for Learning

Category	Number of answers referring to this category
It is mobile / easier to carry around than lots of handbooks / you can take it with you everywhere.	423
You have quick access to Internet, handbooks and other sources / everything in one place.	323
It is easy to use.	95
You can stay up to date with new technology.	46
You save paper, save on printing.	41
I t is more cost effective, less expensive than textbooks.	40

Some of the interesting answers showing a positive attitude to using a tablet for learning were:

"Our generation is exposed to technology, it would be the easiest way to complete tasks given in class or even at home"; Having it with me anywhere so I have no excuse not to do what's important"; "It will make learning easier, it will save money (you don't have to print out notes so often). You also don't have to carry your heavy books to university or school every day"; "Tablets in schools are becoming a big thing, I think it holds more advantages for students than disadvantages". Though 122 students felt that taking notes will be difficult using a tablet (see table 3), one student wrote: *"It is very easy to take notes and highlight important work".* There were also 21 students who felt that there were no advantages. Some answers were: "*Nothing I won't use one" and "I think there are no advantages*".

6. CONCLUSION

A large portion (90%) of the students have had regular exposure to using computers on school level, but in this day and age one would've liked to see this number closer to a 100%. Bearing in mind that South-Africa is still a developing country, especially on the ICT front, one can understand this. This underlines the necessity for computer literacy courses on first-year level and the continuing need to educate learners in the use of computers. As can be seen by the questions on tablet ownership and use, less than half of these students own a tablet, and it will be very difficult to use tablets as a medium for delivering educational content. For such a strategy to be considered, the cost of issuing each and every student with a tablet will have to be included in the cost of education. Overall the response from the students to the questions regarding their online skills, have been very affirmative with close to 90% of them agreeing to positive statements regarding their online skills. It appears that the students will have sufficient skills to participate in a mobile learning course. One has to keep in mind that the students participated in this questionnaire after completing a compulsory computer literacy module. On many of the questions regarding blended learning readiness, the outcome has been positive from the respondents, with only the statements of "reliable access to a high-speed internet connection" and "comfortable with discussion forums", standing out as potential problem areas that have to be addressed. From the results of the interpretive analysis it can be seen that students feel that mobile learning have some disadvantages. Mentioned by most students was the distraction of other aspects such as social media and games, a short battery-life, that taking notes and making summaries are more difficult, that Internet access is not always available and that some students still prefer books. Possible advantages mentioned by the students included mobility, access to different sources in one place, ease of use, staying up to date with new technology and saving paper and lack of money.

From all of the results it is clear that though most students feel that they do have the necessary skills for online and blended learning, however, there are still a few students who have doubts about their own skills in these areas, even after completing a computer literacy module. Furthermore, less than half of the students own tablets and had regular access to computers before entering university. All of these factors have to be taken into account by institutions when planning changes to the curriculum and the delivering thereof.

REFERENCES

Adami, E. (2012). Mobile Media, Mobile Texts: Assessing the Abilities Needed to. *Refining Current Practices in Mobile and Blended Learning: New Applications: New Applications*, 31.

Batista, S. C. F., Behar, P. A., & Passerino, L. M. (2013). Activity Theory and M-Learning in the Teaching of Calculus *Ubiquitous and Mobile Learning in the Digital Age* (pp. 93-108): Springer.

Böck, M. (2012). Mobile learning, digital literacies, information habitus and at-risk social groups. *Refining Current Practices in Mobile and Blended Learning: New Applications: New Applications*, 53.

Cook, J. (2010). Mobile phones as mediating tools within augmented contexts for development.

Corrin, L., Bennett, S., & Lockyer, L. (2013). Digital natives: Exploring the diversity of young people's experience with technology *Reshaping learning* (pp. 113-138): Springer.

Heinze, A., & Procter, C. (2012). The significance of the reflective practitioner in blended learning. *Refining Current Practices in Mobile and Blended Learning: New Applications: New Applications, 175*.

Jones, C. (2013). The new shape of the student *Reshaping Learning* (pp. 91-112): Springer.

Khan, B. A., & Matskin, M. (2012). A platform for actively supporting e-learning in mobile networks. *Refining Current Practices in Mobile and Blended Learning: New Applications: New Applications*, 113.

Pachler, N., Bachmair, B., & Cook, J. (2009). *Mobile learning: structures, agency, practices*: Springer Science & Business Media.

Pachler, N., Cook, J., & Bachmair, B. (2012). Appropriation of mobile cultural resources for learning. *Refining Current Practices in Mobile and Blended Learning: New Applications*, 10-30.

Traxler, J. (2012). Sustaining mobile learning and its institutions. *Refining Current Practices in Mobile and Blended Learning: New Applications*, 1-9.

Traxler, J. (2013). Mobile learning: Shaping the frontiers of learning technologies in global context *Reshaping Learning* (pp. 237-251): Springer.

AN INVESTIGATION OF THE EDUCATIONAL CURRICULUM WITH USE OF FORMAL CONCEPT ANALYSIS

Aliya Nugumanova[1], Yerzhan Baiburin[1], Madina Mansurova[2] and Yermek Alimzhanov[2]
[1]S. Amanzholov East Kazakhstan State University, Ust-Kamenogorsk, Kazakhstan
[2]Al-Farabi Kazakh National University, Almaty, Kazakhstan

ABSTRACT

An educational curriculum is a path of learning that students should follow in their study. It consists of learning modules aimed at mastering skills and developing the necessary competencies within the qualification framework. Each module is logically completed and contains a set of related disciplines which responsible for certain group of competencies. Modularity is an attractive approach to organization of study since it provides variability and flexibility of a learning path. However, modularity significantly complicates the process of curriculum planning and developing. The goal of this work is to propose an efficient tool for planning and analysis of educational curricula, based on the mathematical apparatus of the lattice theory. We use formal lattices as a method of studying the consistency and coherence of an educational curriculum. The advantages of this method are clear algorithmization, restrictions on the inclusion of new entities and concepts, automated construction of the hierarchy of relations, analysis of collisions.

KEYWORDS

Formal Concept Analysis, Lattice Theory, Educational Curriculum

1. INTRODUCTION

The algebraic theory of lattices dealing with partial ordering relations has numerous applications in the fields of artificial intelligence such as conceptual modeling, ontology engineering and data mining. Particularly, one of the popular applications of the lattice theory is formal concept analysis – a method which allows to form hierarchies of domain concepts based on input sets of data presented in an object-feature form (Ganter and Wille 2012; Poelmans et al 2013). The concepts are defined as units of knowledge having a certain volume and content. The volume of concept (extensional) is expressed through a set of features describing the covered objects. Relations between objects and features describing them are expressed through a formal context. In this work we use formal concept analysis for investigation of university curricula.

According to the definition of UNESCO, a curriculum is a systematized purposeful set of competences (i.e. knowledge, skills and judgments supported by assessments), which can be acquired by students through the learning process taking place in both formal and informal situation (UNESCO 2017). In modular building of a curriculum, the learning process is broken into a number of stages called modules each of which contains a holistic limited set of interrelated academic disciplines. Part of modules is invariant, i.e. compulsory for learning, and part of them is variable, i.e. replaceable. The diversity and variability of the learning modules are designed to provide formation of versatile competences of students and thereby contribute to maximum full achievement of the training goals. At the same time, modularity of the curriculum seriously complicates the process of curriculum planning and development, transfers it to a multilink and multiply connected system, the assessment of the consistency and balance of which requires special tools.

Thus, the goal of this work is to develop tools for analysis of a curriculum based on the mathematical apparatus of the lattice theory. According to the set up goal, the structure of this work is as follows. In Section 2, we present some related papers. In Section 3, we provide the necessary input information from the formal concept analysis. In Section 4, we model a formal context of a curriculum and use the formal concept analysis to investigate its structure and content. In Section 5, we formulate the conclusions and plan of the further work.

2. RELATED WORK

The problem of analysis and development of educational curricula using advanced computer tools and methods is a very popular theme among researchers. We can point out a quite great branching tree in this field. Especially popular is the so-called integrated approach which allows to consider planning and development of a curriculum in complex, on the basis of common methodology which integrates all steps from setting high-level learning goals to visualizing the learning outcomes for students.

The integrated approach to curriculum planning and development "combines both pedagogical and organizational change strategies" (Hubball and Burt 2004). There are a lot of studies which analyze these strategies. For example, authors of the just cited work associate these strategies to certain stages of curriculum design and describe each stage in a detailed manner, e.g. "During the awareness stage, curriculum leaders (Deans, committee personnel) across campus were exposed to a wide range of resources … about the benefits of learning centered curricula". Malik and Malik (2011) analyze the strategies by concerning with real cases (e.g. staff development, establishing working groups, organizing teaching materials, etc.). All such studies are helpful when getting started.

Some works are devoted to more thorough investigation of the issue of curriculum integration. For example, Drake and Burns (2004) present the methodological foundation of the process and formulates the basics of good curriculum design. All such studies are useful methodologically. Some works advocate the use of integrated curriculum on their own experience (Van Tassel-Baska and Wood 2010; McKimm 2010; Jacobs and Jacobs 2003). Such studies are useful practically.

There are a number of works focused on technological or modelling aspects. For example, Monette et al (2007), Hnich et al (2002), Chiarandini et al (2012), Ünal and Uysal (2014) investigate the problem of curriculum balancing, which is, in general, related to the aim of our work. The last paper we want to mention is (Škopljanac-Mačina and Blašković 2014). They, as we, use formal concept analysis in the field of teaching. The difference is that they provide subsequent analysis of the examination tasks whereas we investigate a curriculum structure.

3. FORMAL CONCEPT ANALYSIS. BRIEF INFORMATION

A formal context is a triple $K = \langle G, M, I \rangle$, where G is a set of objects, M is a set of features, I is a correspondence between G and M: gIm means that object $g \in G$ possesses an feature $m \in M$. For arbitrary subsets $A \subseteq G$ and $B \subseteq M$, we introduce Galois operators: $A' = \{m \in M \mid \forall g \in A\ gIm\}$, i.e. A' is a set of features which refer to all objects from A; $B' = \{g \in G \mid \forall m \in B\ gIm\}$, i.e. B' is a set of objects which possess all features from B.

Let us explain concepts of a formal context and Galois operators on the example of a set of natural numbers from 1 to 9 and three features of evenness, oddness and primality. We have a set of objects $G = \{1, 2, \dots, 9\}$, a set of features $M = \{\text{odd}, \text{even}, \text{prime}\}$. A formal context can be presented in the form of an object-feature binary matrix: if a number from G possesses an feature from M, we put 1(check) at the intersection of the corresponding row and column of the matrix, otherwise 0 (see Table 1). For a subset $A = \{1,2,3\}$ we have $A' = \{\text{prime}\}$ and for subset $B = \{\text{prime}\}$ we have $B' = \{1,2,3,5,7\}$. As we see, though $A' = B$, however, $B' \neq A$.

A formal concept of a context K is called a pair of the form (A, B), $A \subseteq G$ and $B \subseteq M$ such that $A' = B$ and $B' = A$. As is mentioned above, set A is called a concept volume and B – its content. The two concepts (A_1, B_1) and (A_2, B_2) are called partially ordered $(A_1, B_1) \leq (A_2, B_2)$, if the volume of the first concept enters (inclosed) into the volume of the second one $A_1 \subseteq A_2$. A set of all concepts of a context K ordered by insertion of their volumes is called a concept lattice.

Table 1. An Example of a Formal Context Given in the Form of a Binary Matrix

A	B	C	D
	Odd	Even	Prime
1	X		X
2		X	X
3	X		X
4		X	
5	X		X
6		X	
7	X		X
8		X	
9	X		

In the above considered example, a pair "object-feature" $(A_1 = \{1,3,5,7\}, B_1 = \{\text{uneven}, \text{prime}\})$ forms a concept "a prime odd number", and a pair $(A_2 = \{1,2,3,5,7\}, B_2 = \{\text{prime}\})$ forms a wider concept "a prime number". In the mentioned context of 9 numbers and 3 features we can highlight 7 concepts: a number, an even number, an uneven number, a prime number, a prime even number, a prime uneven number and an empty concept corresponding to the number simultaneously even and uneven (see Figure 1).

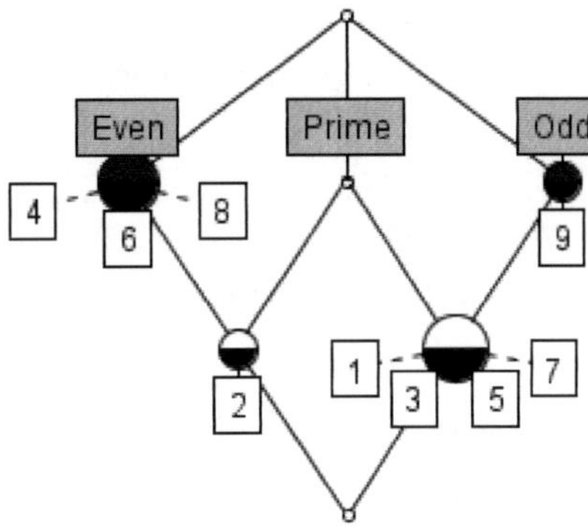

Figure 1. An Example of a Formal Context Given in the Form of a Lattice

A feature implication $B_1 \rightarrow B_2$ is the dependence of features $B_1, B_2 \subseteq M$ such that all objects possessing all features from B_1 also possess all features from B_2. That is, $B_1 \rightarrow B_2$ is an feature implication if and only if $B_1{}' \subseteq B_2{}'$. Feature implications satisfy axioms of reflexivity($X \rightarrow X$), augmentation (if $X \rightarrow Y$, then $X \cup Z \rightarrow Y$) and transitivity (if $X \rightarrow Y$ and $Y \cup Z \rightarrow W$, then $X \cup Z \rightarrow W$) which are also known as Armstrong's rules [1]. An implications basis is a minimum set of implications from which all other implications can be derived by Armstrong's rules.

In the above considered example, a formal context does not allow to determine any feature implication. If a number is prime, it is not necessarily even (numbers 1, 3, 5, 7) and not necessarily uneven (number 2); if a number is uneven, it is not necessarily prime (number 9) and so on. If we extend the considered context by a new feature "square of the number is divisible by 4", we will at once have two feature implications: if the number is even, the square of the number is divisible by 4; if the square of the number is divisible by 4, the number is even. It should be noted that introduction of such feature does not increase the number of context concepts.

The concept of implication in the lattice theory is closely related with the concept of association rule in the data mining. Implication is an association rule the reliability of which is equal to 1(100%) (Bazin and Ganascia, 2012). In the considered by us example one can define the following association rule: if the number is prime, it is uneven. The reliability of this rule is 80%, that is the rule works in 80% of cases (numbers 1, 3, 5, 7) and does not work in 20% of cases (number 2).

4. INVESTIGATION OF THE STRUCTURE OF UNIVERSITY CURRICULUM WITH THE HELP OF FORMAL CONCEPT ANALYSIS

Due to the complexity of the curriculum structure, its formal context can be determined not by a single way. Everything depends on how it is necessary to analyze a curriculum. For example, if we choose academic disciplines as objects of formal context, we must indicate competences developed by these disciplines, terms when they are studies or the expected learning outcomes as features. If the matrix is to be transposed, the objects will be competences, terms or outcomes and features will be disciplines.

Let us consider a competencies distribution matrix in academic disciplines as a formal context. Table 2 presents an example of such context the prototype of which was a competencies matrix of the "Information systems and computer modelling" curriculum developed in one of Kazakhstani universities. The proposed matrix is created by Concept Explorer and describes distribution of the next general professional competencies (PC):

PC1 – students are able to perceive and apply mathematical, professional knowledge;

PC2 – students are able to reason analytically, to make judgments under incomplete information;

PC3 – students are able to analyze and assess the levels of their competencies, to self-learn;

PC4 – student are able to communicate in English, to use professional terminology;

PC5 – student are able to use methods of information collecting, storing, processing, and transporting.

PC6 – student are able to analyze and structure professional information, to highlight trends and core information, formalize and represent information in the form of review, to resume.

The lattice of concepts built on the basis of this formal context allows to assess the competencies matrix visually. So, for example, it is seen in the lattice presented in Figure 2 that competences PC1 and PC6 (formed by 8 disciplines) have the greatest weight.

Table 2. A Sample of a Formal Context for an Educational Curriculum

A	B	C	D	E	F	G
	PC1	PC2	PC3	PC4	PC5	PC6
Decision theory	X	X				X
CAD	X	X			X	X
Requirements analysis	X					X
Intelligent systems	X	X		X		X
Data Mining	X	X			X	X
Experimental data procecing	X	X	X		X	
Control theory	X	X			X	X
Designing of intelligent systems	X	X			X	
Special chapters of math			X			X
Information processes modelling					X	X

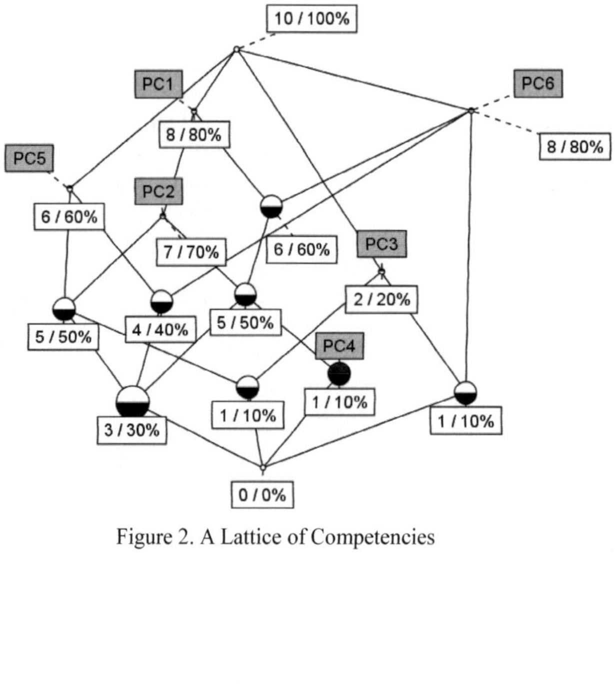

Figure 2. A Lattice of Competencies

On the basis of the lattice, Concept Explorer forms 5 feature implications which characterize interrelations between competencies:

1 < 7 > PC2 ==> PC1;
2 < 5 > PC1 PC5 ==> PC2;
3 < 1 > PC1 PC3 ==> PC2 PC5;
4 < 1 > PC3 PC5 ==> PC1 PC2;
5 < 1 > PC4 ==> PC1 PC2 PC6;

Implication 1 shows that in 7 disciplines the presence of competency PC2 involves the presence of competency PC1, i.e. competency PC1 (ability to perceive and use knowledge) is likely to enter into the composition of competence PC2 (ability to reason). Correspondingly, we can formulate the following rule which we will call the rule of competency absorptions. If in several cases there takes place implication X2→X1, it is probable that competency X1 is not independent but is a part of a more general competency X2. Thus, it is necessary to perform the further analysis whether competency X1 can be excluded from the list of basic competencies and, correspondingly, reduce their redundancy. Anyway, we can assert that competency X2 is deeper than competency X1.

Implication 2 indicates the fact that if a discipline forms competency PC1 (ability to perceive and use knowledge) and PC5 (ability to work with information), then competency PC2 (reasoning ability) is necessarily formed. This indicates that ability to draw conclusions PC2 is part of a more complex competence, which based both on the ability to use knowledge PC1, and on the ability to obtain and process new information PC5. It will be efficient to present all three competencies as components of stronger one which can be treated as soft skills competency. Therefore, we can formulate the following rule which we call the rule of complex competency. If in several cases there takes place implication X2, X3→X1 under the implication X2→X1, it is probable that competencies X1, X2 and X3 are parts of a more complex competency.

Implications 5 shows that if a discipline form competency PC4 (ability to communicate in English for professional purpose), then competencies PC1 (ability to understand), PC2 (ability to reason) and PC6 (ability to conclude and present results) should be necessarily formed. Hence, there is a probability that competencies PC1, PC2 and PC6 are necessary but not sufficient to form one competency PC4. Thus, we can formulate a rule which we will call the rule of necessary competencies. If in several cases there takes place implication X1→X2, X3,..., XN, then it is probable that competency X1 is based on the competencies X2,.., XN.

Reasoning similarly, we can develop a whole number of rules which would allow to reduce redundancy, red rid of circles and duplicates, analyze collisions in the structure of curricula. All this allows us to speak about prospects of the apparatus of formal lattices as a tool of studying the consistency and coherence of curricula. Its advantages are clear algorithmization, strict discipline when introducing new entities and concepts, automated construction of the hierarchy of relations, and also analysis of collisions. In our case we have no collisions but we suppose that the simultaneous presence of two implications of the form X2→X1 and X1→X2 can alert that competencies X1 and X2 duplicate each other (different names of one ability). Also in favor of collisions can indicate the simultaneous implications X2, X3→X1 and X1, X3→X2, which alerting to the presence of methodological problems in the educational program. All this requires further careful analysis, and allows a certain degree of optimism speak about the prospects of development of expert system for the analysis of educational programs on the basis of the proposed apparatus of formal lattices.

As feature implications satisfy axioms of reflexivity($X \to X$), augmentation (if $X \to Y$, then $X \cup Z \to Y$) and transitivity (if $X \to Y$ and $Y \cup Z \to W$, then $X \cup Z \to W$), which are also known as Armstrong's rules, we can determine the basis of implications from which all the other implications will be derived by Armstrong's rules.

5. CONCLUSION

According to the predictions of the World Bank, the structure of the national wealth of the countries in which a smart-society is formed will look like as follows: 5% of it will consist of natural resources, 18 % – of material production capital, 77 % – of knowledge and skills of people which become truly valuable and will determine their future. Correspondingly, the most important question is training of personnel who can create a "smart" environment, produce new values performing "smart" work.

Analysis of formal lattices and all directions of the promising fields such as Data Mining and Text Mining are exactly those smart tools with the help of which a person forms an intellectual space around him. Our subsequent works will be related to the further investigations on the listed tools for analysis of curricula.

REFERENCES

Ganter B., Wille R. (2012). Formal concept analysis: mathematical foundations. Springer Science & Business Media.

Poelmans, J. et al. (2013). Formal concept analysis in knowledge processing: A survey on applications. Expert systems with applications, 40(16), pp. 6538-6560.

UNESCO, 2017. UNESCO. Education: Curriculum. [reviewed 22 March 2017]. Available from http://www.unesco.org/new/en/education/themes/strengthening-education-systems/quality-framework/core-resources/curriculum/

Bazin, A. and Ganascia, J.-G. (2012). Completing terminological axioms with formal concept analysis. In ICFCA, pp. 29-40.

Hubball H. and Burt H. (2004). An integrated approach to developing and implementing learning-centered curricula. International journal for academic development, 9(1), 51-65.

Malik A., Malik R. (2011). Twelve tips for developing an integrated curriculum. Medical teacher, 33(2), pp. 99-104.

Drake S. M., Burns R. C. (2004). Meeting standards through integrated curriculum. ASCD.

Van Tassel-Baska, J., Wood, S. (2010). The integrated curriculum model (ICM). Learning and individual differences, 20(4), pp. 345-357.

McKimm, J. (2010). Current trends in undergraduate medical education: program and curriculum design. Samoa Medical Journal, 1(2), pp. 40-48.

Jacobs, C. and Jacobs, K. (2003). An integrated approach to curriculum at foundation level. Journal of Engineering, Design and Technology, 1(1), pp. 89-101.

Monette, J.et al. (2007). A CP approach to the balanced academic curriculum problem. In 7th International Workshop on Symmetry and Constraint Satisfaction Problems, Vol. 7.

Hnich, B. et al. (2002). Modeling a balanced academic curriculum problem. In Proceedings of CP-AI-OR-2002.

Chiarandini, M. et al. (2012). The balanced academic curriculum problem revisited. Journal of Heuristics, 18(1), pp. 119-148.

Ünal, Y. and Uysal, Ö. (2014). A new mixed integer programming model for curriculum balancing: Application to a Turkish university. European Journal of Operational Research, 238(1), pp. 339-347.

Škopljanac-Mačina, F. and Blašković, B. (2014). Formal concept analysis–overview and applications. Procedia Engineering, 69, pp. 1258-1267.

DATA PROCESSING METHODS FOR INFORMATION SYSTEM TESTING IN AGRARIAN SECTOR

Jan Pavlík, Jan Masner and Jan Rajtr
Czech University of Life Sciences Prague
Kamýcká 129, Prague, 16521, Czech Republic

ABSTRACT

In recent years in Czech Republic there has been steady increase in usage of ICT in many areas. The hardware equipment of general population, business subjects and government administration has improved dramatically. This caused a shift towards higher degree of digitization of government administration. Government information systems were or are being developed that facilitate electronic communication between citizens or businesses and state institutions. One of the new information systems handles communication between farmers and Czech Ministry of Agriculture. The ministry tasked our research team to analyze this information system in terms of usability and operability and to examine end user interactions with this system in detail. Usability testing will be conducted to gather data about user-system interaction when users are performing various tasks. Processing this data will help determine flaws and weak points of the system where users experience difficulties or get stuck. These parts of the IS can then be reworked or optimized for easier operability.

This paper provides some basic information about Czech agrarian background and establishes basis for further research in terms of methodology proposal for data analysis. It also includes some partial results and initial conclusions from pilot testing that took place in specialized usability laboratory during 2016.

KEYWORDS

IS Testing, User Experience, Usability, Eye-Tracking, ICT, Data Processing

1. INTRODUCTION

Testing software and information system with end-users (usability and user experience) in Czech Republic has recently become very important thanks to increase in amount of electronic communication and government administration facilitated through information systems. Applications are becoming increasingly complex and it is necessary to develop them with the target group in mind. This requires expertise in multiple scientific disciplines such as software and system engineering, psychology, marketing and others.

Testing which utilizes end-users as test subjects can be divided into two basic techniques, testing remotely and laboratory testing (Rubin et al., 2008). Distance testing requires users to first start some sort of support application that records their actions (Aterrer et al., 2006), or in some cases turning on the web camera that will capture video footage. This type of testing can have several outputs (video camera recordings, logs from the support software, or logs from the tested application itself) (Andreasen et al., 2007). However, this method is not suitable for testing agricultural information systems in the Czech Republic for several reasons. The first obstacle is bad information literacy of end users - farmers (Vaněk et al., 2015). Installing any support testing software could therefore prove to be problematic.

Another obstacle is insufficient technical equipment of end users, because among farmers in the Czech Republic the use of desktop computers over mobile devices or laptops is still prevalent. Finding suitable users with corresponding hardware equipment for testing is therefore more difficult. Last significant issue is inability to obtain logs from the actual tested software. Complex changes in the software core to capture user activity logs are often not possible because operators of tested software are often large public institutions – in our case that is Czech Ministry of Agriculture. Our team does not have direct access into the tested information system and it does not have suitable logging functionality by default.

The second mentioned method therefore appears as preferable - laboratory testing where users are testing centrally in one place. Hardware and software requirements are secured by equipment in the test lab. The main advantage of this type of testing is the possibility to conduct collective interview after testing utilizing a moderator (Norgaard et al., 2006). This discussion is then a good source of initial findings and it is possible to propose hypotheses on its basis which can later be verified / rejected directly based on analysis of the obtained data, video, and records of eye-tracking (Guan, 2006).

Among other advantages of laboratory testing is higher time efficiency - multiple users can be tested with less effort and further testing may be easier to plan, prepare and have a greater degree of control in the laboratory setting. The laboratory testing allows for creation of tasks that follow a specific predetermined scenario which provides most accurate data about user-system interaction as proven by (Simek et al., 2015). In contrast, distance testing tends to run into unexpected problems that complicate the process (Kaikkonen, 2005).

Laboratory testing is composed of three fundamental phases (Rubin et al., 2008):

1. Design and preparation of the test - it is necessary to develop a test assignment so that the results are representative of the applicability of the tested software or its parts
2. Testing – the actual end-user testing in a lab environment, followed by a group discussion led by a moderator, possibly accompanied by entry / exit questionnaires
3. Analysis of the data and the formulation of conclusions - this part is the most time consuming, it is necessary to process all the data (logs, video, eye-tracking etc.)

For optimal results, it is necessary to test multiple users, but that faces the problem of time-consuming processing of data, especially video. It is therefore necessary to use support tools to automate the processing of video (Harrison et al., 1992). The data analysis and processing is the most difficult part of the entire testing. It is therefore necessary to design and develop a suitable methodology for data processing. This can be achieved by combinations of existing methods and designing our own approaches with regards to the specifics of the agrarian sector.

2. INFORMATION SYSTEM USABILITY TESTING

The main purpose of information system usability testing is to detect issues and errors in said system. These issues may vary from minor or cosmetic problems to critical errors which cause the system to break down. Many agrarian information systems and portals in Czech Republic contained issues regarding usability and accessibility as shown by (Benda et al., 2015). It has therefore become preferable to conduct in-depth testing before the actual system or in some cases use implementation strategy that allows a "soft-start" of the system. Many (but not all) information system are therefore running for several months or years even, before the legislature makes use of these system mandatory. These periods are therefore optimal for testing.

For the tests themselves our research team will utilize a specialized laboratory facility HUBRU (Human Behavior Research Unit). This testing laboratory is part of Czech University of Life Sciences Prague. It is equipped with ten testing computers, several cameras that capture video recordings of the entire testing room, personal cameras that capture video of each individual tested user and microphones. Two of the computers are also equipped with eye-tracking technology.

All the issues of the tested information system can be divided into three fundamental categories:

1. critical errors / blocks – these either cause the system to crash or user to get completely stuck
2. major issues – problems are very difficult, functionality that is unintuitive and causes users to slow down, or get stuck temporarily, issues that require manual to be solved
3. minor issues – small problems that cause only low delays, cosmetic issues

Most of critical errors can be discovered directly during testing. If the system crashes we can ask the tested user what happened or access the video recording at that particular time of the crash to determine the cause of the error. When users got completely stuck one member of the research team who was present noted the exact time and cause of the problem and then helped the tested end user to overcome the problem. We chose this approach because it is logistically difficult to organize these tests and if a portion of users got stuck on an issue and we did not help them complete the test it would be waste of precious opportunity to test as large part of the information as possible.

Major and especially minor issues are harder to detect directly. To determine usability of certain parts of the information system and to localize these issues, we have decided to conduct analysis of data obtained from testing - particularly from individual cameras. Our methodology consists of determining user activity and time spent performing these activities. We have divided user interaction into these activities:

1. Working – user knows what he is supposed to be doing and he is doing it – progressing through the testing scenario
2. Searching the manual – user is searching the information system manual / help page
3. Searching / problem solving – user knows what he is supposed to be doing and is trying to achieve it, he is searching for a solution
4. Being stuck – user is stuck, either not knowing what to do next, or expended all possible options and does not know how to proceed
5. Discussion – since we test multiple users at once, we allow them to help each other when someone gets stuck, we encourage discussion since users may share insights on the spot, which they may forget by the time of the exit interview
6. Other activity – activity unrelated to the testing (using phone, having a snack break etc.)

By analyzing each user's activity we can better locate even minor issues within the information system that are not directly obvious. We are also in the process of developing a specialized tracker application, that would monitor user's movements (clicks, following links, progressing through different stages of the testing task). A log from this application will be helpful when processing the actual data (see next chapter).

3. DATA PROCESSING

In 2016 our team conducted two rounds of preliminary testing. One of the main goals of these tests was to establish if the testing facility HUBRU meets the necessary hardware and software requirements. We proposed several technical improvements some of which are currently being incorporated for the main part of the testing. Another reason for these preliminary tests was to determine the type and amount of data we will be able to obtain from testing. This in turn allowed us to design an initial methodology for data processing and helped us specify what types of outputs we will be able to produce.

In order to determine the user activities as specified in previous chapter we had to analyze video recordings of users during testing. We did this manually – by viewing each individual video recording separately and timestamping it when user switched from one activity to another. To help with this task we developed very simple application in which the analyst plays through the video recording and presses a corresponding activity button when he sees the test subject to switch between activities. Even though this application is easy to use and could therefore be operated by less qualified personnel, the time consumption to analyze these recordings is not optimal. Manual viewing prevents us from achieving better than 1:1 efficiency (if we test ten subjects for one hour, it will take at least ten hours to analyze all the recordings).

Therefore we would like to propose more efficient solution in our further research. We are developing an application that tracks user clicks and movement within the information system. The log from this application allows for easier matching between user activities and testing tasks they are performing at the time. This automation allows us to approach the 1:1 efficiency as closely as possible, but does not allow us to cross that threshold.

During our next rounds of testing we are going to try to utilize our other sources of data such as eye-tracking and voice communication recordings in order to develop an automated analysis method that would compute the results faster which would significantly lessen the workload and allow us to conduct testing on a broader scale. Our initial proposal is to lock users into split-screen that would have the manual in one window and the tested information system in another window. By analyzing eye-tracking data we would therefore be able to determine how much time the user spent looking up in the manual and how much time they spent working inside the system. The log from our movement / click tracker would give us information about user progress and could therefore help us determine how much time the user spent working versus the time they spent problem solving or being stuck. Voice recordings could be used to determine the amount of time users spent discussing with each other.

After we try to utilize this approach we can compare results with the manually obtained user activity logs and calibrate the process to achieve best possible correspondence of both approaches. In case the results of the automated analysis method are too inaccurate we would have to continue the rest of the testing using the manual video analysis.

4. CONCLUSIONS

Our initial testing already revealed several critical errors and major issues with the tested information system. By conducting manual analysis of video recordings we were able to establish a baseline for user activity ratios and also confirm some initial assumptions. Younger users and more technically proficient users had much higher ratio of time spent working and progressing through the testing scenario versus time searching, problem solving and being stuck than older or less experienced users.

In future research we would like to examine the accuracy of computer automated data analysis and determine whether it can be used to sufficiently replace manually examining the video recordings.

ACKNOWLEDGEMENT

The results and knowledge included herein have been obtained owing to support from the following institutional grants: Grant No. 20171008 of the Internal grant agency of the Faculty of Economics and Management, Czech University of Life Sciences Prague titled „Acquisition, processing and evaluation of data obtained from laboratory testing of software usability and user experience".

REFERENCES

Andreasen, M. S., et al., 2007, What happened to remote usability testing?: an empirical study of three methods. *Proceedings of the SIGCHI conference on Human factors in computing systems*. ACM, p. 1405-1414.

Atterer, R.; Wnuk, M.; Schmidt, A., 2006, Knowing the user's every move: User activity tracking for website usability evaluation and implicit interaction. *Proceedings of the 15th International Conference on World Wide Web*, p. 203-212.

Benda, P., et al., 2015. Usability and Accessibility analysis of Czech agrarian portals. *Proceedings of 24th International Scientific Conference on Agrarian Perspectives*, Czech University of Life Sciences Prague, p. 47-54

Guan, Z., et al., 2006, The validity of the stimulated retrospective think-aloud method as measured by eye tracking. *Proceedings of the SIGCHI conference on Human Factors in computing systems*. ACM, p. 1253-1262.

Harrison, B. L.; Baecker, R. M., 1992, Designing video annotation and analysis systems. *Proceedings of Graphics Interface*, p. 157-166.

Kaikkonen, A., et al., 2005. Usability testing of mobile applications: A comparison between laboratory and field testing. *Journal of Usability studies*, issue 1, vol. 1, p. 4-16.

Nørgaard, M.; Hornbæk, K., 2006, What do usability evaluators do in practice?: an explorative study of think-aloud testing. *Proceedings of the 6th conference on Designing Interactive systems*. ACM, p. 209-218.

Rubin, J.; Chisnell, D., 2008. *Handbook of usability testing: how to plan, design and conduct effective tests*. John Wiley & Sons, Indianapolis.

Šimek, P., et al., 2015, Usability of UX Methods in Agrarian Sector - Verification, *Agris On-line Papers in Economics and Informatics*, vol. 7, no. 3, pp. 49-56.

Vaněk, J., et al., 2015, Digital divide and ICT development in rural areas in the Czech Republic. *Proceedings of the 13th International Conference e-Society*. IADIS Press, p. 331-334.

TOWARDS DOMAIN MODELLING IN INVENTORY MANAGEMENT FOR HUMANITARIAN AID SUPPLY CHAIN MANAGEMENT

Mazni Omar[1], Tey Hui Chin[1] and Kamal Imran Mohd Sharif[2]
[1]Human-Centered Computing Research Lab, School of Computing
[2]School of Technology Management and Logistics, Universiti Utara Malaysia
06010 UUM Sintok , Kedah, Malaysia

ABSTRACT

The domain modelling is a conceptual framework that enables researchers and practitioners to focus on the semantics of a problem domain. Various models had been proposed to address the general issues as well as specific issues within the humanitarian supply chain. However, there is still lack of domain model that can guide software developers to develop a humanitarian aid supply chain management specifically on the centralized inventory management. This paper is focused on identifying the requirements of domain model for a centralized inventory management in the preparedness phase during disasters. The initial domain model has the potential to be developed further by researchers and practitioners to address other issues in the preparedness phase of the humanitarian aid supply chain management.

KEYWORDS

Domain Model, Humanitarian Aid, Supply Chain Management, Humanitarian Logistics, Inventory Management

1. INTRODUCTION

With the expansion of information and communication technology (ICT) around the world, communication and information sharing has been made easier. This is especially true whenever disaster strikes as humanitarian agencies are able to get the necessary information from the disaster affected areas and also coordinate among the multiple parties involved. However, to date, there is still lack of domain model for a centralized inventory management for decision makers of humanitarian organizations to make quick decisions on the deployment of emergency supplies. The lack of a domain model may cause information system developers to overlook certain insights or rules that are specific to the problem domain during the development phase (Broy, 2013). By having a domain model, the requirements for a centralized inventory management will be captured more clearly. Without clear requirements, information system developers may not be able to develop useful information systems to assist in humanitarian aid operations. Therefore, this study has proposed a domain model that reflects the disaster preparedness phase in the humanitarian aid supply chain. A centralized inventory management is the focus of the proposed model.

2. RELATED WORKS

A domain model is a conceptual model designed to capture the attributes and characteristics related to a specific problem domain (Broy, 2013). It is also able to depict the most important types of objects in real-world entities and the relationships between them (Leffingwell et al., 2014). Besides that, a good domain model is able to let different parties that may be involved such as domain experts, software developers and business visionaries to have a common understanding of the problem domain. In order to produce a domain model, researchers are required to understand the environment of the problem domain space including rules and operations (Bruegge & Dutoit, 2010; McGuire, 2015). Due to the unpredictable demand for humanitarian relief operations, the preparedness phase in the disaster management cycle is considered as one of the key success factors for successful humanitarian relief operations (Larson, 2012; Iakovou, Vlachos, Keramydas, and Partsch, 2014). Based on the literature review of humanitarian logistics research by Leiras et al. (2014), a total of 75 researches were found to address the preparedness phase from the 228 researches in humanitarian logistics that had been examined. The high number of papers covering the preparedness for disasters compared to the mitigation, response and recovery phase have shown the importance of the preparedness phase.

Typical preparedness activities in the disaster operations management include the prepositioning of warehouses in facility location issues and the management of inventory for critical emergency supplies (Leiras et al. 2014). Based on further literature research, papers published for the facility location issues were more popular compared to the inventory management issues with publications as recent as 2013. It has been found that inventory management systems were typically proposed for specific organizations and the researches were quite dated with the most recent at year 2008. According to Overstreet et al. (2011), there were only eight articles found from 51 academic articles that focused on inventory management. Researchers were focused more on planning, policies and procedures where as much as 27 articles were found. The trend of research in humanitarian logistics that focused on the planning, policies and procedures were most likely due to the complex coordination and collaboration between major actors within the humanitarian supply chain (Tatham, Spens, and Kovács, 2017) as shown in Figure 1.

Figure 1. Major Stakeholders Within Humanitarian Supply Chain

From the findings of the challenges in the inventory management and the coordination and collaboration issues, it can be noticed that there had not been a model proposed to address both inventory management and coordination issues at the same time. Organizations such as the United Nations Humanitarian Response Deport (UNHRD), International Federation of Red Cross and Red Crescent Societies (IFRC) and the United States Agency for International Development (USAID) have prepositioned warehouses located strategically around the world with prepositioned emergency supplies that can be deployed quickly. However, in the event of a disaster, the deployment of emergency supplies to the disaster-affected area is not tracked in a centralized manner in order to reduce redundancy and maximize efficiency and transparency.

3. PROPOSED DOMAIN MODEL

Based on the reviews in the literature, an initial domain model that addresses a centralized inventory management domain model is proposed in this study. The candidate actors, attributes or properties of the actors, responsibilities of the actors and the collaboration or association between the actors were identified in order to construct the domain model. Besides that, two experts in humanitarian logistics and inventory management were consulted in order to understand the domain clearly.

The centralized inventory management is designed to capture all prepositioned warehouses around the world by different organizations and governments. However, it is limited to the monitoring of the inventory levels. Each owner of the prepositioned warehouses is responsible for the replenishment of emergency supplies in the warehouses they owned. Besides the inventory level, the system is also designed with the intention of being used as a centralized emergency supplies order management. This is because in the event of a disaster, humanitarian organizations, governments, NGOs and other humanitarian actors will form a working committee that will act as decision makers for the humanitarian relief operations. Since the decision makers will be given feedback from the ground workers on the needs assessments and actual conditions in the disaster area, it will be helpful to have a centralized inventory management to shorten the time needed for decision makers to decide what emergency supplies to utilize, where the supplies are available and which organizations are requesting for the emergency supplies. This will prevent any duplication of emergency supplies being expedited to the same disaster area, which may be ordered by different organizations. Hence, the targeted end user of this centralized inventory management system is the decision maker of any humanitarian aid operations. Figure 2 depicts the initial domain model using class diagram of Unified Modeling Language (UML).

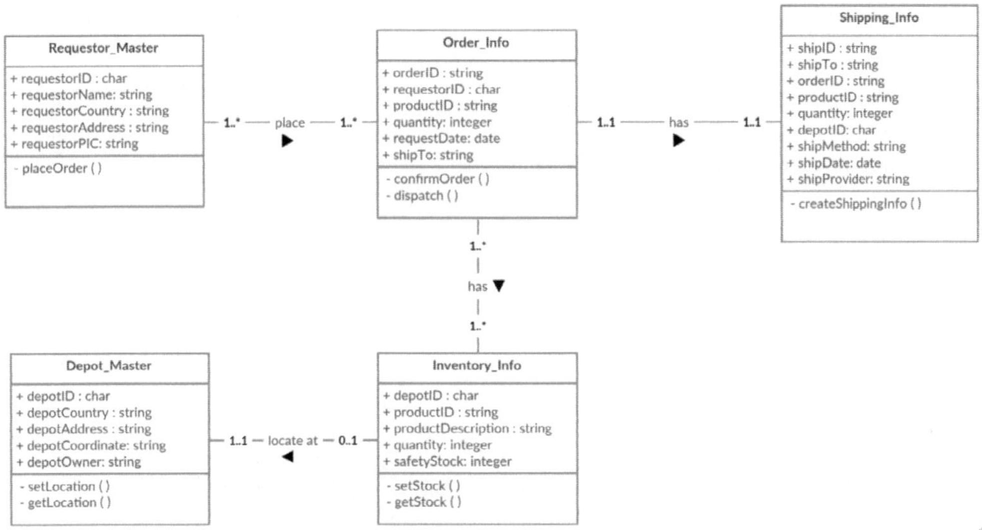

Figure 2. Class Diagram for Centralized Inventory Management

Table 1 explains the roles of each class in the domain model.

Table 1. Roles of Classes in Domain Model

Class Name	Roles
`Requestor_Master`	i) Keeps a record of emergency supplies requesters ii) Any requester can place an order for the emergency supplies
`Order_Info`	i) Keeps a record of emergency supplies orders by requesters ii) Checks for emergency supplies availability
`Inventory_Info`	i) Keeps a record of emergency supplies available in all registered depots ii) Displays the inventory of emergency supplies iii) Updates the balance inventory based on shipments made
`Depot_Master`	i) Keeps a record of depots
`Shipping_Info`	i) Keeps records of shipping details of emergency supplies based on order received

The administrators, which can be staffs attached to humanitarian organizations that work close to the center of any humanitarian relief operations, is allowed to register new warehouses or depots, new requesters, and also required to update the inventory available at depots accordingly. Meanwhile, a clerical staff within the operations can manage data entry such as orders for emergency supplies from various agencies and also manage shipping information once the shipment from prepositioned warehouses is completed. The decision maker consist of a group of working committee that overlook the entire humanitarian relief operations such as project managers who get updated with the situations of any humanitarian operations happening at the disaster area. Decision makers will be able to make quick decisions on how much and what type of emergency supplies that are needed to be deployed and also find the nearest prepositioned warehouse that can support the humanitarian relief operations based on the centralized inventory management systems.

4. CONCLUSION AND RECOMMENDATIONS

The domain model proposed in this paper is a generic model for the centralized inventory management for the humanitarian relief operations. The proposed domain model is able to provide a one-stop easy monitoring of the flow of emergency supplies to decision makers, thus promoting better coordination, collaboration and cooperation among humanitarian organizations, governments, military and NGOs, and also aims prevent wastage and redundancy of emergency supplies. There is vast potential for this initial model to be validated by experts and enhanced further in the future to include other requirements such as fleet management, asset management and human resource management.

REFERENCES

Broy, M., 2013. *Domain Modeling and Domain Engineering: Key Tasks in Requirements Engineering*. Springer-Verlag, Berlin.

Bruegge, B., and Dutoit, A., 2010. *Object-Oriented Software Engineering Using UML, Patterns and Java.* Prentice Hall, USA.

Iakovou, E., Vlachos, D., Keramydas, C., and Partsch, D., 2014. Dual sourcing for mitigating humanitarian supply chain disruptions. *In Journal of Humanitarial Logistics and Supply Chain Management,* Vol. 4, No. 2, pp. 245-264.

Larson, P., 2012. Strategic Partners and Strange Bedfellows: Relationship Building in the Relief Supply Chain. In *Relief Supply Chain for Disasters: Humanitarian Aid and Emergency Logistics* (pp. 1-15). Business Science Reference.

Leffingwell et al., 2014. *Guidance - Domain Modelling* (Scaled Agile, Inc.)[online]. Available at: http://www.scaledagileframework.com/domain-modelling/ [Accessed October 15, 2016].

Leiras, A., de Brito Jr, I., Queiroz Peres, E., Rejane Bertazzo, T., Tsugunobu, H., and Yoshizaki, Y., 2014. Literature review of the humanitarian logistics research: trends and challenges. *In Journal of Humanitarian Logistics and Supply Chain Management,*Vol. 4, No. 1, pp. 95-130.

McGuire, G., 2015. *Handbook of Humanitarian Health Care Logistics: Designing the Supply Network and Managing the Flow of Information and Health Care Goods in Humanitarian Assistance during Complex Political Emergencies in low-resource settings.* Humanitarian Health Care Logistics.

Overstreet, R., Hall, D., Hanna, J., and Rainer Jr, R., 2011. Research in Humanitarian Logistics. *In Journal of Humanitarian Logistics and Supply Chain Management*, Vol. 1, No. 2, pp. 114-131.

Tatham, P., Spens, K. and Kovács, G., 2017. The humanitarian common logistic operating picture: a solution to the inter-agency coordination challenge. *In Disasters*, Vol. 41, pp. 77–100.

DEVELOPING A LEGAL EXPERT SYSTEM FOR THE PALESTINIAN LABOR LAW

Moath Rjoub, Bashar Albakri, Yosef Zatari, Alabas Natsheh, Maysa Dandis and Musa Alrefaya
College of Information Technology and Computer Engineering, Palestine Polytechnic University
Wadi Alhareya, Hebron, Palestine

ABSTRACT

Legal expert system has received abundant attention recently from researcher in the artificial intelligence and law areas. Developing such systems for supporting the judges and advocates decisions improve the reliability and the quality of the taken decisions. The Palestinian labor law consists of 141 rules and represent one of the main fuzzy and difficult issues of advocates and judges. Recently, legal labor cases. The rapid growing of the legal labor cases a high pressure on courts and advocates and a frequent long delay. Developing a legal expert system for the labor law in Palestine will help workers to know their rights and the expected results of the court decision. Additionally, it will help to avoid conflicts and save advocates time as well offer another opinion. In this work, we study and analyze the Palestinian labor law (141 rule) and divided it into three different types: instructive laws, laws related to fees and laws related to achievements. The important features from each group is are extracted and converted into mathematical model. Based on the extracted features, a rule-based expert system is developed and built. The proposed system is tested using simulated and real cases that provided by a specialist advocates and the results are compared with the court decision. The system shows a significant results.

KEYWORDS

Artificial Intelligence, AI and Law, Legal Expert System, Rule Based Legal Expert System, Case-Based legal Expert System

1. INTRODUCTION

The official records of Palestinian courts have revealed continuing increase in litigants who have prosecution concerning with labor law according to (Palestinian central bureau of statistics, 2014). It has been noticed that prosecutions such as compensation, vacations and permanent partial/total disability have regularly been adjudicated. However, the most recent Palestinian Labor Law (No. 7) was ratified in 2000 and replaced the 1960 Jordanian Labor Law in the West Bank and the 1964 Egyptian Labor Law in the Gaza Strip. It was drafted in line with Arab Labor Organization (ALO) and International Labor Organization (ILO) standards.

For the reason of improving lawyers and courts process and facilitating their job, artificial intelligence IA has been deployed in early eighties, (McCarty L., 1990), by discussing fundamentals issues and basics concepts. However, the research primarily discussed tow basic question, the first was ability of implementing practical legal information system which could add considerable value for both layers and non-layers in legal cases (McCarty L., 1983), and the second was argumentation of the process of reasoning legal cases using computational and non-computational methods and techniques.

Over the almost past thirty years AI in law researchers implemented verity of expert systems which covering different areas of law such as: Worker's compensation (Zeleznikow, 1991), Refugee Law (Yearwood et al, 1999) and improving access to justice (JOHN, 2002). According to (James, 1996) Generally, the variant implemented application in legal expert systems refers to three different categories of development of expert systems including: 1) Rule-based systems which first proposed by Buchanan and Headrick in 1970, 2) Case-based systems made by Bench-Capon and his colleagues and 3) Hybrid systems which is eligible in which law is compound of both statutes and cases.

Rule based legal expert system approach can be applied when representing set of facts in law cases, it has been used by many researchers such as: McCarty; Bench-Capon, Kowalski and Sergot; Gardner; and Susskind. On the other hand, case based legal expert system applied when the law is not statute but case law, Mackaay and Robillard proposed to use of nearest neighbor analysis in predicting judicial decision, while Ashley and Rissland used hypotheticals in their case based expert system (James, 1996).

In this research, the motives were basically based upon a large number of legislations, rules and statutes in Palestinian labor law which need to be interrupted and legally represented to litigants and open- texture misleading from litigants side. However, the overall objective of this research is implementing and testing eligibility and adequacy of rule-based legal expert system where there is a set of facts, whether law system is a statute law or case based.

2. PROPOSED METHODOLOGY

Research in AI and law goes beyond an applications area, a critical issue such as reasoning and knowledge representation are considered as most augmenting topics in AI and law. In this research, 141 rules have been critically analyzed with advocates, professors in law school and legislators. Some rules were mathematically represented and others were open textured rules and can't be represented in rule based. However, the proposed system will pass through the following methodology which attempts to represent knowledge extracted from labor law rules. The methodology includes: Knowledge elicitation, knowledge representation and models design, Implementation and Testing and accuracy assessment.

Knowledge was primarily extracted from open texture rule in Palestinian labor law, these include: Vacations, Dismissal compensation, a partial permanent disability, a total Permanent disability and work accident consumption.

What comes after knowledge elicitation is a set of logical models and decision tables to represent the acquired knowledge in a way which all labor rules are mathematically represented. In this research, system has been divided into sub-models in which each model represents set of open texture rules. Figure 1 illustrates knowledge sources and sub-models of the proposed system. Figure 1 presents the main parts of the proposed expert system.

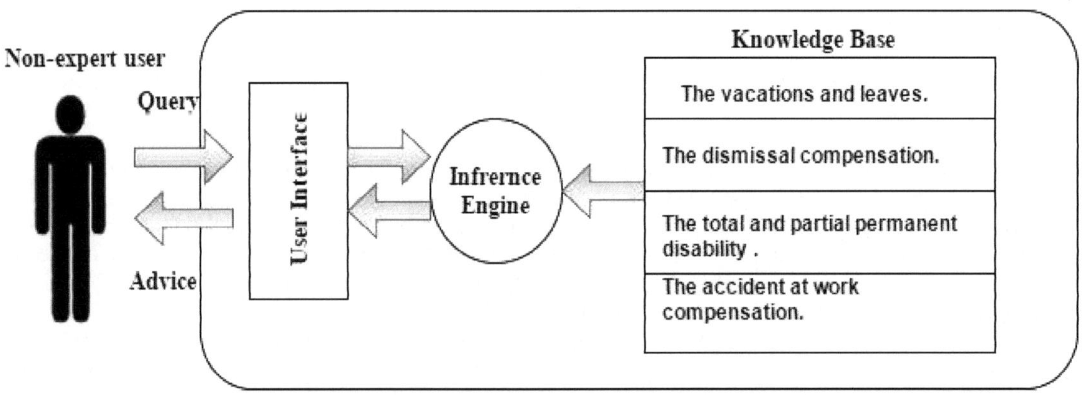

Figure 1. The Main Components of the Proposed Expert System

The following chart is an example of vacations and leaves sub-model. The vacations and leaves rules are analyzed and modeled in the following rule-based model. The proposed model includes rules for annual, sick, bereavement, religious, cultural, pilgrimage and maternity leaves and vacations.

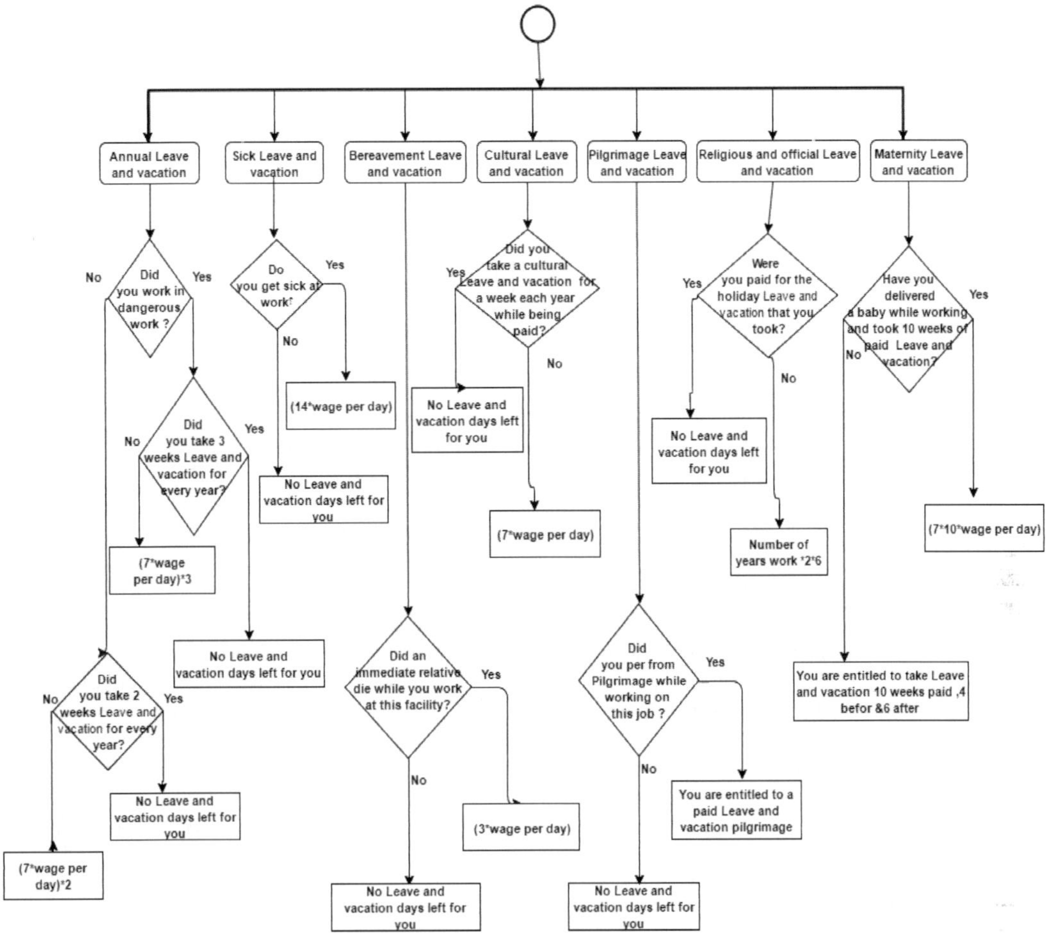

Figure 2. The Rule-Based Flowchart of Dismissal Compensation

3. RESULTS AND DISCUSSION

The proposed legal expert system is evaluated using real cases from the courts and simulated cases that generated from the advocates. The evaluation is done under supervision of specialist advocates in labor cases. The tested cases contain all the information about the labor, employer, and the court decisions.

For evaluating the system, authors used 40 simulated cases (8 cases for each section) that provided from specialists advocates and 47 real cases from the court. The matching ratio between Court Decision (real cases) or the advocate's decision (simulated cases) and the proposed expert system decision is calculated as follows:

Matching Ratio = 100 - Mean (|Court (Advocate) Decision - System decision| / Court Decision) x 100%.

The results of the proposed expert system are illustrated in table 1.

Table 1. The Evaluation Results of the Proposed System

Matching Ratio	No. of Cases	Section No.
96%	17 (9 real cases), (8 simulated cases)	Vacation
88%	18 (10 real cases), (8 simulated cases)	dismissal Compensation
93%	16 (8 real cases), (8 simulated cases)	Partial permanent disability
96%	17 (9 real cases), (8 simulated cases)	total Permanent disability
83%	21 (11 real cases), (8 simulated cases)	Accident at work claim

Table 1 shows that the highest accuracy ratio is achieved for the vacation law and the Permanent total disability. On the other hand, the accident at work got the less accuracy since the workers enlarge the facts about the accidents. The salary compensation and the permanent partial disability sections has some fuzzy rules and requires some human sense and experience.

Adopting the rule-based expert system approach proved to be a powerful tool for the labor law especially the well described rules. Merging the case-based approach with rule-based approach will enhance slightly the results of the rules requires human sense. The system failed to give the correct decisions for special and complex cases.

4. CONCLUSION

In this work a legal rule-based expert system for the Palestinian labor law is developed and evaluated. The labor law (141 rules) is studied, analyzed and classified into five sections (vacations, total and partial permanent disability, dismissal compensation and accident at work claim). The rules at each section are converted into a rule-base model. The system is tested using real and simulated cases that provided from specialist advocates. The evaluation of the system showed a significant success rate. Merging case-based approach with the used rule-based model would enhance the decision accuracy of complex cases. The proposed system expected to play important role for assisting advocates and judges in related cases, as well as assisting labor for understanding their rights.

REFERENCES

Aleven, V. (2003). Using background knowledge in case-based legal reasoning: a computational model and an intelligent learning environment. *Artificial Intelligence*, 150(1), 183-237.

Ashley, K. D., et al. (2003). Law, learning and representation. *Artificial Intelligence*, 150(1), 17-58.

Bench-Capon, T.,et al. (2003). A model of legal reasoning with cases incorporating theories and values. *Artificial Intelligence*, 150(1), 97-143.

Branting, L. K. (2003). A reduction-graph model of precedent in legal analysis. *Artificial Intelligence*, 150(1), 59-95..

Feigenbaum, E. A. 1982. Forward. In Davis, R., and Lenat, D. B., eds.Knowledge-Based Systems in Artificial Intelligence. McGraw-Hill

Greenleaf, G. (1989, August). Legal Expert Systems-Robot Lawyers?(An Introduction to Knowledge-Based Applications to Law). In Proc. *Australian Legal Convention*, Darling Harbour, Sydney.

Incorporated. VOL. 23, No. 15

J. Popple. 1991, Legal expert Systems: The inadequacy of a rule-based approach. *Australian Computer Society* JOHN, Z. (2002). Using Web-based Legal Decision Support Systems to Improve Access to Justice. *Information & Communication Technology Law*, 1-19.

Jackson, P., Al-Kofahi, K., Tyrrell, A., & Vachher, A. (2003). Information extraction from case law and retrieval of prior cases. *Artificial Intelligence*, 150(1), 239-290.

James, P. (1996). *A Pragmatic Legal Expert System*. England: Dartmouth Publishing Company Limited.

Leondes, C. T (2002). Expert systems: the technology of knowledge management and decision making for the 21st century. pp. 1–22, ISBN 978-0-12-443880-4. [3] Luger & Stubblefield 2004, pp. 227–331.

McCarty, L. (1983). Intelligent legal information systems: Problems and prospects. *Rutgers Computer and Technology Law Journal*, 265,294.

McCarty, L. T. (1990). Artificial intelligence and law: How to get there from here. Ratio Juris, 3(2), 189-200.

McLaren, B. M. (2003). Extensionally defining principles and cases in ethics: An AI model. *Artificial Intelligence*, 150(1), 145-181.

Naik, V. M., & Lokhanday, S. (2012). Building a Legal Expert System for Legal Reasoning in Specific Domain-A Survey. *International Journal of Computer Science & Information Technology*, 4(5), 175.

Popple, J. (1996). A pragmatic legal expert system. APPLIED LEGAL PHILOSOPHY SERIES, Dartmouth (Ashgate), Aldershot.. Available at SSRN: http://ssrn.com/abstract=1335176

Rissland, E. L et al, (2003). AI and law: a fruitful synergy. *Artificial Intelligence*, 150(1), 1-15.

Simon, D., & Scurich, N. (2013). The effect of legal expert commentary on lay judgments of judicial decision making. *Journal of Empirical Legal Studies*, 10(4), 797-814.

Song, L. (2015). Research of key technical issues based on computer forensic legal expert system.

Verheij, B. (2003). Artificial argument assistants for defeasible argumentation. *Artificial intelligence*, 150(1), 291-324.

Yearwood, J. A. (1999). The integration of retrieval, reasoning and drafting for Refugee Law: A third generation legal knowledge-based system. 7th International Conference on ArtiŽcial Intelligence and Law (pp. 117–137). *Australia: ACM* Press.

Zeleznikow, J. (1991). Building intelligent legal tools—The IKBALS project. *Journal of Law and Information Science*, 165–184.

Zeleznikow, J. (2002). Using web-based legal decision support systems to improve access to justice. *Information & Communications Technology Law*, 11(1), 15-33.

IMPLEMENTING ARDUINO SENSOR AND ACTUATOR ACTIVITIES FOR MODELING BPMN-BASED INTERNET OF THINGS COLLABORATIVE SERVICES

Kwanghoon Pio Kim[1], Minjae Park[2] and Junchul Chun[1]
[1]*Department of Computer Science, Kyonggi University*
154-42 Kwangkyosan-ro Youngtong-gu Suwon-si, Gyeonggi-do, 16227, Republic of Korea
[2]*Department of Computer Software, Daelim University College*
29, Imgok-ro, Dongan-gu, Anyang-si, Gyeonggi-do, 13916, Republic of Korea

ABSTRACT

The authors' research group has been excogitating an operational architecture and its practical implementations for realizing process-aware collaborative services over Internet of Things community computing environments. In this paper, we try to design and implement two graphical notations and their template control programs to graphically and functionally substantiate the activities of ARDUINO sensors and actuators, and append them to the ACTIVITI workflow platform as designated Internet of Things modeling components supporting the standardized BPMN graphical business process modeling notations. As an operational example, we model an imaginary process-aware Internet of Things collaborative service to be fulfilled by two ARDUINO-sensors such as hygrometer and thermometer, and two ARDUINO-actuators such as buzzer and LED-lighter, and implement their graphical notations and functional control programs. Through these BPMN-based modeling components, we are able to model and enact those BPMN-based Internet of Things services over ARDUINO computing environment and to validate the feasibility of the conceptual architecture of the process-aware Internet of Things, which is the eventual goal of the research and development study of the authors' research group.

KEYWORDS

Internet of Things, ARDUINO, Process-Aware Internet of Things Collaborative Service, ARDUINO-Sensor, ARDUINO-Actuator, Business Process Modeling Notations

1. INTRODUCTION

In recent, everyone knows the Internet of Things, which is abbreviated as IoT, and easily imagines the future society that is brought over from those ubiquitous and smart communications technologies. The meaning of the Internet of Things is to add the mechanism of anything connectivity to the conventional world of information and communications characterized with anytime connectivity and anyplace connectivity for anyone. By completely supporting these three dimensions of connectivity, the literature possibly created an entirely new dynamic network of networks–the Internet of Things–as a future network. That is, the collaborative works of the IoT-related study groups and focal groups of ITU-T (ITU, 2007) like SG13, SG16, JCA-IoT, IoT-GSI, and other European groups such as EPOSS (EPOSS, 2008) and CASAGRAS (CASAGRAS, 2010) have delivered the conceptual idea and its referential model (Bassi, A. 2013) of the Internet of Things platforms, which is called *the conceptual architecture of the Internet of Things platform*. The authors' research group has also proposed a conceptual architecture of the Internet of Things, which is extended from the ITU-T's framework and functional architecture (ITU, 2007) of the Internet of Things, and named as process-aware Internet of Things (Kim, M. et al, 2016).

As one of the validating activities for our conceptual architecture, we have been designing a series of process-aware IoT collaborative services, and implementing these services running on an ARDUINO-based IoT-community computing environment. A process-aware collaborative service is graphically and systematically described by a business process modeling system supporting the standardized business process modeling notation, BPMN. The goal of the service (Kim, H. and Kim, K. P., 2017) is to complete all the procedural tasks, each of which is fulfilled by either actuator or sensor of ARDUINO. In this paper, we devise two types of graphical notations to represent ARDUINO-sensors activity and ARDUINO-actuator activity, respectively, and implement their operational functions with control programs in an ARDUINO-based IoT-community computing environment. As an operational example, we model an imaginary BPMN-based Internet of Things collaborative service that is fulfilled by two ARDUINO-sensors such as hygrometer and thermometer, and two ARDUINO-actuators such as buzzer and LED-lighter. Through the operational example, we are able to practically prove that the concept of process-aware Internet of Things services ought to be a reasonable and applicable concept in any forms of the real Internet of Things community computing environments.

2. AN ARDUINO-BASED IOT OPERATIONAL ARCHITECTURE

Before excogitating a way of modeling a process-aware Internet of Things service, we conceptually illustrate an operational architecture for the service to be enacted over an ARDUINO-based community-computing environment as depicted in Figure 1, which was introduced in (Kim, M. et al, 2017). The operation architecture is made up of five compartments such as modeling part, enacting part, invoked control program part, relevant data part, and ARDUINO Things part. The following are the conceptual descriptions of the architectural compartments:

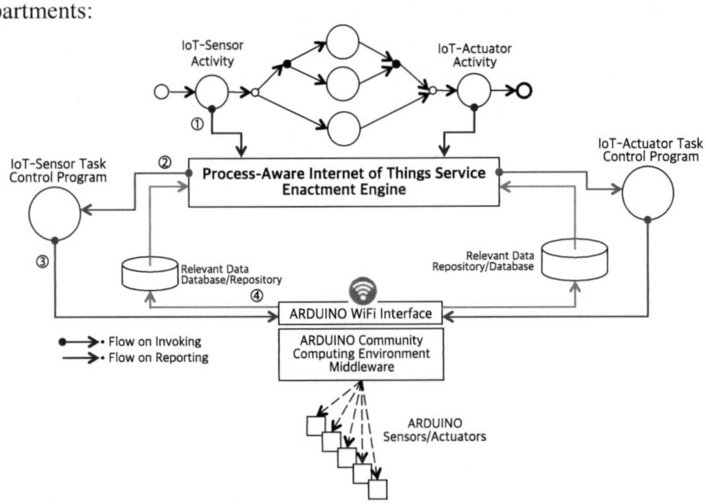

Figure 1. An ARDUINO-Based Internet of Things Operational Architecture

- The modeling part is supported by a business process modeling tool based on the standardized graphical notations of BPMN[1] released by the OMG-BMIDTF[2]. Our research group is trying to devise a new shape of notational constructs to be used for graphically representing the ARDUINO Things' activities as procedural services of a corresponding Internet of Things community computing process model (Ahn, H. et al, 2014).
- The enacting part is embodied by any of the traditional business process enactment engines, and it is able to control, audit, and monitor the Things' tasks in a corresponding ARDUINO-based community.
- The invoked control program part is a group of ARDUINO control programs corresponding to the concrete tasks of the ARDUINO Things' activities fulfilled by ARDUINO-sensors and ARDUINO-actuators.

[1] BPMN stands for Business Process Modeling Notation.
[2] OMG-BMIDTF stands for Object Management Group – Business Modeling and Integration Domain Task Force

- The relevant data part plays an important role as communication channels between the enacting engine and the Things on the Internet of Things community computing environments. It prepares a set of pre-conditional values and a set of post-conditional values to each of the Things' activities and its task. All the activities in a Internet of Things community computing process are able to launch their tasks right after completely preparing their own relevant data predefined in the build-time of the corresponding Internet of Things community computing process model.
- The ARDUINO Things part builds an ARDUINO community-computing environment that is organized by a group of devices, sensors and actuators controlled and supervised under an ARDUINO middleware. For the sake of modeling a process-aware Internet of Thing collaborative service to be described in this paper, we built an ARDUINO community-computing environment that is made up of two types of ARDUINO-sensors such as hygrometers and thermometers, and two types of ARDUINO-actuators such as buzzers and LED-lighters.

3. IMPLEMENTING THE ACTIVITIES' FUNCTIONAL TASKS

In this section, we design and implement the functional details of the notational building blocks by graphically representing ARDUINO-sensor activity and ARDUINO-actuator activity, and by functionally realizing their corresponding control programs. These building blocks are appended to the extended business process modeling tool that is graphically supported by the business process modeling notations (BPMN)[7] released from the business modeling and integration domain task force in the object management group (BMI-DTF).

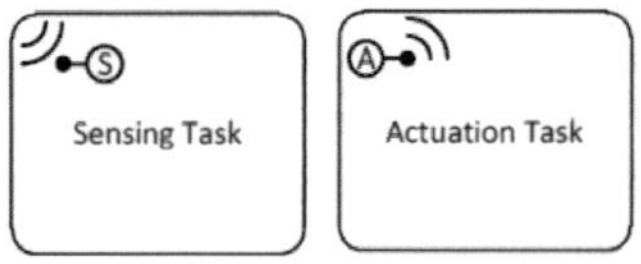

Figure 2. Graphical Notations of IoT-Sensor Activity and IoT-Actuator Activity

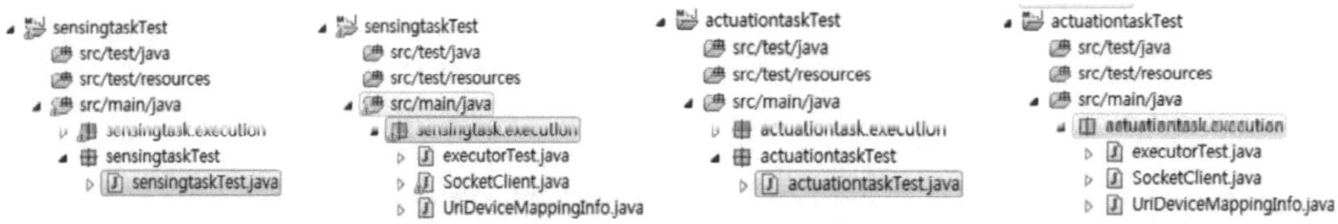

Figure 3. Eclipse-Based Java Control Programs of the IoT-Sensor Activity

As shown in the operational architecture of Figure 1, we build a practical Internet of Things computing environment using ARDUINO building blocks like WiFi shield, sensors (hygrometers, thermometers), and actuators (buzzers, LED-lighters), in order to model a process-aware collaborative IoT-services. Note that it is very important to develop a modeling tool that is able to support all the build-time functionalities from graphically modeling a procedural IoT-service to systematically verifying all the compositional artifacts that are produced from the build-time operations. The authors' research group has already developed a business process management system accompanying an auxiliary graphical modeling tool, which is technically and functionally supported by the open source BPM-platform, ACTIVITI, that supports open standards such as BPMN and DMN (Decision Model and Notation) with open REST APIs for the most demanding human- and system-centric processes. In this paper, we extend the modeling tool so as to deal with the functionality of modeling process-aware IoT collaborative services. Figure 2 shows two graphical building blocks as the manifestations of IoT-sensor and IoT-actuator tasks/activities, respectively, of the operational architecture. Both of them are designed by the ACTIVITI designer, and finally appended into the BPMN-based modeling tool.

Figure 3 also shows the captured screens of the Eclipse-based Java control programs of the IoT-sensor activity and the IoT-actuator activity, respectively. By executing the IoT-sensor activity's control programs, we are able to specify the name, type, IP address, and port number of a corresponding IoT-sensor, and obtain the status and data sensed from the IoT-sensor. At the same time, during the run-time of the IoT-actuator activity, we are able to control the corresponding IoT-actuator by specifying the name, type, IP address, and port number of the IoT-actuator through its control programs.

Figure 4. The ARDUINO-Based IoT Community Computing Environment

4. AN OPERATIONAL EXAMPLE

In this section, we try to model a procedural IoT collaborative service that aims to achieve a goal of an ARDUINO community over the process-aware IoT community computing environment constructed by a group of ARDUINO sensors and actuators. As an operational example, we build an ARDUINO community, as shown in Figure 4, that is able to support an imaginary BPMN-based IoT collaborative service to be fulfilled by two ARDUINO-sensors such as hygrometer and thermometer, and two ARDUINO-actuators such as buzzers and LED-lighters. Of course, we use the templates of the IoT-sensor activity and the IoT-actuator activity coping with their control programs implemented in the previous subsection. Figure 5 is a computer screen window captured from the operational ACTIVITI business process modeling tool and management system. As shown in the figure, the model of a BPMN-based IoT collaborative service is represented by a graphical BPMN process model consisting of five ARDUINO activities, two pairs of gateway nodes (exclusive-OR split and join gateway, parallel-AND split and join gateway), and two event nodes (start event, end event), and all the building constructs are linked by arrows that represent the temporal order of control flows.

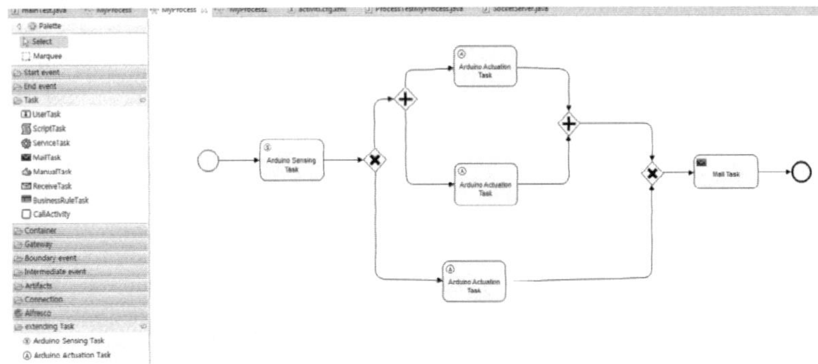

Figure 5. A BPMN-Based IoT Collaborative Service Model

As you can see in Figure 5, there are one ARDUINO-sensor activity and three ARDUINO-actuator activities in the procedural service model. Also, you can see three ARDUINO- actuator activity rectangular shapes with red-colored capital letter, 'A,' inside a circle on the computer screen window. Actually, the screen-window is captured from the monitoring function of the BPMN-based process-aware IoT-service enactment engine that is corresponding to the operational architecture of Figure 1. The red-colored letter of each rectangular activity implies that the corresponding activity is on running status. Additionally, we would stress that all the ARDUINO-sensor task and ARDUINO-actuator task control programs are implemented by the Eclipse-based JAVA programming language and the ARDUINO APIs. The main screen of Figure 5 shows a practical ARDUINO-based IoT community, which is made up of ARDUINO-hygrometer, ARDUINO-thermometer, ARDUINO-buzzer, and ARDUINO-LED-lighter, and we present the snapshots captured by a camera. This IoT community is going to achieve its goal described by the BPNM-based IoT collaborative service model.

5. CONCLUSION

In this paper, we have showed a tangible solution for proving the actualization of the process-aware Internet of Things architecture by designing and implementing a series of advanced IoT-sensor and IoT-actuator activities and their control programs. Conclusively speaking, we proved and verified the feasibility of the process-aware Internet of Things concept and its referential architecture through this modeling work and its implementation on the extended BPMN-based business process modeling tool and enactment engine developed by the authors' research group. As the future work, we have a plan to develop the whole of the functionality that is able to fully support the process- aware Internet of Things architecture and its referential model.

ACKNOWLEDGEMENT

This research was supported by the Contents Convergence Software Research Center at Kyonggi University funded by the Gyeonggi Regional Research Center Program of the Province of Gyeonggi (Grant No. 2016-0174). Additionally, the authors are transferring many thanks to the administrative officers of the science and technology section in the Province of Gyeonggi, Republic of Korea.

REFERENCES

Kim, M. *et al*, 2016. Process-Aware Internet of Things: A conceptual extension of the internet of things framework and architecture. *In KSII Transactions on Internet and Information Systems*, Vol. 10, No. 8, pp. 4008-4022.

ITU, 2007. *ITU internet reports 2005: The internet of things. Executive Summary*, International Telecommunication Union.

EPOSS, 2008. *Internet of Things in 2020: A Roadmap for the Future*. INFSO D.4 Networked Enterprise RFID, INFSO G.2 Micro Nanosystems in cooperation with the RFID Working Group of the European Technology Platform on Smart Systems Integration (EPOSS).

CASAGRAS, 2010. *RFID and the Inclusive Model for the Internet of Things*. Final Report, CASAGRAS: An European Union Framework 7 Project (EU Project Number 216803).

Chiu, H. and Wang, M., 2013. A Study of IoT-Aware Business Process Modeling. *In International Journal of Modeling and Optimization*, Vol. 3, No. 3, pp. 238-244.

Ahn, H. *et al*, 2014. A Process-Driven IoT-Community Computing Model. *In ICIC Express Letters*, Vol. 8, No. 2, pp. 483-488.

Dumas, M. *et al*, 2013. *Fundamentals of Business Process Management*. Heidelberg: Springer-Verlag, Berlin Heidelberg.

Kim, H. and Kim, K. P., 2017. A Process-Aware Goal Description Language for the Internet of Things Community Computing Environments. *In ICACT Transactions on Advanced Communications Technology*, Vol. 7, No. 1, pp. 966–970.

Kim, M. *et al*, 2017, Modeling Process-Aware Internet of Things Services over an ARDUINO Community Computing Environment. *Proceedings of International Conference on Advanced Communications Technology*. Phoenix Park, Pyeongchang, South Korea, pp. 266-269.

Bassi, A. *et al*, 2013. *Enabling Things to Talk: Designing IoT solutions with the IoT Architectural Reference Model*. Springer.

TOWARD A PRESCRIPTIVE CATALOG FOR IT VALUE

Ricardo Tulio Gandelman, Claudia Cappelli and Flavia Maria Santoro
Federal University of the State of Rio de Janeiro UNIRIO, Rio de Janeiro, Brazil
Postgraduate Program in Informatics - Department of Applied Informatics
Av. Pasteur 458, Térreo, Urca, 22.290-240, Rio de Janeiro, RJ, Brasil

ABSTRACT

There is no longer any question as to whether or not IT can deliver value to the organizations: this is already considered a fact. IT value is one of the most researched topics, but little is said about what is "value", most of the research is about IT investments evaluation methods and their classifications. We lack a better understanding of what IT value is, not a single definition but what are the elements that contribute to the IT value. We present our research in progress, whose main objective is to build an IT value Catalog revealing its composition and prescriptions (operacionalizations) on how to obtain contributions to the IT value from each model´s element.

KEYWORDS

IT Value, Business Value of IT

1. INTRODUCTION AND RELEVANCE

The value of Information Technology (IT) has been widely discussed. IT not only supports business operations, but also enables new organizational strategies, delivering competitive advantage (Joia & De Souza, 2009). IT has gone from traditional back-office support to a strategic role (Henderson & Venkatraman, 1990). Information is a key and strategic resource, supported and made possible by IT, which is increasingly pervasive, playing a significant role for organizations and for the economy, being considered a critical and strategic asset (Barbosa et al., 2014; ISACA, 2012; Heindrickson, & Santos, 2014). In the context of this research, IT is related to technologies and initiatives on adopting it; i.e., it is not about a specific area of an organization, as an IT department. Our focus is to understand the value of IT, not of the IT area. Of course, an IT department may use the model to assess its IT adoption and initiatives.

Melville et al. (2004) claim that IT is understood as valuable, but depends on internal and external factors, including complementary organizational resources and business partners, as well as the macro environment and the competitive environment. Kohli & Grover (2008) argue that IT creates value, and this value manifests in many ways (productivity, efficiency, effectiveness, innovation, flexibility, etc.) and at various levels (individually, in a group, in an organization, industry or process).

Businesses that do not even exist in the physical world have been made viable by IT. We can even observe social impacts and their consequences on business value, such as social networks and their potential value, and these initiatives are made possible by IT (Da Silva, 2011). For example, new technologies like big data create significant value to the organizations (Olszak & Mach-Król, 2016).

Large investments have been made by IT organizations (Byrd et al., 2006; Da Silva, 2011), and because of this massive investment, the business value of IT needs to be understood in order to justify this investment (Da Silva, 2011). Measuring the benefits of IT investments, benefits and value are a concern in many organizations and one of the most important issues for senior IT managers (Silvius, 2006; Silvius, 2008).

The goal of the paper is to present our research in progress about the construction of a prescriptive catalog describing the IT value composition in terms of its characteristics, as well as prescriptions and guidelines on how to obtain value for each of these characteristics.

2. THE VALUE OF IT

There is a lot of research on IT evaluation, and this is one of the most researched topics, but little is said about what is "value", i.e., what are the elements that constitute this value. Literature is eclectic with many methods, taxonomies, and classifications of methods (Bannister & Remenyi, 1999).

We argue that there is some confusion between the value of IT and the benefits and outcomes of IT investments. Maybe it is not so clear what is in fact the "value of IT", even a well-accepted definition exists. Understanding the value of IT and, eventually, being able to measure it, is different from evaluating the outcome of IT investments. Silvius (2006) states that value of IT is much discussed and often misunderstood. We lack a better understanding of what is IT value, not a single definition, this we already have.

Lee and Menon (2000) argue that the main purpose of studies in this area was to determine the direct or indirect contribution of IT in increasing the results of the firm, that is, productivity impacts of IT, or the influence of IT investments on organizational performance. Melville et al. (2004) define IT business value as the impacts of IT on organizational performance, including increased productivity, profitability, cost reduction, advantage, inventory reduction, and other performance measures.

Many authors define IT business value as "IT impacts on organizational performance" (Bannister & Remenyi, 1999; Chan, 2000; Kohli & Grover, 2008; Melville et al., 2004; Silvius, 2006; Silvius, 2008; Yassaee & Mettler, 2015) and this is now a well-accepted definition. We lack a better understanding of what is IT value, not a single definition, but what is the composition of this value, explaining what elements may give contributions to it, positive or negative.

3. MOTIVATION AND RESEARCH OBJECTIVES

Although IT investment decisions seems to be based on a sound technical rational basis, the decision-making process uses a large number of inputs, such as, data and techniques, personal experience, organizational policies, personal desires and intuition. Many authors cite decisions also made by "instinct" or "acts of faith". The concept of value is deeper and broader than that considered by economic and accounting models. The alternative is broader sociological and / or organizational models that use a broader concept of benefits and a larger context, with hard and soft benefits (Bannister & Remenyi, 1999). Melville et al. (2004) affirm that linking IT to organizational performance is a complex problem and requires multiple theoretical paradigms.

There are many factors mediating IT and value, key factors and necessary conditions in the IT value chain, such as strategy and IT alignment, organizational and process changes, process performance, information sharing, IT use, etc. However, the causality of IT value is elusive; it is difficulty to capture and assig value to IT investments. The "how" and the "why" have not yet been adequately studied, we are still in the "what". It is necessary to identify how and where IT contributes, so we can measure that contribution, and then demonstrate value (Kohli & Grover, 2008).

Our goal is to build an IT value catalog, based on a qualitative approach, describing all the characteristics that contributes to achieve the desired value and elements that can suggest how to implement it. This catalog should be prescriptive, offering guidelines on how to choose contributions, assisting decision-making process, when there is a need to adopt some technology.

4. RESEARCH PROPOSAL

Chung et al. (2000) suggest developing techniques for designing decisions during the software development process, focusing on the treatment of non-functional requirements (NFR); those requirements reflect software quality attributes, and describe how software will perform something, not what it will perform. NFRs have a qualitative character.

Design decisions can positively or negatively affect a NFR (a qualitative attribute) in particular. This interdependence will be the basis to argue whether the software meets a particular NFR or explain why it does not meet. Likewise, we may use this rationale to assess the impacts of decisions on the use of IT that affect its value, establishing relations of interdependence between factors that affect the value of IT.

Chung defined a framework where the NFRs are represented by a "softgoal", a quality characteristic without a precise definition or criterion to be satisfied, thus called "soft". These concepts are represented in a structure called Softgoal Interdependency Graph (SIG). The SIG represent the relationships between the quality characteristics, positive or negative, their satisfaction levels and their operationalization (the actions to implement a NFR-softgoal) through a graph. The model also proposes operationalization´s catalogs with prescriptions on how to materialize this characteristics into the organization´s context (practices, processes, initiatives, projects, policies, standards and procedures), the operationalization (Cappelli, 2009).

Since IT value is a multifaceted and complex concept with a strong qualitative bias, we identify great similarity with non-functional requirements that deal with quality decisions in software development. Thus, our proposal is based on Chung´s Framework, with the aim to support the assessment of IT adoption decisions with a qualitative approach, during the decision-making process.

We use Chung´s Framework, to formally systematize the IT value characteristics, creating a model that maps the value of IT through softgoals and their interdependencies, as well as the relationship between these factors, expressed by positive or negative contributions. In this model, the IT value is mapped in a cloud of characteristics, the "IT Value SIG", clearly indicating how they contribute to the IT value. The catalog also offers prescriptions on how to materialize these characteristics into the organization´s context (operationalizations). This set of prescriptions (operationalizations), joined with the SIG, would result in an "IT Value Catalog" to provide organizations with ways to generate IT value from their activities when adopting IT.

To use the Catalog, the first step is to identify the characteristics that someone thinks will bring greater contributions to the value, within a specific context. Thus, an expected contribution of the Catalog is to assist in the decision making process when adopting IT, as a tool to be used in a previous analysis, making a sensitivity analysis on the potential contributions of a given technology or IT initiative. The Catalog is not intended to compute a "value". Once we identify the characteristics that contribute to the value of a particular IT initiative, the Catalog will provide prescriptions (operacionalizations) to implement them, so this contribution to value could be actually realized. The second step is to choose which prescriptions (operacionalizations) are more suitable to adopt. Figure 1 depicts the use of the IT Value Catalog.

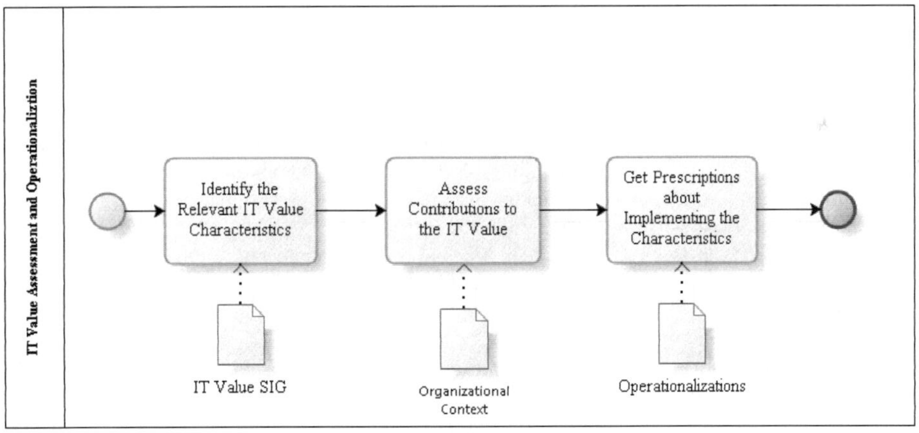

Figure 1. Using IT Value Catalog

5. CONCLUSION AND FUTURE WORK

In this paper, we present a research in progress, aiming at the construction of a prescriptive Catalog for the value of IT. Now, we are working on the Catalog´s construction. The first step is the identification, classification and grouping of the characteristics of the IT value, from an extensive bibliographical review. This step is still in progress. The result will be the "IT Value SIG", representing the contribution elements to the value of IT and their relationships. We argue that this will be a first version that needs to be improved with the contribution of researchers and IT practitioners. One characteristic of this SIG is to be dynamic, and it should always receive contributions to make it more robust and useful. After this, we will work on the construction of the operationalization.

We expect that our Catalog will help the assessment about the adoption of IT or a technology initiative, and assist the decision making process. The Catalog offers operationalizations that can guide IT executives and practitioners in implementing the characteristics identified in the assessment that will contribute to the value of IT; and in addition, let us understand how the value of IT can be created.

REFERENCES

Bannister, F. & Remenyi, D., 1999. Instinct and value in IT investment decisions. Wolverhampton Business School, Management Research Centre.

Barbosa, S.C.B., Rodello, I.A. & De Pádua, S. I. D. 2014. Performance Measurement of Information Technology Governance in Brazilian Financial Institutions, *JISTEM Journal of Information Systems and Technology Management*, Vol. 11, No. 2, pp. 397–414, TECSI FEA USP.

Byrd, T.A., Lewis, B. R. & Bryan, R. W., 2006. The leveraging influence of strategic alignment on IT investment: An empirical examination. *Information & Management*, Vol. 43, No. 3, pp. 308–321, Elsevier.

Cappelli, C., 2009. Uma Abordagem para Transparência em Processos Organizacionais Utilizando Aspectos. Tese de Doutorado, Pontifiícia Universidade Católica do Rio – PUC-Rio, Departamento de Informática do Centro Técnico Científico, RJ, Brazil. Doctoral Thesis.

Chan, Y. E., 2000. IT Value The Great Divide Between Qualitative, Quantitative, Individual, and Organizational Measures. *Journal of Management Information Systems*, Vol. 16, No. 4, pp. 225–261.

Chung, L., Nixon, B, Yu, E. & Mylopoulos, J., 2000. *Non-Functional Requirements in Software Engineering*. Kluwer Academic Publishers. Dordrecht, The Netherlands.

Da Silva, B. A. M., 2011. Decisões do Uso da Tecnologia da Informação: um Estudo sobre o Efeito das Capacidades Dinâmicas. Tese de Doutorado, Fundação Getúlio Vargas, Escola de Administração de Empresas de São Paulo, SP, Brazil. Doctoral Thesis.

Heindrickson, G. & Santos, C.D., 2014. Information Technology Governance in Public Organizations: How Perceived Effectiveness Relates to Three Classical Mechanisms. *JISTEM Journal of Information Systems and Technology Management*, Vol. 11, No.2, pp. 297-326, TECSI FEA USP.

Henderson, J. C. & Venkatraman, N., 1990. Strategic Alignment: A Model for Organizational Transformation via Information Technology. Center for Information Systems Research, Sloan School of Management, Massachusetts Institute of Technology.

ISACA, 2012. *COBIT 5 - A Business Framework for the Governance and Management of Enterprise IT*. ISACA. Accessed: March, 2017. Available at: http://www.isaca.org/COBIT/Pages/COBIT-5-Framework-product-page.aspx.

Joia, L. A. & De Souza, J. G. A., 2009. Linking Information Technology Strategic Alignment Models, *Cadernos. EBAPE.BR*, Vol.7, No.2, pp. 254–269, FGV EBAPE.

Kohli, R. & Grover, V., 2008. Business value of IT: An essay on expanding research directions to keep up with the times. *Journal of the Association for Information Systems*, Vol. 9, No. 1, pp. 1.

Lee, B. & Menon, N. M., 2000. Information Technology Value Through Different Normative Lenses. *Journal of Management Information Systems*, Vol. 16, No. 4, pp. 99–119.

Melville, N., Kraemer, K. & Gurbaxani, V., 2004. Review: Information Technology and Organizational Performance: an Integrative Model of IT Business Value. *MIS Quarterly*, Vol. 28, No. 2, pp. 283–322.

Olszak, Celina M., Mach-Król, Maria, 2016. Big Data: How to Gain Value for Organizations. *Proceedings of the European and Mediterranean Conference on Information Systems (EMCIS) 2016*. Krakow, Poland.

Silvius, A. J. G., 2006. Does ROI matter? Insights into the true business value of IT. *Electronic Journal of Information Systems Evaluation*, Vol. 6, No. 9, pp. 93–104.

Silvius, A. J. G., 2008. The business value of IT seeing the forest through the trees. *Proceedings of the European and Mediterranean Conference on Information Systems (EMCIS) 2008*. Dubai, United Arab Emirates.

Yassaee, M. & Mettler, T., 2015. The Current State of and Possible Future Avenues for IT Value Research: A Review of the Past 10 Years. *23rd European Conference on Information Systems – ECIS 2015*.

Reflection Paper

GOVERNANCE AND CONTROL STRUCTURES FOR IT SERVICE OPERATIONS MANAGEMENT

Veerendra K Rai
Tata Consultancy Services
54 B, Hadapsar Industrial Estate, Pune-411013, India

ABSTRACT

This reflection paper briefly discusses the initial work done on governance and control structures for Information Technology Service Operations Management. It adapts the Viable System Model (VSM) of Stafford Beer to outline the structures in the context of Information Technology Service Operations management. The structures are operations, coordination, command and control, intelligence and policy corresponding to System 1 to System 5 of Viable System Model of Stafford Beer.

KEYWORDS

Governance, Control, Viability, IT Service Management

1. INTRODUCTION

ITIL (2013) defines services as a means of delivering values to customers by facilitating outcomes customers want to achieve without the ownership of specific costs and risks. Services are enabled through configuration items. A configuration item could be any component required to deliver IT services. Examples of configuration items are – hardware, software and process documentation. The goal for IT services is to fulfill business objectives, add value and contribute to business. To ensure provision of services to best meet business objectives, formal controls termed as 'Service level agreements' (SLA) are defined and assessed on a regular basis (Goo *et al*, 2009). Penalty is levied on deviation of services from agreed levels.

2. THE FRAMEWORK FOR GOVERNANCE & CONTROL STRUCTURES

Viable System Model (VSM) is the framework this paper takes as basis for defining governance and control structures for IT service operations management. Stafford Beer's Viable System Model (VSM) (Beer, 1985), (Espejo and Harnden, 1989), (Espejo and Gill, 1989) has been used for decades now to ascertain whether a given organizational structure and communications meets the necessary and sufficient conditions of viability (Hilder 1995).

Viability is a systemic property, which means a system is able to perpetuate its identity in its environment while engaged in purposeful behavior with respect to stakeholders' expectations. VSM is a set of five co-operating viable subsystems conveniently named systems 1 to 5. System 1 is operations- the work an organization performs, which defines its identity as a manufacturer or service provider, for instance. The operations may be spread across product or service lines and therefore we need mechanisms to coordinate the activities of system 1. This is referred to as System 2- the coordination or regulation. System 3 is monitoring, control and synergy between system 1 units where synergy is defined as being the whole, which is more than sum of its part (Beer, 1985). In VSM framework, only system 1 and System 4 interact with the environment. System 1 interacts with current environment for functional purposes while system 4 interacts with future environment and looks for trends in the environment for planning and strategy. System 5 denotes the policy function and puts all components together to constitute the personality of the organization as a whole.

The most important property of VSM is all the viable subsystems 1-5 are contained in each of them. These subsystems recursively build the overall system under consideration.

2.1 Operations Layer

Tickets are resolved at this layer. A ticket is an abstraction of a set of 5 key IT service operations processes (Cannon *et al* 2007) given as follows.

Event management: Proactive monitoring and control at IT infrastructure level and generating alerts in case exceptions are encountered.

Incident management: Restoring availability or degradation in service quickly. Incidents are the issues that cause or can cause disruption in service or degradation of service quality.

Problem management: Determining the root cause of the incidents and determination of any possible changes required to prevent reoccurrence of similar incidents.

Request fulfilment: The process of handling small and pre-approved changes is termed as request fulfilment.

Access management: Granting of rights to use a service also referred to as "Rights management".

Organization of team, classification of tickets, classification of technology stacks, shift planning and support window configuration are key issues to be handled for smooth resolution of tickets. Tickets resolution is constrained by Service Level Agreement (SLA) and service quality. As mentioned earlier in this article operations layer is what an enterprise actually does. Other layers are logical arrangements around operations and tender requisite support to ensure value production for the survival of the enterprise.

2.2 Coordination Layer

Co-ordination may be treated as an extension of operations as coordination ensures operations do not come in each other's way i.e. to coordinate the interfaces of value adding functions. Value adding functions are primary functions of the organizations and constitute the identity of the organization. The primary functions often work on shared resources of the organization. Dependence on shared resources make the value adding functions interdependent of each other. And, therefore, co-ordination of interdependencies is the central task of co-ordination.

The value adding functions in IT service management domain are a set of services provided by IT service management teams that are spread across levels of support and locations. These services include among others event management, request fulfillment, access management, incident management and problem management as defined in ITIL service operations manual. Co-ordination of these services is a complex proposition. There are 4 major sources of complexity- IT service management planning, levels of support, governance rules, and nature of ticket.

2.3 Control Layer

The control layer seeks data from monitoring layer in terms of dashboards, health-check reports, and deviations etc. and performs root cause analysis to identify the underlying cause for any abnormality that may be present in the current state of IT service operations management system. It is also the responsibility of control layer to identify opportunity for improvement in the current state of service management. The improvements could be in terms of continuous improvement metrics that includes cost, efficiency, effort, time to resolve tickets etc. We need to choose optimal strategy which minimizes the cost and risks and produces maximum business benefits. In order to define mathematical relationship between impacting and impacted parameters design of experiment and iterative optimization has been used.

2.4 Intelligence Layer

The intelligence layer explores the external environment to look for scenarios. For instance, a large number of users are going to log into the system on a particular day & time is a scenario and its impact could be high incident volume, reduced meantime between incidents, and impact on workload metrics. The fall out of this impact could be incident dropped, SLA non-compliance, and poor quality of service. Therefore, one needs to design strategies to cope with a scenario if it actually takes place and hence we need to have scenario to strategy mapping or scenario-based strategy design.

However, when we apply a strategy we need to take cognizance of cost, risks and business value associated with a strategy. This requires that we choose an optimal strategy which minimizes costs and risks and maximizes business value. Estimating a point in time impact of a given strategy on service management metrics could be misleading as we do not know how impact of a strategy will unfold in time. Hence we need to generate time series behavior such that behavior of a particular strategy with respect to a scenario could be seen across the duration of service engagement.

2.5 Policy Layer

Policy layer is concerned with setting overall policies for governance and execution of IT Service management engagement. Decision on the overall support structure, number of support layers, escalation policies, assignment policies and preemption policies lies within the scope of policy layer. Besides, any residual issue not handled by others layers must also be handled by this layer.

3. CONCLUSION

This reflection paper outlines a possible set of governance and control structure for IT service management operations by adapting Viable System Model by Stafford Beer. The central objective of these structures is to ensure viability. This paper contains the initial thoughts of the author on the subject. A detailed study is being developed to be reported later.

REFERENCES

Beer, S. (1985). *Diagnosing the System for Organizations*, Wiley, Chichester.

Cannon, D., Wheeldon, D. and Sharon, T.(2007). *ITIL.[4]. Service operation*. TSO (The Stationery Office).

Espejo R. and Gill A. (1989). *The Viable System Model as a Framework for Understanding Organizations*. Wiley, Chichester.

Goo J., Kishore R., Rao H.R., & Nam K. (2009). *The role of service level agreements in relational management of information technology outsourcing: An empirical study*. MIS Quarterly, 33(1), 119-145.

Hilder, T. (1995). *Cavendish Software Ltd.*, Portions © Stafford Beer

ITIL (2013). *Information Technology Infrastructure Library*, http://www.itil-fficialsite.com/AboutITIL/WhatisITIL.aspx.
R Espejo and R. Harnden (1989). *Interpretations and Applications of Stafford Beer's VSM*, Wiley Chichester.

AUTHOR INDEX